ITALIAN LESSONS

JOAN L. ARNDT

RFA, Inc. (Boca Raton, FL)
First Edition

Printed in the United States of America by Knepper Press, Pittsburgh, Pennsylvania.
Publisher RFA, Inc., Boca Raton, Florida (info@levigne.net).
Library of Congress Cataloging-in-Publication Data
Arndt, Joan L.
Italian lessons / Joan L. Arndt
Library of Congress Control Number : 2008934773

ISBN: 978-0-615-23524-0

First Edition: September 2008

Dedicated to the life and memory of my father,
Thomas F. Lombardi
1923 - 1999

Acknowledgments and Author's Note

Our corner of paradise is part of a very small Italian community. We thrive here by the grace of our friends and neighbors to whom we are indebted. They demonstrated ready acceptance of two strangers and it is with tremendous affection and profound appreciation that I have written of our experiences. Real names and places have been used in most but not all instances. The timing of certain events has been compressed for the sake of storytelling.

I owe thanks to many but of special note are Lisa and Albert Davis who agreed to read my manuscript and provide comment to a first-time author. There were times when procrastination seemed my closest friend. Lisa and Albert exercised mighty restraint when physically pushing me forward was their preferred course of action. Thanks also to Clayton Arndt, commercial airline Captain, graphic designer and InDesign expert, who planted himself in front of a computer and worked magic to create a book from a manuscript. To all who read my journals and flatteringly enough asked for more, I send gratitude. You made me believe that another book about Italy was not superfluous. Finally, *grazie* to Roger for without him there would be no Italian lessons worth learning.

J.L.A.

Come mai?

The old woman walking through our olive grove carried a large knife. In most settings flashing a blade would be perceived as menacing but her semi-toothless smile mitigated the threat. While it was spring of 2003, a sepia-toned photo could easily have plunged her into the mid-1800s and a painting would have transported her centuries earlier. Her simple print housecoat was long and tattered; a mismatched kerchief covered her head. She wore dark sensible shoes with sagging wool stockings and carried a burlap sack slung across her chest bandolier style.

My husband Roger wanted me, the Italian speaker in the family, to have a chat with her and find out what she was doing in our olive grove. She lifted the knife as I approached so I was cautious despite Roger's desire for me to be anything but. Her smile remained. She said she was harvesting the greens growing wild among the poppies. She pointed with the knife and while they looked like mere weeds she said they were delicious when boiled and seasoned with salt and olive oil. In Italy it often comes down to food.

She would stay out of the grove in the future but we should know that without fencing anyone was free to enter. We had the ancient Romans to thank for the ready access to unenclosed private property. That explained the occasional motorcycle tracks through the field as well as hunters and their dogs but didn't lessen the sting of intrusion.

Italy is a study in contrasts and our grove wanderer exemplified our many contrasting experiences since we moved to this country. She carried a knife but wore a smile; she was polite and respectful, using the formal *Lei* when addressing me, but to our uninformed way of thinking, disrespectful by trespassing in our grove; she was garbed in what could easily be taken for Middle Ages peasant attire yet inhabited the 21st century; she harvested weeds that were destined to achieve an elevated culinary stature belying their lowly origin. Six months earlier we would have remained indignant by the exchange. Now it became just another notch in our educational belt. We were learning.

Luisa wanted to know more about us – who we were and where we came from. I began the story and her eyes darted between us, a bemused expression on her face. She interrupted with the question we're often asked, *"Come mai?"* Literally it means "how never" but the true meaning is "Why, how come?" She peppered us with all the other questions that follow the simple why - What in the world made you decide to move to Italy? How did you ever find this small town of Colombella? How could you take such a risk and leave everything? Weren't you afraid to move to an unfamiliar place?

We're asked such questions often. After a while, we can see it coming - there's a slight tilt of the head and then in a mildly indulgent tone the question pours out, "What motivated you to do this?" Frankly there are days we ask ourselves the same thing but on those days our questioning is more exasperated, bordering on the colorful, edging toward the profane.

Come mai, indeed. These are certainly valid questions. They involve decisions not to be taken lightly, that impact many people and precipitate many changes. In the end our decision to move to Italy came down to one word, wanderlust. Not an Italian word, granted, but the desire to travel and understand another culture is what led us here. We had traveled extensively, together and independently, personally and professionally. We enjoyed learning about ancient civilizations and historical sites while sampling new foods and wines and the trappings of other lifestyles.

Travel to another country can pique one's interest but living in another country is altogether different. We wanted the full adventure. We wanted to know our neighbors, experience the seasons, plant vegetables and flowers and see things through resident, not visitor, eyes. We wanted more than an occasional peek under the tent. We were itching to learn what life could be like in another land and packing and unpacking bags for limited stays was not scratching the itch.

The wanderlust wasn't new. We married in March 1995 and waited until November, springtime in the Southern Hemisphere, to take our honeymoon in New Zealand. We spent three weeks driving through much of the country and found it enchanting. It's a diverse land ranging from glaciers to tropical forests, mountains to flat expanses of coastline. It is not densely populated; sheep easily outnumber people ten to one. It remains pristine, the people are friendly and there's a high standard of living.

On the southeastern coast of the South Island we discovered the small town of Oamaru, known for its quarries, penguins and tranquility. We found a house, the largest single-story wood structure on the South Island. It had been lovingly and painstakingly restored with attention to architectural details that included Italian marble fireplace surrounds and hammered tin ceilings. The owners lived on site and operated part of their home as a bed and breakfast as well as a fine-dining restaurant.

We lingered in sleepy Oamaru and it wasn't long before talk of purchasing and relocating and commuting began. The breakfast part of B & B gave me an anxious twinge but I didn't have to struggle with the concept for long. Despite all the talk, we never reached a satisfactory deal with the owners and ultimately New Zealand was simply too far from the United States for family, friends and full-time jobs firmly in place.

But New Zealand whetted our appetite. We shortened the distance by looking toward Europe, Spain in particular. We had traveled to Spain often and were drawn to Barcelona and the northern coast. We knew the city well, had friends there, people who offered to help us. Importantly, the language was not a deterrent. Roger had lived in Miami for many years and I was born there.

I grew up in Miami during the sixties, at the time of the earliest influx of Cuban refugees. It was a formative time for the city and for me. I loved the Cuban people; their warmth, their music, their passion for life, their total disregard for a clock, their drive, their perseverance and their dedication to rebuilding their lives in a new land. And then there's the food. I cannot omit the food.

The garlicky smell of *pollo frito*, fried chicken, is forever imprinted on my mental taste buds. The *platanos maduros,* ripe plantains, fried to caramelized sweetness, and the now impolitic *moros y cristianos,* Moors and Christians, black beans and white rice. They became staples of my childhood diet, easily alternating with steak and baked potatoes.

I remember late night parties hosted by my parents, loud music pulsing from the hi-fi. The table in the Florida room was pushed aside to make room for dancing and conga lines. My younger brother and I were supposed to be asleep but there was no sleeping through this excitement. We peered around corners and giggled at our parents' dancing and with that, we'd be discovered. Beautiful women with dramatic make-up and strong perfume would scoop us up, tuck us into bed and cover us with good night kisses. I'd wake the next morning knowing it wasn't a dream; tell-tale red lipstick stained my cheeks. I couldn't wait to grow up and have so much fun at a party.

From the age of five until seventeen I studied ballet with Sylvia Goudie who had taught in Cuba before the revolution. She was a force. A strong, demanding presence who could shower us with affection just as easily as reduce us to quivering puddles with a sideways glance from those enormous dark, almond-shaped eyes. While we vacillated between wanting her attention and remaining beneath her radar, she never lost sight of me. I was her first English-speaking student but no English was spoken in her classes, making me a stranger in my own land. It served me well, fostering a love of the Spanish language and a love of ballet. I eventually declared Spanish as my college major and taught ballet to younger students as I became more accomplished.

Spain is not Cuba but the Latin hook had been set. Spain remained at the top of our list until May 2001 when a three-week trip to Italy changed our minds and altered our lives forever. A week in Florence, one in Rome and one visiting sites in the Tuscan and Umbrian countryside settled it.

Is it possible not to be moved by Italy? Florence, the cradle of the Renaissance, was revealed to us through the eyes of Alessandra Marchetti, a knowledgeable and enthusiastic guide and now friend. We visited Santa Maria Novella, Santa Croce and the Duomo. We lingered in front of the replicas of Ghiberti's bronze panel Baptistry Doors. The originals were washed away in the 1966 flood of the Arno. Eventually recovered and restored, they now remain encased in a museum. We wandered through the Uffizi, craning our necks upward to view the paintings that cover every available space, unable to absorb even a portion of the grandeur. We toured the Medici Chapel and the Accademia. Michelangelo's *David* came to life as Alessandra's true passion was released. Her connection to the sculptor, artist and poet is not only professional. He once owned her home.

As Alessandra did for Florence, Andrea Ruffolo did for Rome. We toured Ancient Rome, the Coliseum, the Pantheon. We visited the Spanish Steps, studied the fountain sculptures, the churches, the hidden courtyards, the keyhole view to the world. We struggled to keep up with our fast-moving guide who knew just how to bypass the Vatican crowds so that our limited time could most wisely be spent studying the ceiling of the Sistine Chapel.

The countryside is no less breathtaking than the works of art. Siena, Arezzo, Montepulciano, Cortona are postcard images come to life – perfect medieval cities preserved through the centuries in stone and brick. The rolling hillsides were filled with abandoned farmhouses screaming for renovation. Roger wanted our driver Giovanni to stop at every one. The ruins intrigued Roger, he wanted to know their history, the cost, the reason they had been left to crumble and decay.

Italian food has its own special draw and we were not immune. Wine-tastings with world-renowned expert Burton Anderson and meals with the freshest of springtime ingredients, the lightest of pastas, the heartiest *ribollita,* vegetable soups, the surprisingly tame sauces of *cinghiale,* wild boar, the *biscotti* with funny but apt names such as *brutti ma buoni,* ugly but good.

The people were friendly. From fruit vendors to waiters to hotel managers to shop owners our interactions were easy going and relaxed. There were no haughty airs, no stand-offish posturing. The attitude translated to the Italian style of dress; not overly studied but clearly refined and up to the minute. It was all on display during the evening *passeggiata,* stroll.

Before we left the country we were under its spell. The defining moment came in Assisi. We stood outside the upper Basilica of St. Francis overlooking the valley of wheat fields and farmland. It was here Roger declared we would have a future presence in Italy. Those were his very words.

Many people dream of moving to Italy but for most it remains just that. We were in the enviable position of making our dream come true. The ties that bind were easy for us to loosen. I left my full-time marketing and public relations job at The Coca-Cola Company in 1998. Since then, I had worked as a free-lance public relations consultant. It was a lucrative pleasure but one that I could easily end. Roger was close to retirement as an International Captain for Delta Air Lines after thirty-two years of service. We could sell our house in Atlanta. Roger's grown children, Clayton and Cameron, could visit. As part of the airline family, we all enjoyed the benefit of pass travel.

It takes a certain breed to walk away from the familiar and wade into the unknown. Many of our friends have told us we're very brave to have made the leap. Are bravery and fear not the flip sides of the same coin? I recently read about a man in Eastern Germany described as courageous after renovating a border house following the reunification of the east and west. He dismissed the adjective. "I think courage is an absence of intellect. The people who really think this through will most likely never do it."

I agree. Words like courage and bravery should be reserved for more lofty matters than an overseas move, especially to Italy. It wasn't as though we'd selected Somalia or Lebanon. But this idea of courage as an absence of intellect struck a chord. If I had any idea what it would take to search for properties, make offers, have them fall through and eventually find and purchase *Le Vigne*, struggle with the sale of our Atlanta home in a soft market, rid ourselves of many of our possessions and then kick ourselves for selling, deal with the antiquated Italian banking system, obtain our *permissi di soggiorno,* permission to stay, from a complicated bureaucratic immigration system, renovate our new home which was not supposed to require renovation, install the most tenuous of dial-up internet connections, wash our clothes in a machine not much bigger than a crock-pot... well, I could go on. If I had any idea it would certainly have given me pause but I didn't. It's just as well.

Courage as an absence of intellect...this idea struck *no* chord with Roger; it smacked of far too much information and intellectualizing. Roger fits the pilot mold well – think large, take charge, decisive, action-oriented. The author Pat Conroy said of his fighter pilot father Donald (known to millions as "The Great Santini"), he was the only person he had ever known "whose self-esteem was absolutely unassailable." Roger's confidence level occupies the same strata; very few doubts or second-guessing and not too many moments indulging in reflective introspection.

Our move to Italy was not a toe in the water approach. We were not going to rent for a few months, get a feel for the area, or weigh the pros and cons of one town over another. There would be no gentle entry of keeping a home in the States with plans for perhaps three months in Italy and nine stateside adjusting the timetable to our comfort level. Moreover, we didn't intend to move to Italy for bucolic retirement. We had a "Project." We were going to host vacationers, operate what's known as a self-catering vacation rental. This wouldn't be a bed and breakfast; I was off the hook for the breakfast part. Instead guests would have bedrooms, their own kitchen and living space.

Projects. In Roger's book if one's good, ten are better. Projects provide purpose, boundaries, definition and order. They represent challenges, successes and achievements. Roger is happiest with rampant activity. There's no such thing as a relaxing day at the beach - makes him crazy, all that sitting around doing nothing. While he logged over 28,000 hours between his Air Force and Delta years there were still tens of thousands of others to fill. And those hours weren't meant for something as mundane as taking in a few rounds of golf or watching a football game or getting caught up on his bird watching. Instead, he filled those hours with projects: organizing hot air balloon rallies, rodeos and concerts; owning hardware stores, nurseries, greenhouses, flower companies, irrigation companies, mobile ice cream parlors and restaurants; staging garden tours; completing massive and multiple housing renovations; creating a high-end cigar and liquor venue during the Atlanta Olympics; selling jewelry and putting together real estate deals.

Retirement was an exciting prospect for Roger. He actually loved his job, the people he flew with, those he met, dinners in the capitals of Europe, the flexibility, the benefits. As a fellow pilot put it, he would miss the rats but not the race. It was too time-consuming. Retirement translated to an enormous infusion of available hours for projects.

I'm a bit of a project person as well. I like the organization, the details, the lists and the satisfaction of completing one event and moving to another. Professionally, my most gratifying accomplishment at Coca-Cola had been orchestrating the first International Olympic Torchbearers Program in 1992. Being detail-minded and organized worked well for me professionally. Personally, I was too precise, too neat, organized to extremes. The traits were mine from the start. My family dubbed me Princess Perfect (though I was far from it) after my exacting father who was known as Peter Perfect (though his name was Tom).

As with any team, we each had our strengths. Thanks to an inborn gift for languages, learning Italian wasn't difficult for me. Years of studying Spanish and French gave me the foundation to quickly learn another Romance language. I decided to study Italian prior to our trip in May 2001. Granted, I was a highly motivated student but the grammar, sentence construction, verb tenses and conjugations came easily. Language was the biggest skill set I brought to our team.

The Italian language represented an opportunity (that's leftover corporate speak for weakness) for Roger. His early vocabulary list consisted of fifty words including such heavy-hitters as *pasta, ciao* and *limone.* For my part, mathematics is and always will be my opportunity. Even as a child, Spanish seemed intuitive while math remained a mystery. In second grade I was selected to appear with other students on a live local public television math program. We were asked to build blocks using certain dimensions. With the confidence of a seven year old, I built my blocks vertically until Miss Dubois obstructed me from the camera's view and in a stage whisper suggested I build out, not up. It was a humiliating moment. I even remember the pink skirt and pink and white checked blouse with gold buttons that I wore.

My numerical acumen did not improve over time. High school geometry was the least logical thing I ever studied and in college, I opted for philosophy courses to avoid math requirements. Over the years Roger tried to teach me about the options market – calls, puts, strike prices, writing covered options – and those seven words represent the extent of what I learned. All the talk of *lire*, Euro and dollars, kilometers and miles, liters and gallons makes me tired, bleary-eyed and cranky.

Roger then is the go-to guy for numbers and I'm the designated hitter for language. Flying taught him that life is better with a crew and as with projects, the more crewmembers the better. I am self-reliant and find it difficult to delegate either because it takes too long to explain or because I think I can do it better myself. Roger is larger than life, funny, memorable and not one to be tortured over making instant decisions. I am much more retiring, subtle and cynical and prefer a "weigh all the options" approach to decision-making. My mother, named Mamma Ruth by Roger's Clayton, believes we deserve each other.

For better and for worse this is our team and this team was moving to Italy. Here is our story, written so as not to forget; to crisply remember the sensations, reactions and emotions of those initial experiences. I want it captured during the short time those experiences are unique because they will inevitably yield to routine which is both the reality and comfort of most daily lives.

Tom, my dad, Peter Perfect, died in 1999. While he was a first generation Italian he had no strong connection to his ancestry. This voyage of ours is not a search for roots. I have no leads. Dad would have loved this adventure not because he would have done it but because we did. I think of him often, wanting to share these tales but it would mean writing to him in heaven. That seems far-fetched and sentimental but there is a thread of symmetry to the concept. We have found a slice of heaven in *Le Vigne*. How very lucky we are to even utter such words and live our dream.

Therefore, I write to anyone who has a dream. It is worth pursuing. But mostly I write to my father in his honor and memory.

Our First Lead

The official search for our Italian home started simply enough with an ad in the *Inky Mirror*, Nantucket's paper, more formally known as *The Inquirer and Mirror*. Whoever placed the ad knew their target market well. Nantucket's reputation as a world-class playground for the rich and famous was solidly established. Although we were neither, September 2001 represented our sixth consecutive year of vacationing on this tiny island.

Nantucket is magical. Those who've never been ask us what we do. Astoundingly for all, but especially Roger, we don't do much. We rent converted fishing shacks on Old North Wharf. The picturesque gravel drive with white, quaintly named cottages, spillover flower boxes and basketball-sized hydrangeas draws every artist and photographer. It's the premier spot, close to town and within easy walking distance to the grocery and shops.

I call it "Adult Camp." Days are lazy, perhaps starting with a walk into town for the paper followed by blueberry pancakes and linquica sausage at the Downey Flake. During breakfast, an intense discussion begins regarding lunch, which might be mussels and Bloody Marys at Rope Walk with further intense discussion regarding dinner. Agreement is finally reached; fresh lobster from the island's sole lobster fisherman who conveniently docks on Old North Wharf. Someone antes up for hosting that night while others contribute an appetizer, fresh corn, tomatoes, salad, bread, and pie for dessert. An important and demanding late afternoon job is established – someone must remain awake to watch for the fisherman's return and purchase the lobsters. The rest have free time before reconvening for cocktails. This strenuous pace continues through dinner after which one or more of us can then be lured to the Club Car for Stingers and piano bar sing-alongs. Conversation eventually turns to tomorrow's activities and the process begins anew.

The core group is ten people – four couples and two widows. Nine of us traveled to Italy in May and it was in Assisi, with this very group, where Roger delivered his life-altering announcement.

So the *Inky Mirror* and Nantucket serve as fitting backdrops for finding a classified ad for *Calarocci,* an old *casa colonica* or farmhouse, with three outbuildings. The home was in the mountains east of Florence, perched on a hilltop with rolling wooded terrain on all sides. The ad read well – lots of land, fireplaces and rustic rooms. We made the connection directed by the ad and determined that an English neighbor was helping the Italian owner with marketing. The neighbor, Jordan, offered to send photos of the farmhouse.

Back in Atlanta, we anxiously awaited Jordan's package. But, as often happens following the glow of vacation, reality hit. Roger plowed through an avalanche of mail while I restored order to a freshly painted kitchen. Of greater concern was the trip Roger needed to make to Dallas to visit Jim, a life-long friend, just hospitalized with the ugly diagnosis of lung cancer. Our search must wait.

Five difficult weeks ensued, pulling our focus from our Italian mission. In shockingly little time Jim succumbed to this horrible disease. Roger changed hats, from friend to executor, and did what had to be done.

When not in Dallas, Roger donned his uniform and flew separate trips to Amsterdam, Rome and Madrid. He also went to Pittsburgh to visit what he charmingly calls "the penitentiary" – the retirement community where his parents Nancy and Dana live. Clayton and his sister Cameron wove through our lives for dinners and lunches - alone, together and sometimes with other friends. I stayed busy with public relations consulting projects.

Jordan's package of photographs arrived while Roger was away. We have a deal. We don't open "good" mail unless we're together. Certain this constituted good mail I waited. On his return we tore into the envelope and found inviting pictures providing a much-needed boost of enthusiasm. Jordan suggested we visit *Calarocci,* staying with him while looking at his neighbor's property and others in the area. He assured us there were buying opportunities worth investigating.

We created a notebook dedicated to our property search in Italy. *Calarocci* became our first entry. Roger combed the internet for houses. We studied them together weighing pros and cons, discarding those that didn't seem to measure up while adding those that made the cut into our notebook. We created a list of criteria for buying a property in Italy so as not to waste time looking at unsuitable places.

We didn't want a ruin. We weren't opposed to some renovation but a roof, doors and windows were necessary. We were not in the market for a handyman's special. We wanted an older building so a renovated farmhouse would strike the perfect balance. We needed a property with space to host guests. This could mean separate buildings or separate entrances.

We wanted land and the right blend of isolation and proximity. Roger needed flower gardens, a vegetable garden, a large lawn, woods and trees.

We had to be close enough to civilization that forgetting the milk on a shopping run wouldn't destroy a day's agenda yet far enough from neighbors to abandon curtains. We needed to be accessible to guests. Having studied maps, we defined a corridor roughly between Florence and Rome. The east/west boundaries needed to be within an hour's drive of the *Autostrada*, the Italian turnpike. Tuscany and Umbria were our targets.

Although we had no sense of price, *Calarocci* seemed to meet our criteria. We shared the photos with friends and they were as excited as we were. I think they envisioned themselves in this setting and who wouldn't? It looked grand. How soon could we leave?

Calarocci

We chose to give up my favorite holiday, Thanksgiving, to see *Calarocci* along with any other properties Jordan might have up his sleeve. Upon our urging, Andrea (our guide during our May trip to Rome), his wife and their three-year-old daughter Bianca agreed to join us.

Andrea is an architect by education, a guide by default since architectural work was difficult to find, an artist at heart and a sensitive, melancholic soul by nature. His English is perfect as is his Italian, Spanish, French and Latin and his knowledge of literature and the arts is profound. Watching him read Virgil's *Aeneid* in the original Latin should not have surprised us but did only because we don't know too many people who spend their spare time in such lofty pursuits. We thought he'd be an asset to us in our search for properties. His familiarity with construction, architecture and Italian law could save us from being taken complete advantage of as gullible Americans.

Jet-lagged but determined, we piled into Andrea's car and made our way north toward Londa, a small town in the foothills east of Florence. As we approached Cortona, a town we knew from our May 2001 visit, we suggested breaking for lunch.

Andrea had never been to Cortona and we learned our first lesson about the provincialism of Italy. Cortona is only two and a half hours from Rome and thanks to Frances Mayes, *Under the Tuscan Sun* and perhaps Diane Lane, Cortona is now known worldwide but it was completely unfamiliar to Andrea. We take great pride in directing him into the town's prime parking area and to a small *trattoria* we knew well. We defined *pici* for them (local pasta made without eggs, shaped like thick spaghetti) and marveled at sharing our two cents worth of Italian knowledge. While we marveled, Andrea didn't find it odd in the least. He defined himself as a Roman first and, only if globally pressed, as an Italian.

Nearing Londa, we agreed to meet Jordan in the main *piazza*. This short, talkative and entrepreneurial Englishman led us to his home, *L'Olmo,* The Elm. Fifteen minutes from the *piazza*, *L'Olmo* sits on one of the surrounding hills at the end of a *strada bianca,* literally white road but actually a gravel or dirt road. Their land is dotted with olive trees and Jordan and his wife Lilly were in the process of harvesting.

Lilly greeted us. Attractive, blonde and as talkative as Jordan, she immediately made us feel welcome and helped us get settled. *L'Olmo* is lovely. A former *casa colonica* that has undergone extensive renovation, it exudes warmth and charm yet continues to respect its historical foundation.

The old farmhouses have certain common features. While we find them appealing in their renovated state, they were strictly utilitarian in their conception. Typically constructed as large two-story brick and stone structures, they housed the animals downstairs and the *contadini,* farmers, upstairs. The farmers benefited from the rising heat the animals provided. I suppose rising odors were a secondary treat. The upper level often featured a large fireplace in which several people could sit. The farmers would gather at the fireplace, cook their meals, talk, smoke, and stay warm until bedtime. Like *contadini* we gathered around *L'Olmo's* cozy central fireplace and chatted with our hosts about their motivations for leaving England and moving to Italy.

Lilly and Jordan had high-powered corporate jobs that took them all over the world; lots of stress, little free time and even less time together. Then there was a buy-out and thus an opportunity to drastically change their lives and move to a spot they had always loved. We pummeled them with questions undertaking our own *come mai* briefing. Patiently, they answered. Bottom line...no regrets, tons of surprises.

It was late afternoon; not the best time to visit an unknown property but we insisted. Jordan explained that the owner was a wealthy businessman in the garment industry. *Calarocci* was a second home, a country house used as a hunting lodge. He was selling because country life held no appeal to his family. The owner had sought Jordan's help in marketing the property and we now understood Jordan's involvement. If he facilitated the sale, there was a piece of the pie for him.

The owner agreed to meet us. As we left *L'Olmo*, Jordan pointed to a dark hillside. "*Calarocci* is over there, it should take us about twenty minutes. Follow me." Five minutes into the ride, we learned a new definition of the word remote. The narrow switchback climb up a steep white road seemed endless. The road was rocky and Andrea's car didn't have a low enough gear; the wheels were spinning as we slid around the curves. We giggled nervously while Andrea verbally prodded his car uphill. "We need to whip the horses," he exclaimed, smacking the dashboard. Eventually we arrived at a large grassy opening and found Jordan and the owner chatting quietly, casually leaning against their four-wheel drive vehicles.

Introductions were made and the owner suggested we use the last few minutes of dusk to quickly look outside. There was a lot of land that came with the property but we stayed close to the house admiring views and fencing and wells and plantings. Moving indoors, I was immediately disappointed. Roger's definitely the one with vision and I could sense his disappointment as well.

The inside rivaled the outside for darkness. The kitchen was lit from a single bulb hanging in the center of the room. There was a chest-level fireplace and several rustic pieces of furniture. We wandered through the house looking at dated bathrooms, small bedrooms filled with ponderous, dark beds and sparsely furnished living areas. It was sad and depressing. The house needed a huge infusion of love and light but such attention wouldn't come from us. We made polite conversation, said our goodbyes and followed Jordan to a nearby restaurant.

Tired beyond words, anything would have tasted good but the meal was satisfying and filling. We pulled no punches with Jordan and thanked him, but *Calarocci* wasn't for us. Jordan was nonplussed, "There are other properties and we'll get started in the morning." Lilly asked what we'd like for breakfast as she had stocked up on everything – what did we have in mind? Roger told her he'd be happy with Eggs Benedict. Snappily she responded, "Oh, shit, well, I've got the *eggs* and the *ben* but I don't have the *dict*."

On that note, we trailed home and tiredly climbed the stairs to our rooms. Eyes closed and voices low, Roger and I briefly chatted about what we had learned on day one of our search.

Our precise criteria weren't very precise.

Never look at property at night.

Pictures can lie.

Property Search, Day Two

It was a chilly but sunny fall day and we were up early. Lilly had a hearty soup going in anticipation of lunch. She offered breakfast but we settled for *caffè,* letting her slide on the Benedict.

Lilly explained that as much as Italians love food, breakfast is not a big meal and brunch is unheard of. Italians start the day with only a *caffè* and *panino,* sandwich. Both are consumed quickly. It takes more time to put the disproportionately large quantity of sugar into the tiny cup of coffee than it does to drink it. Meanwhile, the *panino* is not a Dagwood but a small roll with one razor-thin slice of *prosciutto* or *formaggio*.

Italians order coffee in many ways – *corretto, doppio, lungo, macchiato, ristretto, decaffèinato,* with a shot of liqueur, double, long or less concentrated, spotted with a drop of milk, strong, decaffeinated. Ordering a double latte, typically available on every corner in America, doesn't translate into a tumbler of coffee with steamed milk in Italy. Instead it will result in a large glass of milk and a strange look.

Cappuccino is never ordered after eleven in the morning. Italians believe that a *cappuccino*, laden with steamed milk, is too heavy to drink just before lunch as it ruins the appetite.

An Italian *bar* is not a bar but a café or coffee shop. Even the smallest village has at least one *bar* and it's the central information and gathering point, the unofficial town hall. In addition to *caffè, panini*, Coca-Cola and fresh orange juice, the bar sells cigarettes, matches, lottery tickets and hundreds of different magazines. Despite a *bar* not being a bar, they also sell alcohol.

After Roger downed several of Lilly's coffees Jordan presented us with the day's plan. Jordan, Andrea, Roger and I would look at properties while the rest would remain at home. Jordan drove and told us more about the surrounding countryside and how pleased he was with the area. They weren't far from Florence yet distant enough from traffic and congestion. He pointed to the city on the horizon and the glint on the Arno river.

With the absence of any bearings and the Arno being our only landmark, every place seemed extremely remote. Jordan's first offering was a property with two buildings on rock outcroppings. Each was a big, square box – no charm, no appeal, no warmth. One had a large subterranean storeroom filled with farm equipment and implements. It was musty and the floor was covered with animal droppings. All I could think about was the question on the customs form about visiting a farm. Honest to a fault, how would I answer?

We worked our way upstairs. We'd been told that the house had been modernized and noticed another unshaded light bulb hanging by a single threadbare wire in the kitchen. Modernization must mean electricity in any fashion. Roger asked to see the circuit breaker panel and Jordan took us to a closet filled with paint, brooms, buckets, rags and ceramic knob and tube wiring. Jordan didn't think it looked so bad compared to others he'd seen. He and Lilly had rewired their house and now they could operate the tea kettle at the same time as the dishwasher. There were still a few bugs though since the dishwasher and washing machine couldn't run simultaneously and a single blow dryer tripped everything.

The second building was a repeat of the first. Jordan suggested that one building could be our home and the second could be the rental property. Conceptually he was correct but I was doubtful. We turned a corner and entered a room with a screened-in porch. I stopped abruptly, pointing to the upper left corner of the screen, speechless.

The bat was small and hanging upside down, just like the logo from the movie. Did this constitute a barnyard animal or was this wildlife? I didn't scream but I wasn't pleased. Bats have the cutest name in Italian – *pipistrello* – kind of sounds like *Pippi Longstocking*. Jordan (who I'm getting the sense has the market cornered on nonplussed) continued his running commentary; "Oh, well, this is life in the country, you know." I eased out of the room, one eye locked on the logo, the other focused on stairs.

Standing outside between the two boxes, we made the usual small talk. Simply to get a sense of perspective we asked about price. The number was in *lire* with lots of zeros. Mentally I made the calculation. Take the number, whack off three zeros and divide by two. The number was still big, about $650,000. "Are you sure?" we asked. Lots of hemming and hawing and well it could be lowered a little but it depends if you're really serious. *Calarocci* was $725,000. We must have really looked like foreigners.

We retreated to the car where Jordan talked about price. This is Tuscany after all and Florence is nearby and let's not forget about the Arno and anyway the equivalent of half a million dollars won't get you much in this area. Property number two and our original thoughts about price were out the window. We acknowledged that this was indeed a learning experience and adjustments were needed along the way. "OK, Jordan, what's next?"

In short order we visited what came to be known as the Cat House, the Artist's House and the Villa. The Cat House was a post war ruin – no potential but lots of shattered glass and feral cats. I rationalized that they're household pets so no worries with respect to the customs form. Sitting in the middle of a plain in a long valley was the Artist's House. Valley locations are not desirable for the airline captain. He wants grand vistas and first sun.

Next we saw *Villa Celle,* a magnificent building with a grand, wide outdoor staircase leading to the main entrance. There were fountains and enormous terra cotta pots gracing the landing. It was beautifully decorated and wonderfully restored but with little land. There was a functioning wishing well and a *limonaia,* a glass-enclosed room for keeping citrus trees warm during winter. There was a summer kitchen, more doll house kitchen than real, yet fully functional. I had to duck to enter but could stand once inside. Roger looked like he had walked onto the set of *Gulliver's Travels.*

The owners offered coffee in the main kitchen. We sat at a round table and were served coffee and pastries. Clearly, the pastries had been purchased for some other reason but there was no hesitation in snipping the pretty curled ribbon and removing the paper wrapping to reveal a cardboard tray full of sweets. Plates, forks and napkins appeared and everyone talked at the same time. The smell was wonderful as lunch was being prepared and I worked up my courage to ask the woman near the cooktop what was in the pot. It was a pork roast and she acted like I should have known without asking. The wonderful smell overpowered her scowl.

Talk among the men revolved around *vincoli* – bonds, chains, ties, obligations, mortgages. There was something not free and clear with this property and neither Jordan nor Andrea could adequately explain the restrictions. Moreover, the building was just that – one very large building with no potential for division. We had finally seen something beautiful but not suitable.

We talked about renovations. Jordan told us that while Tuscans are willing to let old farmhouses crumble one brick at a time they are not willing to allow building modifications. Dilapidated farmhouses can be reconstructed but windows and doors must remain as windows and doors and new ones are not permitted. Even if land is available to expand it is not permitted. The existing footprint of the structure must remain intact. A loophole exists however. If an outbuilding is destroyed, those cubic meters can be recovered and incorporated into another building.

We returned to *L'Olmo* for *pranzo,* Lilly's steamy, hearty soup, bread, fruit, cheese and wine. Roger and I were ready to look at more properties but two things prevented that. First, Jordan had exhausted his stable.

There was a possibility to look at one other place but the owner hadn't yet returned his calls. Second, nothing other than eating lunch happens at this time. All shops are closed and people are resting. We could venture out again after three.

But wouldn't they make an exception? We were only in the country for a few days and that had to take precedence over somebody's lunch. Lunch only takes an hour and a half. What do they do the rest of the time? How does anything get done in this country? Beginning a search at three when it's close to cocktail hour and nearly dark seemed counterproductive.

We took the path of least resistance, acquiesced to full bellies, sat in front of the warm fire, roasted chestnuts and did the sensible thing – we napped. Later Jordan chatted with the owner of his last remaining lead. Arrangements were made to visit the following morning.

During the late afternoon Jordan offered to drive us around town. We noticed everyone harvesting olives. Encumbered by us, Jordan hadn't had time to resume picking. He drove us to the local *mulino,* mill, where the olives are taken to be pressed into oil. It was dark and the floors were slick and slippery. A dog slept under a desk; its owner nearby. Jordan inquired about a time to bring in his olives for pressing and the owner retrieved a well-worn ledger from the desk. Stubby pencil in hand, he turned faded pages tracking years of pressings and assigned Jordan an appointment for the following week.

At dinner that night we discussed the properties we visited, things we learned, decisions to be made and what we were likely to see tomorrow. If room and space were what we wanted, we'd get plenty at *Badia di Gabellina Beatrice. Badia* means abbey but I didn't know what else to expect. Jordan told us it was a restoration project that would take several years to complete and the owner was looking for partners. While we weren't interested in partnering, Jordan insisted this abbey would be worth our time. We trusted our English host.

The Abbey

Lilly's kitchen was bustling once again as we gathered our bags and loaded the car. Bianca lost her initial shyness, bounding in and out of the kitchen begging for her *babbo,* daddy, to jump up and down the steps with her. He obliges and we had never seen this melancholy man so animated and youthful. After coffee, cookies and some cheese we extended our thanks and farewells to Lilly and promised to keep in touch.

We followed Jordan to the abbey, driving through an industrialized area and up a steep muddy road. Jordan stopped half-way to come back and point out the property lines of the abbey. We're surprised because it looked as though we were entering a *borgo* or small village. Roger came alive at the thought of owning an entire village and as we continued climbing the rutted road, I sensed his internal gears moving.

Jordan introduced us to the owner and his wife. Both have full-time jobs and had undertaken the week-end restoration themselves. One building was completed and dozens of others were in various stages of disrepair. This project is all-consuming and they're hopeful that taking on partners will accelerate progress in turning the *borgo* into an *agriturismo*.

An *agriturismo* is a farm-stay hotel. Travel magazines often paint peaceful pictures of vacations spent on these working farms. The accommodations are modest and inexpensive. In exchange for cheaper lodgings, guests harvest grapes or pick olives or participate in other agrarian delights. After a long day of physical labor, they join the other workers for simple but hearty meals before retiring early in anticipation of another day of manual labor. Think *City Slickers, Italian Style.*

Agriturismo lodgings are decidedly Spartan. There are those who find this appealing and the popularity of the *agriturismo* is beneficial to tourists and Italians alike. Farming was declining in Italy and the government created a plan to persuade farmers to keep the land and still be able to earn an income. As a result, every Tom, Dick and Giuseppe with a grapevine and a couple of pigs became an *agriturismo,* gladly accepting state funds. While there are criteria defining the *agriturismo*, some adhere to these standards more loosely than others.

We toured the *borgo.* The renovated building is small but attention to detail is acute. The owners had done all the work; electrical, plumbing, masonry, carpentry. The building consists of several apartments each with a bedroom, bathroom and small kitchen. The kitchens are quite clever – free-standing closets, armoires really, containing miniature cooktops, fridges, sinks and cabinets outfitted with dishes, flatware and a few pots and pans. Instead of a Murphy bed, he's created a Murphy kitchen. The surrounding buildings were to be renovated in similar fashion for a total of forty rooms.

The centerpiece of the property is the abbey. It is enormous and our walk-though should have required hard hats. There are steps leading nowhere, drooping ceilings, precariously balanced wooden beams and hastily cobbled barricades limiting access to areas even more dangerous. We entered a large room with a tile floor and were advised to keep to the perimeter. Here, the roof is intact but the floor was covered with a single layer of olives, drying before being taken to the *mulino* for processing. Andrea bent down, picked up an olive and took a bite. Once in Jamaica, my brother made a similar face after sampling some awful-tasting fruit that locals conned him into eating. Olives require three months in *salamoia,* a brine solution, before they are no longer bitter. I'm not quite sure what prompted this brilliant man to partake but I don't believe he'll do it again. Perhaps the Roman had spent too little time in the country.

Roger thought the abbey would make a fabulous resort. He visualized the circular, brick-paved drive in front, fountain in the center, gardens surrounding the building, parking to the left. His enthusiasm was infectious and the owner's eyes brightened. Both men were engaged and through translation pinballed ideas off each other.

The owner saved the best treasure for last. He asked if we'd like to see inside the church. We got the distinct sense this offer is not made to everyone. While the abbey is no longer a fully functioning church, it is a stop on a pilgrimage trail so at least once a year a service is held. The carved wooden doors to the church were locked and the owner didn't have the keys. He led us back into the abbey, this time with a flashlight and words of caution about steep steps and no railings.

We arrived at the roof level, breathless. The owner crouched and removed a small wooden panel from the stone wall. By turns, he had us each kneel and peer through the opening as he shined the flashlight inside. Far below were the altar and remains of wooden pews. It was dizzying and disorienting as the weak light cast beams on different objects. The stained glass windows were intact. He then revealed the true reason for this adventure - frescoes covered the walls and ceiling of the church. I was transported to the swinging rope with Juliette Binoche in *The English Patient* as the man who defused mines hoisted her into the rafters and she carried a torch and illuminated paintings few would ever see. It was unexpectedly beautiful. How did the owner ever find the panel and know to remove it?

We carefully descended the many steps and covered our eyes as we stepped outside. The trip back down to earth also brought our sensibilities back to an earthly level. While the church is part of the *borgo* and the entire *borgo* is for sale the church still belongs to The Church. Further we seek no partners and this really is too extensive. As much as Roger loved the idea of owning an entire village and creating a restaurant and resort, the *vincoli* with the church and the price were enough to deter us. Applying the calculator and mental abacus to *lire* conversions, the owner asked for a pre-restoration sum exceeding a million dollars. We thanked him for his time, for the secret of *Badia di Gabellina Beatrice* and wished him tremendous good fortune.

It was time to say goodbye to Jordan. Unflappable to the end, he would continue to look for properties and contact us by email. He directed us to the *Autostrada* and we left Londa and the view of the Arno in our rearview mirror. It was time to return to the States and revise, refine and re-examine this grand plan.

Retire and Regroup

Roger had three trips before his January 1, 2002 retirement date – Stuttgart, Madrid and another Stuttgart. The final Stuttgart trip was his retirement flight as a Delta Captain and I was joined by Cameron, Clayton and several other couples to celebrate this momentous event. Of course December also included Christmas and New Year's activities, parties, dinner engagements and one final highlight - a catered retirement party for Roger.

Seventy invitees gathered to recognize Roger's aviation career and congratulate him upon entering this new phase of life. Not a soul thought that retirement would mean a reduction in activity. Cameron, Clayton and I were concerned about how he would fare without ten crewmembers at his beck and call. Frankly, I was the one most concerned. Typically Roger would return home from his flight demanding an update on activities during his absence, barking out rapid-fire questions. Then he'd proceed to rattle off orders as though conducting a briefing for flight attendants or a run-through of the pre-flight checklist. I'd let him blather for a while before pulling out my handy custom-made sign, "I am not your crew." Slowly he would decompress, loosen his tie, remove his coat and remember he was now on terra firma with us mere mortals.

In recognition of the diminution of crewmembers he was about to experience, his children and I presented Roger with a united front. We donned customized tee-shirts with my slogan, "I am not your crew" except the word 'not' was modified to 'now.' Roger loved it, embracing the concept whole-heartedly. Wisely, neither Cameron nor Clayton ever wore theirs again. That left me. I hoped I wouldn't regret this light comedic gesture.

Everyone was interested in our property search. We shared pictures and experiences and listened to suggestions. During Italian class my instructor asked about *Calarocci*. I told her it wasn't what we hoped for and while I was struggling through this complicated phrase, she dragged her pointer finger below her eye. *"Che significa questo gesto?"* I asked, knowing that gestures are laden with meaning and importance. *"Furbo,"* she replied, meaning clever, cunning, wily, sly, crafty. The gesture is a warning to be attentive.

We were learning. Our list of criteria became more precise. As Tuscany's prices were astronomical, we put a little elastic into our price limits. We spent more time on the internet creating our own "comps" and familiarizing ourselves with what was available. We were on the lookout for *furbo* and could now decipher "enjoy the quiet countryside" (meaning remote) and "helpful neighbors nearby" (meaning share a common wall). We refused to be uplifted by the word "restored" having learned that any work post WWII falls into that category. We prepared ourselves to see the omnipresent hanging light bulb as "modern" electrical engineering. We urged Andrea to locate a real estate agent to help with the search. We were excited and ready once again.

The Second Journey

It was late January when Andrea arranged for us to meet Bernardo, an agent in Cortona. He's young, tall, handsome, in constant motion and unable to speak a word of English. This was now our second house-hunting trip to Italy and I was feeling comfortable with my Italian until I meet Bernardo. He speaks as fast as he moves and when he moves it's a blur. I'm utterly lost, miserably discouraged and can't imagine how Roger feels.

Roger is equally lost and tries to take control of the process. He asks Andrea to translate after each sentence spoken by Bernardo and to advise the agent to pause, allowing translations to take place. Everyone agrees to the plan. Roger takes a deep breath and asks Bernardo what he's prepared to show us. Andrea duly translates and we patiently await the brief reply. The plan has lasted all of five seconds. Bernardo is talking non-stop and Andrea's asking him intervening questions which Bernardo is forced to answer and Roger is looking at me saying what are they saying and from what I can tell they just seem to be repeating themselves. Roger asks Andrea to stop and Bernardo hasn't yet stopped and finally they all run out of breath at the same time. Andrea tells us what we're to see, Roger begs him to stick to the translation plan and we all pile into Bernardo's car in search of the first house.

Bernardo drives the way he speaks. His dash is covered with post-its with numbers written on them. He's constantly on his cell, asking his secretary to contact the owner of property number 62509 or 33400. In between we try to learn more about the first house while adhering to the translation plan. It never happens. Roger's frustration level is sky-high; not being in control is a difficult and unnatural state.

Bernardo dashes us through seven properties that day with a scant lunch of *panini* and *caffè*. It's late afternoon and we're physically and mentally empty and agree to contact Bernardo later. He leaves and the three of us enter Andrea's car, slump in silence and enjoy the momentary nothingness. We've not made any hotel reservations for the night but since we're close to Cortona and it's a known quantity we head there.

On the way we discuss the places we'd seen. Another "restored" ruin; a property that looked great in pictures but was partially attached to a neighboring building; a spot that does a lot of catering, rents horses and has no land; a converted 13th century brick factory owned by a former ballerina; a tiny, dark little house barely seen at sunset and two others that might have potential.

We were willing to revisit the two potentials but Roger was adamant about attempting to control Bernardo. Andrea had nicknamed him The Neurotic and complained he's impossible to control. Andrea whipped out his cell phone and in rapid-fire Italian began imitating Bernardo, demanding files on houses 72384 and 68001. By now tired, hungry and punchy, we thought this the height of hilarity and begged Andrea to keep doing The Neurotic.

While the days were slowly getting longer, it's still dark by four. We arrived at *Piazza Garibaldi*, the main square in Cortona, and readily found a parking spot, a near impossible feat during tourist season. As we made our way along *via Nazionale* toward the *Piazza della Repubblica* it became clear why parking was available. Everything was closed, shuttered, gated. What are picturesque, narrow, flower-filled corridors in summer become dank, cold and musty alleyways in winter. The one hotel we knew is closed for the season. We entered a tiny market to seek advice. While Andrea spoke to the owner, I spotted a brochure for a seven-room, four-star hotel just outside the city walls. The owner of the market contacted the hotel for us. We're lucky; the hotel was open, two rooms were available and the restaurant was serving dinner.

The drive to Hotel Corys took us along a dark, winding road that climbs high above the outer wall of the *centro*. Unsure of where we're going and how long it would take, we're comforted by the signs that continued to direct us up, up, up. After one final steep turn that had us in the lowest gear we lurched to a stop. Getting the last two hotel rooms in the area, we were prepared to accept any form of lodging. My shoulders relaxed as we walked into a warm, welcoming haven and were shown to our rooms. Dinner was available in the downstairs restaurant. In the meantime, we were provided with a bowl of ice and a small platter of sliced meats, cheeses and olives.

How thoroughly civilized. We're thrilled with the surfeit of ice cubes having struggled at every bar and restaurant in Italy to obtain sufficient quantities of ice. No one seems to have an icemaker. Even ice cube trays are rare. The most common way ice is made is via plastic baggies with honeycomb-pattern indentations. The *barista,* bartender, uses scissors to cut the cubes from their pouches and puts them in a bowl. With surgical precision, he lifts each one with tongs, rinsing the cube under running water before depositing it into a cocktail glass the size of a juice glass. As he twists and turns the cube under the running water, Roger twists and turns on his barstool watching the already small cube become smaller. Three cubes are painstakingly dropped into the juice glass accompanied by a look intended to convey sufficiency.

With our bowl of ice we were off to an excellent start. Our rooms are pristine, the bed large and comfortable, the bathroom spacious and we've relaxed slightly before taking the tiny elevator downstairs to dinner. Renato, the owner, greeted us, led us to our table, offered dinner and wine suggestions and made us feel as though we'd come home. He understands some English and was patient with my Italian. He's an imp – short, glasses perched on the tip of his nose, long dark hair resting in ringlets on his shoulders. He strikes the appropriate level of interest and accessibility to his dinner guests. We explained our presence in Cortona and our search for properties and he offered assistance without any hint of meddling or intrusion.

Roger and I were smitten. Dinner was superb and the wine choices excellent. Andrea asked Renato to lower the music volume which he did without the slightest hesitation. Even our snobby Roman friend was impressed. Sated, we asked Andrea to contact The Neurotic and arrange a breakfast meeting. That settled, we thanked our host, made our way upstairs and slept so very well in our new favorite hotel, Corys.

Day Two with the Neurotic

The next morning's breakfast was an ample buffet with sliced meats, cheeses, breads, marmalades, fruit, yogurt and cereal accompanied by a choice of fresh juices. I was thrilled to have a decaf *cappuccino* and sample the sweet blood orange juice. Roger indulged in the buffet offerings and experimented with various coffees. His favorite is the *macchiato* or spotted which is an espresso "stained" with a drop of milk, cold or steamed. He eschewed the repetitive spoonfuls of sugar the Italians adore but he's adopted their habit of downing the coffee in one rapid tilt of the head - like Wild West gunslingers pounding back a shot of whiskey.

Fortified, we were prepared to face Bernardo who arrived with a folder of various properties. We're impressed with the organization but wondered if this meant we wouldn't get to see the post-it demonstration. We reiterated our criteria but recognized that real estate agents must be the same the world over. They nod their heads in agreement, say they understand and then present exactly what they intended to present. We successfully eliminated some of his suggestions and had our doubts about several others. Bernardo nodded, seeming to agree. We're convinced we were getting the universal real estate brush-off.

We said our goodbyes to Renato and the wonderful Corys and promise to return soon. Agreeing to follow Bernardo, we headed east into the mountains on a dizzying, winding switchback drive that took us through continually changing terrain. Each new curve unveiled different colors, vegetation, rock faces. Even in winter there is lush green landscape. We left the main road and tried to keep up on a muddy path deep in the woods. We climbed in the mud for fifteen minutes and recognized that our criterion of "not too remote" had been blithely ignored. Breaking into a clearing we arrived at a mountain top in sight of three small buildings.

It's an enchanted forest and this is where the elves and gnomes live! The buildings are old, lifted from an illustrated Hansel and Gretel. There's a thatched roof, there are cubby holes and half doors and stairs made of carved tree trunks and low ceilings and smoky fireplaces and copper pots hanging from hooks that threaten Roger's head. It's unlike any mental image I associate with Italy. The buildings are inhabited but not often.

Bernardo suggested using one building for us and two for guests. We passed.

As we left the fairy tale setting on our way to yesterday's two potentials, Bernardo destroyed the only patch of grass on the mountaintop. He undertook the Italian trifecta – driving, speaking on his cell and smoking a cigarette, leaving a fine impression with wheels spinning and mud flying. Andrea growled, "I think I'm going to bite his head." Must be some Roman gladiator custom.

We returned to one of yesterday's potential properties – *Poggiorello,* not far from the Siena – Arezzo highway. These ancient cities carry centuries' old rivalries that still course through the veins of their citizens. A country nationalized one hundred years more recently than ours, Italy's city-states were sovereign independent entities that fiercely resisted unity. Siena and Arezzo epitomize the resistance and their mutual disdain continues. The Siena – Arezzo highway is the perfect symbol for this contempt. Under construction for over ten years, it's not likely to be completed. We've never seen anyone actually working on the road; weeds have grown tall through temporary barriers. Commuting between the two rivals would be easier if the highway were complete but residents are content with the inertia.

Poggiorello is a *casa colonica* on a large plot of land. It originally belonged to a main land holder several hills away. From this vantage point we're able to see its crumbling remains in the distance. In addition to the *casa colonica*, there are two other renovated buildings; a studio and an apartment. The main building is divided in a way that would separate our living quarters from that of our guests. There's a central courtyard, gardens, cypress trees (my new must-have feature) and honest-to-goodness post WWII modernization. It sits on a hilltop, it's not too remote. There are several kitchens, adequate bathrooms, large living areas with functioning fireplaces as well as remaining parts to renovate should we get the itch. It certainly had potential and since yesterday's visit the price had dropped one hundred thousand Euro. We wandered outside and practically ducked as practicing fighter jets screamed overhead for the second day. Just below us, a train whistle blew and in the distance we heard cars attempting to navigate the detour of the Siena – Arezzo highway. *Poggiorello* was quickly renamed *Planes, Trains and Automobiles* and delisted.

As we drove to the next site, Roger, Andrea and I discussed the recent arrival of the Euro in Italy. With the New Year came the public use of the new currency along with confusion and frustration. The *lira* was familiar. The Euro brought a baffling array of coins and bills. Shops and restaurants post government-issued signs with photographs of each bill and coin to help the public identify a one, two, five, ten, twenty and fifty *centesimo* coin along with one and two Euro coins. Paper currency begins with five Euro notes, then ten, twenty, fifty, one hundred, two hundred and finally five hundred. Each note is a different size and color and the notes are slick so they slip out of Roger's money clip. Frankly, they spent so little time in the clip it makes no difference. Andrea contends that the public is outraged because the arrival of the Euro brought an across-the-board price increase to all goods and services.

In another governmental move to assist the public with the transition, every receipt and every item sold indicates Euro and *lira*. The value of the Euro was pegged at 1,936.27 *lire* and as of today that translates to a dollar value of eighty cents.

According to rules of the European Union, each country could design their own currency following strict guidelines and even that provoked controversy. Andrea explained that the French violated the guidelines by including the name "France" along the edge of their coins and unveiling the design prior to an approved release date. Regardless, Italy can lay claim to the most beautiful coin by depicting Leonardo da Vinci's Vitruvian Man. Stellar math student that I am, I was relieved to understand that a one Euro coin had twenty percent less value than a dollar bill. I know it's a moving target but it's still easier to comprehend than *lire*.

We arrived at our second potential which I'll call Mr. Biagi after the kind owner who agreed to meet us at the drop of a hat. The property consisted of two large buildings one of which was quite old and had been renovated. The old one contained an interesting central free-floating brick staircase and other distinctive architectural features; niches and wrought-iron light fixtures. The second building was much newer and decidedly unappealing. Mr. Biagi (the man, not the house) had done all the work himself. There was land, there were views and it wasn't too remote. There weren't enough bathrooms, we would have to renovate just about everything, particularly in the new building. The Neurotic off-handedly revealed that the property was unavailable until after the coming summer season.

We now had two men ready to bite his head. It's early January and this place can't be sold until October? Why are we wasting our time? When had he planned on divulging this minor tidbit? Why isn't it available until the end of summer? We finally learned that the property was rented for the season and the owner wanted the income. Bernardo didn't seem to grasp our frustration but this last surprise was enough to dampen even our mildest interest.

Three properties visited and we'd missed lunch again. We caravanned to the *centro* of the small town of Lucignano and found the only open bar for *panini e caffè*. In an effort to appease us, Bernardo paid. It was here that the answer to an enormous mystery was suddenly revealed. While having coffee in the many bars, I'd noticed men with dark brown stains on the tip of their noses. I found myself staring, concerned about the cause of this pervasive Italian malady until I looked up and spotted a dark brown stain on the tip of Roger's nose.

Oh no, he'd been struck too! We hadn't been here a week. How could this have hit so quickly? Unaware of my concern, Roger asked the *barista* for another *macchiato* which he slams back. Observing his tilted head I'm rewarded with the forensic evidence to solve the mystery. It was coffee splashed on the rim of the cup hitting the nose as heads snap back...purely a function of nose size to cup size.

While I conducted my investigations, Bernardo was anxious to show us one last property. We followed the madman on an hour's drive on the *Autostrada* and then along bumpy gravel roads lined by vineyards. The powdery dust swirled as we pulled into a property marked by the absence of trees. Free-range chickens came from all directions as we met the owner who paid no attention to the fowl. The owner is industrious; he completely rebuilt a *casa colonica* that had fallen into ruin. Only thirty nine thousand bricks remained and he recovered every one to recreate a house in the farmhouse style. The effort was impressive and unobstructed views of the rolling Tuscan hillsides planted with grapes and wheat could be seen from the many arched windows. While the building was indeed large and through some clever maneuvering could be divided for guests, the stark interior and pronounced lack of flora left us unmoved.

Having exhausted Bernardo's supply of properties we returned to Rome with Andrea. Several times during the drive Andrea spoke to Bianca, in France with "The Mother." He told her he's with *il capitano* and "The Daughter" distinctly remembered "The Roger." Andrea's spark burned brightest when talking to Bianca.

Back in Rome, our hotel bartender grudgingly provided three rinsed hailstones splashed with gin. Wistfully, we toasted Renato and his healthy ice cubes and reviewed the places we've seen, why they don't work and what to do next.

On Our Own

In Umbria, on a winding, hilly road between Montegabbione and Montegiove there is *Portici,* which means porches or verandas. The rule of thumb in Italian pronunciation is that the accent falls on the second to the last syllable. In mercurial fashion this works all the time until it doesn't. *Portici* is one of the exceptions and the accent is on the first syllable.

The owner and a calm, soft spoken real estate agent met us at *Portici.* The property consists of four separate buildings, the main one being 150 years old. There are olive groves, goats, sheep, chickens, peacocks, an awful above ground pool, flowers, vegetable gardens and enough projects to keep Roger intrigued for years. The owner no longer lived there but had done all the work and he's as self-effacing as the agent. He had lived and worked in Switzerland as a stone mason for many years, returning to *Portici* periodically to lovingly rebuild this home for his family. His wife was gone and the grown children had no interest so he's selling. He was pruning his olives dressed in knee-high rubber boots and a stained blue work coat resembling a lab coat. Roger was fascinated with the process, inquiring about the methodology, his fingers twitching at the chance to grab the pruners.

The rebuilt building had many interesting features. There was a large eat-in kitchen with fireplace that backed up to an outdoor summer kitchen with a functioning *forno,* a wood-fired oven used for bread, pizzas and roasts.

As spacious as the kitchen is, it is otherwise typical of those we've seen. The refrigerator is tiny and the sink faced a wall. I couldn't imagine anything grimmer than doing dishes looking at brick or stone. A view from the kitchen window had made its way to my must-have list. Mounted on the wall above the sink was an open wood cabinet with spindles serving as a rack for drying and storing plates. This omnipresent cabinet is an interesting piece of furniture, very functional and the reason sinks faced walls. I got it but the cabinet's functional charm didn't outweigh the need for a view.

Two of the remaining three buildings were apartments. The construction was new, the design modest but functional. The remaining building would have made *Home Improvement's* Tim Allen proud - a garage, workshop and storage area all in one. Roger was salivating - farm equipment, garden tools, olive and grape harvesting apparati, vehicles, mechanical trimmers, mowers and blowers - all clean, organized and neat. The purpose of some of the tools was obvious (to those who move in such circles) but there were things with which Roger wasn't familiar and his desire to speak Italian and ask unceasing questions was never stronger than at this moment. *Portici* had lit a spark.

We walked the grounds in the gloomy Euro-drizzle. From certain vantage points the views were beautiful; from others a large furniture manufacturing facility marred the vista. In addition to mental kitchen renovations, Roger revamped the rose-lined drive, expanded the gardens, planted more olives and planned a new pool. He was just getting warmed up.

The same spark hadn't quite caught fire with me yet. Roger saw the property as income producing from guests, olives and grapes and, as an added bonus, maintenance-free. The concept of income producing forced me to tap the brakes on his unbridled enthusiasm. I applied my own mathematical formula known as the Roger Factor. It works via division when dealing with income and multiplication regarding costs and is addressed before applying the flawed concept of maintenance-free.

Mostly my heart went out to the owner. He'd put so much love and labor over so many years into this land and these buildings. He knew that it would be sold yet still came every day to prune his olives, feed the animals and tend the gardens. He asked us in and we declined; our shoes were caked with mud. He shrugged but we hold fast because for the first time in days we're determined to sit down to a proper lunch. We recorded the agent's name and number and promised to be in touch. The owner slowly turned away. He's heard this before but I know we'll be back.

After a lovely wine-filled lunch we made our way to Rome. The real fun started after exiting the *Autostrada* to drive into the *centro*. The trek looked vaguely familiar from Andrea's chauffeuring but doing it solo was harried. Motorcycles slithered in from every direction, horns blared at the slightest provocation, heavy traffic and dusk combined to make this a sporting event. On the ancient *via Salaria* the traffic slowed to a crawl and we worried that an accident would keep us stranded on the outskirts of the city for hours. There was no accident. Instead, a gaggle of hookers with astoundingly little clothing for this cold winter day diverted everyone's attention.

After struggling with the map I finally called Andrea to talk us in. It was a frazzled three-way discussion.

Andrea: "Where are you now?"

Me: "How do I know?"

Roger: "Talk to me, Goose."

With no easy place to pull over and get oriented we simply continued forward. Several roundabouts and a few dozen expletives later we recognized our street, found our hotel and parked. While indulging in our imitation ice cube drinks, Roger pontificated about what's required for driving in the *centro* – nerves of steel, committed aggression and zero eye contact. He's right... we walked to dinner.

We stroll on *via Veneto* (another pesky word with the accent on the first syllable), glanced at the menus posted outside the restaurants and listened to the come-ons from the head waiters luring diners with the day's specials. The waiters worked hard. After all, it was January and the *Veneto* was not thick with easy targets. We finally made a selection and over a subtle *primo* of *tagliatelle con porcini* and a fine Italian red, we agreed to take another look at *Portici*.

Our second visit to *Portici* felt the same to me but Roger continued to find it appealing. Departing from Fiumicino had me humming Peggy Lee's "Is That All There Is?" I wasn't ready to commit to *Portici* without seeing more properties.

A Little Help from our Friends

We loved dining at Antica Posta in Atlanta. The name of the restaurant means Old Place but Atlantans kept trying to change *Posta* to *Pasta* because, after all, it is an Italian restaurant. Marco, the dashing young Tuscan owner, was brave to stick with the name but he really had no choice. His brother Gianni manages the original Antica Posta in San Casciano, a small town just south of Florence. Marco had come to America to establish the New World version.

We sought Marco's advice with our property search and he was gracious, helpful and patient. He offered assistance during our next trip to Italy, scheduled for the first two weeks in April. With spring came tourists and tourists require guides so our moonlighting friend Andrea had other obligations and could dedicate little time to us. Marco arranged for us to stay in an *agriturismo* not far from his family restaurant. It's owned by close friends who he insists will help us with our search. Privately I wondered how rustic the place is but I wouldn't dream of declining and risk insulting him. Marco tells Gianni we'll be coming and wishes us "*Buona fortuna*."

On a sunny Easter Sunday, armed with internet printouts and names of real estate agents we left Atlanta. The rental car counter at the Rome airport was mobbed. It took hours to get a car – a small Fiat with stick shift, a far cry from the automatic wagon we'd reserved. Paperwork and keys in hand, directions to the car in mind, we retraced our steps, carefully steering the *carrello,* cart, so our bags don't tumble. During our previous visits, we were met by a driver and we now realized that's the better way. Our future guests shouldn't have to suffer through this as their initial, jet-lagged welcome to Italy.

Assuming our standard driver and navigator positions we drive north, making a solemn pledge to remain patient for our four-hour drive to San Casciano and not spiral into what our British friends call an R.I.C. – Row In Car. We'd yet to exit the rental lot and traffic was horrid. Already drowsy, we still had to navigate the infamous ring road before getting on the *Autostrada.* We crawled and Roger cursed the manual transmission but we made it to the *Autostrada* and took the first opportunity to stop at an *Autogrill,* the Italian version of a fast food restaurant and gas station. Roger hoped that an infusion of caffeine would alleviate his soporific state.

Autogrills are legend in Italy. Some are built across and above the *Autostrada* providing service for both directions. Ordering and eating at the *Autogrill* should come with instructions. Squeeze to the front of the glass display cases, study the many choices of *panini* and sweets, make a decision, wiggle back to the *cassa,* cashier, place the order and pay. A *scontrino,* receipt, is produced which is then taken back to the front of the display case and placed on the counter. Flag down the *barista* and announce the order. The *barista* will ask if the sandwich should be heated, always a tasty option but more time-consuming. After the order is filled, the *barista* will tear the receipt to eliminate the possibility of someone being *furbo.*

IKEA's forced passage floor plan has nothing on the *Autogrill.* It's a maze filled with pasta, cheeses, chips, jars of olives and artichokes, olive oil, chocolates, cookies, crackers, candies, waters, wine, beer, soft drinks, teas, toys, games, cameras, CDs, DVDs, books, magazines, sunglasses, car deodorizers, maps. All must be passed to exit.

After our *panini* and coffee we tackled the restrooms, marked by international stick-figure drawings. Exiting, we placed a coin, a ten or twenty-cent piece is sufficient, in the dish next to the distracted attendant who exerts little effort to keep the place clean. The attendant only appears distracted. Not leaving a coin earns a scowl, some unintelligible grumblings and a rough jiggle of the coin dish.

Roger was briefly revived by the *macchiato* but after another hour of traffic he struggled to stay awake. I directed him to Amelia only because of the coincidence of easily finding it on the map and seeing a road sign for the town. It's built into the side of a mountain at a dizzying height and even more vertiginous angle. We found a hotel and restaurant perched over a dramatic gorge. As tiny as our car was, we had difficulty finding a parking spot in the crowded lot.

I could imagine how this looked to the clerk at the front desk. His eyes wandered, searching for even so much as an overnight bag. I launched into an explanation of arriving from overseas and jet lag and traffic and all we needed was a little sleep. His demeanor didn't change - he'd heard it all before. While we completed the paperwork and turned over our passports I attempted small talk and asked why there's so much traffic and why the restaurants were so busy. It was Easter Monday, *pasquetta*, or Little Easter, a holiday equal to Easter and Christmas in importance.

After three hours of deep sleep we're back in the Fiat. The drive to San Casciano was long and traffic hadn't improved but at least we're rested. Without too much difficulty we found the original Antica Posta and met Gianni, his wife, toddler son and the family German shepherd, Dino. They were expecting us and since it was too early for dinner, Gianni led us to *Il Manzolo*, our *agriturismo,* where we met the owner's daughter, a freckle-faced redhead who was as welcoming as Gianni. Gianni spoke English, having worked for restaurants in the DC area for several years. The daughter, looking more Irish than Italian, spoke no English and her Italian was distinguished by a strong Tuscan accent.

I remembered learning about this uniquely Tuscan phenomenon. A hard "c" sound is swallowed, becoming a rasping "h" sound. Coca-Cola becomes *Hoha-Hola* and *"Voglio una Coca-Cola calda con la cannuccia corta,"* "I want a warm Coca-Cola with a short straw," becomes "*Voglio una Hoha-Hola halda hon la hannuccia horta.*" It sounds more like hacking throat clearing than the melodic language it is.

Il Manzolo is in the peaceful, hilly countryside of San Casciano. There are lots of buildings, some with lodging and others indicating that this was, first and foremost, a working farm with animals, grapes, olives, tractors, excavators and plows. Our modest room was a former horse stall, equipped with a small kitchen and bathroom.

We settled in, unpacked a few items and realized we were ravenously hungry. We drove to Antica Posta just before eight, the earliest we could even think about dinner. Gianni's kitchen wasn't quite ready for diners but he knew we were starved and accommodated our early-bird-special appearance.

Undoubtedly we're among a precious few who could smile with insider knowledge that the menus in the Tuscan Antica Posta and the Atlantan one are remarkably similar. We tried some new dishes and a few old favorites. It's impressive that Marco can recreate in Atlanta what Gianni can do in San Casciano. Gianni's wine list is longer and includes vintages produced in such small quantities that they're never exported. We ate well, drank well and got lost only once on our way back to *Il Manzolo*.

Star Trek

The morning's first order of business was cash. It was easy enough to get using the English language option on the ATM but the bills dispensed were small - all tens. We wanted larger.

Entering the bank wasn't intuitive. We paraded back and forth but couldn't find any doors. Finally we came across a protruding curved Plexiglas bubble with a large green button to the side. We fumbled for a few minutes, searching for a handle and eventually pressed the green button. Quietly, the Plexiglas door swooshed back into itself like a Star Trek transporter. Only one person could enter. Roger went first and the door closed behind him. He turned to wave at me as a duplicate door on the other side opened to magically transport him and his briefcase inside the bank. I followed. The transporter is not for the claustrophobic.

Once inside, we approached a teller. Fortunately some of my Italian studies covered a few banking terms so I understood the teller's request for our *conto corrente,* account number. Of course we didn't have one and that almost ended the transaction. I explained we wanted to exchange our ten notes for larger bills, a transaction he agreed to. We slid our Euro under the partition and he began counting. These tellers must spend days in fancy counting booths learning the special technique of folding bills and rapidly thumbing them back for the count. Croupiers should be so dexterous. Cash happy, we Star Trek'd our way to our next mission, the purchase of an Italian cell phone.

Everyone in Italy has at least one *cellulare* or *telefonino.* We randomly picked a store and a cute young girl named Rosie helped us. We focused on minutes and roll-over and roaming but Rosie dismissed all that with a wave. Here there are SIM cards and everything is pre-paid. Cost per call was impossible to determine other than knowing that overseas calls were chokingly expensive, cell-to-land line was less so and cell-to-cell was the cheapest. We bought a phone, a charger, a car charger and loaded the phone with one hundred Euro (or as Rosie said, two hundred thousand *vecchie lire).* The phone delivered all prompts in Italian so the language-savvy Luddite got the programming duties.

The bank visit and phone purchase consumed our morning and the attention to language and technical terms left me peckish. It was nearly lunch time which meant all the shops would close until afternoon and we had yet to see property one. We settled on an inviting *trattoria* and once I spoke in Italian the waitress smiled. She offered the daily specials that included the wonderful, hearty vegetable soup, *ribollita* and several *crostini,* one topped with *mozzarella* and tomatoes and another with liver pate. We leisurely drank house wine and watched the locals.

After lunch we wandered the streets looking into shops and businesses. Some were shuttered; others had metal grates locked in front. We noticed several *agenzie immobiliare,* real estate offices so we scanned the postings, gasping at some of the high prices after calculating the exchange from *vecchie lire* to Euro to dollars. San Casciano may not be on the tourist map but Tuscan properties were drawing attention.

Ree-Ree

We drove south to discover on our own. The countryside is changeable and different from the gentle farmlands and rolling hillsides that we'd become used to. Undulation gave way to steep cliffs and sharp rock faces. Vegetation clung to boulders despite the fierce winds that swayed our Fiat; the struggle to survive is strong though not easy. The road is narrow and winding, rising and dipping. Occasionally we see houses set back from the road. Otherwise the area is remote and isolated, nary a grocery, bar or market in sight.

Eventually we arrived in the small town of Campana. Shop owners were raising the metal grates and unlocking doors for the afternoon work period. Here too we saw postings of properties in the real estate offices that dot the narrow brick streets. We stopped in a bar for a *macchiato,* smiling to ourselves at a few brown-nosed patrons. As we left we noticed a large, glass-fronted real estate office and stepped inside. The place was buzzing as women at computer terminals easily conversed with clients in

Italian and English. Phones rang, faxes arrived and people milled about waiting for a chance to speak with the next available agent. This was a happening spot. We studied the metal stands filled with photos of properties with descriptions in both languages. Prices were staggering for crumbling, vine-covered piles of bricks.

A patron left and an agent offered to help us. Her English was perfect and we took a seat opposite her computer terminal. Roger retrieved a legal pad from his briefcase and began describing our dream property and our price thresholds. She smiled indulgently; "You and everyone else." She had nothing to show us. We produced printouts of properties we've seen on the internet. She was familiar with most and told us their flaws, benefits and prices.

A tall, graying man approached and spoke to our agent in Italian. His accent was hard to decipher – English, Australian, South African? She introduced us to Ridleigh, a Scotsman, and the agency owner. She explained our interest and he abruptly and gruffly told us to forget it, give it up, there was no chance of satisfying our laundry list of wants within the price frame we'd arbitrarily and erroneously created. He all but spun on his heels but Roger wasn't about to wave the white flag.

Collecting our scattered papers we trailed Ridleigh asking what he could show us in our price range. He was incredibly discouraging in a matter-of-fact way. He didn't mean to be impolite but this was a seller's market. After fifteen years he knew the area better than anyone. Don't waste his time or ours on something that simply doesn't exist. "Go south," he said, "get out of Tuscany. You don't have a prayer here."

Roger won't be deterred. We decide on an oblique approach, speaking of other things – how did he come to live in Italy, why his agency is so large, why he's doing so much better than other agencies, where do we come from in the States, what do we do there, what careers do we have? We talk about Edinburgh and Perth and Italy and the States.

Roger and Ridleigh, two cranky old cusses, were circling each other, scratching the dirt at their feet. Despite it all, they're finding common ground, slowly building mutual respect. Ridleigh is knowledgeable and Roger was determined to see what's in his stable. We relented and removed price from the equation. Now what can you show us? Don't forget our self-catering vacation rental plan. Ridleigh rapidly thumbed through notebooks, pulling aside a few pages, rejecting most, providing running commentary. He was often interrupted by others seeking advice, a signature, phone guidance. Talk about cognitive dissonance. His accent and the language don't match. I couldn't understand him when he answered his phone – it sounded like Ree-Ree. Roger assured me it was "Ridleigh."

Our schedule was free and we were ready to shop. His schedule was far from free. He couldn't possibly do anything for a week. Roger cajoled then pleaded. Ridleigh caved. He called one of his aides, barked some orders and without the slightest hint of annoyance she agreed to adjust his schedule so we could meet in a few days. That settled, he left us with printouts about the properties we're to see, a handshake and moved on to his next client.

The drive back to San Casciano was sobering. The high that was so infectious sitting in Ridleigh's office was wearing off. We decided to speak to other agents in San Casciano, vowing to remain within our price range. They weren't as negative and we agreed to meet the next day. We found a little market and bought a few basic provisions including a hair dryer and flat iron.

Much to Roger's dismay I collect hair dryers and flat irons the way a philatelist collects stamps. I've dragged the poor man through stores in Europe and Asia and filled our Atlanta attic with an impressive array of appliances worthy of a Smithsonian exhibit. It was easier to purchase dryers and irons locally than deal with adapters, converters, watts, volts and eventual appliance meltdown. He wasn't surprised I'd done it here; just surprised it had taken this long.

The intervening days ran together. The appointment we had scheduled for the following day at 9:30 was cancelled by the agent and pushed back a day. We learned this only by showing up, not by the courtesy of a phone call. More than a little frustrated, we ventured out on our own. We visited *Portici* again while the sad, patient owner alternately led and followed us as we looked at his land, buildings, gardens, olives, animals and pool. Roger was just as fond of the place but I was growing cooler.

We located some of the properties from our internet search and could tell from the exteriors they weren't suitable – too close to the road, little land, great views from one side, poor views from another, partially restored (the photographed part of course). We met other agents, heard similar stories and began to recognize some of the same printouts.

Our time with Ree-Ree proved fruitful. He was interesting, adventuresome and always on the lookout for new real estate even in Umbria. He taught us to talk to the locals, entering the village bar as though he owned it, ordering a coffee and striking up a conversation with the *barista* or patrons. We would hear stories about the carpenter's cousin's best friend's second grade teacher's uncle who wants to sell his house. Off we'd go into the hinterlands in search of the uncle only to find an aunt who knew nothing but she had a friend who told the baker that if anyone was interested in buying an old ruin to let her know.

Ree-Ree's instincts were sound. He could smell a property for sale. We showed him a printout of a house that we had found on the internet, knowing only that it was near Montegabbione, not too far from *Portici.* Ree-Ree didn't recognize it but it piqued his interest. We stopped at a butcher in town to begin the inquiry. The owner, hard at work in the back of his shop, not only knew the property but also knew of a German who wanted to sell his house and one hundred acres. He agreed to lead us to both after he finished what he was doing.

Atop a stainless steel table with legs on wheels was a four-foot long pig, sliced open length-wise, in a shallow roasting pan. The butcher tossed a generous fistful of wild fennel and chopped garlic into the yawning cavity. Already in the cavity was the boiled and chopped liver. Next, he heavily sprinkled coarse salt and freshly ground pepper. Taking a long, curved sail maker's needle, he threaded it with heavy twine and began to stitch the torso closed. Each suture took enormous strength and as he pulled on the needle he would push the torso away with his foot. While he worked, friends wandered in and out: a retired policeman, a former butcher, a neighbor. One picked up a broom to sweep an already clean floor. The easy camaraderie was evident.

Once the cavity was closed, the men rolled the table into another room where they stoked a roaring wood-fired oven. The table was at the perfect height to slide the roasting pan directly into the oven where it would stay for eight hours to become crispy on the outside and moist, flavorful and tender inside. This was a special butcher; one who had just prepared a *porchetta*, a delicacy unique to Umbria. He traveled the countryside in a catering truck and sold *porchetta* sandwiches at the local morning markets. Every afternoon he returned to prepare and roast another pig.

The butcher removed his apron and he and his friends led us into the surrounding hillside to the house that we had only seen on the internet. Owned by a medieval history professor, the buildings were beautiful and fully restored in a dramatic and up-to-date manner. There were outdoor bedrooms and libraries filled with floor to ceiling books and an inviting spot for garden dining. The classical music playing in the background helped set the tone of casual elegance. There were open fields and fenced lands and views of woods and forests. It was spectacular but impossible to use as a rental property. The professor was gracious and welcoming and insisted on serving coffee. We chatted briefly, thanked him for his kindness and proceeded to the butcher's German friend.

The German's property was even more unsuitable and greatly suffered from the immediate comparison to the professor. There were splendid views into the wilderness but the terrain was rocky and sparse. The house had been renovated into little warrens with scant rhyme or reason. The owners weren't dressed for company but we sensed that even if they had known we were coming there wouldn't have been big changes. The pocket on the German's plaid shirt was ripped completely on one side. His wife had the scary red hair that's a top-seller in Europe. They were alone out here and contact with humanity was limited. It was a scene out of Woodstock. They too were gracious and offered us homemade wine. So began a practice that we encountered often. Sometimes better than others but always proudly offered, these vintages had me looking for potted palms or claiming abstention. Bless his heart, Roger drank them all.

Ree-Ree showed us more conventional properties. There was Arturo's chicken farm, made with bright pink bricks; *Cancello Bianco* so named for the giant white entrance gate that opened onto a very busy road; partially restored *Poggio Taverna* owned by an Iranian architect and *Il Molino*, where we appeared moments before the owners returned home and told us we were trespassing. Ree-Ree apologized but told them he thought the house was for sale. Snippily, they told us it had sold that very morning and they were just returning from the *atto,* the closing. Already on their bad side we didn't think it could get any worse by asking the price. Surprisingly they told us. The dump had gone for the equivalent of over 1.1 million dollars and the new owners were English. Welcome to Tuscan-shire! The Brits had invaded, put down roots and in so doing created an inflated market that was quickly slipping out of reach.

We saw acres and acres of olive trees and vineyards, crumbling brick buildings, musty-smelling stone structures, shuttered rooms, salt-encrusted walls stained by rising humidity, converted farmhouses that reeked of the centuries of urine that permeated the floors, unloved houses, dark furnishings, single swaying bulbs, endless wall-facing sinks, decaying barns, scurrying mice, rickety wagons, scrawny chickens, olive oil tanks, demijohns, an impressive specimen-quality bee hive trapped between a window and shutter that pulsed and hummed with kinetic energy. We met caretakers, custodians, owners, farmers, businessmen, heirs, real estate agents. They insisted on personally showing us their properties, presenting every nook and cranny and they so wanted us to love their baby. We drove down many dirt roads, shied away from barking dogs, followed restaurant or bar or bakery owners to properties they knew were for sale as they pursued a finder's fee. We tagged properties with nicknames to keep them straight – Bee's Nest had great views but it was too isolated; War Zone had perfect buildings but no land. And day after day we drank lots of bad, young, pucker-producing homemade wine.

We eventually said our goodbyes to San Casciano, stayed two nights in Pienza and then went back to Corys. Pienza, known for its cheeses, is a storybook version of an Italian walled village. Corys felt like going home. Renato was as charming and welcoming as ever. Even Corys' staff got in on the real estate act. Renato's pouty lipped receptionist took us to a precariously perched aerie whose sole claim to fame was its proximity to *Bramasole*, Frances Mayes' *Under the Tuscan Sun* house.

One sunny but chilly day Ridleigh took us on a long drive south into Umbria. Our destination was the pea-sized town of Acqualoreto, not far from Lago di Corbara, southwest of Todi. The town is not even on our map. The views are dramatic with roads clutching mountainsides and nets covering the rock faces.

Ridleigh wanted to show us *Torre del Tenente*, Tower of the Lieutenant, so named because the house includes a tower that forms part of the perfectly preserved wall of this tiny village. Descending from town center, we turned into the steep and narrow driveway of the house to meet the owner, a refined woman dressed as though she stepped from the Italian equivalent of *Horse and Hound*. We wandered outside admiring the groomed gardens, the abundant lavender, the greening fruit trees, the unique straddling of town and country. The redbuds surrounding the pool were just beginning to bloom and framed a stunning foreground to the distant valley below. An added bonus – there's land to develop so Roger could create his own gardens.

With the ease of the well-heeled, Madame Lieutenant led us inside via the actual Tower. A complete contrast to all the ruins or near ruins we'd trekked through, *Torre del Tenente* is loved and beams its appreciation. Meticulously renovated with attention to historical details that don't conflict with current needs for comfort, the property is a living *Architectural Digest* cover story. The Madame's taste is superb from furnishings to flooring to color schemes to lighting to linens - there's not a false note to be found. The Tower is welcoming and warm and even adaptable to vacation rentals. A connecting walkway to a separate but equally charming building would make hosting guests convenient though non-intrusive. We walked through the many rooms on five levels, marveled at the views and trappings and circled back again in an attempt to orient ourselves. We snapped dozens of pictures but there's too much to take in at once. We couldn't remember what bedrooms were on which floors and which level held the massive linen closets and where the overstuffed casual chair resided, beckoning to be occupied in springtime sunlight. It was in the midst of this giddy, helium-inflated state that Roger casually asked, "Well dear, what do you think?" Awestruck, I replied that it was the most beautiful home I'd ever seen.

The Tower is but one home owned by the Madame. She's most often in Rome and we're fortunate to have found her here today. She and Ridleigh discussed price and her love of the property. Despite having put it on the market, she's quite fond of the Tower and is reconsidering its sale. A friend in Tuscany told her to raise the price, that prices in Umbria were approaching those in Tuscany. The Madame is savvy. Acting the part of a reluctant seller might increase her chances of selling. When she finally divulged the figure we worked hard not to swoon.

We're under the spell of the Siren's song as we return to Ree-Ree's office where we commandeered one of his able assistants to draft an offer. Ree-Ree insisted there was little point in attempting to negotiate. Roger had no idea where such money will come from yet insanely we offered the asking price and, in our hypnotic state, pushed the "send" button on the fax machine.

Hours later, in the calm environment of Corys, we emerged from our communal trance and asked ourselves in panicked tones, "What have we done?" Roger told me it's my fault. Since I told him it was the most beautiful home I'd ever seen he had no option but to purchase. This is a massive confessional moment. I'd just received the secret code. The problem was we'd offered more than we have.

The fax was gone. All we could do was wait.

Carla

We're up early and it was just us breakfasting at Corys. I was content with my decaf *cappuccino* and Roger was relishing the idea of an entire buffet of cheeses and sliced meats to himself. We debated about how soon we could call Ree-Ree and agreed that seven was a tad early. We delayed until quarter past and made the call. Apologetic though we were, he's hard at it and no, he's not heard a word. He assured us he'd call when he had news.

The content of Roger's briefcase had been disgorged onto the breakfast table. We rifled through our documents and notebooks, reviewing properties, rejecting many. One agent's name continued to appear – Carla. Her office was in Montalcino and since it really was too early to call we decided to drive there and call on the way.

There are so many different levels of learning a language and speaking on the phone is a higher rung. There are no visual cues, no hand gestures, no fingers pointing right or left; it's purely a verbal and auditory experience. Imagine me sitting in the passenger's seat, maps unfolded, notebook and pen at the ready and cellphone poised. I call for directions which are delivered in Italian. For some reason, it helps to close my eyes, blocking extraneous distractions. It's a little tough to write that way but Italians are indulgent people and willingly repeat instructions for the map-reading impaired.

As we made our way toward Montalcino, I called Carla's office and spoke with an assistant who kindly provided directions she had to repeat only twice. We arrived without incident and were introduced to a fair-skinned woman who spoke flawless English. Carla's an ex-pat who's developed a steady real estate and ruin renovation business and raised a family during her decades of living in Italy.

We review our paperwork, her property books and our criteria. She's not as dismissive as Ree-Ree but in her stiff Anglo way she works to lower our expectations. We've come to learn the drill and recognized the limits being imposed. Yet she is an agent and she agrees to show us a few properties.

On the way to a hilltop house in Radicofani, southwest of Lago Trasimeno, our cell rings. It's Ree-Ree and my stomach flip-flops before I breathe deeply and respond. The haughty Madame Lieutenant has flatly rejected our offer, having decided she's not asking enough. Foolishly, I ask for the new price. She wants another half-million dollars.

What kind of market is this? How can real estate be managed this way? Are there no rules or laws or even simple courtesies that are honored? Thankfully she said no but that's beside the point. The rejection gives us license to be indignant. Carla is as sympathetic as her aloof nature allows. As quickly as the Tower appeared as a possibility that's how quickly it vanished. Oddly, as we tried to show Carla digital pictures of the Tower we couldn't find them in the camera. It had become a completely ephemeral mirage.

Radicofani is too isolated and the land too barren for our tastes. We drove to Amelia, the scene of our Little Easter cat nap, to a property with a significant amount of land and numerous outbuildings including a huge, screened-in summer porch with kitchen, bathroom and pitched ceiling surrounded by paved walkways lined with roses leading to the pool. The main house dates to the 1650s with brick flooring and wood-beamed ceilings. It was extravagantly furnished and occupied by the owners – two elderly gentlemen aided by their young assistant. Think *The Birdcage,* replete with Agador Spartacus dressed in butler attire and hauling firewood to keep the silk bathrobe-clad owners cozy as they warm their tootsies by the fire. Think too of *Great Expectations.* The dusty dining room table was set for twelve: crystal, flatware, candelabras, napkins, tablecloths and china. Oh what a movie field day we were having but, alas, not a real estate field day. *The Birdcage* could not be configured easily for vacation rentals so Agador showed us to the door.

Carla took us back to our car and we agreed to meet again in a day or so as she would search for more properties. Meanwhile, we would explore on our own in the Perugia / Assisi area based on some of our previous printouts. As long as we didn't have to see *Portici* again I was happy.

Assisi

Years ago, Roger and I joined friends for a portion of a cross-country hot air balloon expedition commemorating the 500th anniversary of Columbus' discovery of America. We arrived late at night in Bozeman, Montana and awoke the next morning to a deep blue sky filled with colorful balloons set against the surrounding mountains. They looked close enough to touch and I suggested we walk to meet our friends. Several hours and blisters later, we rented bikes to continue. The balloons had long descended but we persevered. Several more hours and blisters of a different sort later we gave up and turned around. We never reached the mountains or our friends. They later remembered driving past two people on bikes but didn't stop knowing full well it wasn't us they passed - Roger would never agree to get on a bike.

That little escapade taught us many lessons that I'll resist summarizing here but the most important was this - big things in the distance are nowhere near as close as they appear. That famous Basilica of Assisi with the endless arches is huge and can be seen from many different angles. Getting there was another story.

Assisi was staring us both in the face but that meant nothing. We had made the mistake of exiting the "ring" road that circles Perugia and drove into the frightening city center – a confusing maze of narrow, one-way streets filled with impatient horn blowing drivers. Who knew there was a "ring" road? Why wasn't it a perimeter or a beltway? If Roger said, "Talk to me, Goose," one more time I would scream and in the meantime our cell kept ringing but wouldn't connect.

With darkness approaching I suggested we exit the highway in hopes of finding help. At the bottom of the exit we were faced with a confusing wall of signs for towns, businesses, hotels and restaurants all with arrows. The drivers behind us knew exactly where they wanted to go. Roger turned just to stop the horn blowing but the tension remained. We were in an industrial park with lots of dead-ends but no people and no hotels.

We retraced our path and came upon a roundabout. The detailed signs posted at every roundabout are printed for those familiar with where they are, not for poor souls like us. Here we discovered our favorite street sign. It's thin, long and has white lettering on blue background: *"Tutte le Direzione"* – all directions. How comforting. Destination Tokyo, Miami, London or Milan - go this way. There's nothing to worry about; can't make a mistake. Why oh why were there so few of these signs? And the cell kept ringing and not connecting.

Uncle! That's it! We stopped at the first hotel and declared the day over. Dinner was mediocre and the hotel was overrun by wild teenagers who were part of a soccer team, but we were out of the car. We could study the map calmly and plot our next move. We were tired and frustrated and depressed/relieved that our sole offer had been so ignominiously rejected.

Salcotto

*E*ither Rosie sold us a lemon or we're missing some important data from our cell technology knowledge bank. After breakfast, we sought help from the front desk manager and despite pressing all sorts of buttons he had no better luck than we did. He suggested we go directly to a nearby *TIM (Telecom Italia Mobile)* store, our service provider. Patiently, he provided directions which were so much easier to understand when not seated next to a person behind the wheel driving 140 km/hour.

After conquering several rotaries we found the *TIM* store and made friends with Rosie Two. Armed with my dictionary, our contract and receipts we began a protracted, tedious and painful discussion about our phone. Rosie One hadn't sold us a lemon. Our phone was simply out of money. I'd forgotten everything about the crucial detail of replenishing the money on a pre-paid phone. Rosie Two set us straight, gave us lessons, showed us how to convert our phone to speak in English and most importantly, how to *ricaricare,* reload, our phone with *soldi,* money. We learned that only the person initiating a call is charged. That explains why no one likes to return phone calls.

Armed and reloaded we found messages from Carla who has a property in the Cortona area she'd like us to see quickly. We'd spent the morning on phone duty, never managed to see the properties we intended to see in the area and were now running late. To save time we agreed to meet at a gas station on the highway and follow her to Cortona.

We knew Cortona well and a sense of familiarity was appealing. As Roger drove, I made lists of the many contacts we had near the town. We were so engrossed in our list making that we missed our exit to the gas station only realizing it as we whizzed by Carla's car.

It must be the years of piloting and the requirement of spot-on instantaneous decision-making that prompted Roger's next move. To my utter astonishment he made a sharp U-turn and drove in the exit ramp toward Carla. The maneuver earned him an Italian driving award but had it been witnessed by the *Carabinieri* it could just as easily have resulted in a fine or worse.

Carabinieri are the equivalent of State Troopers. They prowl the roadways and have frequent random checkpoints flagging down motorists with lollipops - black sticks with red circles on the end. Stick down, the lollipops are conveniently housed in their mean looking knee-high black boots. *Carabinieri* rarely speak English and can't abide the humiliation of being unable to do so. Quick learners that we are, we only speak English when stopped which typically results in being waved through with the lollipop.

Mercifully, the drive to Cortona was uneventful. We approached our target property, *Salcotto,* by way of a *strada bianca* with the famous visual of Cortona forming a backdrop. We parked under a green shade cloth that must earn its keep in the summer months. A husband and wife, both veterinarians, greeted us and began to show us around.

Multi-listing systems, lock boxes, flyers, brochures, caravanning, open houses, for sale signs, pre-inspection tours, escrowed monies and other norms of the U.S. real estate market were not the norms in Italy. In Italy, it was perfectly acceptable for the seller to reject an offer at the asking price. In Italy, walk-throughs were often conducted by owners or caretakers, rendering the agent superfluous. At *Salcotto* the owners took charge and preened about the house and its heritage while Carla trailed us, offering an occasional comment. The vets' pride and depth of knowledge was evident as they talked over each other or finished each other's sentences.

A former *casa colonica, Salcotto* included four additional outbuildings, three of which had been renovated, respecting the style of the old farmhouse. Rose bushes climbed the arched doorways and windows. The house looked comfortable and well-lived in and the furnishings tended toward rustic period pieces. A well-worn carpenter's bench displayed antique tools and farm implements. An old chestnut door turned horizontally functioned as a handsome headboard. A massive fireplace surrounded by the smooth, gray sandstone known as *pietra serena* formed the focal point of the living area. Roger had already begun negotiations to include certain furnishings. We had learned that such early discussions were important. Horror stories abounded - people entering their new homes expecting to find furnishings intact and discovering that not only were they gone but basics such as sinks, toilets and fridges had been unceremoniously removed as they weren't part of the deal.

The three renovated outbuildings were former hay stalls or pig barns and were already in use as rental apartments. The owners had been successful in marketing *Salcotto* for vacationers. There was a pool surrounded by olive trees and additional land available to plant more. The small stall near the parking area that had yet to be renovated could be rebuilt as an additional rental apartment. A project like that piqued Roger's interest as did the chance to move walls in the main house and add rooms, create different levels, put in an additional kitchen and a second floor balcony.

There were lots of positives about *Salcotto* and compared to the dozens of properties we had seen to date, a potential for more. As we walked and chatted with the owners, Carla determined the asking price and we agreed to think about it and talk again soon.

We followed Carla to a bar in Camucia, the town in the valley below Cortona, to discuss details. She was certain the property would not remain on the market long as Cortona is the Holy Grail for ex-pats. Not only was it her advice to move quickly but to offer the asking price. We reminded her of our last experience in offering the asking price and our reluctance to do so again. She agreed to speak to the vets to confirm their resolve in selling *Salcotto*.

Roger and I dined at Corys and again converted our table into an office with paper, maps and calculators. We created spreadsheets to compare purchase price, amount of land, views, number of additional buildings, benefits, income stream, expenses, improvement costs and return on investment between *Salcotto* and *Portici*. We made lists of questions about utility costs, improvement opportunities, ready availability of labor, timing of move, coordination of current bookings and more. All the hard numbers tilted toward *Salcotto* but there was also the gut feeling, the intangible, favoring *Salcotto*. We would wait to hear from Carla.

Tahiti

I was excited and had trouble sleeping. Carla called early the next morning and confirmed the vets' interest and reiterated her sense of urgency. Of course she was in a hurry. A quick sale would line her pockets with very little effort. We were learning that commission comes from both the seller and buyer, normally three percent from each, and that the agent doesn't share the commission with anyone. We were gun-shy and called our only adviser, Andrea. He agreed to take the train from Rome and arrive in Camucia late morning.

The vets and Carla agreed to a meeting at the sacred lunch hour of 13:00 at *Salcotto*. We introduced Andrea and walked the property, finding it as intriguing. We then gathered at the massive wood dining table, covering it with papers. Questions were asked, some were answered. Translations were given, some understood, some lost. There was lots of talking at once and long delays waiting for translations. Roger reminded Andrea of the Neurotic rule and urged him to apply it now. We thought having an English-speaking agent would help us but we were only marginally informed. We made lists of the furniture we were interested in keeping, discussed vacation booking issues and agreed upon a date for occupancy. They wanted the first of September and we wanted the first of June. We compromised on the first of July. Finally, we agreed to offer the asking price.

Three hours into the discussion we began talking about a deposit. The first step in an Italian real estate transaction is a *compromesso* or preliminary agreement. It's the document that accompanies a deposit and states the agreed upon purchase price. When the *atto* or closing actually takes place weeks or even months later, the *compromesso* is then destroyed as the *atto* contains only the declared value of the property for tax purposes.

The logistics of arranging a deposit were complex. The vets wanted Euro and we didn't have the cash on hand nor did we have an Italian bank account. Carla agreed to open an account in our name in Montalcino so we could transfer funds for distribution. It was Friday and Carla would open the account early the next week. She had copies of our passports and her name would also appear on the account. With the settlement of this final point, Lady vet stood, grabbed liqueur glasses, a bottle of the sweet dessert wine *Vin Sant*o and a package of *biscotti* and we toasted our mutual good fortune.

In the relaxing moments that followed, Andrea asked the vets where they were going. They planned to move to Tahiti. Andrea couldn't help but ask, *"Come mai?"* They had been once before and found it beautiful and it promised a relaxing, tropical and other-worldly lifestyle. The vets were moving a world away just as we were.

We gathered our papers and said our goodbyes. Carla would be in touch. In Camucia, we stopped at a florist and bought the most gorgeous irises for a pittance. They were wrapped as a work of art and we returned to *Salcotto* with the flowers and a note, "*Adoremo la tua casa come voi l'adorate,*" a feeble attempt at saying, "We will love your house as much as you do." The sentiment must have conveyed as Lady vet embraced me, kissed me on both cheeks and we drove to Rome with Andrea, who regaled us with tales of The Daughter.

Divesting

After all the trips and all the houses and ruins and white roads, we had found our house. There was little time to savor the moment as we tried to work our way back to the States. Flights were full or cancelled and routing through other European cities looked tight. Not only could we kiss first class goodbye, we were facing the strong possibility of kissing each other goodbye and taking separate flights.

Eventually, we made it to Atlanta together, landing at midnight. Despite our exhaustion we were up early the next morning to pack. When we weren't packing we were making lists. When not making lists, we were making phone calls. It was already mid-April and that meant we had a mere ten weeks to dismantle our lives. This first week was a blur of boxes and phone calls and meetings with shipping companies and Anita, our real estate agent friend who would list the house. Arranging doctor appointments and emptying a storage unit of things that we had forgotten we even owned consumed hours. There were rounds of meetings with financial advisers, bankers, accountants, friends and family. We wrote hundreds of emails and spent days on the phone. We received hundreds of responses with the most wonderful sentiments of congratulations, envy and admiration.

In Italy, Carla worked on the bank account. There were forms to be completed by all three of us and we handled ours via fax. Painfully, we began divesting certain treasures to create ready cash – an antique 1967 Mercedes 250SL convertible at a fire-sale price, books with hand-painted color plates that were coveted by an antiquarian dealer in town, collectible coins, lots of Coca-Cola stock. We visited an estate sale conducted by two women who were experts in the field and held an impromptu yard sale of our own that yielded little money but disposed of useless junk.

On Monday morning, April 22, Carla called us from Montalcino. We had wired money and expected to hear from her about its distribution and the *compromesso*. I was reading the paper in the kitchen and Roger was at his desk when the phone rang. After the initial exchange of pleasantries I heard nothing but silence and it lasted a long time, too long for comfort. I slid my chair back from the kitchen table and joined Roger in the office. He was pale and his mouth was wide open but nothing came out. I mouthed the words, "What's wrong?" and he closed his mouth, frowned and gave me a thumbs-down gesture. As a pitcher to a catcher, he shook me off as I tried to glean more information so I just stood there.

He hung up and delivered the blow - the purchase of *Salcotto* had fallen through. Carla was sorry, this had never happened to her before and she knew how we must feel as now it wasn't just a rejected offer but an accepted offer reversed. We were stunned, speechless, shell-shocked. What possible excuse could there have been to justify this behavior? Carla was embarrassed to even tell us. It wasn't the price, it was simply that the vets had put the house on the market but didn't think it would sell that quickly and they weren't prepared for its sale.

Isn't that too bad? Don't they realize what we've sold in order to generate this money now sitting in a bank in Montalcino? Don't they know we were putting our house on the market? Don't they have to honor the sale? Since the money hadn't made it into their account and the *compromesso* had yet to be signed, by Italian law they could indeed back out. But what about the flowers and the kisses and their word, did that count for so little? Apparently so.

I went to exercise class that morning but didn't listen to my Italian tapes on the way. I arrived late and worked out in the back of the room, avoiding "my spot" and my friends. I had yet to digest this bitter fruit and I didn't quite know how to share it with anyone else. I went through the motions but my mind was far removed from the pulsing beat. I put away my step and ducked out of class early with a quick wave to avoid someone asking about Italy.

Late in the day Clayton called and Roger delivered our news. Out of his young mouth came sage and sound words. "It really is going to be for the best. Maybe not now but in a while you'll be glad the deal fell through. There wasn't enough land for you, Dad, and you weren't at the top of the hill. There'll be something else and it will be better."

It was too soon to think about something else. I still needed to mourn *Salcotto* but as the days went by, it became clear that Roger had reservations about the place that he had not shared. I was stunned. Here was this massive move, this colossal uprooting that we were about to undertake and we had not been in synch the whole time. I thought we had understood each other's desires, goals and standards but he had been disappointed with *Salcotto* all along. So why did he agree to it? He thought we were running out of time and options and I seemed happy and he wanted me to be happy. How selfless and generous but what a burden to think he would be settling for less than an ideal. I felt betrayed by this magnanimous gesture and not a little selfish knowing that I would not have done the same – witness *Portici.*

We plugged along with our lives in the States. We kept having yard sales. We traveled and hosted. I continued consulting projects and potential buyers looked at our house. I kept my eclectic Pilates, ballet, yoga, step exercise routine and socialized during cooking classes.

We gingerly shared our disappointment with friends and resisted looking at properties on the internet. Carla continued to send emails alerting us to other places but we were slower to respond, having been so recently scorched. Our notebook languished for days until finally we began to pull ourselves out of our slump. Italy is a large country, there are other properties and we never did see those places near Assisi and Perugia though the thought of driving anywhere near the ring road gave us hives.

The idea of moving to Italy was still appealing. We wanted to stay mad and pout but it was false. We couldn't ignore the lure and in mid-June we returned. We had a pact. Both of us had to love the property equally, no more selfless gestures. It was agreed.

Our plan was to spend one night in Rome before working our way to Corys. We had learned not to rent a car on arrival. This time we took a train to *Roma Termini*, the main station in the heart of Rome then a cab to our hotel. Rome was hot, our room even hotter. Andrea insisted we come to his apartment for lunch with Bianca. The busy streets of Rome were quiet now: it's the hottest time of the day. Even with Bianca and her white rabbit, we're poor company, struggling to keep our eyes open. Finally we succumbed, returned to our rooms and fell into that deep sleep that only a trans-Atlantic flight can induce.

I should never trust my initial judgment after these flights. I'm disoriented and want to go home, wherever that may be. I would readily break if subjected to sleep deprivation techniques. A nap and shower do wonders. The early evening was cooler. Andrea introduced us to a lovely new *trattoria* where we ate well and enjoyed our wine. He listened to our sad tale of *Salcotto* and he too shared his reservations. He never divulged his concerns because we had made up our minds – it was too late but he agreed with Clayton. Something better is out there.

A Day of Brits

The next morning we picked up our rental car and drove north. Carla arranged for us to see two properties before lunch. We met near Chiusi and were introduced to a lovely, elderly British couple living in a remote home with a pond and out buildings and land and grapes and olives and stunning views and interesting architectural features and absolutely no potential for vacation rental. Roger was impressed with the gentleman's organizational talents and that's saying something. Every piece of equipment and every tool had its place. Wood was stacked properly and all was in order and not just that way because the property was being shown. The upkeep is just too demanding and they wanted to return to England. We were sad for them; theirs would not be an easy sell.

We left Chiusi and followed Carla to the town of Bosco, off the E45 in the direction of Gubbio, to see *Le Vigne*. This was the property we had attempted to see when we became so lost in the Perugia/Assisi vortex in April. We had seen *Le Vigne* on the internet off and on since last fall but it was never very clear how the main building was partitioned and whether the current owners intended to remain after the sale. There was a period when *Le Vigne* couldn't be found on line and we assumed it had sold.

Carla explained that *Le Vigne* had been on and off the market for quite a while and listed with different agencies. There had been a deal but it had fallen through and it was only recently that Carla's agency got the listing. There is only one main building, a renovated *casa colonica*. The upstairs portion is suitable for vacation rentals and the downstairs is the owners' living space. The current owner, a British woman, had no intention of remaining once the property was sold.

Driving to Bosco was no easy feat even though we were following Carla. We left the main road, drove past a small cemetery and climbed our way up a steep blind hill past a small church following signs in the direction of *L'Università per Stranieri*. The University for Foreigners is world famous for its language school. Based in the city of Perugia, it boasts many other disciplines but its language renown remains. This wasn't the main campus, rather an old villa adjacent to *Le Vigne* used for conferences and off-site meetings. The school was a good neighbor and owned an enormous amount of surrounding farmland.

Passing the entrance to the University villa we entered the village of Colombella and came onto a rocky, white road that eventually led to the umbrella pine-lined drive of *Le Vigne*. Carla got out of her car and buzzed the intercom to the right of the imposing wrought iron gates. The gates began to open out and she had to quickly back up which forced us to do the same. Roger grumbled that whoever owned this place should switch those gates to open inward to avoid certain catastrophe.

His grumbling didn't last long. We entered to find a wall of magnolias and a herringboned brick driveway that circled an irregularly shaped glistening pool. Behind the pool was a jewel: a beautiful renovated brick and stone farmhouse with various levels and terraces and staircases and steps leading to more patios and views. We both (and I mean both) found it jaw-droppingly beautiful. It was imposing and made a dramatic statement. Entering the gates meant entering another world.

Le Vigne sits atop a ridge with a 270 degree panoramic view of surrounding farmland and hillsides. There was a breeze at this high point and shade from mature trees. We met the owner, Franny, her daughter Sue and a number of scruffy dogs who had the run of the place and had both women wrapped around their little paws. Despite being mother and daughter, Franny and Sue were the Pigeon Sisters straight from the set of

The Odd Couple.

We walked part of the grounds before looking inside. An enormous live oak protected by a low brick and stone raised garden planted with hydrangea and covered with ivy accented the *piazza*. There were two five-foot tall terra cotta pots filled with cascading red geraniums. Each pot was dated 1898 and while one was cracked and held together with wire, they were both impressive. A low privet hedge separated the pool grounds from the *piazza*. Next to the pool was a muslin-covered gazebo shading a rectangular metal table and six chairs. A bocce court paralleled the pine-lined drive and farther down a steep embankment was a lighted, clay tennis court surrounded by seventy-seven mature olive trees. A twelve-foot tall green metal pigeon coop with a fluted roof sat on a tile pad with several large birds in residence.

Paralleling the back of the brick *piazza* were five large trees that we couldn't identify. Franny called them ancient lime trees or *tigli* but they weren't citrus. They had straight trunks leading to branches of broad green irregular leaves. A smattering of fruit trees – apple, cherry, fig, peach, apricot, pomegranate, persimmon – all on another steep embankment, led to a huge evergreen hedge that divided the garden from farmland.

Continuing down from the lime trees the *piazza* sloped into a concrete pad that led to another gate beyond which were two green metal sheds containing yard equipment. To the right, before approaching the sheds was a small stucco building with a wooden lean-to housing pumps, filters and other pool equipment.

We walked back to the *piazza* and Franny invited us into the house. All dogs followed. The large green shutters were closed so the interior was remarkably cool though dark. For our benefit, she opened the shutters so we could see not only the interior but the spectacular views from every position. The main entrance or *ingresso* was marked by staircases. There was one to the left leading down to what she called a "glory hole." All it takes is a phrase like "glory hole" to confirm that the British and Americans do not speak the same language. Rather than display our ignorance we followed her down the steps. To Americans, it was a combination pantry and laundry room. To Italians, it was a *cantina*. There was a small, poorly screened, barred window that allowed a slight breeze and filtered light. There were piles of laundry and a small washer was churning. The ceiling was low, presenting a hazard to Roger as did the hooks that randomly protruded from the plaster. The rest of the room contained canned goods, wine bottles, a generator, dog food and pails, candles and rags, pigeon food and scoops – the odds and ends of a house with no better place to live. Even though the room was below ground level, it didn't smell musty.

As we walked through the house I asked Franny why she wanted to sell *Le Vigne*. Asking this question in the States usually elicits a filtered response since conversations are restricted to agent and buyer not owner and buyer. Here was a chance to remove the filter.

Franny had owned *Le Vigne* for three years. Prior to that, she owned a home for twelve years near Montone, twenty minutes north. She loved Italy but wanted to return to England to have her last rose garden. I pegged Franny in her late fifties so this sentiment seemed a little melodramatic but it was her speech. When she bought *Le Vigne* three years ago she was married. Shortly after the purchase, on New Year's Day, her husband walked out and she was left to cope with not only the emotional distress but the enormous burden of a property like *Le Vigne*. Enter daughter Sue to lend a hand. Having spent many years in Montone, Sue knew the language and thought she might meet an Italian man of her dreams, get married and settle here. It hadn't turned out that way. Men weren't so readily available and she wanted to get on with her life. While the women had help from an Italian property manager and his brother, the responsibility for *Le Vigne* rested on their shoulders and it was just too much.

While Franny spoke we walked down to the kitchen and a room called the *soggiorno,* which Franny described as a summer living room. Roger had to duck under the header above the steps. Two archways separated the kitchen from the *soggiorno* – one a pass-through and the other a door. The *soggiorno* had huge arched windows and doors leading to tiled patios and views of Perugia in the distance. A small diagonal fireplace anchored one corner of the room and oddly, a large side-by-side refrigerator occupied the other. The kitchen was full of light and the sink actually faced a window with more views of hillsides and farmland. It appeared to have been updated and had its own fridge.

We climbed back to the *ingresso* and entered a huge room with nine vaulted arched ceilings supported by four brick columns. Franny called this the rustic salon or *salone rustiche* and explained that it had been stalls for the cows when *Le Vigne* was a farmhouse. Entering the *salone rustiche,* like entering the kitchen, required some finesse on Roger's part. The farmers must have been under five feet tall to comfortably walk from room to room. The rustic salon no longer looked rustic. It was formal, commanding and appeared difficult to decorate. There were large arched windows, exterior doors on two sides and a fireplace. Franny had partitioned each vaulted room into an office, a gym and sitting and dining areas. Running from column to column were wrought iron rods connected to exterior cleats to provide earthquake reinforcement.

Returning to the *ingresso*, we ascended steps to a landing that led to two bedrooms. These rooms and a hallway had parquet flooring while the rest of the downstairs portion was clad in dark brown, hand-made, clay tiles. The first bedroom was small and had a low ceiling while the second bedroom, the master, was very large with a pitched concrete beam ceiling. It was bright and sunny with four windows, one of which looked out on the steepled skyline of Perugia. There was a tiny bathroom and it too had a window. A small wood stove occupied a corner of the master. Franny assured us it was functional.

Leaving the hallway and returning to the landing we climbed yet again to find the rental portion of the house. There are three full-size bedrooms, two ensuite plus a single bedroom and additional bathroom. There's a large living area with a fireplace that has interior benches and an eat-in kitchen. More windows, more views. The ceilings throughout the apartment are distinguished by massive wood beams. The front door to this apartment leads to an outside staircase for private guest access.

Franny and Sue had renovated the apartment and had some success in renting. They shared the guest book and while it was sparse, all comments were positive. The setting was comfortable, quiet and peaceful. The pool was inviting as were the gardens of lavender and roses. Franny and Sue claimed *Le Vigne* was originally a 12th century convent before it became a farmhouse although it was never clear which part was convent.

In addition to the *casa colonica* and the gardens, *Le Vigne* came with three large parcels of farmland. The total amount of land was six and a half hectares which, at 2.47 acres to a hectare, Roger calculated to be just over sixteen acres. The fields were maintained by farmer Grasselli and had been for years. He farmed most of the land in the immediate area, including the University's.

Franny was willing to include certain furnishings and other trappings in the sale of *Le Vigne*, perhaps even a vehicle or two. We struggled to keep emotions in check but this all seemed too good to be true. Day two on this trip and we were looking at a property that met so much of our lofty criteria. Pine-lined drive, white road, land, a habitable renovated property configured for rental, some rental history, excellent hilltop position, easy access to major roadways, secluded yet not remote, historical, plus downright stunning. Just as Clayton had predicted, *Salcotto* was proving to be the best disappointment ever.

The owners spoke English, the agent spoke English and we spoke English so we assumed, "glory hole" notwithstanding, we were all speaking a common language. Roger was direct. We have been looking at properties since last November. We've made two offers and both had fallen through. One offer forced us to sell holdings we can never recover. We're not interested in gamesmanship but we are interested in this property. That said, many things must fall into place before we will make an offer.

Seemingly, Franny and Sue were direct. The property had been on the market for a long time. They were burned by the previous owner, having to pay for a debt that was left behind in order to have title to the property. They were burned by a previous real estate agent. Two deals fell through – one from an "Italian Stallion" and one from a "Fake Sheik" (it rhymed when they said it). They were not interested in gamesmanship but wanted to sell this property. That said, many things must fall into place before they will accept an offer.

The lines were drawn. It sounded as though everyone was singing from the same hymnal. Next step? We planned to be in country for two weeks and this was only our second day. We had other properties we had committed to see and based on our previous experiences we'd be foolish not to honor those commitments. The possibility of furnishings was appealing. We asked Franny to identify what she intended to include.

An overwhelmingly complex and confusing discussion about price began. Franny wanted to receive payment in pounds. We were purchasing a property in Italy thus the purchase had to be in Euro. Of course we calculated everything in dollars while Franny and Carla counted in *vecchie lire*. The conversions changed daily and the U.S. stock market was hitting a slump. The dollar was slipping against the Euro and the pound remained very strong against the dollar.

Numbers. My head hurt. It was hot. We were hungry. We loved *Le Vigne* but were tentative and not about to be burned again. They would work on the furniture list. We would follow-up within the next several days and check their status. And with that, we left.

Villas, Villages and Disco Balls

*W*e returned to the welcoming comfort of Corys. A bowl of ice was at the ready and we needed it and the gin that went on it. We were giddy and in agreement. *Le Vigne* was spectacular! While sipping cocktails we created spread sheets, this time with the added dimension of the pound. We scoffed at our naiveté, thinking back to last September and the price limits we'd set. We had rocketed through them and now planned to liquidate more and more in order to make a deal work.

The heat continued as we moved from house to house, refusing to leave any stone unturned. Ruins, villages, converted stables, a pristine villa with no rental potential, a former customs building that straddled Umbria and Tuscany unsuitable even for camping, we saw it all. New agents, misleading photos, shimmering heat, scorched seats in our rental car, miles traversing the countryside, our clothing damp and sticky.

Each evening we returned to Corys to shower and sit on the terrace for dinner. We reviewed our notes, the status of the dollar, pound and Euro and cringed at the slide of the Dow. The elevation of Corys offered cooler temperatures and a breeze. The sun wouldn't set until ten and the views of the valley and a sliver of Lago Trasimeno were dreamy. Swallows swarmed and dipped and circled and remained busy until last light and by then our dinner had ended. At our insistence, Renato would pull up a chair and regale us with jokes I translated for Roger. Many involved politics and everyone was fair game. However it was clear Renato was a staunch capitalist and while he often hosted the former president of Italy at Corys, he didn't fancy the man's communist leanings.

Everyone knew someone who wanted to sell a property. Renato introduced us to Aldo. He wasn't a real estate agent but he knew about a unique property on the top of a hill overlooking Passignano and Lago Trasimeno. It certainly had elevation; it was above the tree line. Our requirement of a white road was definitely met. It lasted miles and was bordered by thousands of lavender. The drive crossed the line from remote to isolated.

At this height the temperatures dropped and the wind was so strong I had difficulty standing. We were greeted by a custodian and cleaning lady who alternately led or trailed us explaining the property. The enormous house had been razed and rebuilt using original materials. A vapor barrier surrounded the house to eliminate moisture problems. When Aldo unlocked the door to reveal the three foot wide opening between house and barrier walls, the wind swirled and whistled until the door was again locked. There was a sauna, mansard library, bedrooms with ensuite baths equipped with hydromassage showers, masterfully outfitted kitchens and secondary kitchens and *cantinas*. There was even a dance floor with a disco ball.

As impressive as it was, the property offered no rental accommodations. We followed Aldo to a bar in Passignano where he sought our feedback. While we had little interest, we remained polite, asked the price and raved about the distinguishing features. The ritual to extract the price from Aldo was exhausting. His heavy Tuscan accent made comprehension difficult and he didn't want to readily divulge the number. It was as though he wanted to defend the high price in advance of sharing it. Finally, after much dancing, the two million Euro sticker price was anti-climactic and irrelevant. We extracted ourselves from Aldo's clutches by promising to call him after keeping another appointment with yet another real estate agent with whom we saw yet another unsuitable property. Our hearts were elsewhere and we needed to return to that spot.

Back to Le Vigne

In between the various trips with other agents we were in touch with Carla, Franny and Sue. We overcame our phobia about driving around Perugia and returned to *Le Vigne* several times to take pictures, ask questions and familiarize ourselves with the layout, the grounds, the potential furnishings. We wanted to make sure *Le Vigne* continued to feel right and that an offer would not produce another case of buyer's remorse. Regarding this property, we had no doubts. Every visit evoked the same sense of beauty, comfort, serenity and certainty. Yes, this was it.

Despite our certainty we had doubts about the owners. One day we made a verbal offer and waited outside, strolling the grounds while Franny, Sue and Carla remained in the rustic salon. Roger wasn't happy, they were taking too long, the process should be straightforward. Eventually they emerged, accepted the verbal offer and we all went to lunch at Castellaccio, a hotel and restaurant known for fish and seafood – an anomaly in the landlocked region of Umbria.

We considered the meal a celebration. The euphoria lasted all of twenty-four hours as a meeting the following day was filled with a change of terms on their part. Now Franny wanted to keep all the furnishings and sell only some of the trappings. Questions about ownership and maintenance of the white road around *Le Vigne* produced vague answers. Requests for utility costs and property maintenance schedules were summarily rebuffed. The ability to conduct any type of home inspection was dismissed by the owners as well as Carla – it's not something done in Italy. How did things turn sour so quickly?

And whose side was Carla on anyway? It turns out she was on her side as her negotiated commission comes from the buyer and the seller. We finally agreed on a percentage and Franny insisted we pay the seller's portion as well. Shouldn't that come from the purchase price? Don't confuse her with the facts. Franny has a dollar amount in mind, actually a pound amount, and that figure is what goes to her. Other fees and expenses are to be paid by us. What other fees are there? Duty stamps and land taxes and value added taxes and *notaio* costs.

Notaio costs? A *notaio* is not a notary though that's part of the job. A *notaio* is similar to an attorney but requires more years of education. Being a *notaio* is a license to print money as every single transaction conducted in this country requires the work of a *notaio*. The *notaio* creates the document that formalizes the sale or purchase of land, property and vehicles. Each official covers a specific territorial area and once named as *notaio*, holds that position for life. The position is so lucrative, desirable and vaunted that generations of families have been *notaii*. So the *notaio* costs associated with the sale of *Le Vigne* would not be insignificant.

There had been too much talk and too many verbal changes. We needed something in writing, something to at least serve as a starting point from which changes could be made. Based on our discussions we wrote a new offer that included furnishings and trappings. We reviewed it with Carla though it wasn't clear what role she played. At times we dealt directly with Franny, other times Carla served as intermediary. At long last we sent our offer to Sue because she had the email address and the Pigeon Sisters were as one. The message included a July 5th acceptance deadline, a description of furnishings, a November 1 move-in date, a payment schedule and finally a price, in all relevant currencies. The two-week time frame gave all of us some breathing room. We wouldn't have to hover over a keyboard looking for a response and they wouldn't be pressured into providing a knee-jerk answer.

It was a relief to send the email. They could accept or not but this property was it. We had made four overseas journeys, visited over sixty properties, dealt with numerous agents, suffered through lots of superfluous explanations, logged countless miles on the *Autostrada* and we had found the spot we wanted to be our home. If it didn't work we would be severely disappointed but we had tried our best and as much as neither of us wanted to admit it we had invested enough emotionally. We had to know when to call it quits.

With the click of the send button the weather broke. Rain arrived and instead of generating steamy, muggy street scenes it brought lower temperatures and cooling winds. Could this be a good omen? We went to Siena with Carla to meet Franco, the designated *notaio.* Franco was young, bright and commanded a fawning staff of several women. While sitting in the reception area Carla told us that she had heard from the owners of *Salcotto.* They asked whether we were still interested in purchasing their property. Roger almost choked. I can't remember his exact words but there were references to Macy's window and kissing a fat lady's ass.

Franco called us in to his office. He spoke some English but stuck to Italian when communicating with Carla. I could understand but I still worried that wool was to be pulled over our eyes – Carla's loyalties were clear and discomforting. Our intent in meeting with Franco was to better understand the purchase process. To say our knowledge was limited doesn't begin to describe it.

Franco explained that there are two key documents in the sale/purchase of a property. The first is the *compromesso* or purchase contract. It details the actual purchase price between buyer and seller and is normally accompanied by a deposit of thirty percent. Should the owner back out after signing the *compromesso,* he must return twice the deposit to the prospective buyer. Penalties apply to the buyer as well. Should the buyer retreat he forfeits the deposit.

The *atto* is the deed and also the name of the closing event. The document details the parcels of land, the types of buildings, the names, addresses and birth locations of purchaser and seller and the tax to be paid on the property sale. The sales price must be at least five percent higher than the previous recorded sales price. Recorded is the operative word. The *atto* does not include the purchase price. In fact, once the *atto* is signed, the original *compromesso* is given to the purchaser. It's not to be filed or put in a vault or copies made and hidden in secret drawers. It is to be destroyed.

We provided Franco with all our particulars – passport copies, our Italian banking information, current mailing address, email address and multitudes of phone numbers. He would create the *compromesso* in both our names as requested.

Finally, as frightening as this sounds, we had Franco create a document providing Carla with power of attorney. It was not likely that we would return prior to the *atto* and this document allowed her to act on our behalf. The legal document is deceptively benign looking. A lined piece of paper is folded in half to open like a menu. It begins by naming the parties and the rights provided to Carla by us. For as many words as it takes an Italian to answer the simplest question you'd think that hundreds of pages would be required to convey power of attorney. Not so. We had given her free reign in less than two pages.

We left Franco's office with promises to keep in contact with Carla. As Roger drove to Rome we each silently wondered whether *Le Vigne* would be ours but didn't dare utter the words. Navigating the insanity that defines the streets of Rome we met Andrea for lunch at Tullio, a fabulous restaurant packed with locals, mostly businessmen. The *carciofi alla romana* – artichokes with their tender long stems intact, steamed and seasoned in olive oil, can't be resisted. Andrea accompanied us to our hotel and with kisses on all cheeks we left our friend and the next morning, Rome.

A Rocky July

The 5th of July came and we received a favorable response from the Pigeon Sisters. It wasn't a pure acceptance but enough to move forward with tasks that overtly said we're moving to Italy. A lock box went on our front door and a For Sale sign went in the front yard. Caravans, flyers, brochures and virtual tour photos, repairs, maintenance and the ritual of keeping the house spotless at all times kept us occupied. I remained tentative about telling people that we were moving to Italy but Roger had no such reservations and he spread the word by phone, mail, email and in person. He carried pictures of *Le Vigne* and shared them readily.

Carla provided some explanatory documents about the purchase and moving process. They raised more questions than answered but one thing was clear – we would need visas for a stay longer than three months. We spent untold hours on the phone and the computer in an effort to determine the process for acquiring a visa. The websites are operated in the same way much of Italy operates. Translations are awkward and no one responded to our email inquiries. FAQs primarily dealt with people moving to Italy for business reasons. Phone calls to Consulates in the States produced few results. Because of our Georgia residence we were required to deal with the Consulate in Miami.

After weeks of research and ultimately an in-person visit to the Italian Consulate in Miami we learned that visas are issued only by the Italian Consulate in the United States. To qualify for a visa there must be either proof of ownership (the famous *atto)* or a long-term lease. We couldn't just conjure a fake lease as these details are checked and we couldn't acquire our *atto* until the closing actually happened. The *compromesso*, already in hand, wasn't sufficient. This meant we would move to Italy, purchase *Le Vigne* and return to Miami with our *atto* to apply and wait for our visas in order to return to Umbria to live in the house we just bought. Did Joseph Heller write these rules?

The visa application process required not only proof of ownership but proof of financial solvency (so as not to be a drain on the state), proof of good health, proof of health insurance, proof of lack of a criminal record plus the completion of endless, senseless, complex forms in duplicate with photo IDs and a fee. We were attempting to comply with all the rules. It might be easier to do it illegally.

None of this dealt with the problem of acquiring the vehicles as part of the sale. We couldn't own a car until we were residents and we couldn't become residents until we had visas and we couldn't get visas until we had an *atto* and we couldn't get the *atto* until the *atto* happened. How could we drive these cars? We called our friendly *notaio* who created documents giving us Franny's permission to drive the cars which we would insure. This now sounds so simple but to arrive at this point was agonizing.

Meanwhile, we remained in contact with Sue. Proposals went back and forth, twists and turns, banking issues, money to an off-shore account, the mechanics of money transfer, establishing conversion rates, a push-me pull-me regarding furnishings, informational requests and more. In late July we received an email from Sue that essentially ended our deal: a change of heart about furnishings yet again and a demand on her part that we pay additional commission fees.

More than shocked we were angry and a fierce battle of emails ensued with subject lines alluding to deals going down in flames and phoenixes rising once there was hope of resurrection. When Roger gets going with a keyboard it can produce heart-pounding results. It's a wonder his space bar isn't indented as hard as he hits it with his thumb. One Roger salvo began, "You have overestimated the depth of our desire for this property." Sue fired back in similar fashion. Ultimately the rhetoric died down and finally by the end of July we came to an agreement and directed Franco to create the *compromesso*.

Three Months and Counting

Directing Franco to create the *compromesso* was easy but it was a full month later before all parties had signed it. Carla faxed us the document with her translation and we marveled that something that took so long to create was once again so short and simple. The Pigeons now had a deposit.

We created a new notebook to organize the various tasks to accomplish prior to the move. The whole visa nightmare warranted its own section. Marketing *Le Vigne* as a tourist destination and vacation rental required yet another. With a signed *compromesso* in hand even I dropped caution and announced to anyone who cared to listen that we were moving to Italy. I wrote copy for a website to promote *Le Vigne* as a vacation destination. Clayton designed our logo. We combed the Sunday *New York Times* and *London Times* travel sections for Italian rental properties, looked at websites, studied price structures, booking seasons, terms and conditions. Our experience with a villa rental during our 2001 trip to Italy convinced us we could do it better. One roll of toilet paper, one slim bar of soap the size of a butter pat and one flimsy bath towel per person isn't a luxury vacation experience. Our goal was to create an environment that would satisfy our demanding, discerning and discriminating standards.

Another notebook section dealt with possessions – what to sell, keep, trash and give away. I spent days readying clothing for charity or the consignment shop. The shop staff resembled low flight-risk prisoners released on work programs. There were lots of rules about what clothing they accept, its condition and style. I was offended when they rejected some of my favorite outfits. It made me defensive; I took it personally; it hurt my feelings. I wanted to explain where I purchased the humiliated dress with oversized shoulder pads, where I had worn it, what good service it provided. I couldn't quite bring myself to do it though. We had our own private moment, that dress and I.

We made hard decisions about furniture, tools, lamps, books, photographs, kitchen items, china, silver, rugs and artwork. Much of our furniture simply wouldn't fit style-wise at *Le Vigne* so we decided to sell it in an estate sale or give it to Clayton or Cameron. Sentimental pieces, photographs, my torch from the 1992 Barcelona Olympics and other odds and ends that we couldn't part with and couldn't take were imposed upon Roger's best friend Don to store. We sold silver, jewelry and old coins to dealers in Atlanta. We decided to ship artwork, rugs, china, stemware, a large mirror, one special chair, some books, some photo albums, clothing and some hand tools. We couldn't take any appliances due to the different electrical current so we would leave behind the microwave, washer and dryer. We struggled over the decision to ship our beautiful bed, a cherry sleigh that was long enough for Roger and so comfortable. We never left the house empty-handed and we never entered without a hefty supply of liquor boxes and newspapers for packing.

We contacted professionals who conduct yard sales and visited sales they had organized. We decided on a couple, Sherry and Joe, and selected the weekend, Friday to Sunday, October 25 through 27 for the sale. Sunday afternoon was our departure flight to Rome. The couple assured us theirs was a turnkey operation – they would write the ad, price everything, display it, staff the sale, handle the money and dispense with anything that had not sold and provide the appropriate tax documents. We paid for the ad and they took a percentage of the sale with a certain amount as minimum. They preferred we not be present during the sale. It was their experience that people became attached to their possessions and couldn't let them go. That smelled a little fishy to us. We intended to be there to help and also answer questions. They weren't thrilled but had no choice.

That settled, we contacted moving companies and requested estimates, finally selecting an international firm with extensive experience in corporate relocations. Sam was our relocation expert. He recommended we not ship lamps, phone or computer equipment. We took his advice and lived to regret it. I'm not sure how one becomes a relocation expert but if Sam had actually relocated he would know that lamps can be rewired and computer equipment merely requires an adapter.

Crews would build crates for large items like the gilded mirror from Aunt Mary or the cast bronze statue of a dog and her pups. Crews could do it all, down to the trash in the wastebasket but we would pack many things ourselves and in fact already had. That was a problem as the moving company wouldn't insure what they hadn't packed. I dreaded the thought of unpacking so we agreed to pack only non-breakables and allow them to inspect boxes already done. Our goods would travel in a container by ship and take two months to arrive at our *Le Vigne* door. The shipping fee was calculated by volume and the cost of insurance.

Insurance was a frightening topic. Sam provided a folder with forms and paperwork and explanations and customs issues and codicils and exemptions. The cover of the folder pictured a rusty iron freighter pitched on its side in a boiling black sea that made *The Perfect Storm* look as calm as a cup of cream soup. Everything, and I mean everything, must be itemized and assigned a value for insurance purposes. A box can't simply indicate "clothing" nor can it just list "six pair of pants." It must identify "six pair of women's silk pants" with six values assigned. This is the kind of task that is so overwhelming and time-consuming it induces lethargy. Who do you think had to count and pack and make up values? The same one who became very inventive at estimating the value of a tap and die set when she didn't know what it was. I resisted collapsing on the couch because the movers would arrive early on Friday, September 6th whether we (yes, that's a royal we) had completed this onerous task or not.

How do you prove you're not a criminal and have no police record? Trying to communicate with someone at the Atlanta Police Department was no easier than trying to communicate with the Italian Consulate. Menu prompts that led nowhere, unanswered calls, less than helpful civil servants and finally a trip to City Hall East led us through the maze of procedures that resulted in receiving something known as good conduct records. Apparently the police generate these on a regular basis. Not having much experience with police matters (other than my new buddies at the consignment shop) it was news to me. Anyway, we could check that off the list.

The movers arrived as scheduled with a truck, a crew and equipment to build crates. Over one hundred numbered and labeled boxes later, the prompt and efficient professionals left shortly after lunch. If the freighter didn't sink we would see our possessions in Italy in two months. It was hard to believe that all the months of packing had been swept from the house in a few short hours. The house looked empty and it echoed. The timing was right to get out of Dodge.

Going North

*T*wo days after the movers finished we began a month-long farewell tour of the States. It was an opportunity we might not have for a long time. We didn't need to drive south to Florida. Mamma Ruth had agreed to come to Italy with us for six weeks. It would make our transition smoother and she would have firsthand knowledge of our new home.

Roger's idea of travel requires a minimum of two jet engines and 37,000 feet of altitude. He hates to drive but if ever there were a car that screamed "road trip," it was our red Cadillac. We had arranged to sell it to our friend and realtor Anita but that would happen shortly before our departure. For now, we glided the highways and settled into a comfortable driving routine. We took turns driving every hour. The time passes, the miles tick away and for someone who's not a fan of driving it breaks the monotony.

Our first stop was Elkins, West Virginia where Roger spent three years in college before transferring to Duquesne University in Pittsburgh. Apparently Elkins had not experienced the growth spurt that characterizes many small college towns. No, Elkins had remained unchanged. Notice I didn't say unspoiled. There were few places to stay and even fewer places to eat. We found the only hotel in town, the former morgue. At the reception desk we asked for suggestions for dinner and the clerk suggested McDonald's. The man checking in behind us overheard and said we'd be better off at C.J. Maggie's but we better hurry because they would soon close. It was only 8:30 when he led us there and we decided to eat together.

Our dinner companion was an alumnus who remained involved with his fraternity. He was several years ahead of Roger and not in the same frat. They knew some of the same people and our guide regaled us with stories about which frats had been kicked off campus and which had lost chapter status. For a girl who never set foot in a fraternity house in college, my eyes glazed over at the first Siss of his Boom Bah. Elkins didn't improve much in the cold light of day but it proved a nice trip down memory lane for Roger.

From Elkins we drove to Pittsburgh to visit Nancy and Dana, arriving just in time to attend a cocktail party they hosted in our honor. Friends of Roger's parents who now had become our friends came to wish us well on our new journey. The following night we attended yet another cocktail party and private dinner graciously given by our contemporaries. A commemorative menu marked the date and sent us to our next stop with full stomachs and heavy hearts.

After Pittsburgh we drove to Williamsport, PA (home of the Little League World Series) where our friend Rich was competing in a golf tournament. It was a beautiful, fall-like afternoon but so windy the ball frequently blew off the tee. Through sheer will, determination and great skill Rich hit his drives where he wanted the ball to go. His girlfriend Rita, Roger and I politely golf-clapped as Rich finished the day in first place. This secured Rich the earliest tee time the following morning so only Rita joined us for dinner. We stayed at a B & B she recommended, an old Victorian home decorated in fusty chintz and lace and doilies. She and I had a nice little giggle fest about the owner. Clearly the woman had made the wrong career move going into the hospitality business; she was sour, dour, officious and humorless. The visit served as an object lesson as we were about to plunge into the hospitality business ourselves.

From Williamsport it took two days to reach Hyannis by way of New Jersey and a dinner visit with Roger's dad and his wife. Hyannis was our first experience driving onto the ferry to Nantucket and rounding the arrival harbor at Brant Point was exciting. We spent three glorious weeks on the island and raced back to Atlanta.

Less than a Month

Our road trip had lasted one month and we had less time than that before moving. Days were filled with the office work of life - banking arrangements, address changes, subscription cancellations, changes for utility companies, taxes, consulting work. Evenings involved farewell dinners and parties. Wood Fire Grill had just opened around the corner and we became regulars and good friends with chef/owner Michael Tuohy as we dined with couple after couple to say goodbye.

We continued our communiqués with Carla and the Pigeons but they had become routine and administrative as opposed to emotional and gut wrenching. A date was selected for the *atto*, Tuesday, October 29, late afternoon at Franco's office. While house issues were going well on the eastern side of the Atlantic, Lenox Road was proving to be a difficult sale. A year earlier it was a seller's market but the worm had turned. Anita tried many tricks from her real estate repertoire but there were over ninety homes for sale in our area. If the house didn't sell prior to our departure (a highly likely scenario), Cameron would move in.

The centerpiece of our final countdown week was the yard sale. By Wednesday, Sherry and Joe had yet to bring in display tables, organize books or records or artwork or tools or price any items. We were antsy. They assured us that all would be organized on Thursday and the sale would be in full swing by 8:00 a.m. Friday morning. They urged us to remove ourselves from our home to let them handle all arrangements and negotiations. Again, we rejected the notion.

Thursday morning was beautiful. We were awake early, settling into our usual morning routines, habits that were about to change forever.

Roger sat in the office at the computer. When I passed him on the way to the carport door I ran my hand across his shoulders. He shrugged in silent acknowledgment. I walked down our sloping drive to pick up our last morning paper. Returning to the kitchen, I sat at the table wondering how much it would garner at the upcoming sale. Rather than stripping the paper of ads, I went straight to the classifieds to read Sherry and Joe's ad. I took a sip of coffee from my favorite mug, the red one with white hearts, and simultaneously read the ad and spewed coffee. I yelped and a stunned Roger shouted, "What the hell was that?" I slid my chair back across the wood floor and he rolled his desk chair away and as we converged in the dining room I read the ad and watched his face blanch, then redden.

Our yard sale "professionals" had misrepresented (in other words, lied) about some of the items for sale. They turned certain possessions into antiques when they weren't. They ascribed characteristics to others that weren't accurate. But worse than the lies was a huge and glaring error - the address was wrong.

Now what? The bottom line is we fired them. They were full of unsatisfactory excuses but we didn't trust them. For a moment, time stood still. Whatever schedule we had organized evaporated like flash paper. Inertia soon gave way to panic.

The local paper could run a correction but it wouldn't appear until Saturday. We posted signs throughout the neighborhood with the correct address and simply hoped people would figure it out. We called friends Linda and Mike and asked them to come early Friday morning to help us with this monster. We began organizing and pricing, displaying and merchandising.

All hands were put to work. Don had traveled from Kiawah to spend some quiet time with us before we left for Italy. Shaking his head, mumbling under his breath, "Roger, what have you gotten me into now," Don worked the way he always does on Roger's projects. There's a certain amount of awe, a lot of griping and ultimately a tremendous effort to make whatever Roger does successful; he is a true best friend. Gary, a neighbor, friend and relative of Don's, arrived to grumble as well and then pitched in.

There wasn't enough room in the house to display everything so we used the carports. Tools, file cabinets, old phones, extension cords, radios, records, wicker baskets, pots, dishes, posters, napkins, serving trays, Coca-Cola memorabilia, stuff – all displayed on doors supported by sawhorses. At first, things were placed in orderly fashion but as the clock ticked and we realized how far behind we were, any semblance of order was lost. We covered all the displays, backed cars into the driveway and hoped things wouldn't disappear until they were supposed to.

By ten that night, Don, Gary, Clayton and Cameron had left and Roger and I continued until midnight when we fell numb and exhausted into bed. At three we awoke, inventing prices until darkness yielded to morning rain. Linda and Mike appeared early bearing coffee and doughnuts, eager for instructions. At 6'6" no one would mess with Mike so he was in charge of the cash box. Linda would answer questions and roam the rooms to make sure things didn't grow legs. Don, Gary, Cameron and Clayton returned and while we put together a game plan the public arrived.

Despite the incorrect address and the rain, the hardcore yard sale dealers found us, asking for Sherry and Joe. When told they were no longer involved, some walked out while others asked to see certain pieces referenced in the ad. Several said they would wait until the next day. We pieced together our "professional" team's plan. Items would be priced exceedingly high on day one only to be drastically reduced by day two, to be grabbed at depressed prices by their dealer pals. It was now clear why they didn't want us around during the sale. The dealers were thwarted; rules had changed.

There were a lot of tire-kickers and our time could be consumed with someone dickering over a fifty-cent discount on a candle. It was chaos and unrelenting. We sent a runner for snacks and later one for sandwiches. People came in waves so occasionally we experienced a lull. During the ebb, we regrouped and modified our sales strategy. Any furniture that didn't sell would go to the kids or be stored at Mike and Linda's house for a subsequent yard sale in their neighborhood. Much to Mike's dismay, Linda kept putting aside items that she wanted to buy. In the end many became gifts – small payment for their display of deep friendship.

Friday and Saturday blended into one. I know we went to sleep Friday night but I don't remember. Early Saturday morning brought the dealers again and some bought but not at the prices they anticipated. By mid-day, one of the Friday visitors returned to buy our bed. A deal was struck, the mattress was left behind and we watched sadly as the dismantled sleigh was carried out the front door.

Yard sales draw some strange folks. Some wanted to pay by check but not provide any identification. One offered to leave a deposit and mail a check later. One man who bought a lot of furniture in the morning returned in the afternoon, badgering me to drop the price on some remaining items. When it became clear there would be no change in the pricing, he hounded Roger and then Cameron. Clearly underestimating the united front he faced, he was summarily rebuffed and left angry. He returned several hours later but this time didn't make it in the front door.

By late afternoon, Mamma Ruth had arrived by cab from the airport. She looked fabulous and I told her so. "Wish I could say the same for you," was her honest assessment.

Another honest assessment was that too many things remained in the house and they weren't going to sell. With a discount from FedEx readily available, we packed five large boxes with last minute items to ship to Italy. Mike drove Roger to the closest drop-off point. Even discounted, the shipping cost was staggering but the stuff was gone.

How can the most organized people we know (ourselves) have deteriorated into such dervishes of disorganization? In the midst of all this mayhem, we planned one final dinner at Wood Fire Grill. How I dressed and what I wore is a mystery. I know we ate well because we always do but that detail is also lost. My key memory of the evening was Roger paying the bill – in estate sale singles.

Returning to Lenox Road that night was depressing but we were so tired we blocked the thought. Our bedroom was reduced to a mattress, old sheets and a few suitcases. There were no lights or hangers. Mom was spared this dismal environment as Gary had graciously offered to board her for the night.

Sunday brought more rain and a few people to look at the remains from the sale – a pitiful sight. The coffee pot had sold so Don brought coffee on his way back to Kiawah. Cameron arranged to donate many items to a charitable organization assisting battered women. I sat on the cold tile floor itemizing the donation. After five pages I was overwhelmed and finally quit after Mamma Ruth, Cameron and her best friend Kindra all said, "Joan, it's time to take a shower and get ready to go. There's no more you can do here."

Stripping off my black pullover and baggy cotton knit pants was symbolic. Roger hated that outfit and it gave him great pleasure to throw it away. Cameron loaded her Explorer with our suitcases and she and Kindra drove all three of us to the airport. By now the rain was torrential and the weather mirrored the mood of those we were leaving behind. As we arrived and unloaded the luggage, Cameron, who had been so stoic, lost her reserve. She collapsed into her dad's arms unleashing tears that matched the pouring rain drop for drop. Kindra slipped Roger two notes and with final hugs and a slight abatement of tears the girls pulled away.

And that was how we left Atlanta.

The New Life Begins

Alan Bean, the Apollo 12 astronaut, had it right when he walked on the moon - "I'm really here, I'm really here." While our landing wasn't otherworldly, it seemed so. We're equally enthusiastic about being on Italian soil and practically jump up and down with shouts of "We're here, we're really here!" There were miles to go before even setting foot in our new home. A busy but twitchy week was ahead that would include the *atto*, administrative meetings with the owners, a small cocktail party to meet some of our new neighbors, running errands and a search for lost baggage yet again.

We began our week at Corys since it was closer to Siena where the *atto* would be held. Moreover, we wanted Mom to meet Renato, his wife and the others who had helped us, fed us and taken good care of us during the previous months. Renato has a ready smile and an even readier, throaty, smoker's laugh. Short and reed thin he's unbridled nervous energy, a perfect host and knowledgeable, life-long restaurateur. Years earlier he owned a restaurant near Lago Trasimeno and his expertise grilling the perfect steak earned him the rhyming title of "*Renato, Bisteccaro,*" Renato, the Beefsteak King.

Renato chats with us periodically while we ate the wonderful meal his kitchen prepared. He calmly responds to dozens of questions tumbling from us in rapid succession. Where do we go to buy plates, flatware, glassware, linens, cookware, utensils, wines, food? What about furnishings and how do we find laborers and who's going to do all the laundry and why didn't we ask any of these questions earlier?

Our anxiety level was rising but Renato was unflappable. With regard to our culinary purchases, he told us about METRO, a restaurant supply house close to our new home. He offered to take us there as he has a *tessera,* a membership card, and METRO is open to the trade only. We set a date and Renato agreed to stop by *Le Vigne* first and see the property. We want him to feel welcome in our home as he is the embodiment of our welcome to Italy.

Discussion continued and we freewheeled our way through topics. We need to offer tours and babysitters and maybe painting and language classes and oh, definitely cooking classes and perhaps Renato's brother, the chef at Corys, can conduct the classes for us. Roger and I rambled and were slow to realize Renato had become silent and pale. I asked what was wrong and began translating for Roger and Mom. Renato struggled for words as did I.

Late at night in early July, Renato and his brother left the restaurant in two separate cars. His brother led the drive down the mountain and at a T intersection was broadsided. His brother died as Renato helplessly witnessed the entire tragic accident. This happened shortly after our last trip to Italy. Only now did we learn of the horrible months they endured.

How achingly sad. We put our forks down, all of us in tears as Renato recounted the event that forever changed his life. An already small family has become even smaller. Laura, Renato's wife and a former elementary school teacher has now taken over the responsibility of the kitchen. Renato's mother, whom we call *Signora* but Laura calls *Generale,* has lost a son and Renato has lost his only brother and best friend.

Somehow we got through the evening. Renato shrugged his shoulders saying, *"Va bene, è così, è la vita,"* OK, that's the way it is, that's life. We expressed our sorrow as best we could. Language wasn't the barrier here - perfect fluency would not have been sufficient. We made the effort, finished our meal and walked the short distance to our rooms. Tomorrow would be our closing.

The Atto

Next to the *notaio's* office is a bar where we deposited Mom with several Euro, a cup of coffee and her book. She wished us good luck and wanted to know when roles reversed and she became dependent on the children for transportation and communication. I could tell by the look on her face that she hoped we wouldn't forget her. We reassured her and walked into an experience that was part Fellini, part Kafka. The *atto* was a conveyor belt and we were simply along for the ride.

A secretary escorted us into a meeting room with Franco, Carla, Franny and Sue. A long central table was filled with papers and folders and the room was surrounded by bookshelves containing multi-colored plastic boxes that represent the Italian filing system. Carla served as translator while we relied on my language skills to cross check. We had no attorney, no friend, no knowledgeable compatriot to hold our hands.

Just as with the power of attorney, the *atto* is equally simple and straightforward. Both our names appeared on the deed. Our intention was that we jointly own *Le Vigne*. The reality is that Roger owns half and I own half though which half is which is not at all clear. Later Roger tells me he owns the house, swimming pool and tennis court and that I own the woods, fields and bocce court. I'm not concerned.

There used to be a FedEx commercial featuring a balding, mustached actor who spoke incomprehensibly fast. Franco is his Italian counterpart, reading every word of the *atto* out loud. This rapid recitation must be part of the fundamental schooling to become a *notaio*. I'm concentrating, using my finger to follow along in the *atto*, trying not to giggle at the absurdity. At this rate I'm certain to leave with a blister. Franco barely draws a breath and when he finishes, holds out a pen with a flourish for our signatures. We asked a few questions about the odd joint ownership concept, private roads, property lines and the meaning of land classification categories but ultimately we signed and the *notaio* left the room.

This was our signal to discuss the real purchase price. Through a complex series of international banking transactions we had wired funds to Franny's account eleven days earlier. A few tense moments ensued as Sue privately contacted Franny's banker to confirm not only the arrival of the money but a satisfactory exchange rate. Huffy comments like, "I knew it would come to this," (pre phone call) gave way to calmer demeanor (post phone call). If the Pigeon Sisters were satisfied it could only mean we had somehow been screwed. Carla said nothing. She too had received her money in advance so she just wanted to get through this without any glitches. We were given the original *compromesso* with instructions to make it disappear.

The *notaio* returned, intuitively sensing the money discussion had ended. We tied up loose ends. Franco provided a receipt for his services. The power of attorney was destroyed and we received documents giving us possession of the vehicles and confirming that Grasselli made no claim to the land. Copies were provided and the originals would be mailed. Having the originals was key. They represented the missing link in our visa application process and later our Italian residency.

Everyone now stood and handshakes and *auguri,* best wishes, were flung around the room. It was well after six and darkness had descended while Franco had been reading. The Pigeons were aflutter and all smiles as we walked back to the bar where we met a relieved Mamma Ruth and Carla bought *prosecco,* Italian champagne, to celebrate.

After all the months of searching, all the money invested and all the ups and downs, we were now the fourth very proud owners of *Le Vigne* since World War II. In the backward way that things seem to work in Italy, the Pigeons still held the keys and occupied the house. They would allow us to move in at the end of the week.

Orientation Briefing

We moved from Corys to Hotel Castellaccio to be closer to *Le Vigne*. We would miss Renato – he was our umbilical cord to the familiar and it was hard to let go.

Just like the first day at school or starting a new job, we attended orientation, spending two days with Franny and Sue as they transferred bills, documents and knowledge. We had pages of questions: Where's the grocery store, the dry cleaner? Where do we buy a computer, a telephone, a television? Who installs and fixes those things? Who cleans the house? Where do we take our trash, buy clothes, find a doctor? Where can we find a branch of our bank? How do we pay our bills? Who harvests the olives, where are they processed into oil, how much oil can we expect?

I always had a notepad around to jot down the random thought – in the car, outside the shower door, during a meal. The Pigeons supplied answers, showed us how to turn on the lights and set the alarm, how to open the electric gates, which of the hundreds of keys opened which doors and locks, showed us how the heating system worked and who to call for more diesel fuel, explained the relationship with Grasselli, told us what to feed the real pigeons in the beautiful coop, gave us demonstrations on the workings of various appliances and then provided the Italian-only instruction manuals, told us about local restaurants and businesses, suggested where to buy furnishings, shared upholsterer names, car mechanics, nursery operators and other service providers.

Could any of this have been accomplished in advance? Could we have sent an email with a list of all our questions and therefore been prepared and not so rushed to acquire all this last minute knowledge? Certainly, but in this alternate universe we had come to occupy we were not privy to the answers until now. It was only during these post-purchase days that we finally learned the costs of utilities and that bills were received once every two months and were paid at the post office in cash.

We met the local insurance agent so we could pay the premiums. We learned that every door, window and shutter must be closed and locked every time we exit the property, otherwise our reimbursement would be reduced by a third in the event of theft. It would take longer to do that than make a trip to the grocery. Even the Pigeons rolled their eyes at that one.

We met Francesco, the *geometra*. Part architect, part surveyor, a *geometra* is responsible for any structural events - building, construction or renovation. He draws the plans, seeks approval from the various authorities, obtains the *permessi,* permissions and has oversight responsibility for the work. Francesco provided us with drawings of *Le Vigne* depicting all of our land, buildings and property lines.

We dumped our rental car and took possession of one of our two vehicles, a Fiat Punto. Punto means point or period or dot and that pretty much sums up the size of the vehicle. At 6'4", Roger folds himself in half to get into the driver seat and to see him exit is like watching the breech birth of a grown man. I delicately poured myself into the back seat while Mom occupied the passenger seat. She doesn't know what we're complaining about – she's quite comfortable, thank you. This manual transmission business was going to be an issue. Over the years I've tried to drive a stick shift but it's almost like a math problem. I don't sense the rhythm, the concept, where to put my feet, how to stop or when to go so Roger's in charge of driving.

The key learning (more Coca-Cola corporate speak) from this massive data dump was our introduction to Antonio and his brother Enzo. The Pigeons called Antonio their angel and it didn't take us long to discover the reason. He was the *Le Vigne* property manager and had been for sixteen years. He had all the contacts, all the knowledge and all the experience to get things done at *Le Vigne*. Older brother Enzo took care of the grounds including the olives but Antonio was the boss. Anything the Pigeons didn't know – location of our wells, presence of a cistern, location of the septic tank and when it was last cleaned (astoundingly never), how the pool pumps and filters functioned – was directed to Antonio. He knows where all the bones are buried.

We are introduced to a few of the neighbors. Behind us is a young couple, Federico and Catiuscia and their German shepherd Ronnie. Catiuscia is pregnant and Federico works as a mechanic for the trash service. We can see their house across our field through the back doors and windows.

Giuliana and Renato (yes, another one) are the closest neighbors in the other direction, a quarter mile away. Their house is hidden from view; only their chicken coop can be seen from *Le Vigne*. They too have a German shepherd, Yoshi, who is a regal lady. Well, normally she is. After fifteen days with the perfect mate transported from Rome for the express purpose of creating the perfect puppies, Yoshi spurned her imported lover and escaped for a brief fling with a local hunting dog known as Playboy. Two mixed breed pups, Sofie and Ysoto soon followed and they were in constant trouble – running away for days, eventually returning home with porcupine quills painfully imbedded in their faces, eating cans of cat food (I mean the cans), snatching the fresh bread left by the baker, ripping apart anything in their line of sight, destroying lettuce and spinach plants in Renato's garden.

Giuliana is a retired school teacher and Renato a retired bank director. Their property is similar to ours - a *casa colonica* with a four bedroom apartment. They were renting the apartment for an eighteen month stretch to Mary and Don, an American couple from California who recently arrived. Only Mary and Don speak English.

The women shared details about several other families in the area. Farther up the road is Caroline, an American born in New Jersey and married to Augusto, an Italian anesthesiologist. Across the street from Caroline is Gale, Caroline's former roommate at Sweet Briar, also married to an Italian - Ciccio, the owner of a factory in Calabria. After graduating from college, Caroline and Gale traveled to Perugia to study Italian and met two students working their way through school in the cafeteria. The young men were destined to become their husbands. Forty years and five children later, the roommates have remained friends. Caroline was currently in the States as she is every year at this time while Gale was either in Calabria or perhaps Rome where the family also owns homes. Caroline owns a German shepherd named Sam – it seems to be a trend.

Mary and Don hosted a small welcoming cocktail party, a nice introduction to the neighbors. A fire blazed in their wood stove warming the beautiful dining and living room of their spacious apartment. Giuliana and Renato were there and everyone was gracious and kind and pleased that we will be living at *Le Vigne*. Mom is fawned over and has acquired a new name – Mamma Ruta – an Italianized variation of Clayton's Mamma Ruth as the "th" is a difficult sound for an Italian to pronounce. Giuliana invited us for dinner on the first of November. That also would be our first day at *Le Vigne*. I don't think I let her finish the question before blurting, "*Sì, grazie mille.*"

All Saints Day

The first of November is All Saints Day, a very important day on the Italian religious calendar. November 2nd is the Day of the Dead, also important.

Cemeteries were crowded with visitors paying their respects, arms laden with huge pom-pom chrysanthemums, *fiori di morti,* flowers of the dead. Mamma Ruta spotted that trend immediately and we all noted the many florists whose shops are actually located at the cemeteries.

So it is on this momentous day, Friday, November 1, 2002 that we finally moved into *Le Vigne*. We said goodbye to Castellaccio, stopped for coffee and made a trip to Sidis, the local grocery store for a few staples and some wine to take to Giuliana's. We drove around for as long as we could, not wanting to run into Franny and Sue, but by mid-morning we couldn't wait any longer. We approached the front gates of our house and were relieved not to see – we could finally say it – the former owners.

Mom was impressed and we were struck by the same sense of beauty. It still felt right. The moment of self-reflection and contentedness was fleeting as Roger made the same grumbling noise about the outward swinging gates as he did last June. "Make a note Miss Blue," he dictates, referring to the secretary from *Amos and Andy*. At the ready with paper and pen, I made a note and our first official To Do List was underway.

The former owners have left a note on the kitchen counter. It began innocuously enough with last minute instructions and well wishes but quickly headed south. They apologized for the "slight disarray" but they were unable to find anyone to do a promised deep cleaning. They suggested we have the Isuzu Trooper checked because they just discovered a "spot of oil" underneath the vehicle. And as a final "hope you don't mind" they'd adopted five kittens now calling *Le Vigne* home. We could expect the felines to gather outside the kitchen window about five every afternoon. There's some dry food in the *cantina* but the "sweet little things" really prefer the boiled chicken and pasta Franny prepared each evening. They hoped we would do the same. And with a cheery, scribble of names and a *Ciao* the note ended. The kitten part has Roger gnashing his teeth at the bold presumption and unpleasant predicament imposed upon us. Either we're Simon Legrees by letting the kittens mewl and whine and fend for themselves or we're slaves to five o'clock feedings of animals accustomed to a diet rivaling ours.

We tabled the problem, moving from room to room taking inventory, shaking our heads and finally rolling up our sleeves. The "slight disarray" was laughable. Towels and bed linens are not only in the washers but also on the clothesline and we begin our first official shopping list – item one, a clothes dryer. It's drizzly and we know winter is the rainy season. If we've any hope of getting these sheets onto beds tonight the sun better shine.

It eventually did but rain followed. Before day's end the linens would be well-traveled, making the trip in and out of the rain three times.

Roger and I began in the *cantina* and quickly discovered that the Pigeons had left a lot of, how shall I phrase this, crap. We created categories and sorted accordingly – toss, keep or move elsewhere. Everywhere we turned there was a project and it in turn uncovered another one or five or a dozen. Mom and I attacked the kitchen, discovering pots and pans thick with grease and stuck to newspapers. Tumbleweed-size dust bunnies filled with dog hair spun through the house. There are two vacuum cleaners but one doesn't function and the other has parts missing and a frayed cord. Item two on the list. Mom's afraid to use the frayed cord and goes to work with a limp broom and cracked dust pan. Roger has no such fear, using it to swallow tiny black bugs that seem to be hatching spontaneously from the blue Murano glass chandelier in the *soggiorno*.

The mere task of plugging in the vacuum cleaner was a project. Outlets are few. Once found, we discover receptacle configurations don't correspond to the appliance. That sent us searching for another outlet with the correct number of holes but nothing is close. That in turn sends us searching for extension cords. Ultimately we discovered a kitchen drawer bulging with adapters and old photos of *Le Vigne*. Scenes before there was a pool or *piazza*, views of skinny saplings supported by poles and string that we now know to be sturdy thirty-foot monoliths, neighbors with much younger though still recognizable faces. While it's tempting to linger over these historical connections and study the contrasts, we grab a fistful of adapters instead. Re-wiring goes on the list.

We moved through the house creating piles and sorting things. I shuttled between the *cantina* and the apartment washing machines. Three flights of stairs and two landings each trip. The machines are tiny, front loading and the cycle seemed to take forever. Intrigued, I watched a sheet and a pillow case through the glass window as they spun in one direction for a few slow revolutions and then rested. After a minute, they spun slowly in the opposite direction and rested again. This had been going on for two hours. A trip to the Tiber with a heavy stone, some lye and a scrub brush might be quicker.

During a break in the weather, Roger and I left Mom scrubbing and cursing in the kitchen. Roger wanted to move the Trooper from the brick *piazza* to the grass to check the "spot of oil." We performed an awkward little dance. I started on the right side of the vehicle with Roger on the left. Simultaneously we remember the right-hand drive and circled clockwise, repositioned ourselves and climbed in. Roger started the Trooper which smoked and heaved like a tank. Not surprisingly, there's more than a "spot of oil" and Trooper repair goes on the list.

We walked down the wet hillside passing trees laden with ripe Granny Smith apples. Roger wanted Mom to make her famous apple pancakes, taking advantage of our land's bounty. Perhaps we could shoehorn that activity in at five the next morning.

By now we've reached the two green aluminum sheds and the stucco technical building. The sheds hold more stuff – broken tiki torches, tools, molded plastic tables and chairs, old doors and shutters, cracked pots, baskets, tiles and bricks, rakes and shovels, dog houses, feeding bowls, a few dead mice, old hornet nests.

I'm reminded of the Joan Baez song about the Union soldiers in Virginia, "The Night They Drove Old Dixie Down," especially the lines, "You take what you need and leave the rest. But they should never have taken the very best." The women left things when there were duplicates but took the very best. The lawn mower, the vacuum cleaner, even the beautiful 19th century terra cotta vase that holds such a prominent position in the garden overlooking Perugia and the valley below is the cracked one.

The plastic tables and chairs are filthy but sturdy enough and with a little cleaning will be useful inside. We load them and some basic tools into the back of the Trooper and, after dancing our way around the car once again, chug back to the house. This little trip added more to our shopping list – a few basic pieces of furniture and a utility vehicle to scoot around the property. "Let's put a Gator on the list," Roger declares. I received my first lesson in farm life. John Deere makes an open-bed, four-wheel, gas-powered, automatic cart called a Gator, which we must have.

The toss pile was now large enough to require action. The smoking Trooper is pressed into service and we filled the back with trash - some bagged, some loose. We pulled up to the first dumpster we found and after I finally figured out how to raise the lid (not with my hands but via a foot lever), went to work. A man watched us from behind his gates and after grinding his cigarette with his heel, slowly approached. I greeted him with my most upbeat "*Buongiorno*," but receive only a mumbled "*Giorno*" back. Slightly balding and mustached, he's dressed like a farmer; corduroy pants caked in dirt, flannel shirt with a threadbare collar and a highly pilled sweater. His fingers were stained from a heavy tobacco habit and he says in Italian that the dumpster is only for the bagged household refuse. Things like the torches and vacuum cleaners, pots and broken baskets that we've already pitched aren't supposed to go into the dumpster. In the future, they need to be left in a pile next to our property and there's a special number to call for pick-up.

I understood most of the lecture and started to explain it to Roger when the man interrupted me and said in English, "This is only for house shit. No, not shit, garbage." Ah, thanks for the clarification, now I understand. I apologized and we slunk back into the car which was still partially filled with non-house shit, er garbage, and drove away. Day one and we'd already offended someone. We continued driving in search of remote dumpsters to avoid scrutiny, locating a few hidden from the ready gaze of neighbors and quickly unloaded our remaining contraband.

Mom had collected enough dry sheets and towels from the line for us to make beds and ready our bathrooms. We wandered through the house to determine which of the six bedrooms to choose. Logic would have placed us in the master suite consisting of the master bedroom, bath, guest bedroom and hallway. Common sense held sway over logic. To describe the master bath as tiny doesn't make it small enough - the Punto we were driving had more room. The flush lever was inside the shower. The pedestal sink partially hung over the toilet. Everything was either conveniently located or cramped depending on perspective. The bathroom for the guest bedroom was down a set of stairs and made for tricky maneuvering for late night trips. We continued climbing and decided to make camp in the upstairs apartment living area.

The apartment was adequately furnished with beds, free-standing closets, some chairs, a table in desperate need of refinishing and a few lamps. We selected the green ensuite bedroom and Mom took the cream bed and bath at the other end of the hall. By now it was after four o'clock and already dark. I don't know why the darkness surprised us at this hour but it did. The washing machines had stopped hours ago but all our other tasks prevented us from getting laundry on the line. Now it was too late. Stateside, laundry could be done while other activities were taking place. Here it was the main event.

Downstairs in the *soggiorno* next to the kitchen, we'd arranged the clean but hideous plastic tables and chairs. It was cocktail hour and we were about to indulge when shadows pass by the kitchen window and the unmistakable sounds of meowing broke the silence. We desperately tried to ignore the whines but it's Wild Kingdom out there – not just kitten meows but full-size cat ones too. Felines and former owners win this round. Dry food goes into several bowls which we place far away from the house. Maybe they'll get the message.

We hadn't occupied *Le Vigne* a day before Roger launched into what he does best – demolition. All it took was gin and a crowbar for the ugly, out-of-place French provincial style door separating the kitchen from the *soggiorno* to become history. Mom watched wide-eyed and speechless. Dad wasn't the handyman type so this was a new and frightening yet riveting experience. The wood cracked loudly when splintered and nails popped and in mere minutes the door was gone. We could now enjoy easy passage from kitchen to *soggiorno* with the fireplace and arched doors with views of Perugia. There was an additional bonus. Not only would the door make great firewood but it had been hiding an unexpected treasure – a beautiful brick archway. Who would have covered it in the first place and why?

Now we're late. As always, dinner is at eight and we race to shower and find suitable clothes. We've had no time to focus on which of the hundreds of keys unceremoniously dumped in a planter locked which door so we grab the wine, leave the house unlocked and drive the short distance to Giuliana's house. Renato greeted us and accepted the wine. He took our coats and introduced us to his son Massimiliano and girlfriend Elena. Max, as he's known, is Renato's clone except he speaks English, as does Elena. He's an engineer and she's an economist and they both work for her family's company which creates assembly line systems for large dry cleaning establishments. He handles sales and marketing, travels worldwide and has been to the States many times.

Mary and Don came down to join the party. A long dining room table was set for ten with exquisite linens, silver and crystal. I wondered who the tenth dinner guest is when a shadowy figure emerged from the dark, vaulted living room. Actually, the smell of cigarette smoke reached us first. Roger and I couldn't believe it – standing before us is the man who had instructed us in proper trash disposal!

The three of us laugh while Renato formally introduces Augusto. He's transformed from scruffy farmer to neighbor, anesthesiologist and husband of Caroline. The others were curious and wondered how we already knew him. He explained how we met and explained that Caroline can't stand the *bidone*, dumpster, near their house. She's due back from New Jersey in a few weeks and if she finds excess trash around the *bidone* she won't be pleased. What most upset him this morning was that he really wanted to rummage through our trash but was too embarrassed after he had made such a big deal about the trash rules which no one pays attention to anyway. Out of earshot of the others he asks that we let him know about anything else we want to pitch because he might be able to put it to use. Sheepishly he admits to being a pack-rat.

Renato offered small glasses of *prosecco* and we chatted amiably. There's enough English spoken for Mom and Roger to feel comfortable. We notice that no food is offered with our drink nor are any other types of beverages offered. It's not long before we're invited to sit and the passing of platters begins. Giuliana has prepared a feast - the typical meal for All Saints Day. As an indication of the importance of the holiday the same meal is often served for Christmas.

We started with *antipasti* of sliced meats including *capocollo*, *prosciutto*, *salame*, cheeses, roasted mushrooms, stuffed cherry tomatoes and an unleavened flat bread called *torta al testo*. According to the others, the *primo* was the star of the meal – *cappelletti in brodo* - small, hat-shaped, meat and cheese stuffed pastas floating in a chicken and duck broth served with a dusting of *parmigiano*. That was followed by stuffed guinea hen, roast chicken, roasted potatoes, salad, *tiramisu*, cookies known as *fave di morti,* beans of the dead, *limoncello* and *grappa*. Not only was it delicious, she prepared it all and the poultry came from her chicken coop. It's revealed that Giuliana has never bought a boxed pasta. She always makes her own. How would I ever reciprocate and how could I possibly measure up?

Dinner conversation was lively and I worked back and forth translating as quickly as possible. I'm thankful for the other English speakers because I'm concentrating hard to keep up. We bounced from topic to topic and learned about cooking and olives, farming and gardening, roads and property lines, fencing and neighbors. Renato would begin his olive harvest next week and we agreed to help. It will be good to have a training session before starting our own harvest.

In this comfortable setting where labor and food were exchanged, Roger suggested I offer apples from our trees. Giuliana accepts as does Don who planned to make apple crisps for all. Augusto declined what he called our "Grandmother Smith" variety because he has a surplus of his own.

It's late and we'd had a long day. I know my husband. When he's tired, he has to go to bed right away. His eyes drooped but the other guests showed no signs of stopping. Mom and I offered to help Giuliana clean but she wouldn't hear of it. As we rose so did the others. We hoped we haven't broken up the party. They insist that's not the case. Everyone is tired and ready to return home. At the door Giuliana mentioned that she walks every weekday morning with two other women and asks if I'd like to join her. I gladly agree. Being a confirmed gym rat, I worried about what type of exercise I'd get in my new life. "Be ready at 7:30 and we'll walk for an hour," Giuliana instructed.

Goodbyes among Italians take time. We participate in the departure ritual that involves double cheek kissing, women and men alike. There's a prescribed method: always offer the left cheek first by moving to the right. Optional for men: shake hands at the same time and slap each other strongly on the back.

It's been a lovely evening but more than that, a lovely first day at *Le Vigne*.

Days of Discovery

There's very little difference between innocence and ignorance. There was so very much to learn. We didn't know what we didn't know and were clueless on topics complex to mundane. Transfer our Montalcino bank account to a nearby branch of the bank? Difficult, stressful but finally possible. Withdraw money from that account? Close to impossible. Go grocery shopping on a Sunday? Totally impossible. Determine hours of shops and businesses? Forget it.

We were so active that by the time we went to bed we fell asleep immediately, deeply, soundly, contentedly. I had no time to record our many experiences and waited until bedtime to scribble a word or two in hopes of triggering the memory of a particular event. Often I awoke to find nothing but a spreading ink blot next to a nonsensical phrase. Our sleep is the result of that good type of exhaustion - the kind that's defined by a day full of progress. It's accompanied by aching muscles announcing that our hard physical labor is bearing fruit and leading to positive, gratifying results. We wake early but still don't have enough hours in the day. Often Mom had to remind us to break for lunch or think about dinner.

It took us actually living at *Le Vigne* to realize that what we considered "habitable and rentable" didn't measure up to our standards. And that was just the interior. The grounds required scrupulous attention and our project and purchase lists were lengthy. Antonio met with us for hours on end. It must have been painful for him because it was plodding and difficult for me. Not only did I have to understand the technical things Roger wanted to accomplish, I had to translate them for Antonio. Then I had to translate Antonio's comments for Roger. Then Roger would respond and so it went.

My Italian improved daily and my vocabulary grew to include esoteric words such as *zoccolo,* the desirable toe space beneath kitchen cabinets not typically found in Italian kitchens and *trave,* the heavy rough-hewn wooden beams that cover much of the apartment ceilings. Roger's language skills were also improving. His favorite words are *domani,* tomorrow – when he wants work done; *caro,* too expensive – when he's told the price and *sconto,* discount – used at all times.

Antonio had the patience of a saint. He was our *capo,* boss, leader, property manager. He was reliable, competent, professional, knowledgeable and calm. He grasped immediately what Roger wanted to accomplish and how it could be done. They both understood the common language of renovation. We weren't interested in a quick fix. If things were to be done, they would be done right and Antonio appreciated our approach. Antonio knew and recommended the best tradesmen. If they met his standards we were certain to be in good hands.

Lists were divided into categories: gardens, olives, fields, electrical, plumbing, carpentry, masonry, flooring, fuel, furnishings and appliances. Interior work was divided between the apartment and our living space, which called for massive renovations in the kitchen, *soggiorno* and master suite. The apartment required painting, more furniture and appliance upgrades. The entire house was slated for new wiring, new plumbing and new doors. Fifteen French provincial interior doors, so *brutto,* ugly, would become firewood.

Bank Caper

All projects call for money and money leads to banks. The Italians may have invented modern banking in the 15th century, thanks to Cosimo the Elder of the Medici family, but advances since the Elder have been glacial. Last spring we opened our account in Montalcino at the Monte dei Paschi di Siena bank - the oldest bank in the world. We believed such history would translate to knowledge and wisdom and a desire to be at the forefront of technology in the banking industry. We believed branch banking was universal. We believed withdrawing our own money would be simple. Why we made such quantum mental leaps I'll never know.

We found a branch of our bank in Ponte Felcino, the next town south of Bosco. We negotiated the entrance as experts, sending Mom through the bullet-proof Plexiglas bubble first. The interior was unassuming.

There were several teller windows but only one open and a long queue. To the right of the windows were several cubicles, each furnished with plain, utilitarian metal desks for bankers and equally Spartan metal chairs for customers. The desks were overflowing with paper in progress. The shelves behind were worse. Antiquated computer monitors mingled with coin and paper counting machines. *Non aperto,* not open, signs forbiddingly sat at the front of each desk. More metal chairs faced the cubicles and Mom wisely took a seat, ready for the long haul.

Roger and I waited patiently. Fifteen minutes dragged into thirty and Roger sat with Mom. Mentally, I reviewed my Italian banking phrases and felt quite comfortable with how to withdraw *soldi,* money. At the forty minute mark I made it to the window and Roger rejoined me. We presented all of our paperwork from the Montalcino branch and asked to withdraw four thousand Euro. With that our teller closed the window and took off for the bowels of the bank. We weren't pleased but just imagine the groaning from the masses behind us.

The teller eventually reappeared with two other men. Our paperwork was shuffled between the three men while they requested identification. Italian words were flying fast and finally Roger reached his limit and demanded to know what was going on. I tried to insert myself into their conversation when one of the men deigned to address me. He understood we wanted to withdraw money but didn't know who we were. The translation of this sent Roger into orbit. "What difference does it make?" "We want our money!" "Tell 'em, tell 'em now."

I'm frustrated too but trying to smooth all feathers. My stomach hurts and I'm sweating. I try to explain who we are, where our house is, that we've recently moved here permanently from the United States, that we'll be in this bank often to withdraw money when the banker stops me and asks an amazing question – "What do you want to use the money for?" I'm stunned at the request and momentarily speechless. Roger's bursting, "What'd he say, tell me what he said." A split second decision led me to divulge the request. As soon as the translated words tumbled from my mouth I knew I'd made a bad decision. If only I could retrieve the words. Roger was frothing, "Tell him we want to buy drugs, what the hell business is it of theirs what the money is being used for." More sweat, more feather smoothing. I explain we want to buy furniture and appliances and conveniently omit the drug reference. The banker finally relented, instructing the teller to provide us with the cash.

The more senior of the three men introduced himself as the bank director and shook our hands. That's the good news. The bad news, it was his last day. The third man is the incoming bank director – back to good news. We're escorted to one of the cubicles for more discussion about the mechanics of transferring our account, completion of paperwork (just what they need, more paper) and to fulfill our request for checks.

I mentally groaned at the anticipated hassle of acquiring pre-printed checks when the teller provided us with a little booklet of ten blank checks. He painstakingly recorded check numbers in triplicate and wrote our account number on the cover of the booklet. I asked how long it would be before getting checks with our names printed on them. No one understood the question. I took another approach. "What happens when we run out of these checks because with all the furniture, appliances and yard equipment not to mention recreational drugs, we're going to need lots more than ten checks?" Just come back and repeat the process. Apparently we'd never get personalized checks. Now that we're on a first-name basis with the bank director, perhaps withdrawing bucket-loads of cash is the best option.

Taking receipt of the cash is entertaining. Each teller has a drawer with a dial type lock and a timer. Opening the drawer requires finesse as the timer is released every fifteen minutes. We attempted small talk with the teller while awaiting the timer's release. He suggested we notify the bank several days in advance when we want to make a large withdrawal. Eventually the drawer unlocked but alas, there's not enough cash to satisfy our withdrawal. He yells to the teller in the next cubicle and asks for money. That teller's drawer is locked and he can't open it for five minutes so our teller yells even louder to the next teller. The third teller has his drawer open and can provide the cash which gets handed to the second teller who passes it to our teller. All this for four thousand Euro. So much for security, locked drawers and timers.

I've been so engrossed in high finance that Roger has to point out that the bank staff is straight from central casting. They're all switched-at-birth actors. Our teller is Steven Seagal with his tall good looks, high forehead and slicked back ponytail. The new director is Jon Lovitz and then there's Igor (real name Umberto), an assistant director who's a throwback to the Studio 54 days in New York with his swiveling hips and monochromatic shirt, tie and suits. We've named him Igor because his attitude goes with the name.

Days at the bank are painful, always challenging, always stress-inducing. I dread them despite the stories they provide.

More Revelations

Driving proved to be highly entertaining for Mom. All of us could see exactly where we wanted to go but getting there was a challenge. Many times it would have been easier to walk. The mall known as Collestrada is nearby and worth a visit based on all recommendations. A mall for crying out loud! How can you not find a mall? We managed to pass it six times. Eventually we found the exit but got confused in the parking lot. Usually Roger is the fortunate soul with parking lot karma but not on this day. A wrong turn sent us to the rear of the mall and down a narrow alley behind a kennel. Mom laughed 'til she cried. Our stalwart driver was beyond frustrated but finally succumbed to the infectious laughter. In the end, we got to the mall only to find it rather pedestrian, anchored by a supermarket and a McDonald's. As some type of perverse reward for having survived the experience Mom and Roger shared French fries and burgers while I found *gelato*.

Laundry remains a side show. I know the washers are designed to be energy efficient but since they only hold two pairs of panties and a tee shirt more loads have to be done, making the whole effort counterproductive.

We bought a dryer at an appliance store called *TuttoCasa,* everything for the house. As I tried to write a check the clerk said he didn't know us so he wouldn't take the check. I gave him our story while practically sitting on Roger to keep him in line. The clerk suggested I use a credit card; he claimed all Americans have credit cards. Instead we called our friendly bank director who vouched for us. *TuttoCasa* grudgingly accepted the check.

The dryer is quite interesting. It doesn't hold much more than the washer and it's not vented. Currently it resides in the rustic salon until we can make space in the *cantina.* Roger would never read the directions for an appliance whether in English, Turkish or Italian; he'd just turn it on. I on the other hand study every manual whether the appliance is a toaster or a tractor. The dryer manual is written in several languages, none being English, so it took hours with the dictionary to figure out how the thing worked. The design is clever. A tank holds water extracted from the clothes. It has to be emptied after each use otherwise it overflows and the machine won't operate. Nothing goes to waste; I use the gray water for plants and the lint balls for fire starters.

One day we left home with the washer running. When we returned we heard the cistern water pump cycling continuously. We were a little slow on the uptake but eventually discovered the front-loading washer face down in the *cantina*. The little crock-pot had vibrated off its concrete pad during the vigorous spin cycle. The hose had separated and water gushed onto the *cantina* floor. The flooding was already six inches deep. We unplugged the writhing monster, grabbed buckets and towels and called Antonio. Mamma Ruth stood at the bottom of the stairs, arms folded, pinched look on her face and scolding tone in her voice, "You left the washer running while you were gone?" I tried to ignore the post-event helpful advice.

Once Antonio and Roger pumped the water out of the *cantina* and righted the machine they strapped it in place to avoid future leaps. They also agreed to eliminate the cistern and pump system and replace the tiny half-inch supply line with a larger one and bring the city water into the house from another direction.

I actually have managed to do things other than laundry and banking. Giuliana was good to her word and we meet every morning for our walk. While I've yet to go to the gym or find ballet classes, the walks are brisk, enjoyable, educational, gossip-filled gab fests. We are joined by Giovanna whose family owns a local clothing store in Colombella and Liana, an orthodontist. Mostly I listen and soak it all in. They speak rapidly and with the ease of women who have known each other for a long time. I have to focus and if I don't understand a word I skip it to follow the overall train of thought.

All three women are very attractive. Giovanna is blonde and the youngest. She's married to Franco who's in partnership with his brother Giuseppe in the retail clothing shop. Giuseppe is married to Federica, a school teacher who works afternoons at the store. Six months older than I, Liana has long, wavy blondish hair and wears a variety of stylish eyeglasses. She's highly educated. Until recently, to become a dentist in Italy one must first become a medical doctor. While no longer the case, this was indeed her training. Her schedule is strenuous as she travels to different dental offices from Ponte Pattoli to Umbertide to Foligno to see patients, each office being twenty to forty kilometers apart. Liana is married to Massimo, who has his own computer business. Giovanna and Liana each have one daughter and both are in college though not together.

Not only do I learn about their lives, I glean lots of practical advice about where to buy certain goods, that it's important to compare prices and prod owners into discounts. They confirm what we've come to learn – life in Italy is expensive. The advent of the Euro brought with it a bump in prices across the board. Food and wine are relative bargains but everything else is pricey.

The girls ask the *come mai* question and I explain our story. They're amazed we've landed in their small town. Only Giuliana has been to the States (as a result of her friendship with Caroline) and most of their travel has been limited to Italy or other European countries, primarily by bus. Our walks must prove quite a sight. Sometimes Giuliana's dogs are with us. Yoshi can be controlled verbally while the other two scatter as Giuliana refuses to leash them. When the weather threatens we carry umbrellas and the bright colors of the open fabric announce our presence from a distance. Any juicy tidbit of gossip or amusing story calls for the teller to stop in her tracks. The others are also forced to stop as she emphasizes an interesting point. I used the technique myself with the falling over washing machine story. I get a lot of mileage out of laundry these days.

I love being outdoors, starting the day early and soaking in the surrounding views. We vary our walks to include white roads, paved roads, steep hills, grassy and at times muddy slopes. In the beginning I felt like the walks were not as strenuous as an hour-long step class but came to realize they were just as aerobic and I was exercising different muscles. Between walking and working on the grounds I haven't spent this much time outside since I was a kid playing Capture the Flag.

It's restorative. The air is clear. Some days we see our breath as we cross heavily frosted grass that sounds like the crunch of uncooked Ramen noodles underfoot. The terrain is a postcard come to life. The patchwork hillsides change daily – from unplowed fields to roughly plowed fields to neatly plowed fields to planted fields with a hint of green from winter wheat. It's no wonder Umbria is called "The Green Heart of Italy."

November is proving quite changeable. Some days are mild and spring-like, others cold and frosty, some drizzly rain and sometimes heavy rain. We've experienced a *scirocco,* a strong, hot unrelenting south-easterly wind from Africa laden with Saharan desert sand. Two or three days of *scirocco* are always followed by rain that coats our windows pink. Not to be outdone is cardinal point north which brings the *tramontana*, a fierce cold Alpine wind that signals a front and the certain arrival of cold weather. *Le Vigne*'s hilltop position means unprotected exposure to remarkably forceful winds.

Every day we learn a little more. The gap between innocence and ignorance is still yawning before us but our toddler steps denote progress. It's all such fun. We're here, we're really here.

Shopping with Renato

Yesterday was our METRO day with Renato. We suggest meeting him at Bar Tenda (pronounced the way a Bostonian would say "bartender"), a coffee shop at the Bosco/Gubbio exit of the E45, the highway closest to *Le Vigne*. We're pleased with ourselves that we can direct him to this convenient meeting point and once he arrives we lead him to *Le Vigne*. His reaction was all we hoped for. He loved the building, the land, the olives, the fruit trees, the gardens, the setting and most of all, the potential. He finally accepted a bucket of apples and a large branch of *alloro,* bay leaves, to use in his restaurant kitchen.

We drove two vehicles to METRO because after our shopping expedition Renato must return quickly to Cortona. He refused our offer to stay for lunch and we're disappointed. He does so very much for us and we manage so little in return – we must find a way.

As promised, METRO is close and easy to find and what a find it is. It makes Sam's, Wal-Mart and Costco combined look like a mini-mart. Renato is exceedingly patient, helping us with the whole process – where to park, how to retrieve a cart, how to navigate the gated entry (he presents his *tessera* or ID card and explains we're with him), how to work our way through the store, which brands are best, which prices are fair.

Cart retrieval is very clever. All carts are individually chained to a rail near the store entrance. A coin is inserted into the gizmo at the top of the cart which disengages a short chain linking the cart and the rail. The coin is merely a deposit. Once shopping is complete and goods are loaded into vehicles the cart is reconnected to the chain and the coin is returned. It's a sensible solution to an annoying problem - no carts are left to roll around parking lots, crashing into cars or shoppers. Nor do carts travel to nearby apartment buildings only to be abandoned in alleyways or sidewalks.

Before I knew that grocery carts came at a price, I offered some shopper what I thought to be a kind gesture by taking her cart off her hands rather than having to return it to the rack. Instead of doing the right thing, she felt that I was ripping her off with a smile.

Once inside we were wide-eyed, roaming the aisles devoted to produce, meats, seafood, cheeses, pastas, sweets, savories, canned goods, candies, wine, beer, liquors, kitchen utensils, cookware, flatware, stemware, wine racks, storage containers, shelving, waters (flat, fizzy, lightly carbonated), small appliances, detergents, paper goods. We lingered, we dawdled, we ogled, we remarked, we bored this poor man to tears. After thirty minutes of our gape-mouthed, head swiveling action, Renato excused himself, indicating he'll catch up with us later.

We began with an icemaker at the astounding cost of 700 Euro. We're certain to be the only private residence in Italy with an icemaker and it's the same model used by every cutting edge hotel bar that has upgraded from plastic ice bags. After the icemaker we collected items from every aisle. Our cart is the size of a semi and we've filled it and one more. We were forced to stop as our quick calculations had us north of 2,000 Euro and METRO is a cash-only operation. The thought of returning to the bank unhappily came to mind.

Before checking out, Renato collected us and our two semis and led us to the gated entry. While we shopped, he completed paperwork and now has Roger fill in a few remaining blanks. A name was crossed out and Roger's had been inserted. The clerk took Roger's picture, a *tessera* was created and we had now been provided entrée to the trade-only restaurant supply house.

Only two people per business entity can be provided a *tessera*. Renato replaced his brother's name with Roger's. The honor is humbling. Removing his brother's name must have been a stark and final acknowledgment that he's truly gone. Our thanks seem hardly enough. He made sure we knew how to get back home and then he left with promises to see us again soon.

Olive Harvest

*I*taly is harvesting olives and it was time to do ours. The harvest can take place between mid-October and the end of January. Early harvesting yields less oil but higher quality and stronger taste. A late harvest provides greater quantity but lower quality.

While Roger had over a century of genealogical expertise in horticulture on his side thanks to a grandfather, father and Roger himself as nurserymen, none had grown olives so we were new to this together. We got our feet wet at Giuliana and Renato's house one afternoon where we joined a dozen others; family, extended family (everyone seems to be someone else's aunt or uncle), neighbors plus Mary and Don. Not much training was required to participate in this agricultural pursuit so we learned quickly. *Panini* and homemade wine helped fuel us in the cool air. I served as translator and held my own until one of the peasant garbed locals transitioned from Italian to dialect and left me linguistically flat-footed.

Renato is all energy and constant motion. He's thin, wiry and in command of the operation. He sprints from tree to tree stacking crates, delivering nets, moving ladders as though born to the agrarian life. Seeing him inside his rickety *Ape* makes it hard to visualize him as the corporate banker he once was.

A few words about the *Ape*, the mythical utility vehicle that revolutionized the Italian farmer's life after World War II. *Ape* (not the gorilla variant) is a two syllable word with the *"a"* as in "Ma" Kettle and the *"pe"* as in I.M. Pei. Pre-WWII most people in Italy relied on bicycles, walking or horse and buggy but after the War the *Ape* became common, providing even farmers affordable motorized transport. *Ape* means bee and the vehicle sounds like a buzzing bee thanks to the Briggs and Stratton type lawnmower engine that drives it. The *Ape* has three wheels, an enclosed cab and handlebar steering.

The *Ape* remains omnipresent in Italy and reaches maximum speeds of thirty miles per hour. They are barely road-worthy and constantly in the way of faster moving vehicles. Nowadays almost everyone has a car but the *Ape* is still the farmer's utility vehicle of choice and there are some who rely on the *Ape* as their only vehicle. One of my favorite scenes is of a weathered husband and wife pinched side by side on the *Ape's* narrow bench seat on the way to the outdoor market or grocery store or even Sunday mass. During all of our property hunting trips to Italy Roger wanted every *Ape* he passed on the road but now he's settled on the Gator as more powerful and utilitarian. I'm relieved. I couldn't imagine how the two of us would look squeezed into the tiny cab.

Back at our neighbors' harvest, Renato cornered Roger to help with the last of several tall trees. He wanted to take advantage of Roger's height and probably test his mettle. Roger plucked the few remaining fruit within his easy reach but even he had to resort to a ladder at the end. The ladder had seen better days so it wasn't a surprise when ladder and user collapsed together. Bruised elbow, hip and ego survived the fall but not without grand moaning and gesturing, apologies and laughter.

Renato's next assignment for Roger was to help unload the olive-filled crates known as *cassette* from the open bed of the *Ape*. Each full crate weighed fifty-five pounds and Renato had the crates stacked three high and four deep. He asked Roger to walk behind the *Ape,* which had no tailgate. Certain calamity lies ahead but Roger dutifully followed orders, easily keeping pace until they reached the steep drive. Renato gunned the *Ape* and the crates began to slide. Roger tried to block them with his arms and finally thrust his body at the back of the *Ape* in a vain attempt to stop the inevitable tumble. Roger yelled but Renato continued driving, oblivious to the loss of cargo until he sensed the lightness of his load and stopped. Olives rolled down the drive, Roger chased crates and olives, Renato circled back in a wide arc to avoid crushing the precious fruit and Italian and English blended into not-so-mild oaths understood by all. Add strained back and shoulder to Roger's maladies, but his good humored complaining apparently sat well with our neighbor. Together they gathered as many olives as possible, re-loaded the *Ape* (more sensibly this time) and delivered them without further damage. With that, Roger seemed to have passed whatever testosterone-laden Survivor Island challenge had been set.

This frenetic pace served as the perfect counterpoint to our pastoral harvest. The other half of our in-house angel duo, Enzo, held our hand. I found it difficult to understand Enzo so there wasn't as much conversation in our grove as there had been next door. This did not displease Roger. Unsure of our ability and/or willingness to pick, Enzo brought his son Alessio to help in the morning but left him at home in the afternoon once he determined we were worthy.

Harvesting begins mid-morning once the dew has evaporated. Olives shouldn't be harvested wet because they will mold and that will adversely affect the quality of the oil. A large square nylon tarp (six meters by six meters or roughly twenty by twenty feet) is a key tool. The tarp is cut from the center of the square to one outer edge, allowing it to be placed around the trunk and slightly overlapped on the opposite side. Our many steep hillsides require Enzo to use sharpened sticks to prop the ends of the tarp so that the olives don't run downhill and disappear. Roger was frustrated by the inclines, already devising ways to terrace the land to eliminate the *scarpate.*

Once the tarp is in place picking begins. Enzo works quickly and we do the same. Using both hands we run our fingers down each branch and the olives fall onto the tarp. They offer very little resistance as we strip the fruit from each branch. The olives are a variety of colors – green, brown, black, red and mottled and every color goes into the mix. We try not to pull leaves and stems off the branches but some make it onto the tarp despite our best intentions. Once all the branches within our reach have been cleaned, we carefully shift our feet, move to another location and start again. Roger reaches high, I go low and Enzo eventually gets on a ladder or climbs into the crotch of the tree to pick the last of the fruit. Moving on the tarp requires finesse so as not to crush any olives. Even when a tree appears finished, there are always a few olives remaining. Enzo spots them easily, grabs what he can but if a few remain on the tree he says they'll be a treat for the *uccellini,* the little birds.

Gingerly stepping back from the tarp, we gather the ends, forcing the olives to roll toward the center. We lift it above a plastic *cassetta,* one of ten crates we've bought to add to the half dozen we found in the green sheds and dump the olives into the crate, sliding the tarp out from underneath the fruit. Roger wants to fondle the olives and remove stems and leaves but Enzo has already moved onto the next tree, tarp under one arm, sticks under the other. We quickly follow. The full crates are heavy and we use a wheelbarrow to move them, wishing the Gator were a reality.

The sun sets early on these late fall days and the cool night air brings condensation back to the grass and trees. Just as we couldn't harvest in the morning, late afternoons are restricted as well. Olive harvesting is quite a gentlemanly farming experience. Enzo stored the net, the sticks and the empty crates in one of the sheds. He'll return the next morning as soon as it's dry enough to pick.

As impressive as it was to think of picking our olives, the real surprise was watching Mamma Ruta at work. Her exposure to being "in the country" was limited to passing a Cracker Barrel on the highway. She actually did stand on the tarp and pluck a few olives. We have the pictures to prove it but the November chill was simply too much for her thinned Floridian blood. A down vest we purchased did little to keep her warm so Roger assigned her a cozy indoor task in front of the fireplace – remove the leaves and stems from the collected olives and keep the fire burning. This too provided a great photo op as there had been little call for her to stoke a fire in her fifty years of Florida living.

Still wearing the vest and now parked in front of a roaring fire, Mamma Ruta demonstrated her true expertise. She used a small casserole dish to isolate a hundred or so olives at a time. Leaves and stems were thrown into a pail on the right and olives into a crate on the left. Periodically, Roger would come inside to check on the fire and her progress. He'd stand over her exhorting her to work faster, warning her not to make any mistakes. Invariably, stems would go left and olives right and he'd pounce on the poor woman like a cat on a mouse.

Oh, did she complain. "You owe me at least one manicure, maybe more. Plus, I do just fine until you walk in the door and then I mix up olives and stems." We harvested for three days and she cleaned for three days. Enzo and Antonio couldn't believe Roger had given her such a job. No one else bothers to remove the stems and leaves. Enzo said the olives go through a water bath and the big pieces are washed away before the olives are crushed. No matter. Roger reasoned that if the crates contain only olives the oil will taste better so that's the way we did it at *Le Vigne*.

I loved it! The harvest was idyllic, the weather cool yet sunny. I enjoyed the thoroughness, the methodical, deliberate way a tree is cleared, the camaraderie, the bounty, even the soft plinking of olives falling onto the tarp. At first I thought it was just the novelty of it that captured my interest but even after finishing our seventy-seventh tree I was equally enthralled. It's just as well since we'll plant six hundred more next spring.

Now that we had harvested and Mom had cleaned we needed to go to press. Where do we go? Do we just drive to a *mulino* with our olives in the backseat? What do we put the oil in once the olives are pressed? Enzo continued to hold our hand. Even the smallest of villages has its own *mulino* and with everyone harvesting at the same time the mills operate 'round the clock. We heard horror stories about people getting appointments at three in the morning. Enzo handled everything and secured an appointment at the perfectly reasonable hour of ten a.m. at the mill in Bosco. He showed us where to buy a fifty-liter stainless steel container and taught us how to clean it by rinsing it with vinegar, not water.

On the appointed day, Enzo arrived at *Le Vigne* and we loaded his car and our Trooper with crates. The four of us made the short drive to the mill. While unloading the crates, Enzo introduced us to the owners: a husband and wife assisted by their son and a few other family members. Just inside the door, we stacked our sixteen crates onto a large metal plate on the floor – the platform of an industrial scale. The mill was noisy with the sound of heavy machinery. Enzo and the owner spoke rapidly while we found a chair for Mom next to a roaring fireplace.

The mill is an assault on the senses. The aroma is strong, almost acrid. A deep inhale catches at the back of the throat. After several shallow breaths, we adjusted but the deafening noise didn't diminish. Other customers, primarily men, waited as their oil is processed. Some grilled sausages or drank homemade wine from small plastic cups which were then tossed into the fireplace. They sit, they chat, they amble about hands jammed into pockets. Periodically someone sliced a thick slab of crusty bread and toasted it. It was rubbed with garlic, generously sprinkled with salt and drenched in the darkest green olive oil I'd ever seen. Our mouths watered as we're offered a taste of a perfect, pure *bruschetta*. The oil wasn't bland, but fruity and pungent, almost peppery. It's olive oil at a whole new level and with a little *vino,* is the true breakfast of champions.

Roger and I studied the machinery trying to understand how the olives become oil. We took lots of pictures and with no small amount of pride were convinced that our olives looked better than anyone else's. Of course we had no idea what we were looking at. It all became gray paste and brown mush and we thought ours was a prettier color than the last batch. In reality our olives had yet to leave their crates. Our ten o'clock appointment was a little fluid. Other customers arrived, unloaded their crates or burlap bags and quickly left. We're astounded that people didn't remain to watch the magic of olives becoming oil. I guess they'd seen it a time or two.

Finally, the aproned husband began to upturn our crates into a chute directly in front of the weighing platform. Enzo, Roger and I assisted and restacked the empty crates back onto the platform. In this way, we arrived at the total weight of our olives by subtracting the weight of the crates. Normally a mill won't separately process anything less than three hundred kilograms (660 pounds). Fewer olives would simply be thrown into the mix with other small batches, processed into oil and made available for public sale. We were over the minimum and the owner agreed to segregate our oil.

Our photographs began in earnest now that we knew these were truly our olives. The owner commented on the lack of leaves and stems as the olives moved from the chute onto an assembly line trough where water washed over the fruit. Enzo chuckled as he explained Roger's cleaning techniques. He pointed to my down-vested mother and they both laughed. Roger says they can laugh all they want but that famous water bath wasn't as effective as everyone claimed in eliminating leaves and stems. Mom's efforts were not for naught.

After the water bath, the olives proceeded to a huge circular pan where two large granite wheels simultaneously rotated and moved in a continuous circle crushing them. We wonder how the pits are removed until we see that they're not – everything is crushed together. The grinding leads to a mixing trough churned by a corkscrew-like device which creates a dark thick paste. A thin layer of paste is extruded onto a doughnut-shaped hemp (or plastic woven to resemble hemp) mat. Five mats are smeared with paste before being stacked onto a stainless steel cylinder at the center of a moveable hydraulic press. A stainless steel doughnut-shaped plate is inserted below the next mat and the process begins again until all the paste has been smeared and a six foot high stack of olive mat pancakes interspersed with steel plates results. The stack is moved to a far corner of the mill by a hand operated fork lift and placed under a hydraulic press. It's slowly compressed and the oil runs down the sides of the stack into a collection tank. Taped to the press was a sheet of paper with a long list of scribbled names, a line through all but one. The last word on the page was *"AMERICANO"* – there was no doubt this was our oil.

The pancake process lasted the longest, about two hours. We'd become family at this point and toasted bread, drank wine, chatted with the owners and other customers, threw more wood on the fire and kept Mom company. We watched as others arrived and unloaded truckloads of olives. Comparatively, our haul was modest and we marveled at the manual labor involved for all of this effort and came to better appreciate the high cost of olive oil.

At some point, the base around our press was deemed full and the oil was transferred to a stainless steel vat sitting on legs. The vat is a centrifuge and has two outlets – one for oil and one for the separated water. The centrifuge spun for about forty minutes and we're finally asked to put our container in front of the vat to receive our oil. We couldn't take enough pictures and I stuck my finger below the spout to taste the pure, dark nectar. Naturally we believed ours was better than anyone else's but even Enzo and the owners seemed to genuinely reinforce our belief. We're thrilled with the end results: three days of harvesting, three days of cleaning, sixteen crates, 880 pounds of olives, seventy-five liters of oil. Because Enzo had pruned, tended and led us through the harvest, we shared half of our oil with him – the standard method of payment for such services.

We asked Enzo to come home and join us for lunch. He declined but helped us load the Trooper with empty crates and the finished product. At *Le Vigne*, we chopped fresh cherry tomatoes and drizzled them with our oil. We toasted bread and drenched it in our oil. We all but poured it into wine glasses and sang its glory. Oh happy day, we harvested our very own olives from our very own trees and created our very own olive oil.

This is Where We Live

*I*n Italy's central region of Umbria, between Perugia and Assisi, is our speck of a town, Colombella, population 2,000. Our latitude is 43.08 degrees north, on the same plane as Boise, Idaho; Toronto, Canada; Portland, Maine; cities with bitter winters. Thanks to the warm currents of the

Mediterranean, we're saved from such extremes. The Med does nothing, however, to mitigate the short winter days. We would reap the benefit in the summer but until the solstice we continued to lose daylight. It's a fact we never considered in our property search and it's been an adjustment coming from Atlanta's more southerly latitude of 33.76.

For centuries, Colombella has been a farming community and we know that *Le Vigne* was originally a farmhouse. Thanks to a book given to us by Liana and Massimo, written by Massimo's father, we can easily date the property to the early 18th century. The book includes a map dated 1727 featuring *Le Vigne* and several surrounding farms. *Le Vigne* means the vines or the vineyard. Grapes are grown all around us but none remain here today. Our only vines are wisteria winding their way up three sides of the house. It's a beautiful name and we wouldn't change it.

During our first visit to *Le Vigne*, it was described as a former 12th century convent. We're told that the official historical records (known as *catasto*) do exist and can be researched either in the State archives or land registry offices. Someday, after I've brushed up on my ancient Italian and have a full second to breathe, I'll begin the research.

There's some question about the town name, Colombella. Some say it's derived from *colle* and *bella*, meaning beautiful hill and others say it comes from *colomba* or dove – there are certainly plenty of those. Even though we live in Colombella, our address says we live in the town of Bosco meaning woods, the next town to the south. We're told the reason we officially live in Bosco is because that's where our post office is located. I'm not convinced. There's a post office in Colombella. Why isn't that one ours?

Town names are amusing. Some don't mean anything and some are named after people or saints. Some are named based on their location. Three contiguous towns a few kilometers south of us are Ponte Felcino, Ponte Valleceppi and Ponte San Giovanni. *Ponte* means bridge and all three are on the *Tevere,* the Tiber, which originates in Umbria and runs into Rome. *Felcino* has no translation, *San Giovanni* is St. John and *Valleceppi* is a compound word meaning valley and either logs or tree stumps. During heavy rains the river would flood and become clogged with stumps and logs.

Just to our north is Piccione or pigeon, Riccio or hedgehog, is near Cortona and Bastardo is on the way to Rome. To our immediate west is Casa del Diavolo or house of the devil. My all-time favorite town name is Ramazzano Le Pulci, "they sweep the fleas," just south of Casa del Diavolo. Most folks just refer to it as Ramazzano and wouldn't you if that's where you lived? What could possibly be the source of that name? After I finish my thesis on *Le Vigne*'s history, Ramazzano Le Pulci is next.

Street sign manufacturers must make a fortune. Not only are there signs denoting entry into each of these towns, there are signs denoting exit. Entry signs are obvious – *Colombella* in black letters on a white background. Exit signs are as described with a large red slash running diagonally from upper right to lower left – the international symbol for no or not.

Learning to say our website took time. Since there's no **w** in the Italian alphabet, that letter is known as *doppia vu*, or double **v**. In the fast forward speech pattern that is Italian, the requirement to say "*doppia vu, doppia vu, doppia vu*" would make every Italian screaming mad. Instead, they simply say, "*vu, vu, vu*" faster than the speed of light. This little practice should definitely be transported to the States. It's so much easier than the ponderous double u, double u, double u.

Then there's our email address, varkus@levigne.net. It's complicated but not because of any Italian language issues. Varkus is difficult to explain to English speakers. Roger's nickname in Air Force pilot training was Aardvark as he was a tall, lanky guy with a large nose and sloping shoulders. Two syllables being too much verbiage for these pilot types, Aardvark was eventually shortened to Vark. Back in the early 90s, during the Dark Ages of developing email addresses, Roger tried for Vark but that name was already taken. His dear and now departed friend Ray suggested Varkus Americus, unwittingly and presciently turning him into a Roman. Varkus stuck.

I omit the explanation for the Italians and just go right into the spelling using the Italian equivalent of the military alphabet. So instead of saying, "Victor, Alpha, Romeo..." and sounding like June Allyson in that Little Brown Jug movie I use place names and say "*Verona, Ancona, Roma, Cappa, Urbino, Sicilia.*" One exception - *Cappa* is not a place but it's how Italians say the letter **k** even though they spell it with a **c** since **k** doesn't exist in the Italian alphabet.

Now we come to the "at" symbol which is *chiocciola* which doesn't mean "at" at all. It means snail and it refers to the symbol resembling a snail shell. The word is a mouthful and flies in the face of the simplified "*vu, vu, vu*" approach.

The rest is easy, as *LeVigne* follows the *chiocciola* and the "dot" *punto,* precedes net and finally, I'm grounded in tranquil Umbria.

Social Life in Colombella

Life in Atlanta was quite social: dinner parties, new restaurants, old favorites, movies, plays, travel and visits from the children and out of town guests. Life in Colombella keeps us hopping too but for different reasons. Whatever norm existed in Atlanta has zero relevance to any norm we're working to establish in Italy.

Certainly we miss everyone in the States but we're meeting hospitable, warm people who are more than kind, making us feel welcome and comfortable. Our relationship with Antonio may have started with work but he's taken it a step beyond by introducing us to his wife Cinzia and daughters Laura (sixteen) and Giulia (eight). They've invited us into their nearby home, served us coffee and chocolates and Roger and Antonio drank shots of the firewater known as *grappa* while the women vociferously declined to touch the stuff. Without a word of English being uttered, Mamma Ruta bonded quickly with the girls as she speaks a language of unbridled love requiring no translation.

We seek Antonio's advice for everything so when we wanted to buy dishes we turned to him. He offered to take us to his favorite store in Deruta, the ceramic capital of Italy. One Sunday the seven of us made the twenty minute drive south. Both sides of the street are lined with businesses selling every manner and sort of the brightly painted majolica patterns that are eye candy. Every shop looked the same to us but we followed Antonio. There were hundreds of choices but we finally settled on a cheery yellow lemon pattern and bought a set of ten every day dishes, pasta bowls, salad bowls, serving bowls and platters. Cinzia inspected every item to make sure the painting was smooth and nothing was chipped. She rejected some pieces, substitutes were provided and she kept looking. We bought terra cotta feet for flower pots and a sun and a moon and Greek faces to hang on the house walls and garden terraces. Antonio negotiated reasonable prices which improved even further when we offered to pay in cash.

Mary and Don are great fun. Despite attending Italian language classes in Perugia, their schedule was more flexible than ours. They were on a long-term vacation so their free time is spent exploring the area and taking trips to other parts of Italy. If Don had his way, he would be at *Le Vigne* every day working with Roger whether planting, digging, pruning, demolishing, moving rocks or just playing in the dirt. Mary is a *plein air* artist, an accomplished seamstress and a shopper who can sniff out a bargain instinctively. Thanks to both of them, we're rewarded with leads on restaurants, artisans, wine-tastings, specialty shops, bakeries and invitations to their place for dinner. Don's the cook in the family, a fact we discovered when he transformed some of our "Grandmother Smith" apples into tart, crunchy apple crisps.

Language plays a huge part in our lives. I'm in full blown translation mode at all times except when we're alone or with Mary and Don. They struggle mightily with their classes and have posted learning aids around their apartment – conjugated verbs on the fridge, words for kitchen utensils above the sink, dictionaries in every room, homework on the dining room table. They took classes in California and find little connection between what they learned there and what they're studying here. They're frustrated with the instructor and his methodology and fear they'll need to repeat the course.

Roger has no interest in taking a class. He wants to learn Italian without ever having to conjugate a verb. Can you imagine only speaking in nouns? He's such an action-oriented and order-giving guy that he can't survive without saying go, do, make, cook, call, prepare, write, say. He'll ask me how to say something seemingly simple like "our" and roll his eyes when I tell him it depends. "How can it depend?" Those eyes glaze over when I explain that it depends on gender - whether the thing being described is masculine or feminine. He lapses into a flatline coma when I advise that number (singular or plural) has a bearing as well. Eventually he regains consciousness because I just handle the language for him. We're both hopeful that he'll begin to absorb it osmotically, even a few of the dreaded verbs.

While Roger trimmed branches outside our front gate one afternoon he met a Dutch couple driving by, Wendy and Frits. Frits stopped Roger, asking him in English if he were the gardener. Later we learn Frits strongly suspected otherwise, doubting a gardener would so casually sport a Rolex. However Roger said he was *and* he slept with the owner. With that Henny Youngman line, our social circle expanded. Wendy is a beautiful brunette eighteen years younger than Frits. Frits, who is as tall as Roger, is decisive and animated with big gestures and expansive moves. The couple had tired of living in cramped conditions in the Netherlands and yearned for more open spaces and an old building to renovate. They tried living in France but immediately knew it was a bad decision and soon set their sights on Italy. Coincidentally, they too operate a self-catering vacation rental business.

Wendy and Frits actually lived at *Le Vigne* one winter when the nearby ruin they had purchased was undergoing massive renovation. Their tales about the former owners confirmed all we had come to learn. They spent a long, cold season at *Le Vigne* with imposed heating restrictions and two hours a day of hot water.

Glasses of wine in hand, we walked through *Le Vigne* together as Roger described our renovation plans. It was apparent that Frits had done this a time or two and he quickly showed his opinionated nature either by signing off on our ideas or telling us in no uncertain terms to do it differently. His instincts were sound and Roger didn't mind his forthright approach, probably because he's got the same style.

Style. Wendy and Frits are loaded with it. They invited us to their renovated farmhouse that consists of an enormous (900+ square meter, 9,700 square foot) main house with a full-size indoor heated pool, sauna, tanning bed, outdoor pool, fifteen televisions, air conditioners in every bedroom, several outbuildings including a cantina loaded with Italian and French vintages and two separate apartments. They've used old brick and stone and massive wood beams to respect the history of the structure yet incorporated cutting edge design in lighting, fixtures and furnishings. Rooms are neither fussy nor Spartan and we openly share our plans to steal ideas because their taste is exquisite. Not only did they not mind but generously offered to lead us to their various sources. This cuts years of searching out of our lives and saved us from many a Row In Car since there was no risk of getting lost.

Frits likes a project every bit as much as Roger and if one renovation project is good, three are better. He's bought another property within sight of their current house, just as large, just as complex - a complete ruin. As only a mother will do, Mamma Ruta thinks *Le Vigne* is more beautiful and more livable and believes our improvements will render it that much better. We graciously accept her compliments while still planning to profit from their hard-earned knowledge. They're fun and we enjoy dinner together or sharing a bottle of Umbrian wine and talking about the mutual experience of living in Italy as ex-pats.

Giuliana and Renato continue to keep us in their social loop and since Mary and Don are living above them, the six of us are often together. A new restaurant opened at the bottom of our hill and we were part of a group of eighteen inaugurating it on opening night. My morning walking buddies and their spouses were there, relatives of theirs and friends of others – according to Liana, *un sacco di gente*, literally a sackful of people. That night we met Fabrizio and Rita, friends of Liana and Massimo's. Both physicians, Fabrizio is a cardiologist who speaks a small amount of English and Rita is a general practitioner – no English. Fabrizio had a fine time speaking to Mamma Ruta about South Florida with which he's familiar because he's attended so many medical conferences there. I'm thrilled to have a cardiologist on call for Roger. Everyone extended *complimenti*, compliments, to Mom. She's so beautiful and sweet and youthful looking and she demurs when I convey all these kind words.

Not surprising for an opening night, the service was slow but the food was tasty and abundant. We'd left it to the Italians to order and we received *antipasto* after *antipasto* to the point of overload. There was an Umbrian specialty that I describe as pork and beans, followed by lamb parts and other organ meats, *polenta* with mushrooms, a warm unleavened flatbread called *torta al testo* (looks like pita) sliced horizontally and filled with a single slice of *prosciutto*, fried olives stuffed with ground meat and seasonings, breaded and fried onion rings, artichoke hearts, *capocollo, salumi* and other aged meats sliced paper thin, potatoes baked in the cinders of a wood fired oven. Liana told us not to eat the skins as the potatoes had been sitting directly in the ashes. Unfortunately, she shared this only after watching us eat the skins, having remarked to Rita in Italian, "Well, they just didn't know." She's right, we didn't know but the skins tasted just fine. *Antipasti* were followed by *gnocchi* (not liked by the locals, too big) and *pappardelle* (wide ribbon pasta) with *cinghiale* or wild boar sauce (well liked). At this point, the Italians wisely declined to order *secondi,* second courses but somehow lost their senses by ordering *biscotti, panna cotta* and other desserts and then dessert wines like *Vin Santo* and *passito*.

Veteran's Day

On the Italian Veteran's Day (a week after the U.S. version), we attended a special *pranzo* or lunch honoring the veterans of Colombella. Much of the same dinner crowd attended and Renato led the way as we caravanned on the thirty minute drive to the restaurant in Valfabbrica. Parking was tight and creative and for once Roger was happy to have driven the Punto. We entered the restaurant and found a band (heavy on drums and horns) playing to our immediate left. Directly in front were long narrow tables that stretched to the far end of the cavernous room. Over four hundred people filled the seats and the noise and chatter and laughter were already loud. There was some confusion as to where to go next but Giuliana quickly took charge, leading us to a partially empty table in the center of the room, seating us near her.

Once in position, we remained there for four hours. Bread, water and wine were already on the table and Giuliana poured for all of us. When she tired of her white wine and had no other glass, she simply poured the remains into the table's centerpiece much to Mom's amusement. Another non-stop feast began - hot and cold *antipasti* including *crostini, polenta* cakes, beans, tuna, delicate sandwiches, sliced meats, mushrooms in pastry puffs, roasted peppers on bread, tomato and *mozzarella, bruschetta* followed by two types of pasta: huge *ravioli* with truffles and *tagliatelle* with mushroom sauce followed by pork with garlic and rosemary, lamb and chicken roasted with potatoes (no skins), stuffed tomatoes and zucchini, fennel salad, cheeses, cake, fresh fruit and finally coffee. All delicious, all abundant and all served by the sweetest, most mild-mannered agreeable, non-stressed young girls we had ever seen in the most difficult setting. Everything was served by the waitresses – nothing was left on the table family style. The distance between the tables was minimal, the distance between seats even more limited. We couldn't help but think about all those Stateside "servers with attitude" making this cheery demeanor all the more impressive.

Periodically people would squeeze between the seats and the waitresses to visit with Giuliana and Renato. She or Renato would introduce us and Roger would slide his chair back as much as possible to rise and shake hands. I would do the same and try to translate but it was a difficult, cramped environment with poor acoustics. Giuliana unabashedly plugged her ears each time the *Bandaccia* (affectionately but literally, the bad band) boisterously launched into their next tune. She claims they sound a lot better outdoors. No one could explain why polkas dominated the playlist or why *Roll Out the Barrel* was the most popular. The several couples who had found an available corner for dancing enjoyed whatever the *Bandaccia* chose to play.

Despite the clamor, we met Don Gilberto, the priest of the little church in Colombella, who asked us to attend mass. We met the *Maresciallo* of the *Carabinieri,* marshal of the local police, a good man to know according to Renato. We met Maria, the grandmotherly woman seated next to me. She was more interested in Mamma Ruta and frustrated that she had to work through me to communicate. A sweet old thing to us, she displayed her feisty side to the waitress because all she wanted to eat was *maccheroni* and when was she going to get it. We met some of the *combattenti* or veterans wearing faded ribbons and medals. We met Giuseppe, the bandleader of the *Bandaccia* who wanted to know how we ended up in Colombella. He asked Roger if he had served in the military and in what capacity. Roger talked briefly about his flying history in Viet Nam and his thirty-three years as a commercial pilot. He wanted to know whether Roger liked it better on the ground or "up there" pointing skyward and he smiled when Roger said he liked it best here, on the ground, in Colombella.

During a break in the food orgy and polka playing, the bandleader ceded the microphone to a representative from the local town hall. The *combattenti* were introduced and recognized for their service, receiving resounding applause. Don Gilberto led a prayer for those who had died in service to their country (*caduti*, the fallen ones) and those who passed away since last year's *pranzo*. Though unspoken, we all recognized that their numbers would only continue to diminish and at an ever increasing rate. The representative called for attendees to support the organization and we spent twenty-five Euro to become card-carrying members of this national association that maintains the many war memorials and works to keep the veterans' contributions alive in the minds of an appreciative public. Roger reasoned that in addition to all the altruistic advantages, the new card coupled with the personal introduction to the *Maresciallo* will keep us in good standing with the *Carabinieri.*

More speeches followed until the bandleader reclaimed the microphone to make announcements of local interest. He urged us to attend another upcoming *pranzo,* this one to support the tennis club in Colombella of which he's president. He introduced his fellow band members and several significant people in the audience and then I felt my face flush. He started to talk about us; the newest members of the Colombella community. He described the property we purchased saying it's the house where the singer used to live. Interesting...it's as though the Pigeon Sisters never lived there. He acknowledged Roger's military contributions and finally thanked us for choosing their small town as our new home. I grabbed Roger's hand and explained what was happening. We noticed all the heads turning in our direction and the smiles and welcomes and congratulations coming our way. As Giuseppe finished, the hundreds in the room toasted and applauded us. In a word, we were stunned.

Fortunately the *Bandaccia* began to play diverting attention from us. The whole room started to sing along to the rousing tune they had chosen. Giuliana explained that it was a song of the resistance fighters saying goodbye to their sweethearts as they marched off to war. Despite its somber theme, the melody was cheerful and even the Americans sang: *"O bella ciao, bella ciao, bella ciao, ciao, ciao."* Desserts appeared, more mingling took place and an older man tapped Roger on the shoulder. Again, Roger struggled to rise in the constrained space and the man shook his hand, continuing to pump it fiercely while he spoke. Roger looked inquisitively at me while I explained that he was thanking Roger for those Americans who had liberated Italy from the Germans. It was a tribute that we could only accept on behalf of our parents. The room was awash in appreciation of the United States' role in Italy in World War II as evidenced by others who expressed similar sentiments.

As the dessert plates were being cleared, it seemed as though the entire room stood at once. All the chummy camaraderie evaporated in an instant as guests pushed and shoved their way to the front door. There are no lines in Italy, only funnels. It was mass confusion – everyone jockeying for improved positions that netted zero advantage. Adding to the disorder, it had started to rain. Renato motioned to Roger to follow quickly so they could retrieve the cars and pick us up at the door. They tried to slip ahead as Giuliana, Mom and I inched our way toward the entrance.

Making little progress, we watched the band break down their equipment and stow their instruments. One of the band members looked my way and smiled. I returned the greeting and continued to slowly move forward. He looked at me again and said he was sorry. Perhaps I had misunderstood; why would he be apologizing to me? I moved closer and again he said he was sorry and I asked why. He looked up toward the ceiling and said because of the Towers, because of what had happened on September 11th. All I could manage without tears was *grazie.*

The following Sunday Mamma Ruta wanted to attend the morning service so we went to mass at our little church in Colombella. The church occupies a prime position on the hillside surrounded by stunning views. Mount Subasio looms ahead as the largest mountain in sight, Assisi in the foothills. While there has been a church in Colombella since the 12th century, this church was built in the mid-1800s. It is small but beautiful, not overly ornate and there are lovely frescoes that fill the walls and the central dome. The crucifix is carved from a single piece of wood, highly polished; Christ's suffering evident in the face.

On this sunny but chilly morning we find the church filled with young and old and we squeeze into the last pew. Roger towers over the crowd, probably the tallest person in Colombella. Mom follows the service easily while I catch bits and pieces of the announcements and Don Gilberto's sermon dealing with the Advent of Christmas. The mass moved quickly and we were out the door by noon. On the outside steps, several of the parishioners greeted us. Feisty Maria (of "where's my *maccheroni?"* fame) quickly brushed past me to re-connect with Mamma Ruta who continued to be fawned over. The priest Don Gilberto shook hands and asked us to return. Our next-door neighbors Catiuscia and Federico stopped to chat and offered their assistance if we needed anything.

Thanksgiving

The following Thursday we enjoyed our first Thanksgiving dinner in Italy. Don and Mary hosted the meal and in communal fashion we all contributed. Giuliana and Renato supplied the turkeys from their coop, offering us the opportunity to witness the execution and plucking. Don and Mary watched but I declined, preferring a little more distance between me and whatever animal in the food chain I planned to eat. Don thought the turkeys looked a little scrawny so he purchased a large breast at the grocery store to augment the meal. We were sworn to silence so as not to offend Renato.

In addition to the roasted turkeys, Don prepared the stuffing, gravy and potatoes that were supposed to be sweet. We all searched for sweet potatoes – at various groceries, local outdoor markets, METRO. *Gio* (pronounced Joe), a specialty shop in Perugia claimed to have sweet potatoes but they weren't. We supplied the other side dishes including mashed potatoes, breaded and baked cauliflower, Mamma Ruta's zucchini pie, a strange Brussels sprout concoction that I invented and even a cranberry sauce, albeit canned. *Gio* came through on that last item. Max and Elena joined us and as we ate and gave thanks, the Italians asked me to explain the holiday.

I talked about the difficulties of the first English settlers in America (struggling over the word for Pilgrims) and the friendships that had been made with the Indians. Thanksgiving was a time to give thanks for having overcome difficulties, rejoice in the bounty of the recent harvest and share that bounty by eating together with family and friends. That was all fine but they wanted to know more. *Is this a religious holiday?* No, it is a secular holiday not associated with any one particular religion. *To whom do you give thanks?* We thank God, whichever god one worships. *Doesn't that make this a religious holiday?* I thought of the iconic Rockwell painting but said not necessarily. *Why isn't every day Thanksgiving?* Well, it certainly could be and probably should be but this is the one day set aside when all of the country focuses on these gifts for which we should be thankful daily.

The Italians accepted my responses but unanswered questions still floated in the air. They allowed them to drift by, concentrating instead on the food and togetherness. They found it odd that we ate everything on the plate at the same time rather than in courses. Even so, all plates were cleaned and no one was shy about returning for seconds. The homegrown birds had more than enough meat and were loaded with juicy flavor. The uneaten breast would make great sandwiches over the coming days. That night we had achieved the sated feeling that signifies the perfect Thanksgiving dinner. Only Roger wished for the traditional Dallas Cowboys game.

After dinner we made the short walk to Caroline and Augusto's house where we had been invited for dessert. They too had hosted a Thanksgiving dinner though theirs was for twenty-five and included Italians, Americans and English. Their modern home exudes a lively, convivial atmosphere and it's the first time we actually meet Caroline. We didn't know quite what to expect. Her reputation as watchdog of the *bidone* preceded her but we immediately found her charming. She's warm and inviting and highly entertained by the story of our initial encounter with Augusto. "Please don't tell him when you're getting rid of more junk. He'll take it all." She's desperate not to have more *roba*, stuff, come inside their gates.

Caroline slips easily between English and Italian, introducing us to so many people that we lose track. I envy her facile manner of translating – neither the speaker nor the listener feels uncomfortable or interrupted. I wonder how long it took her to become so limber. Caroline makes sure we're provided apple or pumpkin pie or both. I ask where she's found many of the Thanksgiving staples and she explains that she brings most back from the States - can't always depend on *Gio*.

Everyone was relaxed; the perfect ending to a sociable, bountiful Thanksgiving Day. It was late when we returned to *Le Vigne* but the best time to call the States. We heard TVs in the background; Macy's Thanksgiving Day parade in New York, football game chatter. Most were in the midst of food preparation, huge birds in the oven, the big meal still ahead. Ours had ended but we predicted theirs would be good. And while they were missed, we hoped they would be comforted knowing that we too had enjoyed this special holiday and were happy in our new life.

Not All Play

It may seem that life here is nothing but a social whirl but that's not the case. If it appears we do nothing more than move from one four hour meal to the next, it's merely a charade. There were days we felt so overwhelmed with projects and plans and had so much to accomplish that we were frozen into an inert state. Sometimes the minutes required to prepare a sandwich, boil water for pasta or open a can of tuna couldn't be found in a twenty-four hour day. Mom rescued us from the hunger we didn't even realize existed until the smell of her apple pancakes or some other treat reminded us the lunch or dinner hour had long passed.

Our renovation plans were in full swing. We met with Antonio at least twice a week to review lengthy lists that I translated in advance. It wasn't unusual to begin our sessions at three in the afternoon and end after six. My brain was fried. Sometimes we walked the property together in the cool late afternoons. Roger would point out work to be done: replace the entire border of the pool to eliminate cracked tiles, expand the tiled area surrounding the pool, build raised flower beds, survey future garden sites, determine functioning wells, hose bibs, cisterns.

On days without marathon meetings Antonio was here actually doing the work. All external doors were keyed individually. Now they're identical and we eliminated nine unnecessary keys. He installed our ice maker, added new electrical outlets in the cantina for our dryer, replaced light fixtures, repaired shower doors, toilet seats and towel bars. He removed the sail cloth covering for the gazebo for indoor winter storage, located and secured masons, electricians, plumbers, a *geometra,* a carpenter and other contractors. He directed us to tile, flooring, and building suppliers, arranged for the rental of a cherry picker and operator to remove dangerous dead limbs from the centuries-old pines lining our entrance drive, helped us interview various heating fuel suppliers to convert from diesel to the more economical GPL, located a supplier to provide olive trees in the spring, coordinated with farmer Grasselli to aerate the land for olive planting, located a supplier of interlocking concrete blocks to build terraces to eliminate the sloping *scarpate* and increase the level footprint of our property.

Antonio's brother Enzo is as much a fixture at *Le Vigne* as Antonio. Once the olive harvest was complete he transplanted six apple trees to a better location, planted olives that had been in pots outside the *ingresso,* cut down pines that produced too much shade, fertilized potted lemon trees and brought them indoors for the winter, removed unneeded and unattractive fencing, chopped firewood, trimmed, mowed and pruned.

Antonio led us to Giovanni, a *geometra* who works for a building company supplying tiles, brick, bathroom and kitchen fixtures, flooring and fireplaces. We visited his showroom, studied samples, reviewed catalogs, exchanged ideas and watched this talented man sketch designs as a preferred method of communicating with the Americans. Eventually he visited *Le Vigne* and with Antonio we spent more hours reviewing concepts and plans. His pencil drawings littered the floor of our master suite, kitchen and *soggiorno*.

During one of his many house tours, Giovanni is prepared to review the costs for renovating the master bath. We offer a cup of coffee but he disdainfully raises an eyebrow. He sees it's American coffee and therefore weak and doomed to be served in an oversized *termos* instead of an espresso cup - *brutto*. The so-called ugly thermos was simply a regular coffee mug.

Waving his own *termos,* Roger directed Giovanni to a seat. At our request, Giovanni developed two estimates – one very elaborate bathroom renovation and a second more moderate one. He sketched as he spoke and we were all in agreement on design concepts. Roger held the document containing the quotes and I noticed a slight tremble as he looked at the numbers. As Giovanni explained the figures, Roger became uncharacteristically quiet. Eventually regaining his voice, he asked me to explain that these were big decisions and we needed to take some time alone and review them further. We hoped Giovanni was not upset and he insisted that wasn't the case. Such decisions require much consideration and we should take our time. He was available when we needed him.

After accompanying Giovanni outside and opening the gate, I returned to find a pale Roger moaning to Mom about the extraordinarily high cost of goods in this country. If a cheap bathroom is 380000 Euro and the expensive one is 590000 we will have to rethink all of our renovation plans. In fact, we may have to sell *Le Vigne*, return to the States and abandon our entire vacation rental concept. What's to be done, why didn't we know, where do we turn, how do we cope?

I stood over Roger's slumped shoulders as he reviewed every line item on the hand-written list and discovered the flaw as he called out figures to Mom. Since the numbers Giovanni had written did not contain commas or periods, Roger mentally placed commas before the first three zeroes, moving from right to left. In other words he saw the cheap bath at 380,000

Euro instead of 3,800.00 Euro and the high end bath at 590,000 rather than 5,900.00. And I'm the one with math problems.

Oh, jubilation! We can remain in country. The flush lever can come out of the shower, the shower itself can be large enough to hold a human, two travertine shelves, a bar of soap and shampoo. The room can be enlarged, lighting and electrical outlets can be abundant and we'll still have money for other improvements.

A word about shower sizes in Italy and Europe in general. Tiny. That's the word. Even for me. Shaving legs becomes a yoga balancing act (hence the installation of one of the two travertine shelves). Arms should remain at one's side at all times, bent elbows mean bruised elbows. Dropped soap is a disaster. If the idea of bathing in a vertical MRI machine appeals then Italian showers are nirvana. Tiny.

With the bathroom back on track, our plans for the remainder of the master suite are also. The thirty year-old parquet flooring was worm-pocked and must go. We selected new "parquet" – a term that covers any type of wood flooring. The original was indeed parquet, our new selection wasn't. We chose lengths of cherry that would warm our bedroom, hallway and personal guest bedroom. A clear contrast to the remainder of the house, this would be the only wood flooring in the building.

Headers were next on the renovation list. To say that *Le Vigne* is an old *casa colonica* or farmhouse sounds quite charming but consider the reality. Livestock, primarily cows were stabled on the ground floor while the *contadini*, peasant farmers, lived upstairs, benefiting in winter from the rising animal heat. Land was too valuable to be used for grazing; it needed to be farmed. Even now we see very little livestock on the hillsides other than an occasional flock of sheep. Thus our grand, nine-chambered, vaulted ceiling *salone rustiche*, rustic salon is really a centuries-old barn. Fortunately, *Le Vigne* suffers no residual evidence of livestock.

The *contadini* were short; even modern-day Italians are short, and animals had no need for height to pass from room to room. Four crucial headers between rooms were just over five feet tall making it difficult and painful for Roger to pass. More often than not he smacks into the masonry headers, sees *stelle*, stars, and I await the day he simply attacks them with a hammer and a few choice words.

Appliances

We needed a new kitchen. Other than cosmetic issues such as dated cabinetry and tacky Formica counters, more serious problems abounded. Appliances were faulty, lighting was sparse and electrical outlets few and inconvenient, requiring clunky adapters or spaghetti ribbons of extension cords. The oven was electric and burned unevenly. Perhaps this was the result of the oven door refusing to stay closed. Mom and I devised an ingenious plan of propping a chair in front of it to keep it closed. It can be a little awkward when checking on a roast but if one person grabs the chair and the other allows the door to drop open and pulls out the oven rack it can be accomplished quite nicely. Temperature in centigrade proved a challenge until I posted a conversion chart. Initially I burned everything as 200 degrees didn't seem high enough. Trust me, it is.

One night we prepared a roasted, stuffed rabbit (yes, rabbit). Mom and I made the proper temperature selection and rigged our oven door shut, chair in place. All seemed in order until we heard a loud crack from the oven. Mom manned the chair while I grabbed the hot pad as the door fell open revealing a clean break in the casserole, rabbit juices overflowing. She found a metal pan while I caught the rabbit and made the transfer. Juices sizzled on the rack but we barred the door once again and Thumper continued to cook to a tasty conclusion.

The cooktop was the next adventure. It was gas and had to be ignited by match. I didn't like it but I did it. The burner controls weren't fine-tuned precision instruments. Perhaps I was a little demanding as I sought something between blow torch and dying ember.

A grilled cheese burned quickly; a pot of water took hours to boil. The cooktop was outdone by the fridge. If you like small showers, you'll love Italian refrigerators. I understand the concept – buy only what's needed for the day's meal and freeze little, but ours wasn't much bigger than a standard dishwasher. Speaking of which, the dishwasher was short of standard. When Cortona Renato visited he declared it *"perfetto per Barbie."*

We've priced appliances and the coin of the realm seems to be a grand. Television, a thousand Euro; computer, a thousand Euro; fridge, a thousand Euro; dishwasher, a thousand Euro; stove, a thousand Euro; garbage disposal, surprise, only eight hundred Euro (versus one hundred seventy dollars at Home Depot); cooktop, big bargain at five hundred Euro. Life in Italy, however, we continue to regard as priceless.

Television. In addition to the purchase price, we have to pay the Italian government one hundred Euro a year for the privilege of having television access. Separately, we have to pay the cable company deposits and monthly rentals for cable boxes. On top of this, we paid Lamberto, the cable guy for his work. Lamberto wears more chains and leather than a Harley rider and greets Roger with a pounding Centurion-like, across-the-chest, clenched fist salute that is startling. He was retained to climb on our roof, adjust the satellite, remove extraneous boxes, check all cable outlets, install new ones, be the intermediary between us and the cable company and then teach us how to use all the equipment by way of his English bombshell girlfriend Francesca. This accomplished, the only person who had time to watch TV was Mamma Ruta who seemed captivated by a nightly series akin to *Reefer Madness*, albeit in Italian.

Then there's the computer. It seems we could have easily brought our equipment from the States, used an adapter and operated it here. Instead we sold it and went through the agonizing process of buying equipment from Mario who operates a computer consulting business in Perugia. We were directed to him only days before we learned of Massimo's expertise in this area. Naturally, we got lost on the way to Mario as we navigated the streets of our favorite hive-inducing city.

Programs in Italian, commands in Italian, error messages in Italian. *Scheda madre* is motherboard, *stampante* is printer, *tastiera* is keyboard. The keyboard is formatted in an Italian pattern making typing slow and error-ridden. Frustrating, frequent inconclusive contact with the phone company to improve our dial-up connection leaves us both mad as snakes. Roger demands satellite. Are you kidding? Then he insists on ADSL. Not yet available in our area. We're stuck with intermittent dial-up function, only a slight step up from juice cans and string. Roger expects Mario to be available for on-site consultation 24/7. Mario has a different view. The computer, our lifeline to the States and for marketing *Le Vigne,* has become a major sore spot now ranking second to banking for inducing hours of gut-wrenching frustration.

Valter

Speaking of what we should have shipped, we finally received our shipment. It arrived intact and on time, suffering none of the Titanic-like catastrophes that were forecast. It happened early one morning just as I returned from my walk. Roger was in a panic as there were three messages in Italian on the phone. The Neapolitan truck driver had managed to get as far as Enrico's gas station in Colombella. Rather than talk him through, we jumped in the car and led the truck back to *Le Vigne*. Six hours and one hundred boxes later, the driver and his assistant extended *complimenti*, wished us *buona fortuna* and left.

In the days that followed, we unpacked, we sorted, we wondered why we shipped certain things like my collection of crystal, ceramic and stone turtles and cursed ourselves for not shipping others – the bed we sold, our lamps, tools, dressers. Without furnishings, our rooms continued to seem cavernous. Rugs helped, artwork helped, mirrors helped but more was needed to dampen the continuing echoes. We left our clothing in the wardrobe shipping boxes because *Le Vigne*, as every other *casa colonica,* was bereft of closets. There was only one thing to do - go shopping!

Walter (pronounced Valter) is a used furniture dealer in the *zona industriale*, industrial zone of Ponte Felcino. Several people had directed us to Walter but it took weeks of aborted attempts before we actually found his place of business. A junkyard is too upscale a word for Walter's. Sanford & Son looks tidy in comparison. It was so unappealing that Mamma Ruta refused to get out of the car so Roger and I promised to make it quick.

The area outside the building was a jumble of ceramic tables, wrought iron chairs, carpentry equipment, metal shelving, staircases, gates, barber chairs, automotive parts, motorcycles, helmets, bricks, tiles, marble scraps, fountains, flower pots, carousel horses, appliances and many more treasures. It was chilly and I'd seen enough so I walked through the narrow front door into a warehouse that proved to be easily ten degrees colder than outdoors. Mom was wise to remain in the warmth of the car.

There were no fire codes for this building. Aisles were narrow and some simply dead-ended forcing a retreat. A thick coating of dust covered the mostly dark wood furniture – armoires, desks, tables, benches, side boards, book shelves, bed frames, chairs with missing legs and torn seats, sofas with springs jutting through torn upholstery, bread cupboards. Items were precariously stacked on top of each other and magazines and books sprawled across any flat surface. Primarily worm-infested and distressed, it was a stretch to find the few furniture jewels.

Walter was as jumbled a character as his establishment. Gregarious and talkative, he allowed us to roam as we wished (or could manage) and would tell us prices when asked. If we inquired about the type of wood used in a desk or a chair, the answer was invariably walnut. If we asked about its age it was always very, very old; an antique.

Walter wanted to know our story and once he learned Roger had been a pilot, an exciting new area of discussion and hand gestures evolved. In addition to being a used furniture dealer, Walter is a pilot. Years ago, he raced cars and motorcycles competitively but crashed so often and broke so many bones that he gave it up. One hopes his piloting skills are more measured.

While chatting, we persevered with our search and beneath the layers of dust, found several must-have items. A rustic narrow wood plank table became our new dining table. Walter said it's made in the style of the *frati* or brothers, so named because the *frati* would line up on either side of such tables for their meals. A tall wood hutch with glass doors above and wood doors below would store glasses and silverware, plates, placemats and napkins. Much to Walter's surprise, it was filled with old table linens that he threw in as part of the deal. A long, low dark wood 19th century sideboard with open shelving as well as drawers and carved doors would become our new bar. And a wood *sedia a dondolo* or rocking chair unlike any we had ever seen due to the built-in, curved foot rest protruding in front became Mom's new reading chair. Not surprisingly, everything except the rocker is made of walnut and is an antique.

Walter was amenable to bargaining and we haggled until we agreed on price. We had no way to transport our treasures but he gladly delivered them after detouring to a nearby furniture restorer to drop off the *dondolo* for repairs. Ferruccio, the restorer, promised to have the rocker ready within the week and deliver it.

Walter was full of *complimenti* about *Le Vigne*. Before entering the front door, he asked *permesso* as do all the Italians, a polite custom where one seeks permission to enter a home. Once granted we talked about where to place everything and he and Roger muscled the furniture into the house. Walter took no money for the delivery but accepted a glass of wine, downed as quickly as an *espresso*. Before he left, we asked if he'd take a few items we wanted to unload. The large side-by-side refrigerator that still occupied the *soggiorno* was a candidate as was the toilet that would soon be torn from our master bath. He agreed to take anything and pay us once it sold. The prospect of making a few Euro was secondary: the real beauty was to jettison the junk without telling Augusto.

The symbiotic relationship Roger and I developed endures; I can't drive and Roger can't speak. Whether it's a trip to the hardware store or the grocery store, we do everything together. It's a toss-up as to which is more fun. I can't find fake eggs, ground decaf coffee, dryer sheets, zip-loc bags or pecans. Stuffed rabbit, fresh mussels, truffles, *cinghiale* sauce, breads from wood-fired ovens, hearty bean soups and fresh pasta are readily available. In Atlanta, I created a three-ring notebook filled with my favorite recipes. It's such a treasure that I hand-carried it on the flight to Rome. I wouldn't trust it to the shipping company or checked luggage. Whether because our lives are so hectic or the kitchen so mutant or the foodstuff so varied or all of the above, I'd not yet glanced at the once coveted book. We were simply eating differently.

On the hardware side, the Gator had been ordered and we'd purchased a chain saw, leaf blower, fencing, ladders, shovels, mulcher (*biotrituratore* - try saying that with confidence), grinders, saws, shelving for the cantina, lamps, more furniture, vacuum cleaners. Tile and bricks and blocks and sand and bags of cement and reinforcing wire for concrete foundations, and equipment arrived in anticipation of renovation work. Antonio brings the masons, electricians, plumbers and other contractors over to familiarize them with the work ahead. They're filled with *complimenti* for Mamma Ruta (it's a wonder the woman hasn't floated away with a swollen head), for *Le Vigne* and for the planned improvements. They laugh when I say Roger wants it all done *domani.* The plumber said, *"Anche ieri,"* yesterday, even. Now, there's a man who knows how to get on Roger's good side.

People come and go all day long and other than Mario, they are responsive and punctual. Take the man who delivers our heating fuel for example. We knew it was time to order more fuel only because we had no heat. In a bit of a panic, I called to say we're out, not low, but out. He rearranged his schedule and arrived that day. He's an older man but quite limber. He propped a ladder against the gate behind the house. He snaked the fuel hose through the gate, climbed over the ladder, jumped down on the inside, grabbed the hose and filled the tank.

Tank full, he provided the bill, naturally in the thousand Euro range and I got the pleasure of writing a check. I practiced on scrap paper first so as not to make an error on one of our few precious checks. I'd learned this the hard way. Dictionary by my side, I painstakingly wrote the amount in long hand and then the numerals, placing commas and periods in odd places. A check for 1,456.80 Euro is written*: millequatrrocentocinquatasei/80.* I asked him to sign off on what I wrote, hoping he wouldn't take advantage of the ignorant American.

Le Vigne is a big house, tough to keep clean now and will be even tougher once renovation starts. We were going to need help so I asked my walking buddies but they had no suggestions. The women who clean for them were booked and while Giuliana raves about Liliana who cooks and cleans and feeds their chickens, she made it quite clear Liliana had no available time. At our request, Giuliana mentioned our predicament to her son Max whose company hires many Filipino workers for their factory. Max came through and brought us Mick; nineteen years old, quiet, Tagalog and English-speaking (when he speaks), polite, shy and willing to do anything. Mick had recently arrived in Italy so was just learning to speak Italian. He left his homeland to find employment as did his brother Carlo, his mother and her partner Cesar. Mick lives in Perugia with his family. He arrives by bus at seven every morning. Mick was a blank slate and we held the chalk – it was up to us to teach him everything about cleaning a house and maintaining a property.

If we're in a position to teach someone anything that must mean we've learned something ourselves. It's more likely that the three of us will continue learning together. Our house, let alone the whole of Italy, continues to hold mysteries. We still haven't figured out light switches. Several times a week I walk into the apartment's single bedroom when I really mean to come downstairs to our living space.

We awake early each morning and attack the line items on our many lists yet Roger is not satisfied. "We need to get focused," he implores and storms out of the room. I say nothing but feel my shoulders sag. I think we are focused. What have we been doing all this time? Is this not considered "focused?" I finally work it out. He means we need to finish with these lists and create new ones dealing with marketing, promoting and advertising *Le Vigne*. He means all this renovation work will be for naught if there are no bodies occupying apartment beds next summer. He means this is merely a means to an end.

I remember one of Roger's favorite quotes. The words, carved into a small piece of black granite, stare back at him from his makeshift desk. The stone has rested on every desk he can remember owning. Thomas Edison's words drive an already driven character; "Show me a thoroughly satisfied man and I will show you a failure." Based on such criteria, Roger is a stunning success.

All right then. The message is clear. Let's get focused.

December

When our friend and guide Andrea drove us around Umbria and Tuscany during our early days of searching for properties we would often encounter roads under construction. Yellow signs and blue arrows foretold the narrowing of the lanes from three to two. Traffic would slow to a crawl and we could easily watch the men in orange jumpsuits move tools and heavy equipment in an effort to improve road conditions. As fluent as Andrea is in English his description of the situation was a direct translation from the Italian, *fano i lavori*, they're making the works. The phrase is now ours - at *Le Vigne* we are making the works.

We had the good sense to hold off really making the works until the day after Mamma Ruta returned to America. 'Twas a sad day when she left. Antonio, Enzo, Giuliana, Renato, Mary and Don all came to say goodbye. She promised to return in warmer weather but that means she won't get to wear her ubiquitous down vest. She had become a fixture here and was universally greeted with adoration and respect. From the plumber to the masons to the neighbors to the shop owners, no one was immune to her warmth. She awoke every morning to kiss us and then let us go about our crazy business of the day. She was easy, requiring no maintenance or entertainment. She tended the fire, hemmed our pants, cooked our meals, cleaned the kitchen, ironed our clothes and more than anything, showered us with buckets of pure, unconditional love. It must be hard for her to think of the physical distance between Boca Raton and Colombella but she lets none of that show and simply supports our move, our choices and our decisions generously and openly. Our experiences are heightened by her enjoyment and we like the idea that she can picture what we're doing, where we're going and with whom. Never again will we look at the *sedia a dondolo* (or an episode of *Reefer Madness*) without thinking of Mamma Ruta.

But, as Antonio said, it's a good thing she's not here while we're making the works. She's not one for dust and this would have been unsettling. Our *soggiorno* as she knew it? Gone. Our fireplace in the *soggiorno*? Gone. The pass-through separating the kitchen from the *soggiorno*? Gone. Our kitchen, master bedroom, bathroom, guest bedroom? Gone, gone, gone, gone. Things are no better outdoors. The cracked tiles around the pool? Gone. The grass on one side of the pool? Gone. We may have hired Mick to clean the house but Roger has instituted his life-is-better-with-a-crew rule and commandeered Mick to move wheelbarrows full of rubble, rock, brick and cement to distant parts of the property for future use.

Other than the rustic salon, we've given up any pretense of living in our part of *Le Vigne*. We continue to occupy the green bedroom in the apartment but now have fully transitioned to the upstairs kitchen; at least the oven door closes. During the few hours that I can steal him, Mick works hard to keep the apartment clean but dust is insidious. It gains uninvited entry despite originating two floors and three closed doors away.

There are no studs or drywall at *Le Vigne*, only brick, stone and mortar. To raise the star-inducing headers requires the kind of demolition that men are so fond of and our *muratori*, masons, clearly love their work. Sergio and Luca destroy with brute force and then rebuild with deft touch. During destruction mode, they whistle or sing and during rebuild mode, talk companionably but incessantly. They are pleasant, prompt and professional. They would have to be, otherwise Antonio would never have suggested they work for us. On weekdays, Sergio and Luca appear at our gate precisely at 2:30 and work without a break until seven. On Saturdays, they arrive at seven and work until one. Much to Roger's dismay, no one works on Saturday afternoon or Sunday. Occasionally, they work seven to seven with a two-hour lunch break. Roger was a happy man on those rare days.

The masons call Roger *padrone,* or owner. They've come to admire his ideas and appreciate the fact that he gets his hands dirty working side-by-side with them. I'm also in the thick of it, working and translating. "Tell them I want..." is how Roger starts, hundreds of times a day followed by lots of discussion, gesticulation, sketches, confirmation, changes. He is unaware when I soften his demand; "Roger *vorrebbe,* Roger would like" rather than "Roger *vuole,* Roger wants."

The discussion about the headers took hours and called for the boss or *capo,* Antonio. These are important structural supporting walls and demolition of the headers would require the insertion of iron I-beams or *trave*. Exactly how high must they be raised? Anywhere from eight inches to a foot and a half depending on the header. Using a scrap of charcoal Roger marked a spot on one of the headers to indicate the height that would give him safe passage. At long last there was agreement and Roger scribbled his initials in final approval. Before this header is eventually demolished, the masons will complete the charcoal sketch by drawing a head with ears and they too initial their work.

When the masons break for lunch, we do as well. I run upstairs to reheat soup or slap something on bread and call it a sandwich. It's eerily quiet, no sledgehammers or jackhammers, no shovels scraping against tile floors loading buckets or wheelbarrows with bowling ball size pieces of concrete or plaster. No teeth-drilling whine of a saw blade slicing through brick. The silence lasts fifteen, twenty minutes at most before Mick, Roger and I quickly finish lunch to clear debris in a lame effort of staying a few steps ahead of the masons. Soon they are back, along with the noise and mess.

We were making progress but sometimes it was difficult to discern since building techniques can be so contrary to those we know. Our master bath is a perfect example of two steps forward, one step back. To enlarge the master bath two walls had to be demolished. The next step was to rebuild the two walls in their entirety in the expanded locations using only bricks and mortar. But what about the glass brick that we're installing on part of the wall to allow for more light? What about electricity and plumbing? What about tracks for wiring and pipes? What about the doorway? All of that goes in later. But how? Jackhammers, chisels or other brick and mortar destroying tools would be wielded against the freshly built walls to lay wires and pipes, insert glass bricks, create a doorway.

We spent many frustrating hours in that room with Roger saying, "Tell them they still need to get electricity into that wall," or "Ask them why build it first only to destroy it again later. Wouldn't it be easier to build the wall to a certain height, lay in the wiring and pipes, then continue building the rest of the wall?" No amount of cajoling or pleading would dissuade these men from their normal approach. This is the way it has been done in Italy for many, many years. Unaccustomed to not getting his way either through persuasion or edict, Roger simply left the room muttering four words he's come to know well – *Mamma mia* and *che casino*. Meanwhile, the masons, plumber and electrician call out to him, "*pazienza*" before the jackhammer stutters into action again.

Mamma mia – yes, they really say that. *Che casino* – what a mess though *casino* literally means brothel. And *pazienza* – well, that's pretty obvious and we hear it daily. Roger has learned the word but not the concept. No one has seen a December with so much rain...*pazienza.* When is Grasselli going to plow our fields...*pazienza.* The plumber didn't show today... *pazienza.* The hardware store won't allow Roger behind the counter to touch all those nails and screws, to fondle tools and equipment, make comparisons and then change his mind...*pazienza.*

Despite the frustration with the master bathroom wall, Roger is impressed with the talents of our *muratori.* Much of their talent is a dying art. While that sounds a bit dramatic, it could conceivably happen. Young people are pursuing other careers. The knowledge required to create the nine-chambered vaulted ceiling in our *salone rustiche* is limited to a few. The ceilings are typical in *case coloniche*, churches and other historic buildings and the techniques used to create the curved vaults were secrets known only by the masons.

Utilizing the four most expensive words in renovation, "while-we're-at-it," we decide to add chestnut beams to the ceiling in the *soggiorno*. The ceiling calls for six large beams (thirteen inches square and fifteen feet long) accented by twelve smaller cross beams (four inches square and thirty feet long) that will be cut and placed at right angles to the larger beams. The dark-stained, irregularly shaped beams will go a long way in returning this property to its roots as a traditional Italian farmhouse rather than the layered Anglicized Italianate villa it had become.

Antonio liked the idea and helped us find the wood. Together we drove to the industrial zone of Bastia, a small town near Assisi. It's late afternoon, already dark as tar and we're relieved Antonio's with us. We visit several lumberyards, review inventory, discuss scheduling and finally settle on a supplier. The price is fair, the beams are in stock, they can stain them the proper color and deliver them before Christmas. Arriving at a price is a process. It appears we can't get a straight answer from the owner because he's taking an inordinately long time to calculate the amount. He's pressed his calculator into overtime, still struggling with the conversion from *lire* to Euro. "Almost a year," he says "and I still can't get used to the new currency." He's not alone.

The beams do arrive before Christmas but just barely. Late afternoon on the eve before Christmas Eve, the open bed truck arrived with the eighteen beams. Maybe it was the time of day or that the driver and his assistant had to work on the eve of a holiday or maybe it was the rain – whatever the excuse, the boys were in no mood to be accommodating. The assistant operated the *gru* or crane that is a standard part of most transport trucks. Roger tried to get them to unload the beams inside our gates but the truck wouldn't clear the roof over the gate. Roger motioned for them to lift the beams over our fence. They rejected that idea and simply began unloading the beams, one by one against the fence line, making little effort to avoid the mud.

We would have to move the beams inside the gate and these men were not inclined to help. Roger asked me to call every able-bodied man we knew to join the fun. Federico, Antonio, Don and Enzo came immediately despite the rain, darkness and unpleasant task ahead. They arrived garbed in hats, slickers and heavy gloves while the deliverymen beat a hasty retreat having pocketed the cash payment, barely grumbling a *Buon Natale* in their wake.

Three Italian men, two American men and I stand in the rain. And they say women talk a lot. Federico is 'strong like bull' and the youngest. He could carry the larger beams like toothpicks if the others' egos would allow. Instead, an ingenious transport method is devised. It's decidedly low-tech but fuel efficient and calls for a wheelbarrow and wedge-shaped piece of wood as a lever. It takes several attempts but the men settle into a well-oiled system of heaving, leveraging, wheeling and unloading. An hour later, all beams are neatly stacked in a small corner of our *piazza* and everyone's worked up a fierce thirst. They all decline my invitation to dinner but readily accept a glass or two of wine. They leave with heartfelt Christmas greetings and promises to visit over the holidays.

The Hair Salon

After almost two months in country it was time to color my hair. What would normally not rate a mention constituted a reportable event. I had waited as long as I could and finally gathered my courage to arrange for color and cut. Why courage? Red is a very popular color in Italy these days. Not a soft looking natural auburn but a screaming iridescent red bordering on purple or sometimes an orange not reproducible in nature. It was too commonplace to be an accident so women were actually requesting these freakish hues. I needed the courage to take the plunge knowing there was a risk of red or purple or orange if I didn't clearly communicate my desires. All I wanted was my normal brown hair with its natural auburn highlights minus gray temples.

I decided to go to Arturo, a scruffy but talented young man recommended by Giuliana and Renato. Arturo had already cut Roger's hair, though Roger didn't seem to suffer any of my angst. During her visit Mamma Ruta had fearfully undergone a wash and blow at the same place with good results. I called Arturo and was surprised at being able to schedule an appointment so quickly, at three the following afternoon. He told me to arrive about an hour and a half earlier for the color. Already I was confused. Wouldn't that mean my appointment was at one thirty? Why aren't they closed at one thirty for *pranzo*? Too afraid to question the stylist, I said I would be there at one thirty.

I prepared myself. I translated the instructions and color formula from my last salon in Atlanta. I carried my dictionary and photos to show the cut I preferred. I rehearsed unfamiliar phrases from the hairstyle section of the pocket Berlitz book. Roger and I arrived five minutes before the appointed hour. Wishing me luck, he left saying he'd return in an hour. I suggested he make it two in the event I had to murder someone for a crime against humanity. He laughed but I didn't, fearing an outcome that could only be corrected by shaving.

I entered the unmarked building through a door covered by dangly, beady curtains so common in Italy. It's noisy, stuffy and smoky – the occasional customer and stylist are smoking. To the right are two barber chairs and Arturo and to the left are six other chairs, four lab-coated employees, three wash stations, two old lady helmet hair dryers and a banquette of vinyl-upholstered seats. Every seat is taken and people are standing. All eyes turn to me as I've entered. Are they running behind, do all these people have an appointment, am I late, am I too early? I stand still, looking from left to right and finally Arturo takes pity on me and suggests I have a seat. But there are no seats. Arturo asks a purple-haired patron to make room which she graciously does. I grab a copy of *Oggi*, the Italian equivalent of *People* and settle in. Reading the gossip in Italian is just as cheesy as it is in English but I can do so legitimately, claiming an Italian language lesson.

Eventually, one of the cute lab-coat girls beckons to me. I stand but look back toward Arturo confused as to why she would be calling me. She's touching my hair while another girl grabs a color book. I pull out my color formula, point to Arturo saying I have an appointment with him. By now, all the other lab coats have gathered around, talking in unison, lifting strands of my hair, reading the formula. I tell everyone I'm very afraid and they're all quite reassuring but Arturo remains on his side of the building. I finally understand that the blonde lab coat is going to do the color and later Arturo will cut my hair.

So here's the system in Italy or at least in our corner of Italy. Hair cuts require an appointment while color, wash, blow, set, highlights, perms, extensions are on a first-come, first-serve basis. My appointment was on Friday and on Fridays they don't close for lunch because it's such a busy day – everyone wants to be beautified for the weekend. I watch everyone working in this ant farm of activity. It's a family affair. Arturo, his sisters, his parents and my blonde colorist who's worked here so long she's become family.

What looked to be chaos at first glance is efficiency in motion. There are no wasted movements in this operation. The lack of appointments for everything other than cuts means that customers are on an honor system aided by the watchful eyes of the lab coats. There's little territoriality here; a customer may have her color done by one, wash done by the father, blow dry started by one sister and finished by another. Customers periodically pitch in as well. One answers the phone when all lab coats are too busy. Another grabs a broom and sweeps hair from around the chairs that are never empty. Someone will make an *espresso* and offer to make more for others. Even in a chair, customers help by holding the blow dryer as the operator grabs a clip or searches for a round brush or gathers another section of hair to dry. It's all very communal and as distant from a poot-snoot Buckhead salon as can be imagined.

By the time I get to Arturo's chair, I'm calmer. Even wet, I can tell the color is just fine so that worry is gone. Arturo wraps a cape around me, turns up the music and grabs his scissors. I stop him mid-snip. I want to discuss this cut, tell him what I like (long enough to pull into a ponytail, feathered bangs) and don't like (too many layers), show him the pictures, review the idiosyncrasies of my hair (frizzy when humid, bangs will shrink if cut too short, stubborn wave patterns). He indulges me and nods saying repeatedly, "*Ho capito, ho capito,*" understood, understood. Released from my verbal restraint, he cranks up the music anew and begins to cut. I watch the wet curls fall on the cape and know that it's shorter than I want. At least this part seems consistent the world over – stylists cut the way *they* want to. When I think he's finished, he picks up a different pair of shears, the chunking kind designed to remove bulk but add texture, form and volume. More hair surrounds me; covering the cape, cascading to the floor.

Arturo closes his eyes at times, relying on his sense of touch to judge parity. It's as though he's in a trance. He lifts a strand of hair from the right side of my head and a corresponding strand from the left to ensure even lengths. Opening his eyes (thankfully), he snips to make the adjustment. Eventually he's satisfied and begins untying the cape. I protest as he's yet to trim my bangs. "Do I have to?" he asks. "Why wouldn't you?" I say. He's happy to cut bangs to cover a less than attractive face but prefers that I let mine grow and be swept off my face and tucked behind my ears. I appreciate the compliment but persuade him to indulge me. Only now do I allow the cape to be removed.

I look at my reflection with shorter layered hair and last minute bangs. He hands me the blow dryer while he finds a suitable brush. At least it's not purple. In fact the color is perfect. As for the cut – my initial reaction is that it will grow. While he works to blow it *lisci* or straight, my opinion evolves. It's not a cut or a style I would have chosen but Arturo's instincts were right. Cut by feel works for him and beyond merely surviving this experience I judge it a success. Roger's opinion? He agrees but is more impressed with the final, all inclusive price of twenty-six Euro. I tried to add a four-Euro tip but the father wouldn't allow it. He finally accepted the two-Euro coin. As I left, customers and stylists alike wished me *Buon Natale* and *Buon Anno*.

Suitably cut and colored, I was now ready to face the holidays.

Soccer Wars

In the last run-up to Christmas, when our workers are increasingly telling us they'll see us in January, we do what work we can to remain true to Roger's "get focused" plan. Social events slip between the work tasks and offer us new views of our adopted homeland. Close to every Italian's heart is football. Football has nothing to do with the Steelers or Cowboys but has everything to do with soccer. There are entire magazines, newspapers, television programs and channels dedicated to football. The players are celebrities, their every move tracked like Britney's. The coaches, the girlfriends, the illegitimate children, the injuries, the refs, the penalties, the fans, the rumors of fixed games, the confirmation of fixed games all combine to create a frenzied industry that rivets a nation. It is in this setting that we decide to go to a Sunday match with Mary, Don and Renato. Giuliana is not part of a riveted nation.

Renato arranged everything. He purchased the tickets at a mere hundred Euro each in advance and on a cold, gray darkening afternoon drove all five of us to the game, listening to pre-game programming on the way to the stadium. Perugia, the home team is scheduled to play Terni Juventus, the mortal enemy, though any team Perugia plays is the mortal enemy. We left early so Renato would be assured of his usual parking space about a half-mile from the stadium. A gas station, closed on Sunday afternoon, is his parking lot of choice and it's free; no one will shake us down for ten or twenty Euro.

As we approach the stadium, we notice the food, wine and beer vendors hawking their goods. Roger asks if food and drink can be purchased inside but Renato says no, everything must be consumed before entering

Steps to the Basilica of St. Francis 2. Renato at our home base 3. Andrea, friend and guide
4. Paolo, our weekly porchetta vendor 5. This picture got our attention

6. Our first harvest 7. Mamma Ruta harvesting
8. Mom and I sample the first oil 9. New guys in town

10. Roger behind an original door 11. The headers had to be this high
12. Don removing worm-infested parquet 13. Many backs needed to install the beams
14. The hidden arch, the half-wall gone and the old kitchen

15. Don, Mary, Roger & me enjoying the national pastime
16. No water bottles allowed 17. Augusto, Gale, Caroline and Ciccio – together for forty ye
18. Thanksgiving with Renato, Giuliana, Mom, Roger, me, Don, Elena & Max

Cachi (persimmon) in fall 20. Lunch despite the rubble 21. Mick hauled the kitchen debris
22. Talented Mary painted our headboards 23. Umbrella pines in a rare snowfall

24. New Year's Eve 2002 25. With Roger, Clayton & Cameron in Todi 26. We needed a doc
the cantina 27. A normal remodeling day 28. Enzo, Don & Mick working on a new wall si

29. Arrival of the new olives 30. Initial prep of the new olive grove
. Getting the new plants straight 32. Six hundred olives finally planted 33. Annual pruning

34. Luca, Mario, Dani & Mara with mascot Rex at Trilogy 35. Walking with Giuliana
36. Remodeling ideas on a napkin with Frits 37. Preparing to find the fourth-floor leak

the stadium. The four of us are lingering, taking in the sights, smells and sounds but Renato is scurrying through the crowds and wants us to do the same. He's quite protective and is averse to the dallying that we do as Roger, unable to resist food in any venue, buys a *panino* and beer.

The crowd is decidedly male, loud and rowdy. The red and white Perugia team colors are proudly worn, banners are carried, faces and chests are brightly painted and taunting between fans is bordering on litigious. For some reason I think of ancient Rome and the Coliseum. Roger downs his sandwich and beer as we arrive at our gate. Renato provides our tickets and we're immediately greeted by the police who check our coats and bags for illicit items. Politely, they confiscate my twelve ounce plastic bottle of water as contraband. It could be thrown on the field or used as a weapon. Renato quickly apologizes saying that I didn't know. He's more upset about the situation than the police who allow me to pass unarmed.

Our seats offer an excellent view of the pitch. The seats themselves are the plastic bucket type molded to perfectly fit the rear of anyone under five. We notice the seating several rows to our right, cold cement slabs. Renato, ever the responsible bank director, takes his regular seat on one such slab. It's half the price but we decide the buckets are worth what we paid for this special event. The wind picks up and there's an imminent threat of rain. We're glad to have worn corduroy pants, scarves, coats, gloves and hats and thankful for the slight overhang that covers our seats.

Since we're early, we have time to watch the fans enter the stadium and the practice taking place on the field. The end zones or *curve* are already filled with the most enthusiastic fans (read thugs) who chant, cheer, incite, insult, dance, unfurl banners and never stop taunting the opposing team. Aurally sensitive flower that I am, the announcer's endless, screaming pre-game announcements make me wish I had brought ear plugs. He's reading through a list of sponsoring advertisers – paint shops, car parts, electrical supply houses, travel agencies, irrigation companies, garden centers – at a pace that gives each one scant but equal recognition. I'm worried. If this is pre-game announcing, what racket lies ahead?

The game eventually begins and just like any eight year old playing football, I'm more intrigued with the action off the field than on it. I know this is heresy but it all seems like a lot of running back and forth, forth and back, falling down, getting up with shin-grabbing histrionics to rival any Oscar performance; substitutions, flag throwing, cheering, booing and the one second you take your eye off the pitch is the one second someone scores. I keep thinking the announcer will tell us what's happening and I can translate what's taken place but he's yet to say a word since the game started. No play-by-play, no color commentary, no injury report, so my attention to the game is minimal.

What has really caught my eye is Perugia's *curva nord,* on the north end of the stadium. Both end zones are hotbeds of activity but the home team hosts the nastiest, most vocal, most volatile fans. Posters must be created on the spot, many filled with bawdy references to body parts and the weak nature of particular team members. The *curva* is illuminated like the Washington Mall on the 4th of July. Netting in front of the fans is completely ineffective as they toss flares, cherry bombs and other incendiary devices onto the pitch. And I can't carry a plastic water bottle into the stadium? How did the *curva* arsenal pass the gate security?

Repeatedly, the game is suspended while firemen in full battle gear descend to collect flares and douse flames. These are the only times that the announcer finds his voice. In calm, soothing tones, he asks *curva nord* to "kindly and gently" refrain from throwing burning items onto the pitch. His requests are summarily ignored; the ritual continues.

In the end, Perugia lost 1-0, a result widely blamed on bad reffing. Renato is even more protective of us as we leave the stadium avoiding the *curva* on our way to the gas station. We quickly settle into his car, appreciating what we now consider to be spacious seats. We thank Renato for all the arrangements but he barely acknowledges us due to his rapt focus on the radio's post-game report. As Roger says, it was fun but attending a football match in Italy can now be checked off our list.

'Twas the Week Before...

Mamma mia, the holidays. Not surprisingly in this overwhelmingly Catholic country, Christmas is huge. The religious aspect is of utmost importance but traditional foods, gift-giving and holiday decorations are significant as well. In general, Roger and I are Grisham *Skipping Christmas* fans. Here we had other excuses not to participate in the revelry – recent arrival in country, lack of familiarity with local customs, no knowledge of where to buy a tree or where to put one in a partially demolished house, where to shop for gifts, appropriateness of gifts, whom do we gift. No matter. We are woefully unprepared but are swept into the season regardless.

Our first clue to the pervasiveness of Christmas should have been the calendars. Beginning in early December every merchant, delivery man and business establishment participates in the gift giving tradition of providing customers with calendars for the coming year. From the bank to the ladder-climbing heating oil delivery man to the Commie Mill to the tire store to the electrical supply house to the seamstress – all give away calendars. Some are staid and conservative (the bank), others racy enough to rival *Penthouse* centerfolds (electrical supply), some show the entire year (the seamstress' dish towel), some are surprising in their banality (Commie Mill). Each is presented with ceremony and solemnity as though the naked lady calendar is the only one we've received this month. I'm not sure what we're supposed to do with all these calendars. Everyone gives them and everyone gets them so re-gifting would be inappropriate. We'll probably pitch them, except for naked lady who's already found a home in the utility shed.

The Commie Mill requires some explanation. At the bottom of our hill is the *Molino Popolare*, a cooperative warehouse where farmers have joined together to sell their goods at lower prices. It's a convenient place to buy shovels, ladders, chain saws, crates for olives, pesticides, animal food, fencing and other must-have items. Perhaps in its heyday it was more "*popolare*" than it is now; these days it's often empty. It took us awhile to understand that at its core it is a socialist organization – hence our nickname. In today's world the *Molino's* interests tend more to the capitalistic bent and they celebrate the Christmas season with calendar-giving gusto equal to any other business entity. Disappointingly, January is filled with upbeat daily horoscopes and advice for the lovelorn instead of strident "Workers of the World, Unite" slogans. Time has rounded the sharp edges of socialist zeal.

Our second Christmas clue should have been the limited workdays in December and the spillover into January. Every other day is a holiday; businesses close for weeks, not just days, deliveries cease, orders can't be taken. It's difficult to 'make the works' under such circumstances. We do what we can but succumb to the season.

In addition to Antonio's many other talents he raises Christmas trees, something Roger did in the mountains of Virginia. Typically trees are small, unpruned balsams sold with a root ball. It's illegal to cut a tree without permission in Italy and permission is rarely granted. No matter that the trees were planted with the express purpose of being Christmas trees, the no cutting rule rules. Sadly, this is an example of a law gone bad, as the grapefruit-sized root ball is large enough to satisfy the government but hopelessly inadequate to sustain life.

The weekend before Christmas, Antonio delivered our first tree, one that he had pre-selected from his field, the tallest at about six feet. The choice was a lovely gift and came with an unexpected bonus – it spared us the annual R.I.F. or Row In Field that inevitably occurs when spouses walk arm-in-arm, full of Christmas cheer and attempt to agree on the proper tree.

It's common to have at least one decorated tree indoors; Giuliana has two as does Liana though one of hers is artificial. Here they're not called artificial trees but rather ecological trees – an interesting marketing approach. Roger fumes about the many flaws in that theory – how the ecological trees are made of substances that strip and damage the environment, how they're manufactured in non-environmentally friendly ways, how they're transported in fuel-guzzling trucks over long distances. We worry about the effect a spike in popularity of artificial trees would have on Antonio's fledgling side business. He admits to feeling the impact but there are still many who want a live tree.

It was easy to locate the several boxes of Christmas decorations we'd shipped from Atlanta. A tree stand and lights were not so easy. A stand as we knew it was unusable because our tree was equipped with a ball o' dirt and our lights, which wouldn't work with Italian electricity, were sold during our stateside sale. Instead we purchased a plastic pot at the Commie Mill and four strands of lights from our favorite electrical supply house (any excuse for another calendar). The lights came with the reassuring words in English; "perfectly engineered for the 21st century." Each strand has ten different programs but none are synchronized so they flash slowly and then experience a huge adrenaline charge and flash faster and then fade and then twinkle in only white and then in colors and all at different times. It's dizzy, mindless, mesmerizing entertainment. We decorate the tree with some of our many ornaments and grudgingly admire its beauty despite our best efforts not to get caught up in the season.

Our next Christmas clues should have been the decoration of the houses, the specialty foods of the season and the exchange of gifts. It began as close as our next door neighbors. Not only is Giuliana a culinary talent, she's an expert in the decorative arts. She and Mary make quite a pair creating ornaments, centerpieces and wreaths or inventively wrapping packages into frothy confections. This is not my forte but occasionally they drag me out of the *Le Vigne* rubble in search of greenery and other foliage from our woods. One day we collect *pungitopo* or butcher's broom, a dark green shrub marked by tiny but extremely sharp leaves and bright red, cranberry size berries. *Pungitopo* literally means "prick the mouse" and the stinging thorns explain the name. Butchers made good use of the shrub by placing branches atop hanging *salami* and *prosciutto* thus protecting the cured meats from uninvited snacking. The *pungitopo* is difficult to arrange but perfect in its coloring for Christmas and long-lasting when left to dry. It's also a protected species, not allowed to be dug and removed from the wild. Fear of the forestry police (there is such a thing) seems non-existent; everyone's home is decorated with festive holiday *pungitopo.*

On another outing we are in search of *vischio,* mistletoe and *muschio,* moss. Mistletoe casts the same magical kissing spell in Italy as it does in the States. I'm first made aware of *muschio* by precious Lucia, Enzo's youngest daughter who at twelve practices her few words of English with us. She's a bright, vibrant little star who teaches us that the moss is used to create *presepe* or crèche scenes. The *presepe* vary from simple to elaborate. The simple ones remind me of the shoebox dioramas popular in my elementary school days. Slightly more detailed ones might include running water or red colored strips of foil moved by a tiny fan to simulate flickering flames. Living crèches are popular as well and one *presepe* we visited in Santa Maria degli Angeli, the city in the valley below Assisi, was constructed at table-top height in the center of a room. Visitors filed past the *presepe* which wasn't "live" but seemed so in miniature. The scaled-down scene could have been created by Disney; cows mooed, sheep baahed, turbaned Kings crossed a sandy desert on camels the size of tiny dogs following a bright star leading to a manger. The mood was reverent, the room quiet. People moved slowly around the enormous table a second or third time to inspect details missed on the first viewing. They spoke in hushed tones, pointing out water features or the gifts brought by the Kings.

Gifts. Roger and I have a long-standing agreement – no Christmas gift exchanges. We are fortunate enough to gift each other all year long and *Le Vigne* and this renovation are extravagant enough gifts that will last for years. As for everyone else? Don't leave home without one. Enzo brings us a huge *stelle di Natale,* star of Christmas – a bright red poinsettia. Giovanna and Liana appear one afternoon to present me with an assortment of soaps and fragrances from the local *erboristeria,* the Italian equivalent of Crabtree and Evelyn. Antonio and Cinzia provide not only our tree but homemade *limoncello,* concentrated lemon liqueur, homemade *torrone,* a hard candy made with honey and almonds and two fresh golfball-size truffles, one white and one black. Giuliana and Renato give us more *torrone*, olives and preserved spicy mushrooms. Don and Mary give us a dated and inscribed ceramic coffee mug delicately hand-painted by Valentina, a lovely, talented artisan whose workshop is in Ponte Felcino. In return we give plentiful food baskets filled with chocolates, nuts, dried fruits and cheeses.

Kitchens are bustling during this season with the preparation of *torrone, limoncello* and the famous *cappelletti in brodo;* the signature dish for Christmas and All Saints Day. These tiny, filled pastas require an army of women to create. Led by Giuliana, army of one, neighbors and relatives assist in creating the pasta and cooking the delicately seasoned meats blended with cheese to eventually form thousands of hats that are used immediately or frozen. My multi-talented neighbor invited me to participate but I was committed to rubble clearing and translation duty that afternoon. Mary got to play and said it was an experience I shouldn't miss. She didn't understand a single word but language was no barrier. She was able to immerse herself in a process that's been practiced for centuries; knowledge passed from generation to generation. Sadly, this is another art at risk due to a declining population and cultural changes.

Food continues to be a focal highlight of our days. We've discovered the local weekly markets, Ponte Felcino on Thursday and Ponte Valleceppi on Saturday. We buy fresh, seasonal vegetables, cheeses, garden flowers, vegetable plants, kitchen gadgets and *porchetta* sandwiches. Sometimes we buy just the meat, requesting *magra* or lean to avoid the parts laced with fat or cracklin'. December means spinach is abundant and I watch other women buying crates so I do the same. It's not until I get home that I realize how gritty it is. "Triple washed" takes on new meaning – fill the sink with clean water, wash the spinach, rinse and repeat two more times. Saute the crate-loads in a little olive oil, garlic and lemon juice and it reduces to barely enough spinach to feed two but oh, so tasty.

Persimmon is in season and our trees are dripping with the ripe fruit. *Cachi* (disturbingly pronounced 'ca-key') trees are the bizarre ones with no leaves but only grapefruit size, reddish-orange, smooth skinned fruit clinging to dark bare branches. It looks as though the tree has been decorated for Christmas and if the fruit is not picked, it begins to resemble a Dali painting as the orange orbs drip and ooze their way to the ground. Persimmon is dense, viscous, pulpy, gelatinous and not terribly sweet. Sounds appealing, doesn't it? Fortunately, I've acquired a taste for what Don does with our *cachi*. Using a modified banana bread recipe, he creates loaf cakes that he shares with us and his Italian hosts who enjoy these unfamiliar treats. But as Mamma Ruta says "Can't they come up with a better name for that fruit?"

Christmas

The ancient, religious city of Assisi takes on an even more saintly aura at this time of year. The city is located on the side of monte Subasio, a single mountain rising a mere 1290 meters (4,257 feet) above the surrounding plains. In truth, it is more hill than mountain. From the distance, Subasio is a smooth bread loaf outcropping; there are no jagged peaks or Alpine features. The upper quarter appears brown and bald above the unusually low tree line. In winter it's normally covered with snow but with all the rain of late, no white yet appears. We know this only when the fog lifts and the brown pate of a monk's head is visible from all surrounding towns. Continuing three quarters of the way down the hillside on the left is the impressive view of Assisi. The highest and most defensible point of the city is distinguished by the remains of the castle and fortress Rocca Maggiore, a superb example of medieval military architecture. Below the Rocca and to the left are the unmistakable series of arches that characterize the Basilica of St. Francis, composed of two churches, one built atop the other in the early 13th century. We're told that after the Vatican, Assisi is the most visited, vaunted site in the Catholic world. The city has additional significance for us. It was outside the doors of the upper Basilica where Roger predicted our future presence in Italy.

On Christmas Eve we return as part of a group of sixteen for dinner at Hotel Subasio. The ancient hotel is a short walk from the Basilica. The staff has prepared a single long table for our group in a stone and brick corridor. The ceiling is at least ten meters high and vaulted. Unlike in our *salone rustiche*, these bricks are exposed; no white plaster covers the natural pink hues that warm the room. As a side note, Roger and I fleetingly toy with the idea of removing the plaster ceiling in our *salone rustiche*. But before anyone has to call the psych department of the local hospital we recover our senses. "While-we're-at-it" can't be applied here – the job would be too time consuming and costly. It would darken the room considerably and we're already struggling for more light. We quickly dodge that renovation bullet.

Tradition calls for a meat-less Christmas Eve dinner. Our many courses revolve around fish such as dried cod that has been soaked to remove the excess salt, served with tomatoes or brothy soup with tiny pasta, white fish and diced vegetables. We start later than the standard eight o'clock dinner hour because the plan is to attend midnight mass in the Basilica. We linger over coffees, dessert and *digestivi,* after dinner drinks designed to aid digestion. It's only eleven by the time we finish. The staff would politely remain in place until the following Christmas but we want them to be able to leave the restaurant even though they've chosen to work on Christmas Eve.

Our drizzly December continues as we make the short uphill walk to the Basilica in the rain. Not surprisingly, both upper and lower churches are already packed. We learn that seating has been reserved for months and the best we can hope for is standing room only in the most distant reaches of the sanctuary for what is certain to be a two hour service. That made the decision for most of us. Our group of sixteen quickly dispersed. Some headed to a local bar in search of Irish coffee of all things, some returned home and others decided to go to Farneto, the next town north of Colombella where a Franciscan monastery would hold midnight mass.

We are part of the Farneto contingent and have to hurry. Traffic into and out of Assisi is heavy but Giuliana rides with us and knows a back way to the small village. Roger's driving while Giuliana's directing from the backseat urging us to go quickly because Farneto will be crowded as well. The road is dark and narrow and we're thankful to have a guide. We spot the Farneto sign, turn off the main road and climb an even narrower road. We wind and turn and eventually see cars parked on either side. Giuliana urges us to take one of the spots but Roger is convinced his parking karma will hold, especially in the rain. Ignoring her, he continues driving to the front of the church where he creates his own parking lot, earning a *"bravo, Roger"* from an impressed Giuliana.

A Franciscan monastery has existed in Farneto for centuries. St. Francis purportedly passed through this town during his many travels. There is a large, smooth flat rock in the surrounding garden with two deep side-by-side indentations, made by his knees during prayer according to the believers. Tonight, the small Gothic church is filled. From the back, it appears all seats are taken however Giuliana, Renato, Mary and Don stride to the front and indicate there's space and we should join them. It didn't seem like the thing to do. Dozens of people were standing and with the singing underway it seemed as though the service had already started. Little did we know that the service had yet to start, the deep voices of the singing brothers was simply what Roger called pre-game warm up. A young friar dressed in the simple dark brown robe that is the garb of the Franciscans hands me a stack of programs and asks that I pass them to new arrivals. I've now been given a mission from God.

This is going to be a long night. The singing continues, people stream into the crowded little church, I dutifully distribute programs. The sermon contained the standard admonitions one hears at Christmas and Easter - nice to see so many people tonight, but where are you every Sunday during the year? At the seventy-five minute mark, tired of shifting from foot to aching foot, Roger and I both feel the need for a little fresh air. We step outside into the dampness that proves a relief from the stuffy interior. We press our stiff backs against the stone and wonder how much longer the service will last.

An older friar passes and asks what we're doing outside. I explain that we didn't feel well and needed some air. My response met with raised eyebrows and a stern suggestion to go back inside. The obvious question is what is he doing outside and if not for Roger's inability to formulate the words in Italian, would have been impertinently asked. The not-so-obvious question is why weren't we in a bar someplace drinking Irish coffees. Sometimes this language barrier is a good thing. That said we had enough holiness for one night. Mary later told us that *panettone* and *prosecco* were distributed but that would not have been incentive enough for us to stay. Our decision to finally leave at 1:30 was the right one.

Christmas Day began with a broken promise. Our long-standing agreement of no gift exchanges fell apart at the sight of the small gift under our tree. Roger had commissioned Mary to do a painting of *Le Vigne*. The two had conspired for days and agreed it should be done in the spring when the wisteria and roses are in bloom. The little package held a prototype that is as meaningful if not more so than a finished work. I am touched and guilt-ridden. In the midst of our rubble and destruction, Roger had the forethought to arrange a gift while I took our annual agreement as fact. His reassurance that it's really a gift for both of us does little to assuage my conscience. This is Roger at his core, tender-hearted and considerate, generous and thoughtful.

Caroline and Augusto hosted eighteen for Christmas Dinner. All of us contributed – Giuliana brought the famous *cappelletti*, Don brought a chocolate dessert, I brought two casseroles, one with zucchini and potatoes and another with triple-washed spinach. Other neighbors and friends brought breads, more desserts and side dishes. We feasted for hours; turkey, stuffing, corn pudding, and cranberry sauce thanks to fresh cranberries that Caroline smuggled in from her recent trip to New Jersey. The dinner was hearty, filling, tasty and a mix of cooking styles and traditions. The various courses are served and cleared by Lorenzo and Francesca, Caroline and Augusto's dual-citizenship, bilingual children.

Lorenzo, the oldest at thirty-one is an architect living and working in Venice. Francesca is twenty-eight and lives in Viterbo, an hour south of Colombella where she teaches English to the Italian military. They decline all offers for others to help. They are bright, charming, funny, delightful. Not living at home makes them somewhat unique as Italian children. Perhaps they are more independent because their mother is American and they've spent a lot of time in the States. In the States, the boomerang phenomenon notwithstanding, most children going away to college have left home for good. That's not the case in Italy; children attending university typically live at home and do so until they marry. The relationship between parent and child is strong and close, physically, geographically and emotionally. While there are obvious benefits, there are downsides to such extreme proximity.

Italy struggles with one of the oldest populations in the world coupled with the lowest birth rate. The rest of Europe has the same problem but Italy's statistics are the worst. The implications for the future are weighty – who will support the elderly, how will such support be financed, who will lead the government, how much more tax can the public stand (currently over forty percent)? Education is prolonged, full-time secure jobs are limited, marriage and children are delayed. Such issues are mulled by parents and children as they eat their dinners at home, pasta made fresh by *Mamma,* utilities and rent covered by *Babbo*.

Back at Christmas dinner, after the final dishes are cleared, coffee served, *digestivi* finished, the children remove the table linens and Ciccio, Gale's husband insists we play *Mercante in Fiera*, a card game requiring two special decks of cards. The *Mercante* is a trader, merchant, dealer at the fair or market or bazaar. Everyone enthusiastically agrees while Don, Mary, Roger and I have no earthly idea how to play, what the objective is or how to win. No one makes any effort to teach us, everyone is talking at the same time, we've been thrown into open water, the sharks are circling.

Renato is the barker, the ring leader, the *Mercante in Fiera.* He collects five Euro from every player in exchange for two cards. Each card has a figure – perhaps a sailing ship or a swan, a castle or a rhinoceros. The four of us join with the others to play, if you can call it that. After twenty clueless minutes we finally determine that the game is a combination of Fish and Concentration and the goal is to match one's final card with one selected early in the game and placed in the pot. Banker Renato reveals a new aspect of his personality. He's a shady wheeler-dealer urging us to sell cards or buy others. He's convincing and manipulative. His scheming forces the rest of us to make side deals causing the original pot to swell. Through luck, guile and his own Rhett Butler brand of conniving, Roger is one of three remaining players and is rewarded grandly for his effort – he breaks even.

Some of us then play *tombola*, a kind of Italian bingo which Roger dubs Bingolino. Milton Bradley would probably categorize it as "good for all ages" which in reality means "best for four to seven year olds." It's perfect for those of us struggling with Italian, an excellent way to learn numbers. Catch phrases go with certain numbers – 77 is *gambe della donna*, legs of a woman; 33 is the year of Christ. Roger was not as successful with *tombola* as he was in the card shark game. On the other hand, being relieved of his heavy *spiccioli*, coins, change, shrapnel, constituted a win of sorts.

We've now occupied Caroline and Augusto's house for more than six hours and we're expected to make an appearance at Catiuscia and Federico's house. We promised them a short visit, making clear that we will have already eaten a full dinner. Here, there are no English speakers, the burden is on me to greet, introduce, translate and be hospitable to our hosts, her parents, his parents, grandparents, great grandparents, cousins, aunts, uncles, nephews and nieces. The basement contains four tables groaning with food – cheeses, olives, breads, *panini, prosciutto, salumi*, vegetables, salads, desserts, homemade wines, bottled waters, candy. Various family members offer food, trying to prepare plates which are difficult to decline. We both accept drinks – Roger takes red jug wine and I get away with only water.

Catiuscia is exhausted. My poor neighbor is due at the end of January, the baby is kicking her breastbone and she hasn't slept for days. The forty or so people are entrenched but we're determined to make our visit quick. Federico's five year old nephew learns we speak English and is convinced he can speak to us. To the tune of "London Bridge is Falling Down" he repeatedly sings "all the snow is falling down, falling down, falling down," and then explains his performance to the totally rapt family members who are charmed by this bundle of energy. He jumps into Roger's lap, talking a mile a minute in Italian, gesturing, grabbing his ear, pulling his nose, giggling, asking questions. Roger has no clue, simply nods in agreement and finally says, "I'm *vecchio,* old, and *stupido* and I don't understand a word you're saying." With that, London Bridge scampered to the other side of the room to announce with great fanfare and pointing back at Roger, *"Lui è un po' stupido,"* he's a little stupid. The declaration was greeted by barely stifled laughter and half-hearted efforts to restrain his childlike frankness.

Roger took no offense and laughed with the rest of them. It seemed as good an exit line as any but to do so took time. We began the requisite double cheek kissing gauntlet. Federico finally let us go only after we promised to return for a coffee or to watch some television together. Coffee? Doable. TV together? *Mamma mia.*

New Year's Eve

What are the holidays without visitors? Cameron and Clayton made their first visit to *Le Vigne*, bringing boyfriend Cal and girlfriend Shandi to share the experience. Roger's children are seasoned European travelers thanks to Dad's commercial airline career and pass benefits while the significant others are making their first overseas' trips. Again it hits us; we realize how much we've learned when we are in a position to teach someone else.

The *giovani*, young people, have interesting impressions about life in Italy. They are shocked by the amount of time it takes to do laundry. Their jeans are cold and cardboard stiff coming off the line. The pockets are frosty and Cameron uses the interior bars of the *salone rustiche* to hang slightly damp sweatshirts overnight. Shandi and Cal haven't put their cameras down. Clayton is fascinated by all things horticultural and architectural. Cameron renames the Smart cars Tic-Tacs. They're all in high speed internet withdrawal and can't imagine how we survive with some days yes/some days no phone and computer service. English-speaking television is limited, sushi and hamburgers non-existent. They are frustrated at not being able to communicate in their own language, read a menu, order their own meals. Occasionally, they suffered severe attacks of junk food deprivation though I think it was more a case of longing for something familiar and recognizable. They loved our property, the surrounding countryside, the ancient cities of Todi, Cortona and Santa Maria degli Angeli; the pizzas, *salumi*, pastas and *porchetta*. They helped us with our construction projects. Cal spent hours programming our computer while Clayton created a label for our olive oil bottles. All kept us company and brought us up to date on stateside happenings. Without the slightest hesitation they were ready to abandon us and seek adoption from Wendy and Frits upon seeing our friends' heated indoor pool and completed, tastefully decorated renovated farmhouse.

On New Year's Eve we dined together at Lo Spedalicchio in the town of Ospedalicchio, not far from Assisi. The restaurant and hotel is owned by Giancarla, a good friend of Giuliana's. The building dates from the 13th century and has survived many lives. In one iteration it was a way station between the warring factions of Assisi and Perugia. Just as houses, buildings and hospitals in Virginia changed hands repeatedly between the North and the South during the U.S. Civil War, Lo Spedalicchio fell to Assisi or Perugia depending upon who reigned victorious in battle that day.

The structure is impressive – the now familiar two-story vaulted brick ceilings are intact, the narrow openings in the interior façade are wide enough for deadly arrows to fly from the quivers of the armed sentries posted to protect the occupants. Plexiglas floor panels afford a view of the original flooring several feet below street level. The *giovani* are wide-eyed. Giancarla greets us warmly, filled with *complimenti* about the young people. We're all dressed up for this *cenone*, big dinner, and Giancarla looks even more strikingly elegant than usual. She is dramatic, perfectly coiffed, with wide expressive eyes set in an attractive round face. She exudes a movie star demeanor and graciously pours us a glass of *prosecco*. It's as though we're dining in her magnificent home rather than a restaurant.

We are early though it's after nine. The tables are decorated with confetti, foil covered chocolate coins, brightly colored beads, party hats, noise makers and the evening's menu coiled and beribboned. Slowly, the other tables fill and the service begins. We indulge in sixteen courses, countless wines, desserts and *digestivi*. The pace is leisurely; guests stand and stroll from table to table between courses. We meet a cute young couple from Milan and their four year old daughter Francesca who believes herself older and is the ringleader of eight and ten-year-old children who blithely follow her by dancing into the lobby when not dining. At the far end of the dining room is a group of ten including Giuliana and Renato. Our four guests are impressed that we know people or meet people so readily. Frankly, we are too.

The meal is superb and the stand-out item is most certainly the *risotto* which includes pea-size melon balls. The pairing of the fruit and rice is perfect though a combination I never would have come to on my own. After our meat and vegetable course we heard loud popping noises from outside the building and confirmed midnight on our watches. Everyone rose and greeted each other with *Auguri* and *Buon Anno*. Francesca paraded through the restaurant, young soldiers in tow, all carrying the noisemakers, neon-colored beads draped around necks and wrists, sleep a distant, banished thought.

Sleep was not far from Roger's thoughts. He disappeared and when the time away became longer than a mere bathroom break, Clayton went searching for his father. Thinking we were finished and ready to leave, Roger had claimed his overcoat and abruptly went to the parking lot. Clayton found his dad impatiently waiting for the rest of the family and reminded him we'd yet to have dessert or paid the bill for that matter. Father and son returned for dessert, coffee and the guaranteed ribbing that his disappearance provoked.

It was well after one by the time we loaded into the Trooper. Tipsy, sleepy and maneuvering the right hand drive Trooper, Roger paid scant attention until Shandi reminded him to abide by the ten and two rule of hand placement. We laughed, but Shandi's light-hearted voice carried enough of a rebuke to force *Babbo* to listen up for the short drive home. By now we had missed the invitation to Gale and Ciccio's to watch fireworks from their terrace.

Fireworks are huge here and readily available; every local grocery store carrying a full armament. As we approached *Le Vigne*, Perugia and the surrounding small towns in the valley were randomly illuminated by the many multi-colored bursts. The New Year had begun.

La Befana

The holidays were far from over. We had yet to celebrate Epiphany, the famous Twelfth Night and until that event was celebrated we weren't likely to see much of our workmen. The sacred Epiphany is commingled with the secular *Befana*, an ugly witch with a big, hooked nose, wrinkled skin and several facial warts. She brings stockings for children – sweets and treats for the good ones; coal, onions and garlic for the naughty. On the night of the 5th, Clayton, Shandi, Roger and I went to La Boteghita to celebrate. The restaurant sits between Ponte Felcino and Ponte Valleceppi off a narrow, dark road near an expressway overpass. Our pilot made several missed approaches before locating just the right alleyway but eventually we arrived to find hundreds of other diners.

Dinner at La Boteghita was a raucous, expansive, over-the-top affair. One large room led to several smaller rooms where each table was filled and waiters jockeyed for space in the cramped setting. Several menus, each the size of posters, detailed pizza, pasta, beef and chicken specialties as well as the usual offerings of *antipasti*, side dishes and desserts. Our jocular waiter Vincenzo dutifully took our order but hesitated as we continued to order more delicious sounding *antipasti* and *primi*. We should have caught on when he kept saying, "This is your first time here, isn't it?" We glanced at the other tables and seeing the portions appear on Paul Bunyan size platters, we sought Vincenzo's advice on how to scale back.

If we had ordered just one appetizer we would have been overserved. A platter was placed in the center of our table and included *mozzarella di bufala*, tomatoes, wedges of *radicchio*, crescents of melon, onion rings, deep fried and stuffed olives, other cheeses, nuts, honey, and *bruschetta*. We each received plates and our adequate table for four was quickly shrinking with candles, wine, water, condiments, bread and silverware. Before we had taken our first samplings, Vincenzo reappeared with a wrought iron tripod stand that he placed over the original platter. He grinned maliciously at his Boteghita virgins and slipped away only to appear seconds later with a second platter that fit into the ring on top of the tripod.

We groaned, Vincenzo laughed, Shandi photographed and Clayton was in heaven. He called it a meat waterfall. Paper thin slices of aged and seasoned *prosciutto*, various *salumi, capocollo, mortadella, lardo*, and more cascaded in layers from a central support in the platter. I had never seen such a presentation and more was on the way.

As we marveled at these displays and those at the surrounding tables, the restaurant went dark. Perhaps there was a power failure, a frequent event in Italy. Waiters and patrons were undisturbed by the darkness and we quickly adjusted to the candlelight. The large room at the front of the restaurant erupted in laughter and lights began to reappear. We continued to make minimal progress on our two story appetizers when a *Befana* walked into our room complete with cane, warty mask, kerchiefed hair, hooked nose and gypsy-like floor-length skirt. The *Befana* circulated from table to table, greeting customers, terrifying wee patrons and generally causing more tumult in this already rowdy environment. As the *Befana* firmly shook each of our hands and approached the next table we all agreed that this *Befana* was definitely a "he," confirmed when the *Befana* flashed a table of friends.

Vincenzo was in his glory. Not only did he have newbies for patrons, we were there on the night of the Befana. The *orecchiette pasta*, little ears, which he tried to serve from a copper sauté pan was immediately returned to the kitchen before it hit our plates. We begged to *portare via* or take away; a little known and less appreciated concept in Italy. He indulged his first-timers and allowed us to collect our plentiful leftovers after introducing us to the owner. She's from Colombella, knows our property and urged us to return. An attractive pixie and glad-handing politician, she moves from table to table, chatting with customers, collecting money, assisting waiters with tripods, directing traffic from the kitchen all while keeping her eye on the front door and incoming guests. With a wink from the *Befana* on our way out, we can now officially declare the holidays over and once again reapply ourselves to the many tasks we must complete before opening our doors to the guests we know will arrive this summer.

So, like a looming homework assignment ignored during Christmas break, Roger's mantra bubbles to the surface from our subconscious, replaying over and over the three words we've suppressed for weeks. Let's. Get. Focused.

Visas

Not so fast on the focusing business. As much as we wanted to stay firmly entrenched in our combat zone, destroying, slowly rebuilding, measuring progress by decreasing bucket loads of rubble, we had to return to the States. We needed our visas.

Here's the *Catch 22* short course: We can't own a car in Italy unless we're residents. We can't become residents without a *permesso di soggiorno*, permission to stay. We can't obtain the *permesso* until we have our visas. We can't obtain visas until we have a hard copy of the *atto*, property deed, in hand. We couldn't obtain the *atto* until we closed on *Le Vigne*. We can't obtain a visa in Italy but must originate the request in Florida, the Consulate serving Georgia, our former residence. A visa is required for a stay longer than ninety days and while it was hard to believe, we were fast approaching our three month limit for remaining in Italy without one.

Preparing for this departure was difficult. We changed our departure date four times for a journey that would last three weeks and include three visits to Atlanta, two to Florida and one to Pittsburgh. Departure meant organizing the work load in our absence. Mick would move into *Le Vigne* full-time. A steady stream of masons, plumbers, carpenters and electricians ensured activity during the day. Antonio, Enzo and Don would swing through often to provide more movement. Mick had the night shift.

Why were we so concerned with *Le Vigne* being occupied? During these past three months we had heard some disconcerting news about life in Italy – crime, primarily theft, exists. It would be unrealistic to think otherwise but it's a specter we hoped to escape. While the daily news in major U.S. cities often leads with murder, not even large densely populated Italian cities suffer the high serious crime rates that are an unfortunate feature of life in America. But without a doubt, things are stolen here. If one were to believe the locals, Albanians are responsible for all thefts.

Giuliana locks all doors, closes all windows and seals all shutters whether going to bed, running to the grocery store or going away for a week in the Dolomites. It's driving Mary and Don nuts as they're not about to slam click themselves into and out of their apartment during their long-term stay. It's a constant struggle. Giuliana tells me that she would feel awful if something were to happen to Mary's possessions while Mary tells me that they can't live their lives in constant fear. I try to explain both sides to each side but only end up hearing the same arguments. *Basta,* enough.

Le Vigne has nine doors, thirty windows, thirty screens, thirty-eight shutters and an alarm system - all in need of replacement. There's not a snowball's chance that Roger is going to participate in this shutter, door, window, screen closing, alarm setting, key-toting, paranoid exercise. He too has learned the word *basta* and while he'll be prudent and cautious by arranging for a house sitter and installation of a functioning alarm system, he will not be whipped into a froth by neighbors or strangers over this wart on the surface of our bucolic existence. *Basta.*

What does have us whipped into a froth is the planning, organization and lengthy work lists to arrange prior to departure. If there were any way not to make this trip or if Roger could simply send me to handle it for both of us or if it could be postponed until the renovation were finished we would do so. One could not contrive a more exquisite torture for a controlling micro-manager than to banish him in the face of such exciting activity.

Capo Antonio patiently endured meeting after meeting, walks around the property, translated list upon list to learn what was required in our absence. One grueling four hour session left me wondering exactly how much translators are paid. Are they paid by the word or the hour? What about advance work conducted during lunch or dinner? What about over cocktails? What about comp time for lack of sleep due to dreaming about these lists in Italian? This departure was a test. We would learn much about the capabilities of Antonio, the other workers, my translating skills and the fortitude of our resident micro-manager.

Three weeks in the States, three different climates, four rescheduled departure dates and suitcases still nested under a bed. Packing was so far off our radar that it wasn't until midnight prior to departure that I grabbed our bags, throwing in who knows what. As pass-riders we would fly standby and if we were lucky we'd be drinking mimosas with the swells in business class in less than twelve hours. Flying this way is always an uncertainty despite checking the flight mere hours in advance. We were certain about only one thing; our visa documents were completed, organized, checked and double-checked, packed in our carry-on bags and pulsing with anticipation of their visit to the Italian Consulate in Miami.

Antonio drove us to the Rome airport at o'dark thirty affording Roger one final two-hour list reviewing session. Separation was difficult as was my ability to explain standby status and the possibility that we might not get on the flight and he could potentially see us again in two hours. Fortunately we made the flight and he was free of us for three weeks.

The first of our two visa experiences in Miami was not nearly as traumatic as the six months of preparation for the event. We arrived at the Consulate prior to opening and found several others waiting. The offices inside were dark as seen through the closed glass doors. No staff in sight.

Fifteen minutes later several Italian speakers arrived and unlocked the doors, gave themselves access and promptly relocked the doors. No words were exchanged with the officials who carried tiny cups of Cuban coffee (the closest approximation to *espresso*), cigarettes and Danish into the inner sanctum. Another fifteen minutes and one of the officials unlocked the doors allowing the now dozen of us to enter in typical Italian style. It was a scramble to grab a ticket from one of those machines that reside at deli counters everywhere. Again we waited, this time to be called by one of two officials standing ceremoniously behind glass teller windows.

Eventually our number is called and I recognize this official as the one who answered questions and provided forms last summer during my fact-finding mission. We advise that we're here for our visas and he asks to see our completed paperwork. We provide half-inch thick files for each of us that include letters attesting to our good health, financial solvency documents, good citizen (non-criminal) records, photo IDs, passports, original and copies of the *atto* and the forms we struggled to complete in the preceding months. At his request, we each provide a nominal processing fee of $23.19 in cash, exact amount required, no change provided.

I'm nervous while Roger is anything but. He's used to being in charge and has little patience when someone else is. I worry that the forms or requirements have changed since my visit or that something won't be in order or that we've omitted some blatantly obvious document that will slam the door on this bloated bureaucratic exercise. Our burly official, dark hair slicked back exposing a ferocious widow's peak, coffee at his side, cigarette pack open, rifles through our documents at lightning speed and just as quickly seems to find nothing lacking. We're told to provide self-addressed stamped envelopes or return in ten days for our visas. We opt to return. All documents, including our passports, travel in a diplomatic pouch to Rome, are processed there and returned to the Consulate in Miami. Don't call to check on the status; just show up after ten days to obtain the visas. We shake our heads and explain we just left Rome. We ask why we couldn't have handled this process on the other side of the Atlantic. As is the case with bureaucrats the world over we receive a response that's hardly an explanation. "That is not permitted. See you in ten days."

As we walk out the door, relieved to have the first leg of our mission complete, our burly official abruptly summons us back to his teller window. I cringe, Roger groans. "By the way, we're moving the office to Coral Gables next week." I'm grateful to have been advised now rather than enduring the alternative while Roger continues to fume at having to deal with this at all. We collect Mamma Ruta and sprint to the nearest seafood restaurant and plan our subsequent trip to Florida.

Fast forward ten days plus one; we allowed an extra day as cushion. We locate the Consulate's lovely new office building, grab our deli ticket and wait. A customer at the window is nearing panic. Her visa hasn't arrived and her flight is scheduled this afternoon. She's frantically making calls on her cell while a female official is trying to explain that her passport has yet to be returned from Rome so she's not going anywhere. I try not to listen, try not to make contingency plans, try not to get three steps ahead in what-if scenarios. Our mere presence in this place causes Roger to settle into slow burn. Our now familiar burly official calls our number. We smartly approach.

He remembers us and steps behind a screen that does nothing to shield him from our curious eyes. He sifts through various dark blue canvas bags heavy with documents and specialty locks and retrieves our passports. Approaching the window, he cross-checks our names and photos against our faces and with a cheery *buon viaggio*, turns over the passports and sends us on our way.

That's it? After six months of phone calls, visits, paperwork, information gathering, flights into and out of the country, we're finished? Such speed and efficiency impresses us. Waiting for the elevator, we laugh in relief and take back all the negative things we said or thought about bloated bureaucrats. With a sense of accomplishment, we open our passports to study these freshly minted visas. In unison, we slap them shut and blurt out a chorus of "Oh, shit!"

We retract our retractions. Roger's visa has been inserted into my passport and mine is firmly ensconced in his. So much for efficiency. We return to our burly official, this time ignoring the deli ticket and slide our passports into the silver tray of his glass window. We point out the switch. He barely raises an eyebrow and asks when we're traveling back to Italy. Lying through our teeth, we say that afternoon. He asks us to wait. This twist leaves me incapable of avoiding a mental plan B. Roger simmers. This is not something we can discuss.

Our official calls us back, proudly hands us our passports and again wishes us a good trip. The switch has been corrected immediately. I'm reminded of the scene in *The Wizard of Oz* when Toto moves the curtain to reveal the true wizard who's spinning wheels and pulling levers to create the fearsome Oz. All this talk of ten days to process documents, review their suitability, determine whether we've met certain acceptable criteria, travel in diplomatic pouch to Rome – all this is boiled down to a presto-changeo act that has taken a few moments and a little glue to make right. *Pazienza.*

The Questura

The visa experience is streamlined efficiency compared to events at the *questura,* police headquarters, in Perugia. Within eight days of our re-entry into Italy, visas proudly in hand, we are required to appear at the *questura* to request our *permesso di soggiorno*. It is a frightening thought that now, after buying property, obtaining visas and already living at *Le Vigne* we can be denied permission to stay. Everyone agrees this is an exercise, a seemingly ridiculous one, yet absolutely required. Whether an ex-pat or an immigrant seeking asylum, the *permesso* must be carried at all times. We are not citizens and our presence in Italy is at the pleasure of the Italian government.

As with all things unfamiliar, we turn to Antonio for advice. He has made inquiries of a friend at the *questura* who says we must appear on a Monday morning between eight and eight thirty to obtain a number dispensed from long rolls like raffle tickets. We're to bring our visa-equipped passports, the *atto* and four passport-size photos each. Antonio accompanies us and we arrive at 8:01 and are denied access inside a gated area by an armed guard with a bleached tuft of a goatee and dark, reflective glasses. We say nothing but turn to Antonio. Mr. Goatee tells us we're late which is hard to understand since we arrived one minute after the allowable time. He tells Antonio that people have been waiting in line since five-thirty to obtain a number. Beginning at eight, one hundred numbers are distributed. By one minute after, the numbers are history. He's sorry but we need to come back another day and we should come early.

It is brutally cold and windy and we are already here. Antonio is annoyed and calls his friend who's not at home, not at work and not available. Antonio leaves messages and suggests we wait. Inside the gate more than a hundred people are milling about in the cold courtyard with no seating, waiting for their raffle number to be called.

Crying babies, frazzled mothers, creased grandmothers, men smoking; some folks dressed in the garb of their home country, hands filled with papers, some borrowing pens, a mix of races and languages suffuse the courtyard. Mr. Goatee doesn't want us hovering near his domain and tells us to wait in the courtyard where emotions vacillate between boredom and desperation. I can't help but think of the hundreds of thousands of immigrants who suffered the indignities of Ellis Island. We wait and attempt small talk. Antonio's phone rings after forty minutes.

He's received special instructions to enter the building and proceed to the window for European Union and Italian citizens only. Inside, the crush of wall-to-wall bodies has raised the temperature to an uncomfortably humid level. We're jostled and pinched together, Roger's briefcase always in our sights. Others stand in front of the EU window and we get into a line of sorts. This process is not for the timid or polite but for the aggressive and assertive. Roger's height and heft provide decent coverage and protection. Eventually we arrive at the front and a woman behind the glass ignores Antonio's efforts to catch her attention. Some internal mechanism triggers and she finally deigns to focus on him.

Antonio explains the situation and she hands us each two identical forms. We are to complete them in duplicate; carbon paper or copy machines unavailable, at least for the huddled masses. We struggle with the Italian forms not so much because of the language but the lack of clarity. Arrival in Italy? Our most recent arrival or when we bought *Le Vigne*? We pick most recent and hope that's what they want. Date of issuance of visa? We insert the month/date then realize we should have used the European style of date/month and roughly mark through what we've written. By the time we finish, the forms look like they were completed by messy six year olds.

We fight our way back to our officer and wait. Again, some mechanism triggers and she collects our paperwork and photos, reviews the *atto* and visas and stamps one of the duplicate forms for each of us that provisionally gives us permission to stay. We're advised to return no later than two months from this date, on a Tuesday or Thursday to obtain our *permessi.* Now we're free to be fingerprinted, something we can do today or at a later date. Fingerprinted? Who said anything about being fingerprinted? Return at a later date? Better a root canal. We need to end this today.

We push our way into another line in front of a closed door. A handwritten note indicates we must have our provisional permission, passport and a passport-size photo. Great consternation ensues. We have the first two items but we've just surrendered our four photos each. Are we supposed to provide another photo or do we retrieve one of the four from our last friendly official? Antonio doesn't know, we certainly don't know, there's no one available to ask. My vote is to err on the side of caution, no big surprise. Roger's been patient up to this point but he's getting cranky and spoiling for a fight. So far, this makes going to the bank look like a day at Canyon Ranch.

Outside in the courtyard there's a photo booth, the kind that dispenses four grainy photos on a little strip. Instead of making goofy faces, surrounded by as many friends as can fit in the cramped space, we scrounge for exact change and get four more passport-size photos. Antonio's held our place in line while we generate pictures that reflect our mood, making driver's licenses look like glamour shots. It's taken us fifteen minutes to deal with the photos and while we worried that we'd lose our spot and the opportunity to be fingerprinted, Antonio's not advanced an inch.

Eventually we're permitted entry to a tiny room and the door closes behind us. There are two uniformed, gun-toting officials who ask to see our documents. How dangerous can fingerprinting be? We present our documents and new photos, thankful that we went through that exercise and are asked to stand against a wall marked in centimeters to measure our height. Roger approaches the wall and the two guns jovially wonder whether there are enough centimeters to cover Roger's height. We need the levity.

I'm up first for fingerprints and an added bonus - palmprints. The official pays little attention to the proximity of the ink and the cuffs of my jacket which I've not removed because I never thought I'd be palmprinted. Black ink is precariously close to the jacket when I'm finally excused to the bathroom to clean up. Imagine the level of cleanliness in this tiny, overtaxed facility ill-equipped to handle hundreds of people each day. I quickly scan the room. There's not a scrap of paper in sight. There might be a crumpled tissue or two in my jacket pocket but I'm not really in a position to prospect. I stand in the middle of this room, arms extended like a scrubbed surgeon except my hands are black and there's no toilet paper, tissue or paper towels. With my elbow, I depress the stainless steel button on the sink and on this bitter cold February day, there's no hot water. No matter. I run my hands under the freezing water and start rubbing. And rubbing. And rubbing. Nothing is happening; nothing good anyway. Black ink is smearing and beginning to bleed up my wrists. While rubbing and trying to come up with a solution, I spot a bucket on the floor that is filled with a sort of sandy goop. I'm compelled to dig in and the gritty petroleum is a saving balm, slowly causing the ink to vanish. I'm so relieved that I've forgotten the icy water and lack of paper.

Shaking my hands, I spray water drops around me like a dog after a bath. Roger really needs to know about this latest adventure before entering the bathroom with his blackened hands. He declines a used tissue. I hold his jacket and wait. He returns shaking his head and flicking water from his hands, mumbling, "This has got to be one of the most primitive things I've done since Air Force survival school."

As we collect our paperwork the official shouts past us, advising those attempting to push their way in that they'll only accept another three or four people. We grab our documents as pandemonium erupts. The dozen or so waiting rush the door, each with their own rationale for why they should be accepted today – elderly parents, sick children, baby sitters, employment commitments. We consider ourselves fortunate, lucky that we accomplished what we intended. Lucky that our paperwork was in order. Lucky that we finished the fingerprinting process. Especially lucky that Antonio was there to hold our hand. We may have been lucky but Roger says he's never going to do this again.

Progress on the Home Front

For the moment, the *questura* and all the indignities are behind us. The good news, the very good news, is that our workers did a fabulous job during our three week absence. The time invested in meetings and lists and translations paid off. Important infrastructure modifications took place: eliminating the cistern and water pump system, inserting a GPL line to eliminate tanks of gas for cooking, installing new drain lines in the *cantina*, rewiring the house and adding two plug types at every outlet to be rid of shoeboxes full of adapters, installing a new alarm system.

More visible and tangible renovations took place. Scaffolding had been erected in the *soggiorno* for the *muratori* to install the chestnut beams and fill the spaces between them with plaster. The masons chiseled deep square openings on one side of the room and slightly less deep square ones on the opposite side. The large beams were hefted to the ceiling, inserted into the deep hole and then eased back into the shallow hole on the opposite side. The scaffolding traveled the *soggiorno* as the masons worked first on inserting the six large beams, then the twelve smaller ones and finally adding the space filling plaster.

The master bath was almost finished; the tile was in, the electricity complete. The shower had been installed but a door must be ordered and the vanity created. The cherry flooring had been laid in the master suite though it hadn't been sanded or finished. Five inch diameter holes were drilled into the bedroom walls for air conditioners. While the diameter of the holes isn't impressive, the length is. A special piece of drilling equipment was brought in to bore through the two feet of stone, brick and plaster walls, each air conditioner requiring two openings. The kitchen/*soggiorno* pass-through was demolished to below ground level. Since we live in an earthquake zone Antonio is very particular about supporting beams and foundations. A trench was opened and rebar was covered with poured cement for a reinforced foundation. Antique brick was laid and is the perfect complement to the dark, irreplaceable floor tiles that cover the rest of our living space. Alfio, our carpenter, had slowly begun replacing all fifteen interior doors with rustic, custom-made Russian chestnut doors. Eight hundred decorative nail heads cover the dark, massive doors built in the old Italian farmhouse style.

One of the many headers that was raised violated the floor space of our personal guest bedroom. Roger had the masons create a bench in this opening perfect for a suitcase or a place to sit. Alfio reworked a lovely two inch thick slab of walnut to become the top of the bench and the masons covered the exposed sides with hand-painted Florentine tile.

The masons stayed busy. They repointed the brick archway that Roger uncovered on day one. To provide added definition, they dug out a small opening about hip high, a *nicchia* or niche designed as a resting spot for Roger's evening cocktail. They built another *nicchia* of brick and stone in a spot that will be perfect for holding a rack of *espresso* cups.

The rains that marred most of December ended during our stateside visit. Grasselli finally plowed our fields, a task possible only after a run of good, dry weather. He planted winter wheat and the tiny sprouts are already showing a hint of green through the clumps of dark brown soil.

Enzo began the intensive process of pruning our olive trees, another agricultural task requiring decent weather because the pruned limbs can't be exposed to damp, rainy conditions. The red clay tennis court was given its winter treatment of mounding additional clay over the tape lines and removal of the net. The bricks on the outside staircase leading to the apartment were repointed. Rusted and broken glass in the fourteen lamp posts around *Le Vigne* were replaced. A trench was dug around three sides of the tennis court – a foundation for *blocchetti*, concrete blocks, that will be used to build retaining walls to make future olive harvesting easier. Roger, truly a man of vision (but sometimes I slip and call him a man of visions), has extensive plans for these terraced retaining walls that will increase our level footprint and decrease the many *scarpate*. Finally, and this merits a drum roll, the *cancello*, entry gate doors that provide the initial striking impression of our home, were reconfigured to open inwards so as not to crash into waiting vehicles. That grumbling phase of our lives has been put to bed forever.

But we are grumbling over something else - a bad decision that's our fault. The *camino*, fireplace, in our *soggiorno* is not what we envisioned. Our *geometra,* Giovanni, had directed us to his associate Domenico who was also a happy sketcher. His drawings didn't match the reality of the fireplace that was being installed. The dimensions were off as was the style. His was tiny, another Barbie-like appliance. It was too modern looking, out of place in the rustic setting we were creating. The workmen he chose exhibited no artistry, no care in the selection, angle and placement of brick and stone. We were spoiled by the craftsmanship of our masons.

Roger and I struggled with this problem. We ran the gamut from it not being so bad and something we could live with to let's rip it out now, fire Domenico and bring in our own masons to do it right. We talked and talked, over lunch, during dinner. Occasionally I would catch Roger staring into the *soggiorno* at Domenico's partially completed work. We didn't sleep well. After several fitful nights we arrived at the same conclusion. The fireplace was the focal point of the *soggiorno* and we were going to spend a lot of time in this room. If we didn't correct the problem now it would forever be an eyesore and disappointment. Despite the cost and the loss of time, it had to go. We slept.

The new fireplace was another Roger vision. It would be open on two sides and raised well off the ground at countertop height with a large opening below for firewood storage. The height was important because he planned to grill in this fireplace and had no intention of bending or stooping. The mantle would be substantial; five inches thick, dark chestnut, like our interior doors and six feet off the ground. Roger designed a light to shine into the fireplace so he could easily check on his grilled meats. In the brickwork on one side of the fireplace he created a special opening with a narrow door to house the slim BBQ tool kit Clayton had given him.

Getting rid of the fireplace meant getting rid of Domenico and also saying goodbye to Giovanni. My morning walking friends and advisors suggested another building supply company just north of us in Piccione - family owned, well respected and approved by Antonio and the masons. Their advice: make sure they know we referred you so that you receive a good price. It was a good tip. Ristori treated us fairly, supplying us with all the inner workings of our redesigned fireplace and the tile for our kitchen.

Our kitchen. The old kitchen was already gone. The sink, fridge and various cabinets were recycled and built into the *cantina* which had been tiled and painted. Despite the removal of all the appliances and cabinetry, the footprint of the kitchen remained the same. Roger spent hours with graph paper and charts in an effort to squeeze more out of less. No matter how the kitchen was laid out, we gained nothing without added space. The only way to add space was to take down part of a wall.

Removal of the wall was another Roger brainstorm, one we had discussed over several days but finally rejected as too difficult. The wall in question is part of the stairwell leading to the *cantina*. Access to the *cantina* is achieved by traveling up and down a series of stairs. If we close the stairwell and break through the wall, we gain ready access to the *cantina* and an opening in which to put a larger refrigerator. With the fridge fitting precisely in this opening, we free valuable space to use for deep, long countertops, a cooktop, oven, sink and dishwasher. No overhead cabinets would be built, leaving open wallspace and a sense of roominess impossible to achieve otherwise. Shelving in the *cantina* would be used to house canned goods, baking goods, and other foodstuffs that tend to be squirreled away, long past expiration dates, in standard kitchen cabinets. And there would be an added bonus; Roger could convert the closed stairwell into closets, providing sorely needed storage space in a *casa colonica* that has no built-in closets.

These were indeed big visions. Late one Saturday as Antonio and the masons were wrapping up some sort of demolition, Roger gesticulated his idea. Antonio immediately embraced the concept. His enthusiasm became infectious and everyone started talking at once with Roger calling for simultaneous translation. We'd need a chestnut *architrave* or lentil because the wall required reinforced support, we needed more antique brick and stone for flooring, to build a step and to cover the exposed wall openings, we needed to increase our tile order to accommodate an expanded kitchen and we needed to place an order for more chestnut ceiling beams to create a uniform look flowing from the *soggiorno* into the kitchen.

Such unfettered support was all the prompting Roger needed. By Monday the wall was demolished and revised kitchen plans were underway. The search was on for antique bricks. During our driving excursions, Roger's radar honed in on piles of bricks stacked at crumbling old farmhouses. Since we remained joined at the hip for every outing, he wanted me to ask the owners if we could take their bricks. No one had yet relinquished any from their property but we hit pay dirt at an old building site. Hesitantly, I approached the workmen asking if we could sift through the five-foot pile of rubble. "*Certo*," sure. My mother would be mortified to know her only daughter was picking through piles of trash. Still, the yield was significant.

The wall opening is a fabulous idea that delayed our completion date and created a new round of controlled chaos. Sunday was our only day to breathe. There are no workers; it's strangely quiet. We catch up on computer work when our tenuous connection holds. Otherwise, we are clearing debris, running errands, consulting on paint colors, organizing deliveries of beams or sand or *blocchetti* or brick or cement or tile or rebar. *Le Vigne* was a beehive that included Antonio, Enzo, Mick, electricians, plumbers, carpenters, gate and alarm specialists and our favorite *muratori* whom Roger calls Morey and Torey, having taken his corrupted Italian to a new low.

The rubble we've created never ceases and the dust is thick. Mick, Roger and I clean and re-clean, wash, vacuum, dust, attempt to seal off the apartment from the downstairs and do it all over again and glare at anyone who tracks in dirt and mud which is every last one of us. It's no wonder Oklahomans looked fondly at the glint of a sharp knife during dust storms. Wendy tells me that at her house, even a year after completion, dust still filters from cracks and crevices. If keeping Roger away from renovation activity was his form of torture, living in this dust-filled environment is mine. *Pazienza.*

If we're not clearing yesterday's debris, we're running errands. These trips are made in the mornings because our workers arrive in the afternoon and our involvement is hands-on. We expect nothing less from a micro-manager. Besides, everything closes at mid-day, something we tend to forget until we arrive at a locked door. We drive around our neighboring cities, get lost and eventually locate various businesses for purchasing kitchen appliances and more furniture. Wendy and Frits direct us to a furniture import warehouse where a chain-smoking rough character named Anna rules. Anna claims Frits always beats her up on prices. Roger tells Anna he and Frits are brothers so he's looking for the same pricing. She believes this tale, moans about the bargains we drive and then decides that Roger and Frits are indeed brothers, right down to their identical big noses. We buy tables, sofas, armoires, chairs. Ferruccio, our talented furniture restorer, works his magic on damaged wood or missing hinges. Once returned from his workshop, we cover the goods with sheets in a vain effort to obstruct the dreaded **d** word.

During the morning errand runs, we've discovered that shops are freezing; sometimes colder inside than out. We approach a store and the lights aren't on. Are they open? Have we misjudged the lunch hours once again? Is this their *turno* or closing day? Actually, these are cost-saving measures. Electricity and heating fuel costs are high. Business owners conserve where possible. While selecting kitchen appliances, the owner greets us in a muffler and heavy coat, plumes of vapor escaping his mouth as he speaks. He walks through the store, turning on lights so we can actually see the appliances. When he writes the final order we form a tight cluster near his desk, seeking warmth from a small space heater at his feet. I sign the paperwork, never removing my gloves.

Homeowners are equally conscious of energy costs. On the spur of the moment I stopped to visit a new neighbor. She wasn't home but her husband was, sitting at the kitchen table, reading the sports section in the dark. He turned on the light only after inviting me inside. Huddled over the paper, he was dressed in layers; socks and slippers, a scarf and two sweaters. The room was cold and bordered on depressing. Fuel costs are indeed high and we too have learned a few of these parsimonious lessons. Every morning on waking we turn off the heat and don't turn it back on again until early evening. Yet ours must be the warmest house in the neighborhood as the Italians say *che caldo*, how hot, right after seeking *permesso* to enter.

Conservation and parsimony are ingrained in our Italian neighbors. No one has a clothes dryer; either choose laundry day wisely or expect several days of drying time. We're doing the same thing, putting the dryer to use only under extreme circumstances and then feeling guilty about it. Every glass jar, every tray from cookies bought at the bakery, every plastic grocery bag is saved and put to a secondary or tertiary use. We see our workers utilize scraps that we would normally discard. A former door jamb becomes a straight edge for our masons. Enzo and Antonio cut a pallet in half to fit in a corner of one of the utility sheds. The other half is saved. The pallet itself was never disposed of having come from the *blocchetti*. This frugality gives us pause, causing us to consider the too-often disposable lifestyle from whence we came.

Parsimony aside, we are spending money. As we near completion on certain projects, others spring up unexpectedly. We awoke one recent chilly morning without heat. We're savvy to this problem – it often means we've run out of fuel. But this time was different as we had just received a thousand expensive liters of propane (GPL) following our switch from diesel. We were certain that not even as Americans could we burn through fuel so quickly. Antonio answered our panic call and confirmed that while we did have fuel we had problems with the furnace that required replacement parts. He appeared that afternoon with the parts and a technician, spent hours in the furnace room and made two trips to the *zona industriale* of Perugia. Antonio sadly informs us it's time to purchase a new furnace and water heater as this old equipment is not likely to survive another season; it's been patched for too many years. If anyone could squeeze more life out of this rusty clunker, Antonio could. If he says it's given up the ghost, we believe him. Ka-ching.

Another substantial investment we make is in Roger's new *giocattolo,* toy. A different Ferruccio, the fastest talking Italian I've met and the head mechanic at Bavicchi, the premier lawn and garden center in Umbria, called to say the Gator had arrived. I begged him to slow down, *piano, piano*. He had to tell the story three times before I understood. When Roger heard the news, he grabbed a stack of Euro monopoly money, jumped into the Trooper and drove to Bavicchi to pay for it. This he did without waiting for me, asking me to join him, taking his wallet or his license. We were separated for one hour; the most time we had spent apart since moving to this country. I guess language is no barrier when it comes to toys. Another ka-ching.

I can't possibly begrudge him this vehicle. The Gator has already proved invaluable. We've lined the bed with a rubber mat and transported loads of rubble from the house to the tennis court area where we're building the first retaining wall. The walls require backfill and since we don't have enough dirt for this purpose, Roger uses the rubble instead. The Gator replaces the wheelbarrow which makes all of us happy, especially Mick, since Roger plans on teaching him how to drive. In America everyone his age has been driving for years. The prospect makes him anxious and excited at the same time.

The bright green Gator with yellow accents is equipped with an hour-meter on the dash that tracks usage. It's there to let the user know when to conduct various maintenance events such as changing the engine oil after the first twenty hours or lubricating front king pins every fifty hours. Roger's found a secondary role for the counter – he likes to calculate vehicle cost per hour, reveling in the rapid reduction, fortifying a high price/value ratio. Frankly, there's no need for so much rationalization – he likes it, it's functional, it's a time and therefore money saver, plus it's cute as a beaver.

Ka-ching means more trips to the bank and that means more stomach churning, teeth clenching experiences. The staff is friendlier as we're there once a week but the monetary exercises remain difficult. A strong Euro and a weak dollar combine for a double whammy when calculating losses for every transaction whether it be deposit, withdrawal or cash conversion. We received our first bank statement that covered three months of activity and despite hours with a dictionary and a calculator I was unable to make progress in deciphering the six-page document. Roger found it hard to believe but this wasn't my standard math learning disability at work. We took the statement to Jon Lovitz, our bank director, who struggled to explain every line item and the various fees. In the end, he couldn't do it and begged us for *pazienza.* He'd try to reduce or eliminate some of the fees. Meanwhile, the account in Montalcino remained open and the funds had yet to be transferred to Ponte Felcino thus generating duplicate costs. When we asked about the status of the transfer, Jon provided us with a very technical fiduciary explanation; "They're late."

Often we would tap the tellers of their limited resources. When faced with our withdrawal requests, they call out to each other, "Sara, Marco, do you have any five hundred, two hundred or one hundred Euro notes?" *"Sì, no, sì,"* before bills would fly across glass partitions from all directions. Was this not a bank? Didn't people come here every day and expect to get money?

After struggling to collect enough cash, Sara has to count the bills before documenting the transaction in triplicate, stamping the forms and shoving them into trays already sagging with reams of paper. To assist in the cash count process is a clever bill counting machine. Bills are neatly stacked and a lever is pressed. Invariably, the machine jams and Sara starts over, re-stacking the bills, re-pressing the lever. Sometimes it counts the bills without a hitch but more often it jams again and Sara repeats the process a third or fourth time. Since Sara can't trust the machine she hand counts the bills in that fancy Italian teller way with thumb and forefinger flying. If that count happens to match the total from one of the many previous attempts with the counting machine, then we're able to obtain our cash. Sara goes to great pains to provide us with a *busta,* envelope, for the money. A wad of cash this size can hardly be discreetly concealed in a flimsy envelope but I graciously thank her and shove it in my purse.

The Sunday Times

*I*n between all the manual labor activities, we've put a toe in the marketing waters. Lest we forget, our real goal is not renovation but operation of a self-catering vacation rental. We now have a website created by Abigail who was referred to us by the former owners. Abigail and husband Ralph live in Tuscany and operate a vacation rental. Friendly, helpful and knowledgeable, they've been willing to share much needed advice. In addition to developing the website, we've listed *Le Vigne* with several vacation rental agencies and placed the following ad in *The New York Times, London Times* and other publications:

Italy – Umbria, near Assisi 4/3 villa with pool,
tennis, bocce, maid, air conditioning, full kitchen,
weekly rental. American owners – speak English,
Italian, Spanish, www.levigne.net

Seeing these words in print is a bold reminder that guests will arrive (hopefully) and we'd be wise to impose a deadline on renovation. Roger has selected April first, April Fool's Day. This doesn't bode well. Designated family worrier, I not only worry about meeting the deadline, I'm concerned about whether our ads will deliver results.

If we build it, will they come? We're holding our collective breath.

Spring

So much for that deadline. April first came and went and we remained in the weeds. But what beautiful weeds they were. The weather is changeable as spring is everywhere. Some days cold, windy, sunny, clear. Others bring rain or sleet. A dusting of snow stopped Mick in his tracks. Eyes wide, hands outstretched, he turned to Roger with the announcement, "It's my first time, sir." The *neve*, snow, is always brought by the *tramontana* and it flies by *Le Vigne* horizontally leaving little vertical cascade. Morning walks are spectacular. Some days I can't leave the house without my L.L. Bean long underwear, out of service since the Lillehammer Olympics in 1994. By noon, it's a lightweight cotton tee and jeans. Evenings are chilly enough for fires but there's no mistaking the lengthening and warming of these fresh days which bring more sun than rain.

Nature at *Le Vigne* is enchanting. The sky is intensely blue and the air so clear that I can count the windows in houses in Perugia. The night sky reveals stars pulsing vibrantly, free of haze and city lights. Apples, apricots, peaches and plums are puff balls of pink and white flower sprays. Hazelnut trees unfurl tightly coiled leaves the color of the old Crayola Crayon called Sea Green. The hillside carpets of winter wheat darken to emerald and as the tender shoots spread and stretch, the soil is no longer visible. The five tall *tigli* lining a portion of the *piazza* and five English walnuts are covered with swollen leaf buds. The two Japanese magnolias near the pool are coming into purple flower and pale green buds hint of the leaves to follow. Daffodils, tulips, forsythia, quince, crocus, paperwhites, primrose, mimosa and other, as yet unidentified plants complete the palette that defines a burgeoning spring. Outside the immediate garden area, we learn that the thorny trees with white blossoms bordering our woods are *spino bianco,* literally white thorn but really wild prune. Their heady perfume is powerful and far-reaching.

But the real horticultural stars of spring are our new olives. Antonio directed us to a grower from Pistoia in Tuscany who supplied us with six hundred four-year-old *piante*, plants. Italians refer to olives as *piante* not *alberi*, trees, because plants must be pruned annually and such is the case with olives. Plants or trees, we are smitten. These silvery green matte-finish evergreens catch light all winter long.

We're told that Tuscany provides the best olive plants while Umbria provides the best olive oil. A forty-kilometer stretch of land known as the

Silver Coast is this country's heartland for exceptional olive oil. *Le Vigne* sits in the center of this sea-less coast where the soil, weather, sunlight, rainfall, altitude and general *terroir* combine in the right proportions to produce liquid gold. We've selected a mix of five varieties: *pendolino, leccino, moraiolo, frantoio, picholine* for pressing into oil. A sixth, *ascolano*, is walnut-size and primarily grown as a table olive because it contains little oil.

Late one afternoon the grower arrived, his truck ingeniously and tightly packed with the five foot tall olives. They look like little colts, spindly and young. Each tree arrived in a small black pot, staked with a slim bamboo pole tied top and bottom with green plastic cord. Placed at an angle and tied with rope, the six hundred trees occupied only a third of the truck bed. It didn't look like much. While four of us unloaded the trees in less than an hour, it took five of us over a month to plant them. Looks can be deceiving.

Farmer Grasselli plowed the five acre field we selected for the grove using two different pieces of heavy machinery. The field is **L** shaped and visible from most rooms of the house. There are no steep inclines but many undulations and dips so there are times that the far part of the field disappears. Grasselli's first aeration broke the earth into large boulder- like chunks, dark and clay-shiny. The second plowing produced smaller clods that appeared smooth from a distance. Up close the field was anything but smooth. The soil was rocky, a perfect medium for olives. Walking in the field was like wading through the ocean in lead boots. After a month, we knew every inch.

Our biggest initial challenge was laying out the dimensions for planting. We were advised that each tree should be five meters (about sixteen feet) apart in line and row. Thus the long arm of the isosceles triangle formed by the right angle of three trees should be slightly more than seven meters in length. The author of the preceding sentence believed there was no practical use for high school geometry. It may have taken thirty years, but she was eventually proved wrong.

We began with the short leg of the **L** and spent days placing and replacing the initial stakes. One of us held one end of a twenty meter tape measure while another sprinted the twenty meters to mark an end point and the three, five meter intervals in between. You can guess who did most of the sprinting and who did most of the holding. The process was a real lesson in quality control tweaking and adjusting that resulted in error after compounded error.

The first and second rows were fine; stakes were placed five meters apart and as a cross-check the distance between the stakes forming the long arm of the triangle was indeed seven meters. But the farther we progressed the distances began to vary slightly. By the time we staked the third row, the minor fudging we allowed in rows one and two had became major. We weren't smart enough to have simply staked the ground marking the spot for planting. Instead, we actually planted trees and by the third row, we were pulling trees out and replanting to correct our errors.

I remember family summer vacations and road trips through central Florida. Dad and Mom in the front seat of the station wagon, my brother and I sweltering in the back – air conditioning was not allowed; mile after boring mile of citrus groves with perfectly parallel rows and evenly spaced trees. It never occurred to me what effort would be required to accomplish this task. This was important. All eyes of Colombella were upon the Americans and we would be the unflattering talk of the town if we didn't get this right.

We finally realized that each of us involved in staking and planting marked the start, end and intervals slightly differently. One of us might start at the zero on the tape measure, another just this side. One might plant a bamboo stake at the five meter point but another might mark it on one side or the other. Over time and distance such seemingly petty differences were revealed in big ways. Eventually, we became consistent with measuring and staking and finished unscathed and free of ridicule.

By the time we began the largest section of the field we worked as a well-oiled team. Don came over to play almost every day, joining Enzo, Mick, Roger and me. The cute-as-a-beaver Gator proved its worth and was an integral part of the team, carrying thirty recently watered trees at a time. On a good day, we can get thirty trees planted by *pranzo*. Once the ground has been measured, two-meter bamboo poles are driven into the earth. A tree is placed next to each pole and the two green cords are untied from the trunk and left on the ground to re-attach the planted tree to the sturdier bamboo.

Olives maintain superficial roots and shouldn't be planted too deeply. The hole required for planting is shallow - about eighteen inches deep and two feet in diameter. The tree is placed in the hole, the dirt shoveled back around the plant, square knots are used to re-attach the two plastic cords, the pot is collected as is the slender bamboo cane along with rocks, roots, shards of pottery and bits of glass and then we do it again. We do it again six hundred times.

There's a lot of time for reflection in a five acre field with six hundred trees. I think about my dad often, he's on my shoulder while I'm working. He was truly a city mouse and would not have had the slightest idea what to do here but would have gladly joined our team in this thoroughly country mouse experience. Oddly, I also think of the *Green Acres* theme song, "You are my wife. Good bye, city life." I'm struck by how much our lives have changed. Dad raised a city mouse but I've adapted well to this outdoor, rural existence. Roger tests my limits though. Lately, he's been talking about converting a plot of land into a chicken coop. Fortunately there are so many other projects underway that it's easy to divert his attention from chickens, ducks, geese, turkeys. I believe there's an important reason they're known as fowl.

Unplanned projects continue to intervene and impede our progress. During the olive planting project, Roger discovered standing water in one corner of the grove. Further inspection revealed the source to be the drain field serving the never pumped septic tank. I'll skip the gory details but we installed a new system, tank, fifty meters of tubing and a deep drain field filled with gravel. We contacted a septic service and scheduled annual cleanings after promising to create new access to the tank, currently obstructed by hedges, narrow pathways and soggy terrain. Hours were spent discussing the various possibilities for reaching the tank, none of which were satisfactory to the driver. What a translation and logistical nightmare dealing with unappealing subject matter. Surprisingly, there was a silver lining.

To create the new drain field and hole for the tank, Antonio arranged for Agostino, a backhoe operator, to dig all the holes and trenches. A long ugly pine hedge, rusty fencing, posts and concrete foundation pads blocked the way and Agostino removed the offensive treeline in a few hours. His skill with this equipment was remarkable. Don was certain Agostino could pour a cup of *espresso* with the bucket of the backhoe and not spill a drop. Removal of the hedge delivers our payoff - an unobstructed view of the grove and an additional ten meters for planting olives.

Meanwhile interior work continued, begging for our attention, but it was hard to remain indoors during these brilliant spring days. To say Roger is a strong advocate of pruning is putting it mildly. He never leaves the house without his Felco pruners holstered on his right hip, the leather worn shiny from years of use. We spent days pruning apple, peach, apricot, plum and fig branches. We collected the fruit branches in the back of the Gator along with the olive branches Enzo had pruned earlier. While the

Italians burn their olive cuttings, Roger decided to mulch them for composting. We worked together feeding the *biotrituratore*, mulcher, finding it a time-consuming task since the machine was flimsy and toy-like, not akin to the heavy duty mulcher we once owned in Atlanta. We took turns feeding the 'bio' thing and scooping up buckets of scraps and dumping them into a compost pile near the two utility sheds.

Within days of mulching, Roger sprouted red welts on his arms that quickly spread to his neck, trunk and one nasty spot in and around his eye. I was next, developing the same rash on my scalp and lower back. The itching was constant and we tried to restrain ourselves from scratching. We went to sleep covered in cortisone cream, drowsy from Benadryl. We had no other symptoms but the welts and itching lasted for days. There were far too many projects and a new deadline to have to deal with a health matter. We tried to ignore the problem.

Eventually we discovered the source of our discomfort. At a dinner party celebrating Wendy's birthday several guests were discussing the Italian health care system. One described a trip to the *pronto soccorso*, emergency room, after a full day of pruning fig trees. The staff was unimpressed with the mean-looking blisters covering his arms, face and neck. "Happens every spring," they told him. Allergy to the sap (but not the fruit) is quite common. A mere brushing against the end of a cut limb produces impressive welts, itching and redness that takes two weeks to disappear. There was little else they could do but treat him with cortisone cream and Benadryl and the advice to avoid the sap next spring. Roger and I made eye contact across the table and smiled wryly. Our medical mystery has been solved.

Despite the lure of the lovely outdoors, we did turn our attention inside. We'd set a new, hard, we-really-mean-it deadline of April 30th. A thirteen day tour including a week-long barge trip through the Netherlands with our friends calls for us to be in Brussels on the third of May. The tour would begin on the fourth. After the trip our friends planned to return with us to *Le Vigne* for a week's stay. This meant all work must be completed, bedrooms ready, living space habitable, painting done and most improbable to envision, everything clean, in order to host our first real guests. Roger awoke every morning discharging his focusing battle cry. Pressure is an effective, albeit uncomfortable motivator.

We delighted in the progress being made. We made the right decision by removing the ugly *camino* and rebuilding to our specs. The cherry flooring in the master suite had been sanded and varnished. This took longer than anticipated as it had to be done twice. The first attempt was done with the windows open on a windy day resulting in a gritty, rough surface. We weren't pleased with the results nor were the workmen thrilled with the idea of re-work. The vanity in the master bath had been installed, all kitchen appliances had arrived, dozens of light fixtures were put in place, we'd selected and received the kitchen tile, tiled behind and repainted radiators, applied plaster skim coats to wall surfaces in anticipation of painting, built the *ingresso* closets that Roger designed, installed custom-made screens on all windows, graded new roads on the property to eliminate *scarpate*, removed non-functioning pipes, rabbit hutches, lean-to's, partially broken troughs, wagons and pots and planted flowers, herbs and vegetables. We installed a safety opening to allow for the escape of gas from the *cantina*. The preceding sentence looks innocuous enough but it took days to accomplish and kept Antonio in a ditch for the entire time.

The retaining walls around the tennis courts had been completed using more than three thousand *blocchetti* each weighing thirty-five pounds and requiring untold Gator-loads of sand, fill, rocks, bottles and dirt. A second retaining wall was created to form additional flower and vegetable gardens. It wasn't until we started the second wall that we realized the entire first wall was constructed with the blocks placed upside down. Over time it won't matter as ivy will grow to cascade over the blocks. And finally, as a true mark of seeing light at the end of the renovation tunnel, we contacted several cleaning agencies to provide *preventivi* or estimates for the not inconsequential task of deep cleaning our interior space.

Oh Sheet

Another clue to our progress was the need to shop for finishing accessories such as bed linens and towels. We also needed two beds; one for the master and the other for our personal guest bedroom. The apartment was already outfitted with three kings and a twin. The kings were not single mattresses but rather twin mattresses side-by-side, the frames hooked together. The headboards and footboards are decorative wrought iron painted with attractive floral designs. Each king can be split into twins so the quantity of bed linens required was growing at exponential rates creating inventory and storage challenges. Conservatively we needed ten sets of king size sheets, fourteen sets of twin sheets, twelve mattress pads, twelve pillows, twenty-four pillow protectors, twelve blankets, six bedspreads and eleven decorative pillow shams. I thought about Jean Marsh playing the role of housemaid Rose Buck in the TV series *Upstairs, Downstairs.* Key ring clanking, prim uniform in place, she managed the groaning linen closets familiar only to the domestic servants.

In the States, this shopping assignment would have taken a few hours at Target. Not here. My stateside notions about where to go, what to buy and ready availability of goods had no relevance – there is no Target. Every suburban strip mall in America includes a mattress store; not so in Italy. Even the terminology is different. There's no distinction between king, queen or full sizes. There's simply *matrimoniale* which is roughly a king and *singolo* which is a twin. To further complicate matters, the three kings we inherited were not identical so I had no sense of standard.

Understanding towel sizes and uses brought its own challenges. I wanted to buy bath towels, hand towels and washcloths. The Italian bath towel is an enormous, unwieldy bath sheet, bigger than a pool towel. An alternative is a bathrobe with hood. I couldn't picture anyone over the age of two using this drying technique. A third option is a towel smaller than the bath sheet that is perfect for me but too small for Roger or any other American male. It's known as a *viso* which means face. By American standards, it's huge for a face towel but too small for a bath towel. Next is something called *ospite* which means guest and approximates the size of a hand towel. Finding washcloths is impossible. While Americans use washcloths inside the shower or for face washing, that's not the case in Italy. Soap alone is used in the shower and both washcloth and soap are considered too harsh for facial use. Then there are bidet towels...

Escaping construction and olive planting for one entire day, Mary and I went shopping. I left Roger with translated lists and *un sacco di gente,* including masons, plumbers, electricians, Antonio, carpenters, backhoe operators and gasline workers. Mary and I hadn't pulled out of the *piazza* before Roger called seeking language assistance. This could be a very long day.

In the weeks preceding the shopping excursion, I had collected recommendations from various sources: a home show we attended, my morning walk advisors, magazine ads. I created a matrix listing the bedrooms and bathrooms and linen needs for each. I included the dimensions of the mattresses and the general color scheme. I had pictures from books and magazines. Filled with great resolve we headed to Foligno. The second I entered the first shop I was struck with input overload and all but swooned. Mary kept me on task. She was in the enviable position of spending someone else's money and with her love of shopping and her trained artist's eye, this was pure fun.

The staff was helpful and patient. Custom-made bed covers and pillow shams could be made to my specifications within the time frame required. Rich colors, heavy fabrics, complementary designs combined to produce unique accessories that couldn't be duplicated at any of the big box stores. Eventually we found a source for towels, sheets, bath mats and bedside rugs despite the size variations.

Once fabrics were selected we could proceed to paint selection. Our advisors directed us to Max Color and Enrico who introduces us to the wacky world of painting in Italy. We quickly locate accent colors for the apartment bedrooms; colors graphic artist Clayton suggested would make the rooms pop. Things got a little messy though when we turned to our bedroom. Roger's bias surfaces quickly. He once owned a paint store in Miami and is now used to Home Depot and the risk-free assurance that a paint chip in Atlanta can be duplicated with one hundred percent accuracy in Pittsburgh. Not so in Italy. Pre-mixed paints or true paint color formulas don't seem to exist. Paint is created by blending some powders, adding a touch of black, throwing in some water and stirring.

Enrico knows Enzo, who along with a friend, is going to handle the painting. Accommodating Enrico urges us to take home a bucket of this mixture and have Enzo test it on a wall, let it dry and then decide. Enzo enters our bedroom, armed with a brush we shipped from the States and opens the paint bucket. Roger and I scramble to find cardboard to cover the cherry floors, while Enzo slaps watery paint on a large section of bedroom wall. It's horrid and we reject it immediately. Enzo urges *pazienza*, "Wait until the paint dries." We do but it's no better.

We make another trip to Max Color, armed with dictionary, paint brush samples, color chips and Italian painting vocabulary. We wanted to achieve an oatmeal color with a slight green cast. This was the neutral color of the skim coat of plaster the masons had applied. Sounds awful but it wasn't. Another round of mixtures and Enzo testing. Once again we're disappointed. Enzo is unfazed; this is the norm. More trips to Max Color. I explain Roger's paint store history to Enrico. With a slap on the back and a declaration that the two are now *colleghi*, Enrico invites Roger into the lab where we discover testing boards. We convince Enrico to test various color combinations on the boards in the lab rather than on the walls of our bedroom. A selection is made just to keep moving forward. We buy bolts of clear plastic, dozens of rolls of masking tape, cover the cherry floors and hope for the best.

We are so far behind that Roger pitches in to paint. This is a big deal. He has no fear of physical labor and is happy to work with his artisans but painting is different. Roger's stock phrase, "I'd rather paint a house," is his equivalent of preferring a sharp stick in the eye for any unpleasant task. But here he was, painting a house, with paint that behaved unlike any he had ever used. These were not fun days. *Pazienza*, my ass.

Taking a Break

But we do have fun days and fun nights. Our most relaxing dinners are movie nights at our house with Mary and Don. We collaborate on meals, sit in front of the TV, fire roaring and catch up on movies in English. While paint selection and banking are primitive, movie rental technology in Italy is advanced. We discovered a store front in Ponte Felcino with DVD movie rentals. Not unlike Blockbusters, we provided a deposit and were issued a rental card. Here the similarity ends. Outside the store is a booth with touch-screen displays. Think ATM for DVD. Insert the rental card and sort by category; new releases, actor, director, comedy, drama, action, most popular rentals. Select a film and read a brief description, run time and availability in English. All this and the benefit of avoiding lines and marginally helpful clerks. Mick is the youngest person we know so he showed us how to operate our DVD player and remains on call for technical assistance.

Our favorite restaurant for special events is Lo Spedalicchio. We had put it to the test for New Year's Eve, Valentine's Day and most recently, *Festa delle Donne* or Ladies' Day. Giancarla consistently creates varied menus and innovative, flavorful cuisine using seasonal ingredients. Ladies' Day is an annual holiday originally established to recognize women's right to vote and the ability to work outside the home. Over the years it's evolved into more of a girls' night out. Restaurants cater to large parties of women some promising more entertainment than others. I found a flyer advertising a fixed price dinner and the "Full Monty Sexy Strip" for twenty-five Euro. We resisted this tantalizing offer and the usual Colombella crowd opted for a more refined dining experience with our husbands. After the meal the women received a spray of delicate yellow mimosa, the traditional flower for *Festa delle Donne* and the men received the bill.

A great intro to local color was the birth of Catiuscia and Federico's baby girl. The family hosted an informal party inviting neighbors, friends, co-workers and family. Catiuscia was tired after a long and difficult labor. We visited briefly, left our gift and excused ourselves from the grandmother line-up surrounding sleepy mother and child. Outside, the new *babbo* tended the BBQ grilling sausages, beefsteak and kebabs. This was an interesting grill, unlike any we had seen but common in Italy. The grill platform was long and narrow with hot coals spread below the grate. A long piece of wrought iron, shaped like a hockey stick, was used to drag the coals from the back of the grill base forward. The back portion of the grill housed a vertical hopper filled with wood which eventually fell below to ignite and make coals to be dragged forward by the hockey stick. The hot fire felt good on this frigid windy night. Despite the temperature most guests remained outdoors, warmed not only by the fire but generous servings of homemade wine. The savory smells kept the crowd near the grill. Federico noted our hesitancy and called out "C*oraggio*," be brave. We stepped forward with *panini* in hand to receive delicious hot sausages.

Federico asked his father-in-law to look after us while he tended the fire. He took this assignment seriously. He called out Roger's name and obediently, we followed. Italians love to say Roger, they trill the initial **R** forever. My name is impossible. I'm everything from Joe to Joe-ah to John to Giovanna to Ju to Ja. Forget trying to spell it. I'm pleased if I see Jone. Sometimes I'm Signora Roger. Sometimes I'm invisible. I might call a store and say I'm Joan Arndt and I'm greeted with silence even though I'm greeted with kisses in person. Finally I relent and say I'm *la moglie di Roger*, Roger's wife. Ahhhh, goes the bell of instant recognition. I'm doing all the talking. I'm doing all the translating and yet it's this big holster-wearing larger than life RRRRRoger who is RRRRRecognized.

The Dinner Party

Preparation for a dinner party at *Le Vigne* can be a test. We've hosted several as repayment but also because we enjoy entertaining. Truthfully, entertaining in Italy has become less pressured for me but in the early days I was stressed. In Atlanta, I had a routine, my old standards, recipes that never failed, things I could do in my sleep. Here there was no routine and certain ingredients were difficult to obtain. That, coupled with having to live up to my own personal Martha Stewart neighbor, made it a challenge. Granted, this was self-imposed stress but sometimes external events conspired to heap on additional servings.

Here's a typical scenario: We had a dinner party scheduled for a Saturday with Mary, Don, Giuliana and Renato. The menu included crab, artichoke and green chili appetizer; roast rabbit stuffed with sausage and truffles surrounded by potatoes seasoned with fennel; zucchini and cheese casserole; sautéed cherry tomatoes; gorgonzola and walnut salad and apple tart for dessert. Note the absence of a pasta course. I hoped the Italians would survive. Shopping was almost complete.

Food preparation is underway when the masons ring the bell at seven a.m. They are followed shortly by Antonio and his cousin Giuliano, our electrician. I'm immediately called downstairs for translation with the masons. That accomplished, I race back upstairs only to be summoned again for help with electrical problems. Taking the stairs two at a time I try to get back on track. I collect the ingredients for the appetizer and preheat the oven only to hear the front gate bell. Ferrucio, the furniture restorer, his girlfriend Erika, also a restorer and his precious red-headed daughter arrive to return a refurbished desk. Roger wants Ferruccio to walk through the house and inspect tables, mirrors, paintings, benches, bookcases and other items to determine what restoration work is required and how long it will take. We wander through the house while I translate and mentally watch my prep time dwindle. Ferruccio loads certain pieces, we agree on cost and deadlines and I bolt back upstairs to the kitchen. By now the oven is well heated. I'm ready to mix the ingredients for the appetizer when the bell rings again. Wendy and Frits are here because their phone and therefore fax and computer have been out for days. Could they check email and contact the phone company about the status of repair? Surprisingly, we're able to say yes because our computer's actually working. Roger offers them coffee and sweets. I turn off the oven, set aside the appetizer ingredients and organize drinks while Roger listens to their tale of frustration.

Wendy has called Telecom repeatedly, speaking to someone different each time – perhaps someone in Sicily or in Calabria. The representative reviews the records and knows they've called many times. They insist they're working on the problem. They promise to send a *tecnico* within forty-eight hours, except if it's the weekend, which it is, then it's seventy-two hours. There's no opportunity to speak to a supervisor, there's no chance to talk to the last *tecnico* and there's no satisfaction. Frits suspects that a hunter shot through their phone line. The *tecnico* told him this happens with some regularity at the start of each bird hunting season.

They feel marooned without email. All vacation rental bookings happen online. They have a sick family member in the Netherlands and

Wendy's sister is expecting any day. Thankfully, they have the cell phone but emails are their real connection to the world. Would we mind if they stop by again later for another quick check? Certainly not, we're as likely to be in the same position as they are someday and we know firsthand the *bega,* hassle, of dealing with the phone company. Wendy and Frits gather their messages; thank us for the help, and leave.

I clean up the dishes and turn on the oven when the front gate bell rings again. Mary, Giuliana, Yoshi and the two *brutture,* ugly ones, are out for a walk and stop to visit. The two brutes are bounding through the gardens seeking the source of scents they can't ignore. Yoshi nonchalantly sits on the sidelines as if to say these two can't be mine. Giuliana and Mary half-heartedly try to control Sofie and Ysoto who have now discovered that the pool cover can be traversed and rambunctiously splash icy water everywhere. Roger is steaming at the sight of the brutes, their sharp nails threatening to pierce the cover. Politely, I offer coffee and sweets to the girls while Roger chases the brutes away from the pool, away from the gardens and toward the front gate. The girls decline the offer but invite me to join them on their walk. Sure. I've accomplished nothing related to tonight's dinner and simply say, *non posso*, I can't. Cornered at the gate, the brutes are squirming to escape. In her best Italian, Mary calls out to Giuliana, "*Andiamo*," let's go, and as the menagerie bolts we confirm tonight's dinner at our house at eight.

It is now lunch time and the masons, Antonio and Giuliano are preparing to leave. We discuss next week's plans, materials to be purchased, work to be done. Lists are made; greetings of *buona dominica* are exchanged. I'm translating but I'm not paying attention. Mostly I'm watching the clock. As soon as they're out the door Roger announces he's famished, what's for lunch? I nuke last night's leftovers and while we're genteelly shoveling pasta into our mouths, I tell him now's the time to go to Sidis for the last minute items. While Sidis maintains *orario continuato,* continuous hours, Italians tend to remain home at lunchtime so there's a nice lull at the grocery, even on Saturday. Roger offers to run the errand but has the cell phone with him in case consultation is required.

The afternoon blurs. I make good progress on the meal, set the table, clean as much as is possible to clean with such turmoil and jump when the bell rings at five. Wendy and Frits have returned for another email check bearing a bottle of wine as thanks. One thing leads to another and the bottle of wine disappears. So does half the crab appetizer. We urge them to stick around for dinner but no, they have dinner plans with her father. Roger tempts them by opening another bottle of wine and the flow of the juice matches the flow of ideas from Frits on how to spend our renovation money. Drawings on napkins, sketches directly on walls, expansive and expensive modifications emanate and the free association is contagious. Roger develops new concepts and the two of them loudly debate the merits of each. With less than an hour before dinner guests arrive, I decide it would be bad form to remain unbathed, dressed in the same sweater and jeans I was wearing when we herded Giuliana's dogs this morning. I excuse myself and while showering, hear Wendy and Frits leave and then the unmistakable dulcet tones of Roger snoring. Once dressed, I rally Roger who can shave, bathe and dress in seven minutes. I re-plate the crab, presenting it as new and answer the ringing front bell to greet our guests who have promptly arrived at eight. With a calm belying the storm that preceded it, I casually announce, "Dinner is served."

And so another busy day passes at *Le Vigne*. As a final nod to entertaining, here's a recipe for the best crab appetizer ever. It's not the least bit Italian but guaranteed to fly off the table:

Preheat oven to 350 F.
1 can lump crabmeat
1 can artichoke hearts, drained, quartered
1 can chopped green chilies, drained
8 oz. cream cheese, softened
Juice from 1 lemon
1 T. Worcestershire sauce
½ c. chopped green onions (reserved for garnish)

Blend all but chopped green onions. Spread into small ovenproof casserole dish.

Bake for 20-25 minutes. Garnish with green onions and serve.

Language Lessons

When is a gate not a gate? When in Italy and it's a *cancello.* When is a remote, either for the television or the *cancello,* not a remote but a *telecomando*? When is the new faucet we've ordered a *rubinetto*? Same reason. While Roger and I speak English to each other, certain Italian words pepper our conversations replacing their English equivalents without a second thought. We're straddling two worlds; sometimes we speak in meters and kilograms, sometimes feet and pounds.

Less English is spoken in Italy than in any other European country. It's taught in school along with French or German but not put into regular practice. English speakers can get by just fine in the big, tourist-filled cities of Rome, Venice or Milan but that's not the case in rural Italy. One theory about this insularity is that since Italy is a peninsula its people are not forced to learn the language of their neighbors. A similar theory could apply to the United States.

In Italy, Italians speak Italian. They might also speak a dialect and there are hundreds of those throughout the country but our focus is on Italian and the burden is on us. We have no expectations that Giuliana or Federico will be learning English.

Clayton flew over for a short visit and was impressed with his Dad's growing vocabulary. Before he could adapt to the foreign language coming from Roger's mouth he had to first adjust to Roger's new look. With our latest we-really-mean-it deadline looming and the desire not to waste a single minute, Roger's sworn off shaving until the work is complete. As a pilot, a beard was never allowed. As a retired pilot, he sure has one now. It's pure white and he calls himself *Babbo Natale*, Father Christmas. It's not my favorite look. He resembles Skitch Henderson or a white-bearded version of Abe Lincoln. If he develops a resemblance to one of those guys in ZZ Top with their chest length beards, we'll be in trouble, having blown every deadline imagined.

Clayton's not crazy about the beard either. Stepping off the plane in Perugia, exhausted after flying a good twelve hours, he visually ping-ponged between us. Eventually landing my way, he demanded, "Who's the Quaker you brought with you?" He throws out trimming suggestions which Roger rejects. Poor Clayton – he can't quite get a fix on this Italian-speaking bearded man who claims to be his *babbo.*

But *Babbo* he is, with a smattering of Italian. After his original gaffe with Giovanni's renovation estimates, Roger's got numbers down pat. He recites our phone number and understands quotes from suppliers without translation assistance. He talks *intonaco*, plaster, with the masons (who now number three) and *presa e interruttore*, receptacle and switches with the electrician. Antonio may be *capo* but Roger is *capo supremo*. Our third mason is another Enzo, we call him Enzo *due,* two. One day when Enzo *uno* and *due* were working, Sergio asked where they both were. Roger told him the *Enzi* were upstairs – he creatively made them plural, all on his own.

The workers have taught us hand gestures as well as Italian trade words. When Roger asks Antonio if we can build a new shed and the idea is rejected, it's not simply a shaking of the head from side to side. It's accompanied by the pointer finger drawn through the air in a big swirling repeating **S** pattern. This is not a subtle wagging but rather a grand wave beginning at eye level, eventually ending chest height, a continuous series of **Ss**. There's nothing equivocal about a no like that.

Around lunchtime and therefore quitting time we see another hand gesture. It's a variation of a football ref's clipping signal. The right hand is held palm down, at waist level and is tapped against the side of the torso several times indicating it's time to eat. I like this gesture; it comes in quite handy. Roger may be planting olives or monitoring a burn pile in a far distant field but this signal means it's quitting time and food's on the table.

The workmen are polite and mannerly and continue to impress us with their strong work ethic. Before leaving in the afternoon each worker finds us, no matter where we are, to shake hands and say goodbye. We spend so much time in their company we'd like to get to know them better. On a Friday evening we'll offer a glass of wine. Most often they decline but when we insist, they beg for only a *goccio* or drop. Enzo *due* will hold the wine glass while I pour, hand on the stem to lift the glass against the bottle forcefully to indicate I should stop. Instead of a relaxing visit over a glass of wine these men down the wine in one swallow, the same way *espresso* is chugged. There's no tradition of cocktails or happy hour.

The workers love RRRRRoger, his humor, his hard work, his vision. Sergio says Roger's name a hundred times a day, seeking his opinion on the placement of stone and brick. It's not that he needs Roger's approval, it's more that Roger has become a fourth mason, having inserted himself into their worksite and been welcomed. The masons taught us *tutto fa brodo*, everything makes broth, meaning nothing goes to waste in masonry. All building material, whether it be a perfectly smooth river rock, a broken piece of travertine or a small scrap of brick, is put to good and attractive use through their artistry.

Occasionally one of our workmen will bring a *regalo*, a gift. Giuliano brought Roger a bottle of clear, super charged liqueur known as *grappa* from a nearby distillery. He declines a taste as Roger samples the firewater that only recently has achieved a more refined status thanks to quality and purity standards imposed by a family of women who revolutionized the *grappa* industry. Sergio brings an antique drain pipe to use as a decorative vase for dried flowers. As he runs his calloused hands over the oddly shaped pipe he lovingly describes its original purpose on the exterior of an old farmhouse. It's a tribute to Roger that Sergio would entrust this artifact to him – recognition that only a fellow mason would appreciate such a gift. Enzo *due* brings us the occasional bounty from his hunting forays – roasted rabbit or pheasant stuffed with sage and black olives.

Italians are very warm and open. They are forever greeting each other with 'good' something. *Buongiorno, buon pranzo, buonasera, buona dominica, buona passeggiata.* No one dares lift a fork until *buon appetito* is said by all. Even work calls for such a greeting. A wave and a hearty *buon lavoro* are always delivered by our neighbors who see us planting olives or moving rubble. Clayton is correct in his observation that we've really lucked out with our location, friends, neighbors and workers.

Funny language stories are a daily occurrence. In a fit of frustration, Sergio exclaimed, *"Porca miseria,"* when he dropped his trowel into a bucket of cement. It's a mild oath, a wonderful combination of words to express damn. Literally however it means pig squalor or pig poverty. It does not mean misery. *Miseria* is what's known as a false friend – a word that looks like a cognate but isn't. Roger liked the sound of this *porca miseria* and tried to commit it to memory. It was clear he needed a little practice though when he let loose with a lusty "porky pig" after smashing his thumb with a hammer.

During these days with burdensome deadlines, Roger implores the workers to complete tasks not *oggi*, today, but *ieri*, yesterday. Good naturedly, they respond *subito*, right away. Roger's attempt sounded more like "scooby-doo." Once a week Luciano delivers sand and gravel for the masons. He asks me where he should *scaricare la roba*. Do we want to *scaricare qui* or *scaricare li*? Roger asks me why Luciano always says everything is scary, scary. No, hon, not scary, scary; *scaricare*, to unload.

At Trilogy, Roger likes to modify one of the thirty pizzas already listed on the menu. Instead of just pointing to his choice when Dani takes his order, I must order for him – *"Lui vorrebbe avere una pizza Napoletana con salsiccia."* He would like to have the Neapolitan pizza with sausage. Next, I place his drink order – "*Lui preferisce una birra grande.*" He prefers a tall beer. Frustrated at not being able to order himself Roger demanded, "Who the hell's this Louie you keep talking about?" It's you, big guy. *Lui* means he or him.

Truly, he's learning a lot but I am too. While walking the other morning I encountered a spry old woman eager to chat. We talked about the weather, the pretty spring flowers and the admirable pace she maintained despite the hills. I laughed when she proudly told me she was twenty-eight. Pleased with my reaction, she laughed too. I offered *auguri*, congratulations, and turned toward home. As I walked away, it occurred to me that twenty-eight must have been the year she was born, making her seventy-five. She still deserved the *auguri* while I deserved a goose egg.

At the outdoor market recently I ordered two *porchetta,* holding up my pointer and index fingers, giving the butcher a peace sign. He did a double take, "Do you want two sandwiches or three?" All customer eyes turned to me while the butcher glared down from the platform of his *porchetta* truck. My words indicated two but my gesture indicated three. Putting my hands behind my back, I verbally confirmed two and slunk off to the side until they were ready. I still have a hard time counting with my thumb as number one.

My vocabulary has grown to include arcane subject matter relating to tradesmen and building construction, cement types, the names of different shapes of tiles, the varieties of sand and gravel mixtures and their different properties and purposes. Massimo has patiently taught me the language of computers as he invests hours in trying to right all the wrongs of our system. After all his generosity in time and expertise, I unintentionally insulted him by misunderstanding a word.

One night, Massimo loaded our digital camera photos onto the computer. We glanced at various before and after renovation pictures and several shots of Massimo working at the computer. In one, Roger's caught him off guard. We all laugh at the look on his face - he says he looks *stupito*. Soothingly, I come to his rescue saying he doesn't look stupid at all. He chuckles even more once he realizes I think he's said *stupido* but he's really said the other, meaning shocked, surprised, stunned. The more I tried to recover, the harder he laughed. He didn't look stupid but I sure did.

Residency

With so much progress on the language front, we should be residents by now. Well, almost. We had passed the two month deadline and Antonio urged us to return to the *questura* to obtain our *permessi.* Could you just rip my fingernails out with pliers instead? He understood our reluctance and offered to contact his friend to make sure the documents were ready before we wasted a trip. They were indeed and Antonio offered to pick up the paperwork on our behalf. With his guidance, I created a document in Italian giving him the authority to obtain the *permessi.* We liked this idea; anything to avoid another trip to the *questura*.

All seemed in order until Antonio called us from police headquarters. New rules had been instituted that day and the proxy concept was now illegal; everyone had to pick up their own documents. We raced to the *questura* to find a mob scene. Eventually we spotted Antonio who ushered us through to the officer who gave us our *permessi*. After all the previous difficulties this seemed too easy. We were deceived.

Antonio led us from the *questura* to a branch office of Perugia's town hall to apply for our residency. The office was cramped, the waiting room empty. Two clerks seated behind teller windows wore the officious attitudes of bureaucrats the world over. One called us forward and asked for our *permessi*. Proudly, we slipped them into the tray of his window. Silently he reviewed the paperwork and began collecting various forms for completion. Some we completed ourselves such as one requesting the square meters of our house. Every resident must provide this detail in order to be taxed for sanitation services. I guess once we're paying for trash pick-up we can now be considered residents.

The official completed the next form based on information in the *permessi,* some details from our passports and some verbal responses. The oversized form looked like something a town crier would unfurl to announce momentous news. He asked for our mothers' maiden names, our college degrees and specialties. I would answer in Italian but some of the answers were difficult. We adopted a routine where he would ask the question and hand me a scrap of pink paper to record the response. He'd retrieve the pink scrap, record the information onto the big form, wad up the scrap and toss it on the floor.

We were running along quite smoothly with our pink scrap effort when suddenly we screeched to a halt. Our official discovered a discrepancy between my passport and my *permesso*. The *permesso* made me six months younger with a birthday on the first of June instead of the first of January. The documents were headed back to me. Even Antonio, a stickler for rules and regulations wouldn't hear of it, giving him the big swirling **S** finger wag meaning no way. "*Dai,*" he said; "Come on." With our promise to fix the error at some future date, Mr. Pink Scraps reluctantly continued completing the form. The crier announcement inched up the inside of the teller window, practically blocking his unfriendly, bored face from view. Grabbing a series of ever-larger rubber stamps, he pounded the form in various places before setting it aside, providing us with two narrow strips of yellow paper that serve as our temporary residency documents until the permanent ones are ready in six weeks. We're to carry the temporaries at all times and use them to sign up for national health insurance. We must wait for the permanent cards to purchase a car.

More hoops remain. The *vigile urbano*, local police, will visit us to verify that we do indeed live in our house. Our official is unable to tell us when this will happen other than to say it should happen soon, within the next several weeks. Are we to remain indoors at all times? What about trips to the grocery or bank? What about appliance shopping, linen shopping, paint shopping, brick scrounging? What about planting olives five acres away from the door bell? Unimpressed with our busy lives, he tells us, *"è così,"* that's the way it is.

In the days that followed, I got in the habit of leaving notes on the front gate. "Dear Vigile, We're at the grocery store. We'll be back scooby-doo. Thanks." "Dear Vigile, We're in the back of the house planting our baby olive trees. Here's our cell phone number. Call and we'll meet you at the front gate."

Fifteen days after our visit to town hall a policeman showed up while we were both at home. "*Avanti*," we said; "*Permesso,*" he said upon entering. He looked very important, dressed in his dark blue uniform, carrying a clipboard, consulting his paperwork. He confirmed that we were the owners and scribbled notes all the while. He asked basic questions - how do we like Italy, are we being treated well, where are we from, plus the usual *come mai* question. As we chatted, he continued to write on his clipboard, eventually declaring, "*Tutto a posto,*" everything's in order. He offered "*Auguri,*" shook our hands and said our permanent cards should be ready in two weeks.

Fifteen days later we received our permanent residency cards and went directly to Perugia Auto, a private business designed to help people wade through all the red-tape surrounding car ownership. Only now could we begin the time-consuming, paperwork-intensive process of transferring ownership of the Fiat Punto. We didn't know it at the time but visits to Perugia Auto would compete with the bank and the paint store on the frustration meter.

Compared to getting the *permesso,* this residency thing was a bit anticlimactic. Particularly since we learned that we must repeat the *permesso* process at the *questura* in less than a year. At that point, our new *permessi* will be granted for an indefinite period of time. Roger's not one to eat his words comfortably. He said he was never going to do it again. Come February, we'll see what happens.

Doctors

Now, about that national health insurance. Thanks to Roger's former employer, our health insurance coverage is worldwide. Although we must pay at the time of service, eventually, we're reimbursed. Thus we never presumed to be eligible for free medical care, but Liana is very concerned about our ability to tap into the medical system should the need arise. Privately we agree that it's not a bad idea to become familiar with the process whether we're able to take advantage of it or not.

Liana arranged for us to visit Rita, friend, general practitioner and wife of Fabrizio, the cardiologist and our tablemate at the opening night dinner in Colombella. We appear at the *anagrafe* or medical registry office to find the place packed. People were sniffling and sneezing and Rita apologized for the clinic conditions – a new facility is under construction.

The first step toward free health care is to sign on with a general practitioner. Each GP has a maximum number of patients and Rita has reached her limit so she's recommending we sign on with a friend, Dottoressa Angela. She'll arrange an introductory appointment for that afternoon to make sure we're comfortable with her. Before we could blink, beautiful Rita spun out of the room, white coat flared behind her.

Two hours later we were still at the *anagrafe*. The obliging clerk attempting to register us into the system spent most of her time on the phone, running into one bureaucratic brick wall after another. If we were students or employed this process would be a snap. Simply coming to Italy to live made us ineligible to obtain free medical treatment. The only way around this problem was to visit the city office dealing specifically with foreigners (a strange request since we were now residents and landowners) and pledge a significant percentage of our retirement to the Italian government. Roger would sooner spend each Monday at the *questura* than opt for this suggestion.

We kept the appointment with Dottoressa Angela and were impressed. She doesn't speak any English but she's taking lessons. She asked about us, *come mai,* did we enjoy living in Italy, and our health. Periodically, her cell would ring. She'd apologize, take the call and calmly listen to one patient's woes after another's. Every once in a while the nurse would knock and enter seeking her signature on a drug request or referral to a specialist. She never rattled, never displayed impatience, always remained attentive to our comments. She is unconcerned that we are not part of the national system and more than willing to help us as needed. As we left, she handed us a sheet of paper with the clinic hours, her cell phone number and the nurse's name and number. And with this, we've been introduced to the world of medicine in Italy and a new language arena lies ahead.

For now, we continue at the most basic of levels. Learning comes slowly but can be measured the way a child learns – crawling before walking. We may not *capisce* all there is to know but we're now official residents and life's new adventures continue to be a giggle.

The Deadline

Some things are not a giggle. People here are curious about what we as Americans think of Iraq and Afghanistan. Italy has committed troops in both countries and we see the *pace*, peace flags flown throughout the region. It's difficult not to read or hear about anti-war and anti-American demonstrations. We're fortunate not to have personally been targets of any negativity even as we pass on the opportunity to have political discussions.

These are dangerous times. Fear of overseas travel lurks in the back of every traveler's mind. Airlines, hotels and tourism destinations suffer. As much as Mary and Don can't live in constant fear of break-ins, we can't sustain an unrelenting sense of doom. While it's selfish, we go on with our daily lives, emotionally keeping dire consequences at bay.

Our admittedly narrow view is focused on our budding enterprise. A smattering of reservations has resulted from the ads we placed last winter. It appears some are shelving their fears and accepting the challenges of travel in today's world.

What *we* are doing is working and worrying. We've stretched our we-really-mean-it deadline of April 30th as much as we possibly can, to the second of May. We're leaving the country on the third of May; cutting it close. The deadline drifts not through lack of will or desire or competency but because of something called *festa.*

Festa is a multi-purpose word that covers holiday, feast day, saint's day, national holiday, festival or party. In the ten days prior to departing for Belgium, five days were either a *festa* or a Sunday. A *festa* is a day off and no one works on a day off. There are no exceptions. There's no lure of dropping by the office to wrap up a few things when other employees aren't around. There's no willingness to put in extra hours at a second job while getting paid for the first and there's certainly no working for two crazy Americans who have created their own deadline and are desperately trying to meet it.

These days are sacred but not always for religious reasons. Even Mick, who's now officially registered as our employee, making him eligible for all the perks of the national system, does not work on a *festa.* For one thing, the bus doesn't operate. Secondly, *è così.* Alfio, our extraordinary carpenter has never worked on March 19th and never will. That's the *festa di San Giuseppe* and *San Giuseppe,* otherwise known as St. Joseph, aka father of Jesus, is the patron saint of carpenters.

Not only do Italians celebrate the *festa*, they *fare il ponte* or make the bridge. A *festa* falling on a Thursday begs to be bridged, making Friday a day off. Our particular ten-day push included Good Friday, *Pasqua,* Easter, *pasquetta,* Little Easter, Independence Day and Labor Day. Building a bridge was nothing. This series of holidays called for an aqueduct.

We may have been exhausted in the preceding months but we were lively in comparison to our current numbed state. We ricocheted between frantic, dazed, desperate and maniacal. We couldn't sleep, we barely ate. Personal hygiene was at an all-time low. My fingernails served no purpose other than to chip paint, plaster and glue from tiles, windows and woodwork. We literally walked in circles. Roger dropped paint brushes from ridiculously high ladders. I shattered light bulbs and any other glass objects within reach. Roger drove off a hillside in the tractor, stood up, shook himself off and got back on for more.

Our living space was reduced to a tiny corner of the apartment as we systematically painted room after room. We lived in the center of the green bedroom to avoid touching any walls. Who could keep track of what was wet and what had dried? It was safer not to touch any painted surface. Our living quarters were still not complete. The kitchen was ready to be assembled but practically required peace talks to arbitrate negotiations between the granite installer, the masons and the carpenter. Each had done their jobs precisely and that was precisely the problem.

There's not a straight line in our entire house. Nothing's even, nothing's square, nothing's plumb. For support purposes, the base of the building is wider than the top. The back of the house slants inward and our kitchen is on the back side of the house. Differences were so dramatic they could be seen with the naked eye. Each craftsman pointed fingers at the other when his piece of the puzzle didn't slip into place.

The masons had completed the yellow and blue tile work. Alfio, never having built a custom kitchen, struggled but eventually shaved, sanded and modified the under-counter chestnut cabinets to snuggly fit the wavy floor and walls. Vincenzo, the granite man, was next. Everyone agreed he was strange; a little too much marble dust over the years. When the smooth granite slabs speckled with red, black and gray flinty highlights were installed along with the backsplash of the same granite, a gaping inch and a half opening existed between the top of the backsplash and the bottom of the tile. Vincenzo pitched a little artistic fit.

Enter *capo supremo* and translator along with three masons, and one carpenter. Giuliano the electrician stood on a ladder in the center of the room listening to all, enjoying his voyeuristic role, clearly pleased to be part of the action without the responsibility. All workers talked at once, fingers flying, tape measures snapping in and out. Previous sketches were produced from back pockets and waved dramatically to prove points now moot. While they argued, Roger fiddled with his own design and solved the problem. "Vincenzo, it doesn't matter, go make this," as he presented his drawing. All necks, including Giuliano's from on high, craned toward the rough sketch that removed the blame and carried very little burden.

Ingenious. The sketch called for Vincenzo to cut a one and a half inch thick piece of granite, three inches deep. It should be as long as the countertop and be installed in the gap between tile and backsplash. In other words, he created a little shelf around the cooktop; a convenient place for seasonings and spices. Giuliano was the first to blurt, *"Bravo, Roger."* The others chimed in with the masons handing Roger a pencil to sign the sketch. Vincenzo grudgingly admired the concept though it was clear he would have preferred a protracted argument and a little ass being chewed.

Installation of the refrigerator kept me awake. The fridge was destined to go into the old stairwell. Roger had taken these measurements personally and we all knew it would be tight. While I didn't doubt that it would fit, my worry was electricity. Was the cord long enough for someone to slip behind the fridge, plug it in and slip out again before the fridge was slid into its cramped cubbyhole to remain for life? When I did sleep I had a recurring nightmare; I was the someone selected to plug in the fridge and Roger left me trapped back there. I'd wake, gasping for air.

One Final Push

Every morning as is his custom, Roger wakes, grabs a coffee and endures the tedious process of going on line to check email. The stars must be in perfect alignment, fingers crossed and the phase of the moon just right for the dial-up connection to hold. Nothing aligned on this particular morning. After several aborted attempts and lots of "porky-pigs," he gave up, deciding to try again after lunch. Separately, I called to check on the delivery of an appliance but the call wouldn't go through. Instead, there was a recorded message saying I could only call emergency numbers such as the police or an ambulance or the phone company's administrative offices. Oddly enough, we could receive calls.

I contacted the phone company and struggled through a conversation with someone whose dialect bore no resemblance to Italian. Eventually I discovered that the phone company had partially disabled our service since we had not paid our bills. She was right; we had never paid a phone bill in our entire time in Italy. In our defense, we had never received one. Her response, they were mailed every two months. Still defending, they were not being mailed to us. We solved that issue and moved on to our current no service problem.

The operator told me what we owed, suggesting we pay the bill immediately and fax a copy of the receipt to their offices. They would then reinstate our service. Antonio helped me complete the paperwork at the post office and after delivering *un sacco di soldi* we raced to a bookstore with fax services and sent the receipt. Days dragged by without resolution. I called the offices without success and begged Antonio for his help. Finally, he spoke with a supervisor who promised to reinstate our service if we re-sent the fax. Within hours of dispatching the second fax our phone and computer connection were fully functional.

To add to our overloaded plate we planned a celebration party for the Saturday after our return from the Netherlands. I arranged with La Boteghita restaurant to prepare *antipasti* platters of cheese, fruit and sliced *affettati* – the famous meat waterfall from our Epiphany/Befana dinner. We wanted live entertainment and Enzo *uno* negotiated with a local three-piece band. I met with Antonella and Luigi Faffa, proprietors of the eponymous bakery established in 1851 for other *antipasti*, hundreds of sandwich rolls and dozens of cookies. I called all the invitees to advise them of the party date and time. Over one hundred guests were expected for an outdoor event in the *piazza* and around the pool. In the event of rain we'd move into the *salone rustiche* and *soggiorno*.

This was high anxiety. We had worked at a fevered pitch for five months and with these additional pressures we were edgy, irritable and impatient. Precious few days remained before our departure; our panic scores were off the chart. Just as we approached core meltdown, when days could not get any more hectic, when one more crisis would have tipped the scale to some unpleasant end, we were saved. Miraculously, everyone took vacation at the same time.

In the end, *ferie* saved us. Day and night, side-by-side, we toiled, one eye on the calendar. Spare moments were devoted to buying furnishings, arranging deliveries, exhausting trips to the paint store or the bank. When the workers stopped for the evening, Antonio remained for meetings, lists, translations and assignments.

At ten o'clock on the night of the second we tried to change our departure. "Please give me one more day," Roger growled to the computer. No other flights were available. At midnight we relented and began packing, realizing that our *capo* would have to oversee all that remained to accomplish. Relinquishing control and recognizing that we could do no more was painful. We felt like the losing team at the end of the Super Bowl. Time was our opponent and it had won.

Once again Antonio drove us to the airport, calmly enduring another two hour session fraught with loose ends, minor details and major headaches. He took it all in stride, as unruffled as one human can be. In his heart of hearts he had to be thinking, "Hang in there, they'll be gone in two hours, it's almost over."

As organized as we were, having placed all the various linens on each bed in plastic wrap; labeled all the curtains for re-hanging; arranged for furniture, beds, appliances and other deliveries prior to our return; coordinated between the carpenter, plumber, electrician, masons and granite maker to finish the kitchen; designed planters and platforms for the gardens and ordered the flowers and vegetables to fill them; ordered and installed the gas lines; arranged for the installation of a new furnace and water heater; left Mick pages of work instructions that included weeding large circles under the seventy-seven mature olive trees; provided instructions for completing interior painting; planned a party for one hundred guests; booked the cleaning agency to work their magic in this dust-filled, paint-splattered, flooring-distressed abode - there was still much left on Antonio's list.

Did we actually go on vacation for ten days? Did we travel on a barge through dozens of locks in the Netherlands? Did we awaken early to see the flower auction in Aalsmeer? Did we travel by train to Bruges? Did we spend Mother's Day surrounded by millions of tulips in the Keukenhof? Did we marvel at the North Sea-stopping, man-made wonder known as Delta Works in Zeeland? The itinerary and pictures say we did. But we also spent lots of hours on the cell phone with Antonio trouble shooting and problem solving. Some things were progressing, others lagging and still others moving in reverse. Roger and I discussed worst-case scenarios if *Le Vigne* were not habitable upon our return. We would cancel the party and book hotel rooms in Colombella for everyone, including ourselves.

We returned to Rome on a glorious, warm spring day. As we left the airport, we removed the sweaters and jackets necessary in Northern Europe. The return to Rome with these friends closed the loop of a unique circle. These were our traveling companions from our May 2001 trip to Italy, the one when Roger announced our future presence in this country. We had even arranged to have our same capable driver and friend, Giovanni, squire us home to *Le Vigne*.

The two-hour drive from Fiumicino seemed to take days. Roger used Giovanni's microphone acting as tour guide, pointing out towns of interest from an insider's perspective. He and I were like children, ants in our pants. The anticipation of seeing *Le Vigne* was almost more than we could stand. The culmination of two years since our initial trip, including eight months of searching for property and five tumultuous, labor-intensive months of renovation came down to this single moment. Finally, we arrived and were greeted at the front gate by Antonio, Enzo and Mick. They had worked non-stop and were putting the finishing touches on clean up with raking, blowing and sweeping.

Le Vigne was transformed. We had never seen it look so beautiful, so clean, so organized. Piles of rubble were gone, flowerbeds in their place. Furniture was in every room, beds were made with custom linens, the cotto tile floors were clean, rooms were dust-free, the kitchen was assembled with appliances and the all-important spice shelf, curtains were hung, the house was stocked with staples. Antonio and the crew had made it all happen. Even Cinzia, Giuliana, Mary and Don had contributed their time and graceful touches; fresh flowers filled every room. It all appeared seamless. Only Roger and I knew the extent of this remarkable transformation. I could have cried from relief.

That night, after dinner at Giancarla's restaurant, Roger and I climbed the stairs to sleep in our bedroom for the first time. This was not the green bedroom in the apartment but our very own room. The large window faced south, framing the skyline of Perugia. The scent of wisteria and roses wafted into this calm, spacious retreat. We left the windows open, the gentle breeze reminding me that I was a child the last time I slept without air conditioning or heat.

I picked up a book to read before drifting to sleep. Roger told me he didn't realize I had brought the book with me on this trip. Quickly he recovered, "Oh, I forgot. The trip's over, we actually *live* here." I understood the sensation, this newness, an unfamiliarity tinged with the pleasure of nascent discovery.

Months ago, Giuliana stood nearby while I emptied a wheelbarrow full of rubble. She was elegantly dressed while I was powdered from head to toe in chalky dust. "Soon enough," she said, "the work will be done and you'll be sitting poolside, *gambe all'aria*," legs in the air. At the time, I never imagined the work ending. Could it possibly and finally have come true?

The Party

Returning to a transformed *Le Vigne* felt like an ongoing vacation with blissful days of discovery. We unpacked dishes and silverware, pots and pans, stemware, crystal, platters, vases and urns and stored them in spacious new homes. The new kitchen was a showcase but I had no idea how the appliances worked. From the Bosch dishwasher to the Miele microwave to the Ilve brand cooktop and oven – each was an adventure.

Even the toaster was a learning experience. It was the only one we found that released toasted bread at the end of its cycle. How do Italians know their toast is ready? Did they just keep popping it out to check it? Margherita, a Courteney Cox look-alike and husband Michele, her Matthew Perry, owners of a small electrical appliances store, searched for weeks to find such a toaster. They never heard of it but were impressed with the concept. Location of this novelty proved such a difficult mission that when Margherita finally found one, she called to say, "It jumps, it jumps." The drip coffee pot we purchased for guests to make American-style coffee has fins and flares and looks like something Judy Jetson would use. Our cartoon animated existence extended to decidedly low-tech objects like a paper towel holder designed to hold a Flintstone-sized roll of paper towels, literally two feet in diameter.

The Miele coffee machine has yet to expel its first drop. The Italian language instruction book is eighty pages. I contacted the *numero verde*, the Italian toll-free equivalent, to request an English version. Despite my urgent plea it will take three weeks to arrive. Meanwhile, we'll make do with Judy Jetson.

We played tourist along with our friends, taking them to Todi, Deruta, Montefalco and Cortona. We shopped at Valentina's ceramic store, we ate cookies at Faffa's, we had fun at Sidis, we ate in, we ate out, we drank everywhere, we walked every morning collecting wild flowers and green wheat stalks. Not surprisingly, there was precious little time poolside with *gambe all'aria* especially in advance of The Party. We shopped at METRO filling two flatbed carriers to overflowing with beef tenderloins, sausages, wheels of cheese, olives, chips, fresh fruit, fresh vegetables, beer, wine, soft drinks, waters, napkins, plates, forks, cups. We bought cheerful sunflower dappled fabric to decorate the plastic tables. We borrowed Federico's famous grill for the sausage and beef and arranged with Corys Renato to have a friend man the grill. We mowed, bought flower pots, planted flowers and herbs.

While there was much to do, all seemed organized and ready. We were prepared with chilled drinks, drink stations, seating, table arrangements, forks wrapped in napkins tied with ribbon, lined trash containers, electricity for the band and food deliveries. A phone call the afternoon before the party threw us a curve. The *Befana* restaurant, known for its Bacchanalian *antipasti* platters really wasn't set up to do catering and suggested we make the platters ourselves. Why did she take the job? Out the door we bolted to buy meats and more cheeses. We rushed to Margherita's shop to buy a meat slicer, a toy Roger has wanted since arriving in Italy. We sliced for hours and bagged *mortadella, prosciutto* and *salami* and *pecorino* and *cacciota* cheeses in plastic, ready to be plated at serving time. Crisis averted.

Party day arrived and the weather was perfect. *Le Vigne* sparkled. Magenta roses were in full bloom and the geraniums around the pool were a luminous, blinding red. Guests were invited early, at four, to accommodate Renato's restaurant dinner schedule. Four o'clock came and went and no one appeared. Now I worried. I had invited everyone verbally. Had I used the wrong words, had I invited people on the wrong day? Did we unwittingly schedule our *festa* on a *festa*? In our continuing education course that is life in Italy, we needed a few lessons about parties. Four o'clock was an awkward time. Some people were at work, others were resting and still others were watching a *partita*, soccer match.

I audibly sighed upon seeing Enzo *uno* arrive with the band. *Piano, piano*, slowly, slowly, guests trickled in, by ones and twos then six or eight at a time and then in droves. Greeting everyone became a blur. Our neighbors, masons, carpenter, electrician, plumber, paint supplier, painters, my walking friends, vendors, retailers, people we had come to know - Wendy, Frits, Abigail, Ralph and everyone's attendant family members, wives, husbands, children, parents streamed in. It was just as Caroline and Augusto predicted – people came *bussando con i piedi*, knocking with their feet. It means that guests' arms are so laden with gifts that they can't knock in the usual way.

Naturally, we specified no gifts. Our words went unheeded; the generosity was impressive. Flower arrangements, potted hydrangeas, spathophyllum and a braided money tree, cookies and the platters they came on, *prosecco*, liqueurs and wine by the caseload. A very pregnant Valentina brought a lamp we had admired in her shop. She had her own discovery on arrival. Years earlier she had painted the blue and white ceramic "*Le Vigne*" tile that is attached to the brick column supporting our front gate. Until today she had never seen its home.

Giuliana and seven other women commissioned a two-foot tall, hand-painted ceramic urn from Deruta inscribed with the date, their names and *Le Vigne*. Seeing the gift explained a lot. Giuliana had repeatedly inquired about the guest list. I'd review the names of those she knew and she'd ask about so-and-so and I'd tell her, yes, she and her family were invited and she'd move on to someone else. Amused by her interest, I told Roger this was quintessential Giuliana, signing off on our guest list. The emotional and humbling unveiling of the urn brought her motives into focus. She didn't want me to offend anyone by omission. I had done the right thing; all gift givers were present.

Wrapping packages in this country is an art. The craftsmanship is applied to items intended as gifts and other purchases. A trip to the bakery must allow for wrapping time. Cookies, cakes or breakfast pastries are placed on waxed cardboard trays with gold foil highlights. Boxes are constructed with internal hoops so as not to damage the contents. The whole thing is then wrapped in branded paper and tied with ribbon. There are admonitions about cautious transport - carry this tray upright and that box this way, don't stack one atop the other. Even pharmacists practice the art whether the purchase is toothpaste, aspirin or diaper rash cream.

Flower arrangements are treated with such precise care that it seems a pity to unwrap them. Netting, ribbons, tulle, fans of coral, shells, velvet, sugared almonds, pastel wrapping papers all combine to transform a few cut stems and greenery into improvements on nature. An unobtrusive sticker discreetly attached to a corner of ribbon includes the name of the florist. I saved all the stickers for future patronage. Housewarming plants include tiny wooden ladybugs as bearers of good tidings. A Zen-like centerpiece from Margherita was draped across a three-legged glass trapezoidal platter – a gift that will last long after the antherium, moss and orchids are gone.

Our next party lesson came in the form of eating. While shopping for groceries, we puzzled over quantities. Tonight, platters upon platters of food were arranged on the tables while Renato supervised the grilling. The smell of sausages and tenderloin was tantalizing. Everything looked delicious but strangely the food remained untouched. What error had we committed this time? I knew Italians ate everything we offered so why was no one eating? I started to calculate freezer space for all the sliced *mortadella.* As I turned to ask Giuliana for advice, a guest approached wondering if she might take a plate of food. *"Certo, sì, come no, prego,"* Sure, yes, why not, help yourself. Roger and I ran from table to table ushering people in, handing out plates, *"Mangia, mangia."* Later I remembered a party at Giuliana and Renato's where a platter of appetizers remained pristine until *Buon appetito* was announced by our hosts. Just as no polite person will enter a house without *permesso,* no one will eat unless invited.

Once given the green light, these friendly neighbors, colleagues and family members moved with lightning speed, funneling into Italian lines, elbowing anyone who got in between them and a sausage. We restocked grilled meats twice and when Renato came to the well for the third time it was dry. I never got a bite of anything from the grill. Cheeses, rolls, fruit, vegetables and cookies disappeared at an equally alarming rate. We underestimated on all the above and overestimated on *salami* and *mortadella* – there were a lot of sandwiches in our future.

As people mingled, poured drinks and ate, I asked the bandleader for the microphone to share a few words. In Italian I explained that the party was a small way for us to recognize the contributions of so many in making *Le Vigne* shine. Roger and I wanted them to know that all their work, time and effort were appreciated. I thanked everyone for making us feel so welcome in Colombella.

As I handed the microphone back to the bandleader, he quickly consulted with the others in the band and before I could step away they began playing our national anthem. Enough Americans were present and we sang *The Star-Spangled Banner* together. While everyone applauded, Roger asked the band to play the Italian national anthem. There was an awkward hesitation followed by hasty consultation before the band agreed they knew the music. The Italians sang their counterpart and there was much applause. The entire experience seemed lifted from a Frank Capra script but it wasn't. It was purely spontaneous, magical, touching.

Graciously, our guests wanted to see the house. The carpenter and masons took obvious pride as they showed family members their many accomplishments. We conducted criss-crossing tours and sent others off on their own to cover the four floors from *cantina* to apartment.

As dusk settled over the *piazza*, we turned on what Roger calls the Village Lights. Normally, four lamp posts provide enough light to illuminate the *piazza* and front gate. Tonight the other ten lights throughout the gardens and back drive blazed while the band played an eclectic collection of tangos, big band tunes, the ever-popular polkas and Italian folk songs. The musicians moved smoothly from *Volare* to *Rock Around the Clock* and the *piazza* was transformed into the perfect dance floor. Everyone danced including little children who delighted in spinning with each other and their parents. Enough wine flowed to convince the three masons to sing. The three tenors are safe. Guests covered their ears, some winced in pain. It was brutal but comical with one American commenting, "That's a slice of Italian culture you couldn't pay to get."

Near midnight, a seventy-person conga line snaked around the *piazza,* into the *ingresso,* down the *steps,* through the *soggiorno,* into the gardens and back to the pool level. Luca, the most boisterous mason, led the charge pushing Enzo *uno* in a wheelbarrow. When they reached the steps, Luca unceremoniously dumped Enzo and abandoned the wheelbarrow. I helped Enzo stand and it was in this mellow state that he told me he appreciated my *discorso,* speech. I said it was sincere and particularly directed to him and his brother Antonio. He patted my shoulder, leaned in and whispered. He knew the words were really meant for just the two of them. I hoped each person felt the same way.

Shortly after midnight, guests began to gather their things to leave. Sleepy babies dozed in strollers or in their parents' arms. We walked people to the front gate, thanking them for their gifts, thanking them for attending, asking them to return soon. The bandleader asked if he should continue and we told him no, they had put in a full night. Soon, only the masons and electrician remained; a fierce game of bocce underway. A final score of *pari, pari*, a tie, left them spoiling for a rematch. Antonio, our perfect *capo,* told them it would have to happen some other time and escorted everyone out the front gate despite mild protests. He smiled back at us and waved goodbye before turning off the Village Lights.

The Party, and all it represented as a culmination of our labors, was a success. We could reflect contentedly on our accomplishments, take a moment to enjoy the satisfaction of a job well done and bask in the richness of our surroundings. Another phase of our lives would soon begin, one without the daily pressure of renovation.

But life with Roger means the work never really ends. The type of work might vary, the project list might shorten but there's always another item to take its place, improvements to be made, block walls to build, the ongoing maintenance issues of a property like *Le Vigne*. Giuliana was decidedly wrong; *gambe all'aria* might happen at someone else's house but it's not likely to happen here.

Nature

"Why isn't doing laundry at home as much fun as it is at *Le Vigne*?" So wrote a friend after a week's stay this spring. Time softens the harsh edges of reality and the part about how long the wash cycle takes or how little the washer holds. Inconveniences fade and only the pleasant, lavender-scented aroma of line-dried clothes remains. I guess she also forgot about having to beat the ants out of her clothes before bringing them indoors. It only takes one ant in a pair of panties to sear that habit into place. The ants have taken to using the clothesline as their own personal tightrope. In the battle pitting humans against ants, the war has been won by a smear of Vaseline on either end of the line.

Let's not forget the sudden hustle of a sprint to get clothes off the line when rain arrives. Storms come from nowhere. Bruised purple skies like those in a Greco painting can just as easily result in frustrated nothingness while an azure blue, cloudless day brings drenchings that stream water into the *soggiorno*. On balance though, the appeal of line-dried laundry, most especially the rough texture and outdoor-fresh smell of a bath towel, outweighs the negatives. It's hard to believe we used to like the limp, insipid feel of a towel fresh from the dryer. We tolerate the limpness on rainy days when we're thankful to have the dryer, but our preference is the clothesline. Laundry remains a big focus in our lives.

The unfolding of our natural surroundings is enchanting. The days lengthen and we rise earlier to take advantage of the cool morning air. The scent of wisteria drifting into our bedroom has waned only to be replaced by the strong aroma of jasmine. The magenta roses climbing the walls now compete with hundreds of other varieties and colors – reds, pinks, whites, salmons, yellows and a mauve straight out of *The Thorn Birds*. Having broken through her gruff exterior, we finally met Marina, owner of the greenhouses at the bottom of the hill. She knows her stuff. Flats of geraniums, impatiens, begonias, petunias, gazanias, dahlias, lobelia, daisies, verbena and zinnias have made their way to our gardens from her greenhouses. Pots outside our kitchen are filled with basil, chives, thyme, oregano, mint and a variety of sage with leaves the size of business cards. The lettuce we planted last December is just ending as we prepare the soil for tomatoes.

The centuries-old oak in the *piazza* casts fabulous shade but at this time of year drops thousands of fuzzy, curly brown strands. Swept together, they mat into Rastafarian dreadlocks requiring a wheelbarrow to remove them from the driveway twice a day. Unless Mick stays on top of this task, the pool suffers from clogged skimmers and filters.

Sweet magnolias are blooming poolside and a milder varietal of lavender is just starting to show color around the tennis court. Wild, white-flowered trees called *sambuco* (not to be confused with the anise-flavored *sambuca* liqueur) line the white roads and fill the woods with a heady scent stronger than jasmine.

Our one cherry tree is bearing small yet tasty fruit. We fight the birds to collect enough and Don makes cherry cobblers to die for. The *tigli* now have leaves and form flowers that dry and spin like little helicopters when they drop. The privet around the pool is blooming and competes with the yellowing broom of the hillsides for strongest, sweetest scent of the month. We saw our first *lucciola* or firefly the other night and Roger, in his ever-expanding and inventive Italian vocabulary has named it a *fuoco mosca,* fire fly. *Mamma mia.*

Grasselli has planted our two remaining fields with *girasole,* sunflowers. No wonder Roger thinks he can create his own language when a word like *girasole* means turn sun. Leave it to him to note that even as tiny green plants, before their cheery yellow faces are formed, they follow the sun's movement. The green waving wheat has started to fade. Soon it will be beige and then a parched golden brown. Giuliana already laments the coming *trebbiatura,* the threshing of the wheat when all that remains is the *stoppia* or stubble, until the next aeration in late fall.

Our focus now was outside the walls of the house and I was developing a *muratore* tan, the equivalent of a farmer's tan, from all the work in the gardens with my head bowed. The retaining walls designed to eliminate *scarpate* and increase our footprint and therefore garden space require

38. April sunrise 39. May roses and the entrance to the rental apartment
40. Wisteria end of Le Vigne 41. Tulips bordering the pool

42. Apartment kitchen 43. With Valentina & Clara at cooking class
44. Anita, Charlie and family 45. Typical arrival night dinner

46. Le Vigne after restoration 47. Lavender on the tennis court wall
48. Monica 49. One of the infamous bottle walls 50. Poppies in the olive grove

51. Self-service for the masons 52. The new great wall 53. Putting my face in the new wall
54. Mamma Mia, that's some cauliflower! 55. First planting behind the great wall
56. In the giardin-orto 57/58. Cistern garden

). Gazebo pad and travertine pool coping 60. Reed, Miriam, Brad and Ryan loved the Gator
Karen & Freddo at work 62. Don & Roger 63. Locally made bell–a gift from our Pittsburgh
friends 64. When Don left his shorts stayed with Mick

65. Daniela harvests from the center 66. Int'l Harvesters come in for a break
67. Daniela, me, Pat and Luigi harvesting 68. Team ready for another meal
69. All the olives go in the hopper to be pressed 70. Int'l Harvesters – finally finished

71. Getting a fill-up from the wine pump 72. Renato, our piranha
73. Clayton & Shandi at Thanksgiving 74. Shandi helping with Thanksgiving
75. American Thanksgiving at Le Vigne

76. Firemen fighting the hornets 77. Hornet nest finally dislodged into fireplace
78. Marina & Roger celebrate their birthday 79. Demijohns as yard art 80. Sunset over Peru

**Photos courtesy of Albert Davis, Pat Deschner, Mary Baum, Beth Hosking and Roger Arndt*

blocchetti by the pallet load. A standard delivery was eight pallets, each containing sixty blocks. Every few months, we received a new delivery and every delivery to date has brought meteorological phenomena worthy of the Weather Channel. Last winter, we unloaded block in a *tramontana*, with stinging winds and sleet hindering the half-hour process.

Typically, the truck arrives and the driver operates a hand-held panel with joy sticks to control the *gru*, crane, which offloads the pallets. The driver controls the crane, Mick or I slide the arms of the crane into the two openings below each pallet and Roger guides the pallet to the ground and removes the arms so the driver can repeat the process seven more times. In good weather, the whole event would make me nervous as I conjure the potential of so very many serious injuries. When there's wind, sleet, rain or hail and the ground is a slippery, mushy mud-filled mess, my worry meter reaches the red zone. Naturally, Roger dismisses my concerns. Privately, I corner Mick and threaten him with bodily harm should he not hover over the "Boss" when block arrives. He agrees seriously, shaking his head in ascent, several yes Ma'ams in succession.

Each block weighs thirty-five pounds. I can carry one to Mick or Roger's two as we load the Gator to transport block to the various retaining wall building sites. The walls require enormous quantities of dirt, back fill and rubble. Dirt is so precious, so scarce, that we divide it into cleverly named categories based on its eventual role; good dirt and bad dirt. Good dirt is created by sifting the clay-laden earth and removing pebbles, roots, weeds and other extraneous matter. It's then blended with compost, peat moss, sand and soil enriched with fertilizer. Peat, sand and soil are purchased while the compost is created through grass clippings, fruit and vegetable remains and egg shells; our daily contributions. The good dirt's destiny is to be placed in the front of each block for planting ivy, rosemary or lavender that will eventually cover the gray walls.

The bad dirt is used for back fill but even with this arbitrary distinction we still don't have enough volume. We continually search for new sources. We utilized all the scrap created as a result of renovation; wheelbarrow and Gator loads of rock, broken tile and other rubble. We progressed to household items that wouldn't decompose: the hundreds of extra keys we were able to eliminate, the torn screens we replaced, old CDs and their cases, electrical wires, spent light bulbs, nails, screws, toothbrushes, broken pottery, and even a kitchen sink. The back fill beast remained hungry and needed to be fed.

We combed nearby building sites in search of more fill. Roger would drive to a site and leave me with the construction workers. They were impressed when I explained our need for *calcinaccio,* rubble, a word not typically found in an English/Italian phrase book. We helped neighbor Renato by taking his rubble as he and Giuliana have begun their own building renovation project; construction of a small, one bedroom guest house converted from an old pig barn. Yet the beast demanded more.

Eventually we found a way. Roger experienced another one of those vision things. It's an idea that is so creative, so novel, that our neighbor Ciccio thinks Roger should apply for a patent. The answer: empty glass bottles. Roger uses wine, champagne, beer, liquor and liqueur bottles, placed flat and side-by-side behind each row of block as rubble. He sprinkles the top of the bottles with a scant layer of bad dirt before putting another row of block in place. How he arrived at the idea is not apparent but he correctly reasoned that cylindrical glass is impressively strong and can withstand enormous pressure without breaking. It's the perfect shape; like an egg.

In some places the terraced block is nine courses high. This translates into an impressive need for bottles. While we contribute our fair share, we need industrial quantities, not mere household consumption efforts. Our symbiotic team goes to work. Roger drives, I speak. We travel to the three restaurants within a few miles of us asking the owners if we might collect their empty glass bottles on a daily basis. The puzzled looks are consistent, but the owners are willing to indulge our pursuit of *calcinaccio.* We invite them to come see the eventual resting place of their detritus. They do and applaud Roger's ingenious use of glass.

Part of our daily morning ritual now includes a drive to collect bottles; crates upon crates of bottles. We know the best sellers, the most popular whites, most expensive reds. We learn which restaurant has a more upscale clientele and who's catering large parties, weddings, baptisms or confirmations. We know which days of the week drive volume and understand the impact of a soccer match on business.

During the days of clearing the field to plant our olives I thought I might find some ancient Etruscan or Roman artifact. However, the treasures I occasionally encountered were much more contemporary and banal, a shard of pottery from a wine pitcher, a few golf balls, a glass medicine bottle. Our systematic planting of wine bottles leads me to think of future generations and how the discovery of thousands upon thousands of bottles will be interpreted. Perhaps a twenty-second century Geraldo Rivera type will stream live video (or the next century's equivalent) of the great archaeological dig at *Le Vigne.* Roger tells me he's placed notes in some of the bottles – "Joan drank all of these." Knowing this makes me wonder how many ways we've been duped by previous generations. For now, the terraced walls continue to grow, the ivy trails downward and the enlarged level footprint supported by bottles is sturdy enough to drive on. The improvement is apparent and the beast has been sated.

The terracing allows us to plant other flowers and vegetables. We notice the neighbors' vegetable plots contain artichokes, beans and potatoes. We're late on some, timely on others. We zone our garden for mixed-use, planting daisies next to artichokes and mums next to thyme. The neighbors are surprised; they've not seen gardens planted in this style. There are very strict, unwritten rules to planting here, grounded in centuries of farming protocol. A *giardino* is a flower garden while an *orto* is a vegetable garden and never the twain shall meet. The *giardino* is small and its role is *bellezza,* decorative beauty, while the *orto* is large and its role is sustenance. Roger has no compunction mixing the two, telling Giuliana that we have a *"giardin-orto."* Webster-o is going to have a field day with new additions to the dictionary.

If people from Pittsburgh talk incessantly about the weather Italians run a close second. Hailstorms, heat, rain, clear skies, mild temperatures, slight humidity, no humidity – all are great introductory topics, safe conversation starters. Perhaps it's because Italian life was so closely tied to the land and such century-old habits are hard to break. I don't know what the explanation is for those from the 'Burg. We continue to spend most of our days outdoors, so for Roger, raised in Pittsburgh and living in Italy, the weather is of constant interest and comment.

Easter Sunday brought us firmly into the ranks of the weather-talkers. In the midst of our construction frenzy and deadline countdown, with all the other worries on our plate, we experienced a rogue, late spring freeze the night before Easter. Not that we could have done a thing about it, we weren't even home when the freeze hit. We stole a night with dinner and a room at Corys Hotel with Renato. We were living up to the Italian tradition as expressed in the saying, *"Natale con i tuoi, Pasqua con chi vuoi,"* meaning Christmas is spent with family and Easter is spent with whomever you want. While the Christmas meal is usually eaten at home, Easter dinner is usually eaten out. Perhaps it's because people are experiencing spring fever and want to slough off the confines of winter. We were no exception and on Sunday we left Cortona and joined our Colombella friends for a four hour *pranzo* at a Sardinian family's farm. Lamb was the centerpiece of the feast served by family members who had raised and grown the bounty we enjoyed.

It wasn't until we returned home late that afternoon that we saw the initial blighted evidence. The tight purple buds on the Japanese magnolias were tinged brown and hung limply from the tree. Violas were like puppets with the strings removed and tulip stems had turned to green, pulpy mush. As the days progressed and the warmth returned, many plants and flowers recovered. But soon the real impact became apparent.

Olives are resistant sentinels. They withstand most climate changes well, in some cases surviving centuries by adapting to the vagaries of the seasons and the few pests that prove troublesome. But there's one thing that olives cannot tolerate and that is a hard freeze when they are at the critical stage of flowering, of setting their buds. The Easter freeze proved devastating for the olives. They were caught at just the wrong time. The temperature drop didn't destroy the trees but it did decimate the tiny blooms that would have eventually produced our olive crop for the year.

Weather mattered and we joined the chatter in Umbria. At elevations higher than ours, the trees had not yet flowered so they weren't adversely affected by the one-night freeze. At lower elevations the fruit was set. We inhabited this microcosm. Olive growers fretted and indulged in the endless comparisons between yours and mine. "Do you have flowers?" "What about yellow leaves?" "Do you have the fly?" "You can spray for that, you know." "The price of oil will indeed be high this year." "We'll help you with your harvest since we have *poco niente*, less than nothing, to pick." "The mill will have lots of available time this year; no problem getting an appointment."

For the most part, our seventy-seven mature trees were blasted. Interestingly, some of the young ones had flowers. Not all flowers produce fruit but several experts advised us that it wasn't too late to fertilize these trees. An olive's hearty constitution means that it will grow with little water, little fertilization. Despite such strength, a young olive will benefit from the added boost that such sustenance provides. The majority of Italians would allow the olives to tough it out on their own. We decided to help them along.

Irrigation and fertilization can happen in different ways. We had seen the occasional grove laced with above-ground tubing. Black tubes tied and snaked from tree to tree were unsightly, disrupting the feng shui of a sea of silver green shimmering leaves. Underground was our approach and both irrigation and fertilization could take place through the same system. Antonio helped us interview suppliers and collect estimates and we eventually found Silvio who promised to finish the job in twenty days.

This was not a minor task. Heavy equipment was required to dig trenches parallel to the rows of olives. Perforated tubing was to be placed in the trenches and the entire system needed to be connected to a water source, timers, an autoclave and a holding tank for fertilizer. Twenty days came and went. Thirty days passed. The project was still not complete. Roger's *pazienza* had expired but we were committed with our supplier, half of our grove already trenched. Whatever excuses were offered were unimportant. While I continued to translate, very little was required as Roger's facial expressions and hand gestures conveyed all one needed to know about his state of mind. Finally, parallel rows of weeds next to the olives attest to the fact that water and fertilizer had arrived.

Weeds and the occasional volunteer sunflower are not welcome guests in the grove. They pose a risk to the root system of the young olives. My farmer tan darkens as there are days when I spend more time bent over than upright. Roger drives the Gator while I collect weeds in one bucket, rocks in another. At six feet, four inches he maintains that the person five feet, four inches with a lower center of gravity should do the collecting. My only retort is that bent over is bent over, we need to take turns. That lasts all of five minutes before we move onto another project, perhaps creating good dirt.

Natural phenomena continue to impress. We revel in the endless days of blue skies, low humidity, warm breezes. There's the occasional rain or impressive hailstorm but we live, eat and breathe the outdoors from dawn to dusk. Inside, *Le Vigne* is equally impressive. We are learning the importance of shutter management, the opening and closing of the enormous exterior shutters on doors and windows to block the strong sunlight. As with many other things in Italy, from doing laundry to making good dirt, closing shutters is a time-consuming process. The combination of well-executed shutter management and two-foot thick stone and brick walls results in cool interior temperatures. The effect is dramatic; like entering an air-conditioned room after standing in full sun. It makes the process worth the effort.

Recently, we experienced a force of nature we'd just as soon avoid. Just before six one morning I was awakened by a loud noise. Groggy and unable to determine the source I did the only sensible thing. I fell asleep for another hour before my morning walk. During the daily gossip session it was casually revealed that there had been an earthquake. All the girls felt it, their dogs and cats felt it and the morning news confirmed it. I raced home to report the startling development. Roger occupied his standard position at the computer, coffee in hand, completely unmoved by my news. He had not felt it, heard it nor sensed it. His personal Richter scale measured even keel. While that solidifies my role as family worrier, the massive iron supports running from one end of our home to the other are witnesses to the reality of this threat. In 1997, near-by Assisi suffered an earthquake severe enough to kill four people and destroy frescoes in the upper vault of the Basilica. Closer to home, the house next to Giuliana's was destroyed during the same quake. The girls tell me that it's best if we experience several slight tremors that alleviate pressure than to suffer one big shock. I can only presume they are right.

With all the unfolding natural beauty, it's easy to find a deep corner of the brain in which to stuff and ignore an earthquake. It's far more satisfying to allow the surroundings and yes, the weather, to envelop us day in and out. At the bottom of the hill, in the town of Colombella, there's a fresh pasta shop, bakery and butcher shop. I often walk to town, pick up a fresh loaf of bread, still warm from the bakery. At times, I carry home trays of lemon ravioli as delicate looking as daisies and particularly tasty with minced fresh sage, olive oil, *parmigiano* and a grind of black pepper. Making my way up the steep rocky hill, passing the little church of Colombella, its bells tolling the hour and then the lilting refrain from *Ave Maria di Lourdes*, I pass fields of swaying grain and volunteer poppies sprouting on the roadside. I hear chickens clucking in the distance and pass a neighbor out for a stroll with her leashed puppy. It sounds far too bucolic to be real but thankfully it is. This is our life in Colombella.

But this too is our life...we've discovered a leak in the apartment kitchen. The outside of the stone and brick wall is damp and Antonio thinks an internal drain is cracked. The masons have returned and are constructing two stories of scaffolding in order to jack-hammer a targeted area of wall in hopes of locating the leak. One of our two pool pumps has died and the high-priced replacement has its own leak, bedeviling Antonio as he tries to repair it. There's no water pressure in one of our two functioning wells and the antiquated circuit breaker panel that controlled its power has self-destructed and must be replaced. The existing irrigation system around the pool and house gardens has crushed sprinkler heads, misdirected heads doing a fine job of watering the driveway while leaving the privet bone dry, a leak reminiscent of the Manneken-Pis statue in Brussels spewing water from a brick flower bed, cracked tubes, hose bibs that froze during the winter months, newly planted flower beds not receiving any water. These are merely the standard issue maintenance problems of an old property.

And what about our self-catering vacation rental business? We have seven weeks of firm reservations for the season but of course, we're seeking more. Abigail, Ralph, Wendy and Frits have been in the business for years and are impressed with our seven bookings. Abigail tells us it took two years before they were full and we should exercise...*pazienza*. We pursue all leads, establish ties with travel agents, mine our rolodexes for potential contacts and work on ways to differentiate *Le Vigne* from the thousands of rental offerings that exist in Italy.

Meanwhile, we enjoy this life. We take turns dining outdoors on our respective terraces with Mary and Don when they remain in town long enough to play. Our circle of acquaintances grows. People are kind, generous, friendly. Our accountant is coming for dinner this week and we'll repay him for the property tax he shelled out on our behalf last December. People who attended The Party are inviting us to their homes for dinner. Margherita and Michele entertained us in their tiny apartment where we feasted on a fish and seafood meal. Our place settings were charmingly labeled, Roger and Jone. Caroline and Augusto host a dinner party that draws us into a group of their lifelong friends; a mix of Americans, Italians and French who seamlessly transition from language to language.

So it is in this contented, *tranquillo*, relaxed, blissful state that we move forward into our first summer season of life in Italy.

It's All About Clothing

Emerging from our renovation cloud gave me a chance to open my eyes to our surroundings. Not the natural beauty but the fashion and design surroundings that contribute to Italy's worldwide trend-setting stature. Milan may be the originator of this standard for the country and much of the world but the unmistakable handprint of style is everywhere. One would expect the *centro* of Perugia to be loaded with high-end designer shops but even tiny Colombella keeps its eye on fashion. Two large clothing stores, less than a few kilometers apart, are our town's anchors.

One store belongs to Giovanna and her family. We don't know the family owning the other but both stores stock enormous inventories including men's, women's and children's clothing, outerwear, lingerie, accessories, shoes, purses, and the occasional bath towel, shower curtain and bed linen. The stores must market to neighboring towns because Colombella's small population can't single-handedly support such shopping enthusiasm. The parking lots are always full yet the inventories never seem to diminish. The clientele indulges in just the activity the designers want – shopping to revamp wardrobes each and every season.

Seasonal revamping is important. Twice a year, in early January and late August, massive *saldi,* sales, are held throughout the country. Last season's clothing is offered at drastically reduced prices to make way for the latest fashions. Semi-annual discounting is a different approach from the States where any day can be called a sale day. Here, the limited sale dates percolate customers' pent-up shopping momentum six months at a clip. By the time January and August roll around, the steady simmer converts to full boil and shoppers bolt from the starting gates ready to gobble up the bargains.

Our ongoing education of life in Italy extends to fashion. Sizes have no correlation to anything familiar. While size six may be the new fourteen according to *The Devil Wears Prada*, imagine what the style mavens would say about size forty-two. Sometimes goods are labeled for sale in other European countries and an entirely different numbering system from the Italian one is used. Until the numbers become mentally imprinted, it's best to simply try on a pair of pants and move up or down in size depending on fit.

Fit is a subjective concept. It's usually accompanied by the word tight. Constrictingly tight is the goal and Italian women large and small embrace the style. I've learned not to rely on any advice from a salesperson who insists I'm wearing clothing at least one size too large. I don't want to achieve baggy, just enough room to avoid the look of a sausage. I hold my ground but I'm not the norm.

The stereotype of a big, fat Italian mamma is unfounded. For the most part, Italians are trim and fit, obesity is rare and exercise is incorporated into daily life. Walking to the far end of a property, riding a bicycle to the market, household chores, gardening, hanging laundry all combine to eliminate the need for an hour of spinning at the local gym. It's a lifestyle different from that of a typical sedentary American.

Sizing is a problem for Roger. Take shoes for instance. Roger wears a fifteen and while not all stores in the States stock fifteens there are enough fine ones that do. His favorite, most comfortable shoes are made of supple leather that molds to his feet. The irony? They're made in Italy, in Le Marche, a region a mere two hour drive east of Colombella. A trip to the manufacturer resulted only in frustration. We learned that while they do indeed manufacture his favorites in his size, all of them are immediately exported to Nordstrom which is where he buys them in Atlanta, Boca Raton and San Diego. There's simply no market for a size fifty in Italy.

Women's shoe sizes are different but easier to discern than clothing sizes. Thirty-five equals size five, thirty-six is six, forty is ten. There are no half sizes. In terms of style, pointy toes have been supplemented by ballet flats with rounded toes yet Italians remain enamored with the points. Women insist that the pointies are comfortable because one's toes never extend all the way into the pointy part. This translates to an extra two inches of length. The pointier the better. The look is excessive, exaggerated. If I make the concession that pointy shoes are indeed comfortable, I still need to learn how to walk in these things. Climbing steps is a challenge. The additional inches force the foot farther back on each stair tread. I could walk on my tip-toes but the points get in the way. I can crabwalk or walk in a modified second position, feet pointing ten to two or do a combination of both. Practice is required not to trip or scuff the points.

Once steps are mastered, heels become another concern. They're as narrow as the front is pointy. They are also high - skyscraper, Jimmy Choo, Manolo high. And they catch in the brick and cobblestone streets paving every medieval village. All these points, heels and height could explain why the second most popular shoe style in Italy is the glorified, beautified, stylized, face-lifted, no relation to a Ked, sneaker.

But as tricked out as the sneaker has become it can't compete with pointy high heels during *passeggiata*. The *passeggiata* is the early evening stroll on the main pedestrian street of town. In Perugia, the *passeggiata* takes place on the *Corso Vannucci*, the beautiful wide boulevard bracketed by the *Rocca Paolina* and the *Fontana Maggiore*. It's where double-cheek air kisses reach an art form, where one goes to see and be seen, to have a coffee, to eye one another up and down, to grudgingly acknowledge an elegant look or cattily deride an unwise choice. It is the ultimate pay-off, the reward for exquisite wardrobe selection, revamping and execution.

There's an open air shopping arcade officially known as The Mall just south of Florence. It's built with tourists in mind; shuttle buses run continuously between Florence hotels and The Mall and there's no closing for lunch. A small café on site offers a quick, light lunch so as not to disrupt the inveterate shopper. All the big names are there – Armani, Gucci, Valentino, Loro Piano, Bottega Veneta, Ferragamo, Perla, Yves Saint Laurent. Bargains can be found but a seven thousand Euro Valentino gown only looks marginally more attractive at the rock bottom price of thirty-five hundred.

The glaring omission in The Mall's cavalcade of fashion stars is Prada. Not to despair. Prada and labels that are part of the Prada family (Miu Miu, Jil Sander, Helmut Lang) are available at the only Prada factory outlet in the world which happens to be in Tuscany. While road signage is plentiful and clear for The Mall, signage for the Prada outlet is non-existent. So confident are the owners that they will be found, they expend no effort in advertising their location and they're right. Despite the attempt at anonymity, Prada is the worst-kept secret around. The building is unmarked, non-descript. Regardless, it's as though the shoppers have homing devices leading them directly to the end of the rainbow.

At the other end of the fashion spectrum are the weekly local markets. Shoe-horned between the live chicks and the *porchetta* wagon is the occasional clothing vendor offering jeans, sweaters, jackets, underwear, scarves and pajamas at low prices. Week after week, the same goods are displayed in wire racks and inverted open umbrellas, changing only when the seasons change. The booths are always packed. Customers do the Italian line thing and elbow each other out of the way, grabbing the same scarf or denim jacket they man-handled last week. It's a little circus with the vendor promising high quality and the customer insisting on deep discounts.

Closer to home there is a cashmere and knitwear outlet in the *zona industriale* of Ponte Felcino. The men and women's clothing is finely constructed; confirmation that the Made in Italy label still matters. The goods are exquisite; not too trendy, not too Mrs. Doubtfire. Exceptional detailing in the form of buttons, ribbons or pockets, inventive use of fabric and yarns, colors ranging from bold to pastel and reasonable outlet prices combine to make Tricot Longhin a frequent shopping destination. Three raven-haired beauties work at the outlet, one of whom is the print model for the most recent line of clothing. We feel as though we know a star.

In contrast to the elegant promenade that is the *passeggiata* is a stroll at the seashore with the Italians. It's apparent that the collective Italian psyche possesses a healthy self-image as evidenced by bathing suit choices. Women, regardless of age or shape, are confident enough to wear a bikini. Not a demure two-piece, not a tankini, not a bikini top with a modest little skirt to cover bulges that exist on everyone except air-brushed centerfold pin-ups, but rather full-on, flesh baring, love me the way I am bikinis. Even men wear those tight Speedo swimsuits. Here's a thought. Let's put U.N. resources to good use and institute a mandatory worldwide ban of Speedos outside of Olympic competition. As trim and fit as Italians tend to be, some are more suited for bikinis but no one other than a water polo player is suited for a Speedo.

Fashion and weather are related but not just in the obvious ways. In Italy, the calendar trumps the thermometer. November first calls for bundling. If a balmy day happens to break through the typical winter gloom, an Italian will not shed a single sweater let alone a coat. Redundant, tautological philosophy is at work here: It is November therefore a sweater and coat are worn. The same reasoning would apply on the twentieth of March. That day still qualifies as winter even if it's sunny and warm. Do not jettison the jacket and be prepared to hear about it if you do.

Roger runs hot, he's just built that way. He favors short-sleeve shirts and padding around the house in bare feet even in winter. The Italians are appalled, scolding him mightily, gesturing with a finger under the throat and making fake coughing sounds. They believe there is direct cause and effect: walking barefoot in the house in winter will result in illness. It is a certainty. One will be struck with either a *raffreddore*, a cold without fever or worse, *influenza,* a cold with fever. Every change of season brings forth an entire population sneezing and sniffling and the cause is always the result of not having dressed warmly enough for the calendar.

An integral component of proper bundling and swaddling is the omnipresent neck-protecting scarf. Men, women and children wear scarves. My friend Miriam noted that if you don't have a scarf upon entering the country, one will be issued to you at the border. Scarves serve a dual purpose. They make a fashion statement and function as a medical device. They add flair and at the same time offer protection against the dreaded *mal di gola* or sore throat. Little did Burberry know that by blanketing the population in their trademark plaid scarf they could also make health claims.

In terms of style, the prescribed way to wear scarves has evolved based on arbitrary fashion dictates. Last year, scarves were placed in front of the neck and the two ends were then circled behind the neck and brought back to hang in front. Out of nowhere, a massive simultaneous mind-meld occurred and a new procedure was implemented. Now the procedure is to double the scarf, place it behind the neck and loop the loose ends through the opening in front of the neck. How did everyone know? Who issued the memo and why didn't I get one?

Italian clothing can be very complicated. Not just the sizes or determining the fit but the construction of shirts, pants, skirts, dresses. Drawstrings, criss-crosses, rucheing, zippers, latches, clasps, multiple pockets, glittery straps, metallic studs, ribbons, bands, flares, asymmetrical lines. Do the straps go over the shoulders or behind the back? Do the zippers stay zipped? Are shirt tails in or out? Are belts worn at the waist or on the hips? Are they even belted? There's a generational thing going on and if I were young I'd know this by sheer osmosis but in the meantime I can't figure out how to get into this gear.

Tee shirts, purses, jeans, hoodies all have writing on them and always in English. "I'm a God Animal," "Wam, Bam, Thank you Man," "Princess Inside," "Stay Single," "Remove Before Flight," "Want to see my Big Bamboo?," "It's so Difficult to Be Calamity Jane." They all beg so very many questions. It's a given the wearer has no clue as to the meaning of the emblazoned words. I know, they ask me. You'd think a designer would seek help with translation before producing a million tees that say "I Only Sleep with the Best."

Despite the semi-annual sales, the Italians we've met don't own hundreds of clothing items. They buy fewer items but of higher quality. They wear the same thing on multiple occasions and there's no negativity. Clothing costs and costs associated with clothing care – laundering, drying, ironing and storage are factors in this pared down existence. We too have adopted this approach. Partially it's a result of our different lifestyle. Life at *Le Vigne* doesn't call for much dress-up. Jeans in the winter and capris in the warmer months cover most eventualities. Limited closet space applies to us as well. It's quite a departure. All those special wardrobe shipping containers that we so carefully packed in Atlanta sat untouched for months. By now, we've given most of the goods to charity. They simply have no place in our new world.

Fashion is designed to be a moving target. To remain current and in style, one must buy seasonally, continuously. It takes time, study, effort. It takes being a dedicated shopper to know if exposed midriffs are in or out. Are flared pants the look or stovepipe? Should they drag on the ground or stop above the ankle? Do jeans ride on the hips or dip lower? Are purses tiny or huge? The beauty of living in the countryside with a limited wardrobe is not spending money on clothes that will be worn rarely and thus fall out of favor in a blink. It's almost a relief to drop out of the competition, miss the highs and lows and instead settle on a look that hopefully won't embarrass.

Having said that, I've broken out of the mid-range upon occasion. When Giuliana, she of critical eye and high fashion sense, throws a *molto fru-fru* my way, no translation is required and I know I've arrived at some fashion level achieving an Italian seal of approval. Every once in a while an Italian will ask me for directions. This wouldn't happen unless there was something about me that made the inquirer think I too was Italian. Clothing is the only external clue so my façade must not be screaming, "I'm an American tourist." It's like two toddlers approaching each other for the first time. They sense inherent, unspoken similarities. They've found common ground, something familiar and recognizable and can communicate in their own language. I like the affirmation that tells us we're slowly blending into our environment.

In this land where style ranges from high-end couture to low-brow cotton house dress, I have reduced all the clutter to its pure essence and found my all-time favorite fashion item. It's a bra. It's not particularly revealing or fancy. It's not something Howard Hughes would have designed for Jane Russell. It's rather simple in comparison to so many complex Italian clothing items. And what makes this bra so special? The transparent plastic straps. I know the trend is to wear a brightly colored bra under a white tank and make sure the straps are exposed. I can't quite work up to that look so the seemingly invisible straps are perfect for my tanks, camisoles and other shoulder-bearing tops. When I've worn it in the States, everyone wants to know where I got it since the novelty has yet to arrive. That catapults me to the leading edge of fashion for my fifteen minutes. Considering that's my big style discovery, you might want to turn to *Vogue* for a more comprehensive report.

Meanwhile, I'm trying to convince Roger he needs a pair of capris for the summer. That's a fashion leap he's not likely to make. I'd have greater success getting him to wear mascara. For now, there's little risk that an Italian is going to ask him for directions. Maybe next year.

Summertime

Every newspaper in Europe proclaimed this was the hottest summer on record. The heat wave that swept the continent smothered Italy in unsafe, unhealthy and sometimes deadly temperatures. Endless days of forty degree (110F) heat baked everything, including people. *Che caldo,* what heat, was uttered by every man, woman and child. Even Roger would greet a neighbor with the phrase that proved to be the sum of his Italian meteorological vocabulary. No matter; those two words were enough to keep a conversation going until I appeared to say yet again, *che caldo.*

Farmers were devastated. Sunflowers are supposed to cycle from their peak of full-faced yellow beauty in July to slumped brown mop heads in late September. Their seeds must be fully dried before being pressed into oil. However, these extremes were simply too much and harvesting was in mid-August.

In Umbria, only feed corn and tobacco are irrigated. But wells ran dry. Corn fields were thinned thatch-colored plots and tobacco leaves were filled with holes resulting in dismal harvests. We were lucky. After the repair of the damaged circuit breaker panel, we had two functioning wells and an extensive irrigation system. Constant watering couldn't make up for the lack of rain and the hellish temperatures. The *giardin-orto* struggled as did the ivy, lavender and rosemary seedlings desperately trying to throw down roots on the block walls.

Indoor temperatures were equally stifling. Shutter management was a great concept but week after week at such extremes left us gasping. The air conditioning units that we were so proud of could do little in the face of high ceilings and even higher temperatures. We were arrogant and here was our come-uppance. Occasionally a breeze would build but it was the wrong kind, the unwelcome *scirocco*.

Despite the heat, I liked the summer - daylight lasting until nine thirty or ten at night. I liked the contrast to the early, unexpected afternoon darkness of winter. I liked the low humidity. Roger found this laughable and reminded me of a tee shirt I used to own, purchased in Arizona. It depicted a skeleton saying, "...but it's a dry heat." Having lived in Miami and Atlanta, I knew that high humidity would make this much worse. But he was right; these were the dog days of summer – a fitting phrase considering its connection with the Romans. The ancients could see Sirius, the Dog Star, in the late July and early August sky. The "dog days" became associated with spoiled food, disease, lethargy, failed crops and rabid dogs.

Everyone sought respite in some way. Our morning walks began progressively earlier. All winter long, Giuliana and I scampered up the final hill on our way home. Now we groan through that daily trudge, gasping about our lack of stamina. During the winter, we sought the sunshine. Now we trekked through deep woods. Stores could not keep *ventilatore,* fans, in stock. We bought a dozen, including two standing, wind-tunnel versions. The power company grid shut down for hours at a time. We suffered brown-outs and black-outs that threw our sensitive little computer into a tailspin. We'd jump into the pool, fully clothed because we couldn't resist. We instituted earlier summer work hours for Mick because by noon it was unbearable. Roger would drive to the bottom of the hill twice a day; once to collect Mick and wine bottles and then to drop him off. It was simply too hot for him to walk.

If it was too hot to walk, it was way too hot to cook. Last winter, Giovanna told me to look forward to the summer months when there's a different *sagra* every night and I won't have to cook until early fall. At the time, wrapped in scarves and ear muffs, our breath visible in the chilled air, I couldn't imagine not spending part of every day cooking in my yet to be completed gourmet kitchen. But her prediction proved true.

The *sagra* is a ten-day outdoor festival, a fundraiser held by local communities. Earnings remain local and are poured back into recreational centers that are packed with children year-round. The closest American counterpart to a *sagra* would be a town fair. Every town holds an annual *sagra* that begins at eight in the evening and runs until two or three in the morning. There are carnival rides for the very young, a raffle with the chance to win a donated *prosciutto* or costume jewelry, booths selling candy and balloons. Nightly entertainment varies – from orchestras playing dance music to outdoor theatre to roller skating exhibitions to soccer matches to fashion shows. After midnight, a pub opens featuring a DJ spinning techno and the young people create their own *passeggiata*. It's a view of Italy not often seen by tourists as a *sagra* is the most local of events.

But the real draw of every *sagra* is food. Originally, the food was indigenous to the town and in some cases that remains true. Other towns simply jumped on the *sagra* bandwagon having seen the popularity and profitability of the event. The *sagra della porchetta* is held in Costano, the pig farming center of Umbria. The onion festival, *sagra delle cipolle* takes place in Cannara where onion fields stretch for miles. Meanwhile, there's the *sagra* in Colombella every September where asparagus is the star. While fresh, wild asparagus is widely available in the woods surrounding Colombella in April, only frozen exists in September. Why Colombella chose asparagus is beyond me and everyone else. It would have made more sense to offer *colomba* or dove and play off the corruption of the town name but asparagus it is; in soups, on *bruschetta*, in pasta and *risotto*.

The *sagre dei funghi, degli spaghetti alla carbonara, dei tartufi,* even *della nutella* keep us out evenings, eating mushrooms, pasta with eggs and *pancetta*, truffles, even chocolate hazelnut cream. There are varying degrees of sophistication but the basic premise is the same. Staffed by volunteer labor, the festivals take on an amateur feel and naiveté that can sway between charming and frustrating. We learned to arrive early to avoid the crowds and lessen the confusion.

Tourists would have a difficult time at a *sagra* unless someone were there to guide them. There are no instructions. While the set-up is similar from *sagra* to *sagra* there are enough variations to keep us on our toes and focus on the ultimate reward – the food.

The first thing to do is park, usually in a fallow field converted for just this purpose. Some lots are staffed with volunteers while others are free-for-alls making a mockery of order. Next, choose a seat at a pre-numbered picnic table and leave some assertive or better yet aggressive group member to protect needed seats. Keys, purses, pens or hats zealously guard the spots. Another group member then peruses the menu board to make food selections. There are pre-printed forms to complete using little yellow golf course pencils. Once decided, elbow into line, approach a wooden booth and surrender the form to the volunteer.

The volunteer will ask for the table number, enter it and the menu choices into a computer. The order is electronically dispatched to the kitchen and the customer is provided with a computer-generated copy. This level of efficiency at a bush-league, small town, volunteer-staffed hoe-down when banks can't master account transfers in less than six months, is a marvel. The priorities are clear; when it comes to food, only leading-edge technology will do.

Before returning to the table, drinks are ordered from a different booth. Water, Coke, beer and inexpensive wines are available, paid for and carried back to the picnic table. By now, the assertive one left behind is relieved to see a friendly face after repelling the invaders. Meanwhile, a precious youngster wearing a *sagra* tee shirt has appeared to set the table with paper place mats, plastic utensils and cups. Just when hope is gone, when the surrounding tables have received their food, when the wine bottle is half empty and people are hovering menacingly, another equally precious youngster appears with trays of food. The server cross checks her receipt against ours and once confirmed, collects our copy and chirps, "*Buon appetito*" as we begin eating.

Despite arriving early at the *porchetta sagra*, the place was mobbed. Parking lots were already filled and order gave way to anarchy, resulting in criss-crossed, double and triple parked jumbles of Puntos. Hoarding of entire tables was common. An elderly grandmother was often left behind as the defender. It was a clever ploy. You'd have to be a real jerk to kick out grandma. Truth be told, she could hold her own handily.

Porchetta was a lunch staple for us as we bought the meat sandwiches weekly at the local market. The *porchetta* at the *sagra* reached a new standard. It was the freshest, leanest most savory pork ever. Even the air was scented with the mouth-watering aromas of fennel, garlic and roasted pork. After working our way through the goat rope (or should I say pig rope) of parking, seat selection, table protection, ordering and food delivery we were entertained by a roaming four-piece brass band. The horn players trailed unsuspecting customers, managed to teach dogs to bark in time to the music and showered embarrassed servers with kisses. Reluctantly turning over our table to famished patrons, we followed the brass band as they continued their mischievous antics. When their break came, the orchestra began and seating near the dance floor became just as coveted as picnic table seating had been. Polkas yielded to other partnered dances and then hundreds jumped up to perform the electric slide.

Our favorite *sagra* so far is the onion one in Cannara. The *centro* of Cannara is large and divided into four neighborhoods. Each of the four creates a tented area filled with tightly packed picnic tables and benches. Each has its own kitchen offering a different menu, creating a competitive atmosphere. Fourteen of us caravanned to Cannara with Renato and Giuliana as our leaders. They knew precisely which tent we were to patronize. Despite our best intentions to arrive early, herding fourteen was not easy. Staying together on the highway and in the parking lot was a challenge. The *sagra delle cipolle* must be everyone's favorite *sagra,* not just ours.

The narrow streets and alleyways of Cannara were sardine packed with people. We stuck with Renato as we would never find our way to the proper tent let alone figure out how to get out of town without him. His tent choice was as crowded as all the others but at the far end he found an entire empty table. The reserved signs did nothing to dissuade him from commandeering the protected space. Our mild-mannered neighbor insisted we sit. This *sagra* was at the higher end of sophistication and organization and instead of fresh-faced youngsters serving and clearing, we were treated to hard-boiled waitresses who actually took our orders while we sat and reviewed menus. One such egg spotted us in the act of acquisition and headed our way. Arms akimbo, scowl on her face, finger wagging in that giant **S** shape, she poured forth with a fast-paced litany of reasons why we could not use this table. Renato stood his ground, gave her the praying hand gesture in response to her finger wag, explained that fourteen of us had driven over thirty kilometers for this meal and the reserved guests weren't here and we promised to eat quickly. She grudgingly relented. Life in Italy is the epitome of seeking forgiveness rather than permission.

The *sagra* was a showcase of the onion's versatility. All courses starred onion and each item tasted unique: from onion soup to *schiacciata* (meaning crushed or flattened, it's thin-crust pizza bread smothered in onions and rosemary), to onion *risotto* to *tagliatelle* with onions and mushrooms to grilled sausage and onions to pork cutlets with almonds and onions to roasted onions. There was even an onion dessert though none of us had room or courage.

After dinner we strolled through town. Vendors lined the narrow streets selling braided ropes of onions and garlics of varying sizes, colors, shapes and strengths. Farmers bellowed to potential customers to buy, buy, buy, insisting their goods were superior. Onions were everywhere – purple, yellow, white skins; squat cubes, big round balls, tear drops, tiny pearls, and the promise of flavors ranging from sweet to mild to strong.

The main *piazza* was converted to a theatre with stadium seating. A play presented in dialect caused laughter to ripple through the audience. Even we understood the parody of Italian country life it depicted – a hovering mother, beleaguered father, rebellious children, spunky grandmother. A dance school waited in the wings; three year olds in tutus and eighteen year olds in toe shoes warming up for their performance.

The *sagra* saved us from the heat of the evening kitchen. Sometimes a breeze would stir in one of these hilltop towns providing blessed relief from the torrid days. What proved to be relief for us caused locals to scurry for sweaters and scarves. We learned that such sudden, drastic swings of temperatures are the cause of colds, sore throats and flu just as much as walking in the house barefoot in winter.

The apex of summer is *ferragosto,* Assumption Day, on the fifteenth of August. While it is a religious holiday, it is more secularly known as the start of the traditional summer vacation season. Italians flock to the sea all summer long but particularly during *ferragosto.* They parade along the shore in all manner and sort of the previously described skimpy attire. But many simply remain at water's edge or in lounge chairs stacked like cord wood, not even dipping a toe into the briny sea. Despite the shimmery mirage, Death Valley kind of blistering heat, we notice that the mass of humanity does not readily frolic in the ocean. Why are they not diving in? Why the hesitation?

Summertime old wives' tales rival those of winter. The excuses are plentiful: the air's too hot and the water's too cold or the water will cause a spasm in my back or my ears get blocked easily or the water stings my eyes or I'm just now recovering from a *mal di gola* that kept me in bed for weeks last winter. All the above may be true but in addition to the delicate Italian constitution there is another dirty little secret at play. Many Italians don't know how to swim. The numbers are dwindling as more and more youngsters have taken lessons but it is remarkable that so many people inhabiting a peninsula are not swimmers by nature.

If sea water exceeding the temperature of bath water can cause such imbalances in Italian homeostasis, just imagine what havoc can be created by air conditioning. Typically, homes are not air-conditioned but some businesses are and that spawns chills, spasms, aches and pains. The legions of Pandas and Puntos filling the highways are unequipped with air conditioners but if one should have such a cooling system, it rests untouched. The shock of the cold air after exposure to hot ambient air is certain to cause a stiff neck, sore throat or worse.

The Blessing

It was during the height of the summer, when the heat wave was most intense, that we took part in an unusual exercise. We asked Don Gilberto, the local priest to bless our house. Normally, houses and businesses are blessed once a year. During Lent, as hearts and minds are cleansed the home is cleansed as well. Don Gilberto maintains a busy schedule, published in the weekly church newsletter, traveling from house to house, blessing each home and its inhabitants. We were in the throes of demolition when the priest made his way from Federico's house, passing ours on the way to Giuliana's. He offered to stop but we declined as there was no opportunity to undertake either metaphorical or actual spring cleaning. In a move of procrastination that he hoped would be forgotten, Roger had me tell Don Gilberto that we'd like him to bless the house later in the year when my mother returned.

All chickens come home to roost, including Mamma Ruta and house blessings. Roger and I were treading on unfamiliar ground so I consulted with the experts. My morning walking friends gave advice to *fare bella figura,* to make a good impression. After many question and answer sessions I learned that I should set a small table with a white tablecloth and a single candle. I was to include a small religious item on the table. I should offer the priest coffee and dessert and provide a small contribution to the parish.

It was this "small contribution" that had me stuck and provoked endless discussion. How much is an appropriate amount? Whatever you think.

Yes, I understand, but more or less, how much? That's entirely up to you. OK, but can you give me a general sense; five Euro or one hundred Euro? Anything you want to do is fine. No blasphemy intended but *mamma frigging mia,* can someone not give me a direct answer? Apparently not. We were left to our own devices so we placed a fifty Euro note in a sealed envelope and hoped for the best.

It was a stingingly hot Sunday afternoon when Don Gilberto arrived, well-worn briefcase in hand, shirt stained dark with sweat after driving his modest Fiat without air conditioning. He greeted the three of us politely and we asked him to have a seat at the table in the *soggiorno.* There the four of us sat in palpable awkwardness. Don Gilberto was not a big conversationalist and my fellow Americans couldn't communicate with him on their own. Roger, who under normal circumstances can talk to a paper bag had uncharacteristically lost his tongue; not even a *che caldo*. Neither Roger nor Mom could read my dagger messages, "Work with me people, I'm dyin' here." I attempted small talk, dutifully translating for all parties. I asked the priest about his life and his travels. He asked where we were from in the United States and *come mai* Colombella. The ticking of the kitchen clock filled the room, occasionally interrupted by the great Italian conversation fillers of *insomma* or *allora,* so or then or well. In between Mom or Roger would burst forth with equally sparkling dialogue along the lines of how nice or that's interesting. The beads of sweat pooling on my nose were heat as well as tension induced.

I offered coffee and some of the dessert I had prepared. Don Gilberto accepted only coffee. Perhaps it was the fly, roughly the size of a marble, seeking clearance to land on the dessert, that gave him pause. I now understood the reason for all those half globe food hats at Sidis and kicked myself for not owning a few. We waited patiently and in silence as Don Gilberto added several spoonfuls of sugar to his coffee. The stirring competed with the ticking for aural prominence. Thankfully he drank coffee just like every other Italian and in seconds it was gone. He cleared his throat and suggested we get started.

There was no need to ask twice. I pointed to the table covered in white and the single unlit candle. I mentally stifled a snort remembering what Roger asked when he saw me arranging the table – are we conducting a séance or a blessing? A pinched look covered the priest's face as he gazed at the only religious item I owned. It was a prayer card celebrating the sixtieth anniversary of the priesthood of a family friend. Father Kidwell was a Jesuit and this card in the land of the Franciscans was not welcomed.

I sensed our blessing sliding away. Don Gilberto disliked the militancy associated with the Jesuits. I explained that Father Kidwell was important to us, having offered much-needed comfort at the time of my father's death. This softened the priest's tone and he finally acknowledged the positive role the Jesuits played in education.

While the card stayed, Don Gilberto retrieved a framed photograph of the carved crucifix in the Colombella church adding that to the table. He asked that I light the candle. He held a dog-eared prayer book and explained that years ago the blessings were conducted in every room in the house. More recently, one blessing was made but it applied to the entire house. He asked us to choose. I felt I was on pretty safe ground not translating the question and told him we'd opt for the abbreviated program. He opened the book and with the speed that comes from years of practice and thousands of blessings, he conferred grace on our home and asked God to keep us safe, happy and healthy. *Le Vigne* had been blessed.

As he gathered his things, we gave him the envelope and he placed it unopened into his bag. After all the hand wringing we never learned if our donation was appropriate. Maybe that was the point. The end result mattered; it was a beautiful, touching moment that Mom had unwittingly engineered. The peaceful glow lasted all of five minutes. As we walked Don Gilberto out to the front gate, he said he looked forward to coming back for another blessing next spring. Conveniently forgetting that this is an annual rite, Roger's head snapped back, "You mean we didn't get the lifetime version?" I mumbled some pleasantries to the priest in an effort to mask the surprise in Roger's voice. Perhaps we did.

The Hospitality Business

The hot summer months were busy. Mom wasn't our only visitor. Roger's mother and her Breakfast Club pal Claire came, Clayton and Cameron returned and dozens of friends visited. And there were guests - real, live, self-catering vacation rental, paying guests. Despite the heat, the strength of the Euro, the war, SARS, terrorism, economic downturns, travel fears and all the other events conspiring against us, we had guests.

It's been fun, hectic, fast-paced, challenging and rewarding. Mick, Roger and I have become dynamos at cleaning, laundry and rapid restocking of the apartment. We've prepared dinners, conducted cooking classes and wine tastings, handled pre-arrival grocery shopping, made luncheon reservations, raked the bocce court, dragged the clay tennis court, handled airport transfers, picked up rental cars, conducted sightseeing tours and arranged for guides. We've introduced our guests to our favorite restaurants, towns, *sagre*, drivers, ceramic artisans, vineyards, produce markets, cashmere outlets, bakeries, pasta shops, fish markets and butchers. On any given day we wear dozens of hats; acting as host, gardener, cook, concierge, translator, banker, booking agent, marketer, launderer, pool cleaner, secretary, chronicler, travel agent, guide, photographer, maintenance and repair people. This takes place when we're not building block walls, removing rocks and weeds from the olive grove, replumbing the irrigation system, planting and maintaining gardens, decorating our home, translating documents, reworking the electrical and heating system and generally conducting our everyday business.

We went to the jazz festival in Perugia, the monthly outdoor antique market in Arezzo, the linen shops of Montefalco. We took our guests to Assisi, Gubbio, Todi and Cortona. We went to the charming pink stone city of Spello, draped on a hillside. Beautiful on any day, it is especially enchanting on the morning of the *Infiorata*. Held on the feast of the Corpus Domini in late spring, the streets and alleyways are covered with floral carpets; think Tournament of Roses floats. Not only are the tapestries treats to the eye, the smell of the various flowers and herbs infuses the air with its own beauty.

We went to the small medieval village of Bevagna which holds an archery competition. A centuries-old event, the competition involves the entire town as the inhabitants train throughout the year. Citizens don elaborate period costume and artisans display wares produced in the style of their ancestors – paper, basket and candle making, wrought iron. Meats are grilled over huge outdoor fires. Bands of musicians, drill teams, and men and women on horseback parade through town in colorful pageantry. Amidst the sumptuous velvet and brocade, the chain mail and helmets, the boots, the standards, banners, cross bows and quivers of arrows, it's easy to envision this town as it once was.

We had no idea what we were getting into with hosting strangers in our home. Awaiting the arrival of our very first guests, total strangers from the U.K., we panicked. What have we done? We don't know this British couple and their three boys ages six, four and two. The apartment is not the least bit child-proof. Suddenly, disaster was written over every outlet, cupboard and floor to ceiling shelf filled with china. Why this had not occurred to us sooner made no difference at this point, the guests were due shortly. But from the moment they arrived, extolling the beauty of *Le Vigne*, we calmed. We have been spoiled by this lovely family.

Even the children were angels; in behavior and looks. They adored Roger who entertained them with Gator rides around the *piazza*. They called him B.F.G. and while I was prepared for this to stand for the worst it was simply a reference to Roald Dahl's Big Friendly Giant. We toured together and ate together. The two older boys enjoyed watching us toast each other as we clinked our wine glasses at the start of every meal. *Cincin* is the standard Italian toast. It is short for *cent'anni,* in essence, may you live a hundred years. To them it sounded like *chin, chin* and every subsequent toast had them tapping their chins together.

The summer heat wave broke on the first of September. It was like drawing an enormous shade, making mornings and evenings cool and days mild and breezy. We abandoned shutter management and ate *pranzo* and *cena* outdoors. The true benefit of low humidity became apparent.

We admitted to a little melancholy watching our last guests of the season leave at the end of October. Their departure meant there was no need to rapidly clean and restock the apartment, purchase fresh bread and pasta, prepare a welcoming dinner, arrange for tours or translate menus and cooking classes. It meant we would not hear chairs scraping on the tile floor upstairs as guests backed away from the breakfast table. It meant we wouldn't hear giggling from the children splashing on floats in the pool. It meant our first hosting season had come to a successful end. We had met wonderful people who arrived as strangers but became friends. We already had bookings for next year, not nearly enough as Roger so often reminded me, but a start.

As our final guests pulled out of the *piazza* after hugs and promises to remain in touch, Antonio arrived with several workmen to cover the pool. It was a brilliant fall day and it seemed a shame to lose the view of the glistening water until next spring. The workmen had created a new tarp and this was its maiden run. We leaned out of the apartment window, taking birds-eye view photos as they dragged the blue-green coated plastic across the pool. We congratulated ourselves, taking a moment to reflect on our accomplishments. But the mood quickly vanished as we watched the frustrated workmen struggle with one corner of the cover; it was too short. We abandoned our fourth floor aerie to join everyone poolside. Antonio wasn't happy and Roger started tapping one of those famous size-fifteen feet, a well known symbol of his dissatisfaction. As quickly as the tarp had been unfurled it disappeared into the workmen's truck.

Soon we will celebrate our first year at *Le Vigne*, poised to repeat some now familiar rituals. We're often asked what we miss most about the States. The givens are family and friends. But there are the little things; cheddar cheese, sushi, an American style shovel, extra large work gloves for Roger, first-run movies. We can import the little things and travel to the States to see the people we miss. But the most important thing we've learned and the most gratifying is that we can honestly say that *Le Vigne* has become home.

Drivetime

*L*anguage and driving still had the two of us joined at the hip. I was in no position to demean Roger's language skills when I had made zero progress on driving a car with manual transmission. Roger, Cameron and others had tried to teach me but the glum reality was self-evident; I could probably learn Chinese, and ancient Greek before I'd be driving one of our cars.

The long-term plan was to get rid of the Trooper and Punto. For the near term though, they would be around. The transfer of documents, assurances of insurance, payment of taxes and inspection fees and other bureaucratic matters were nightmares of epic proportions. It consumed months of translation efforts to untangle information and search for missing details. As complex as the process was for the Punto, it was idle time in a sandbox compared to the Trooper. The Trooper had come from England and still had U.K. plates. It remained registered in England though it physically resided in Italy. The previous owners had tried to register it here but failed. We tried as well. It was impossible. That's a phrase that doesn't sit well with Roger but it was true.

The problem revolved around the chassis and the catalytic converter and emission control standards and that this type of vehicle had never been approved for driving in Italy. We had documentation from Japan, paperwork spanning years and we had contacted various agencies, having lost confidence in Perugia Auto. We finally had our paws on the Trooper registration having obtained it in person from the former owners during a summer visit to the U.K. Duplicitous to the end, we learned from Sue that the Trooper should have returned to England for "motoring" or annual inspection – something that hadn't happened in four years thus subjecting the car and driver to fines. It was here that Roger couldn't resist asking Franny how the large 19th century terra cotta pot looked in her current garden, knowing full well that it sat comfortably in Antonio's front yard. Unable to look him in the eye, she replied that she hadn't yet had time to set up her garden; the pot was still in storage in London.

The ugly up-shot of this vehicle trauma was that the Trooper would remain. Neither vehicle had air-conditioning so during the hottest summer in the history of the world, we were miserable. Mainly we used the Trooper so that Roger could avoid being born every time he entered or exited the Punto. We limited our trips to early mornings when possible. Every excursion was faced with gritted teeth, sticky clothing and bad attitudes. We needed air-conditioning or pistols at forty paces.

Through connections we had made at San Egidio, Perugia's local airport, we met Marino, the man in charge of the rental car counter. Marino spoke English quite well but to this day calls me Jane. A former Italian Naval officer, he was enamored with Roger and his career as a pilot. He was fond of saying, "Remember Roger, right or wrong, the captain is always the captain," followed by a crisp salute, as though Roger needs such reinforcement. Marino stood at mock attention in Roger's presence, portraying the John Wayne role from *In Harm's Way.* He'd grab his pant leg, flapping the material back and forth simulating the wind building on the carrier deck as the planes revved their engines for take off. The performance was hilarious and he never tired of reprising it.

Roger gave Marino the assignment of locating an automatic, air-conditioned station wagon for us to purchase. Until he found one, we would rent. Rental day was momentous. The surgery separating us as conjoined humans was a success. Roger no longer needed to transport me to the grocery store but there were times when separation anxiety prevailed. Trips to the hardware store never occurred solo.

I remembered what it felt like getting my first driver's license. This time, the freedom coming mid-life instead of mid-adolescence was even sweeter. I benefited from our mutually hard-earned knowledge after having spent months of getting lost. Topping off all this pleasure was the added bonus of air-conditioning. Running errands became the new favorite activity and we maturely agreed to take turns rather than openly fight over who got the keys.

It should come as no surprise that the process to obtain an Italian driver's license rivaled obtaining our residency with its own brand of bureaucratic insanity. A kind young man at the local driving school explained the absurd procedure. Italy has a reciprocity agreement with certain countries. We perused the list. All members of the European Community appeared,

South Korea was there, Samoa, but not the United States. This lack of reciprocity means that Italy presumes we have never before driven and have no license, yet long-term rentals for Americans are permitted and a driver's license is required. Recognizing the incongruity of all he had explained, the young man simultaneously laughed, shrugged his shoulders and expelled the oft-used Italian *"Bo,"* pronounced as in bow-tie - the verbal equivalent of a shrug.

Just for grins we asked how to get a license. We envisioned spending hours at a strip shopping center, providing proof of residency, taking an eye test, a written exam and then waiting for the license to arrive in the mail. Our vision was optimistic and delusional. Proof of residency is needed and that would be the simplest task. It would be followed by mandatory attendance at a three month driving school that included classroom instruction covering driving rules and engine maintenance. This would be followed by actual driving lessons. All this in Italian.

We had seen the cars with big signs on top screaming *Scuola Guida*, driving school, and a giant **P** covering half the rear window. The **P** stands for *principiante* or beginner and these cars are equipped with a passenger side clutch and brake for the instructor. After three months of schooling there are both oral and practical exams. There's no opportunity to attend school with a translator or bring the translator to either exam. As the final cherry on this bureaucratic cupcake our comedian told us there was a six-month backlog for the school, the administration of the exams and the processing of the paperwork. Inertia may be our best course of action.

We had already learned important driving lessons without the benefit of attending school. One such lesson was not to drive at all in Rome or Florence. Roger could do it; traffic wasn't the problem. It was the electronic surveillance making it an ironclad certainty that any transgression would result in ticketing and fines. In an attempt to limit traffic in large cities, vehicular restrictions are imposed during certain hours, on certain streets and in certain lanes. After receiving multiple time and date stamped tickets for having committed some unknown offense, we finally got smart and opted for train travel.

There were more lessons. Stay in the right lane unless passing. Left-lane travel could be a frightening proposition with cars appearing out of nowhere, flashing lights and blowing horns. Entrance and egress ramps are constrictingly short and often steeply banked. The concept of merging on an entrance ramp is non-existent. Drivers race to the end of the entrance ramp and are forced to sit in place unless the lane is clear. There's no attempt to begin the merging process from the start of the entrance ramp thereby easing into the flow of traffic.

Intersections are equally dangerous. My theory is that the manual transmission is the primary cause of accidents at T intersections. Drivers are too lazy to change gears and in order to avoid the energy-consuming downshift and braking required at a stop, they simply glide into the intersection in hopes that opposing traffic will allow ingress. Tailgating ensues, horns blare, arms flail, fists shake but the driver slips into the stream or crashes - another instance of forgiveness triumphing over permission.

The Grocery

If Italy wants another secure source of revenue it should license access to grocery stores and their parking lots. Maneuvering in the Sidis' lot is playing adult bumper cars without governors. The defined parking spots marked by white lines are ignored. Everyone wants to park close to the door and if a space is not available the easiest solution is to create one. I often come out to find I've been boxed in on all sides and must return to a cashier to ask her to page the drivers of perhaps a blue Twingo and silver Multipla. An owner saunters out feigning surprise before moving the car.

After parking and obtaining a cart, I brace for the skirmish ahead. The grocery cart must serve as the modern-day chariot in the collective memory of Italians. Carts are weapons and so armed, shoppers will eventually achieve ramming speed starting in the produce section. Driving schools are missing a huge opportunity – a *principiante* sign would be more appropriate on a cart than a car.

The cart itself is complicated as each wheel independently turns 360 degrees. Carts are difficult to maneuver, requiring both hands and strong shoulders to maintain forward momentum while each wheel competes for dominance. Throw in ubiquitous cell phone use and an Italian behind the wheel and we're back to adult bumper cars.

Cart courtesy is non-existent. For a people fixated on *fare bella figura,* there's patent disregard for making a good impression in the grocery store. It's as though the person in front might just purchase the last and best *prosciutto* so arriving first is a universal goal. Aisles are narrow and while I struggle to keep my chariot far left or right, others pay no mind. I patiently wait while Signora decides between the *farfalle,* butterfly pasta, and the *strozzapreti,* priest strangler pasta. My reward is to be ignored. Just like on the open highway, if no eye contact is made I'm invisible. After breaking through the cone of silence with a strong "*Scusi,*" I'm met with the most astonished look; one that says, "Have you been here all along, am I really in the way, oh, but of course, I'll move."

The actual shopping experience called for a steep learning curve. The produce section is small but inviting. Only seasonal fruits and vegetables are available so meals are prepared using the freshest of ingredients. Produce is displayed in crates and each item is flagged with its name, origin, price by weight and a code number. Several racks with plastic bags and gloves are strategically placed throughout the section as are scales with touch screen technology. Grab a glove and a bag, fight off a fellow shopper and settle on the choicest, most fragrant cantaloupe available. Bag the melon, put it on the scale and enter the code from the display. Instantly, a sticker will be ejected pricing the fruit based on weight and the sticker can be slapped onto the bag. Failure to weigh and price the produce will result in certain embarrassment at the *cassa,* cashier. Only a foreigner, holding up the check-out line while the cashier races back to the produce section, would create this crisis.

The next stop is *gastronomia*, the deli counter. A tempting display of breads, *salumi, prosciutto, capocollo, mortadella*, cheeses, olives, prepared foods, fresh pastas and cakes awaits. I subdue the grocery cart and out-maneuver others to take a number. A giant display and recorded message counts down the numbers and when mine is called I place the ticket into a little wicker basket on the counter. Attempting to hand the ticket to the clerk will result in an unpleasant look, as though I tried to offload an air sickness bag.

Ordering here and at the butcher counter is a lesson in metric conversions. There's no getting away with a half pound of sliced *proscuitto*. Know hectograms and kilograms or be able to indicate the desired number of slices and then shout, "*Basta,*" when it's enough.

The dairy case contains heavy cream and cheeses, yogurt and butter but no eggs. Eggs are found unrefrigerated in a separate section. Most milk is aseptically packaged and found next to the sugar in a different aisle.

The butcher case contains identifiable as well as mystery meats. Chickens and turkeys are sold with heads and feet attached. Cuts of meat remain an enigma. I can recognize pork tenderloin but have had little success obtaining beef tenderloin.

A fresh fish counter abuts the butcher and our favorite find there has been fish cakes made with white fish, spinach, egg white, *mozzarella*, herbs and bread crumbs. There are lots of squirmy little fish and others to filet but everything we tried has been too salty and bony.

The greatest amount of space is dedicated to pastas and sauces – two aisles in fact. An occasional surprise surfaces: a bag of tortilla chips, a box of McVitie's digestive biscuits, a container of Uncle Ben's salsa. I knew Uncle Ben made rice, but salsa?

Approaching the check-out counter requires an assertive stance. Waiting in line does not offer respite nor the luxury to read the latest gossip magazine. Mentally and physically prepare for the hurried task ahead. Use the time to good advantage: juggle a wallet, unfurl the grocery bags brought from home for just this purpose and locate the frequent shopper card. If there aren't enough bags, they will be provided at a fee of four Euro cents each. When the time arrives, unload groceries onto the moving belt as the seated cashier scans the card and purchases. She slides the scanned items toward the end of a ramp and it is now the shopper's responsibility to bag the groceries and do so quickly. The ramp is divided because the cashier will finish ringing up purchases before the shopper finishes bagging. The next person's purchases will be shuttled to the other side of the ramp. When the cashier calls out the total, hand over credit card or cash. Using a credit card chews up a bit more time which can be put to good use to finish bagging groceries. Change or credit card is returned to wallet, receipt is retrieved from the cashier, and final items are shoved into already overstuffed bags. With a last check of the divided ramp, grab the grocery cart to exit.

A loaded cart is no easier to manipulate than an empty one. Eggs are practically scrambled by the time they're tucked into the car. Another driver is impatiently waiting to take the soon-to-be vacated parking spot. I still have to return the cart to its rightful spot and retrieve my coin while dodging cars and carts. Finally I can leave the lot, a bit dazed. I've been flung from the grocery store orbit.

Sidis frequent shopper program is an adventure in tacky. Rarely do the benefits result in savings but more often come in the form of ordinary quality household items; a hair dryer, a plastic box for storing shoes, a frying pan, salad servers. A catalog displaying the rewards for shopper loyalty sits at the end of every cashier's divided ramp and shoppers gobble up the catalogs to see what their *PuntoDelizie,* delicious points, will deliver. In a clever ploy to make a profit from the delicious points program, Sidis offers higher quality items at higher point value. Knowing full well that no one could have accumulated that many delicious points, Sidis allows shoppers to combine points and cash to acquire a drill or television or outdoor furniture. Conceivably, one could spend more money to obtain a marginally needed item in the interest of using points. Points expire. Points are not cumulative. Point frenzy ensues and rational thought is supplanted by a mania and the threat of lost delicious points.

We admit to having succumbed to the madness on the first go 'round. The usually cramped aisles of Sidis are near impassable during delicious point season. Gift inventory is piled sky high and check-out becomes even more harried as cashiers have the added responsibility of delivering stuff to shoppers. Having studied the catalog, I was prepared at check-out and ready to receive a cake pan. The cashier scanned my card, confirming sufficient delicious points and promptly advised that the pan was out of stock but could be back ordered. For months I carried around the paperwork for my cake pan. It became my responsibility to check periodically with the cashier to determine whether the pan had arrived. Eventually it did but the whole process left me disenchanted. I think I'll pass on future offers.

A Tractor Named Monica

This entire Sidis discussion has veered me off track (note the vehicle verbiage) from the central topic of driving. While I was running errands in air-conditioned comfort, Roger was in pursuit of his own vehicular nirvana. After much research and investigation, it finally arrived in the form of a shiny, brand new silver and black Lamborghini. This was not a purchase provoked by a mid-life crisis. This Lamborghini is a tractor.

Buying the Lamborghini was a ride of its own. On two occasions we met with a character named Romeo, the largest farm vehicle concessionaire in Perugia, bringing local experts Federico and the younger Grasselli, Luca, to advise us. Both visits took place on days of intense heat which might have explained Romeo's lightweight attire: worn leather bedroom slippers, wife-beater tee shirt and ancient, threadbare, faded plaid shorts. He paraded us through the floor plan, extolling the virtues of one tractor after another. Romeo insisted Roger test-drive the tractors and was thrilled with Roger's eventual choice – a model he declared more beautiful than Monica Bellucci, the young, hot Italian starlet.

The discussion on price took place in Romeo's smoke-filled office. We had to work up to the subject of money, first talking about the weather and our reasons for living in Italy. A female gum-snapping assistant stood at

Romeo's side, pen and paper in hand while he regaled us with stories. In the raspiest of Don Corleone voices he proclaimed his love for Americans and his hatred of Saddam Hussein. Just when I thought I would faint from the heat and smoke he began to talk price. On cue, the assistant moved to an adding machine that had seen fifty years of hard service. He barked out numbers that seemed preposterously high until I realized he spoke in *lire*. Her fingers flew as she made the conversions. Cranks were pulled and tape churned. There were add-ons and value-added taxes and fees and delivery costs and eventually he applied a discount and we haggled and he relented, agreeing on a price.

The assistant moved from the adding machine to a Methuselah-era manual typewriter. She spun contract forms separated by well worn carbon paper into the platen. Years of practice at slapping back the carriage return showed as Romeo, still puffing away, dictated the terms of the purchase, pausing periodically to obtain our address or Roger's birth date or some other salient piece of information. He offered Perugina chocolates which we felt compelled to accept. Meanwhile his assistant stamped copies and collected signatures in triplicate. She cut quite the officious presence in her well-rehearsed role. As we escaped the fumes of his office, finding the stifling outdoor air a vast improvement, Romeo slapped Roger on the back and promised delivery the next day.

The Lamborghini appeared on schedule and Roger immediately christened his newest toy. He tilled the large olive grove to remove weeds and poppies and unearth stones and bricks. I missed the volunteer poppies and sunflowers but they became immediate casualties. Italians don't seem to mind the weeds, bricks and rocks. Fields are so laden with stone that one has to wonder how a young root can make its way to soil. Acres upon acres of tilled earth look as though planes have dropped wood chips onto the land. The color contrast is striking – the brown dirt interrupted by the lighter colored stones.

Our *campo,* on the other hand, must be the smoothest one in Umbria if not Italy. Nothing goes to waste as the weeds are composted and the bricks, stones and even pebbles are collected. In between planting or wall-building or hosting, a quiet afternoon can be spent harvesting rocks. The Gator holds various buckets to easily categorize the rocks by size and shape. I've been over this land for months now and still we find more rock, the turned earth continuing to spew forth an endless supply. The largest and best can be used by the masons for future building projects while the scraps are destined for *blochetti* back fill. The neighbors comment about the powdery field we've created and marvel at Roger's passion for the outdoors. They've dubbed him the *grande coltivatore*, the great farmer, and he's identifiable around town by his height and holstered pruners.

Roger had additional plans for the olive grove. It would not remain cocoa powder silty because he planned to sow grass seed. Once wet, the clay-filled soil turns to muck making it impossible to walk or drive the Gator. This will simply not do during harvest time; we needed the grass under our feet for traction and *bellezza*. Grasselli planted seed and once again our field became the talk of the town. Other fields remain rocky. Other fields remain weed-infested. Other fields might have vegetables planted beneath the olives. Those are other's fields.

Small tufts of grass began to sprout and then thrive thanks to the underground irrigation. Growing grass can mean only one thing – it must be cut. In her current state, the Monica Bellucci look-alike became superfluous. We no longer needed to till the field and if we didn't want to put Monica out to pasture, we best figure out how to adapt her for mowing.

Romeo was thrilled to see us as we purchased a mowing attachment for the Lamborghini. It couldn't arrive soon enough and when it did, Antonio removed the tiller and installed the mower. Straw hat in hand, Roger impatiently stood by until the attachment was in place. Roger saddled the Lamborghini to mow; hour after hour, row upon row, disappearing over the horizon until the field was finished. I anxiously awaited his verdict but knew the news was not good as soon as I saw his face. The attachment didn't really mow, it bush-hogged.

Mowing is about as mind-numbing a subject as exists. We don't seem to own precisely the right equipment for the various mowing tasks required. We have two weed eaters, two small lawnmowers with baskets, one John Deere 355D riding lawnmower and now a washed-up Lamborghini with lawnmower attachment. Weed eaters are used on the embankments, the little mowers are used in tight spots such as near the pool, the riding mower is used around the olives near the tennis court and the Lamborghini does its ineffectual job in the new grove.

Roger couldn't sleep with worry about the unsightly bush-hogged grove. There had to be another way. Romeo saw us coming and suggested a Grillo ZTR (zero turning radius) mower. We were getting smarter, having decided to test drive the Grillo on our land before buying. Delivery of the Grillo was impressive accompanied as it was by two factory representatives and a riding technician. The technician was a Fabio look alike. He sported tinted, flowing locks, five o'clock shadow and a black wrap-around work coat so as not to dirty his designer jeans. He mounted the Grillo while still in the large delivery truck, fired it up and backed it down the ramp as though perched atop a prized stallion.

Fabio was quite a sight turning the Grillo on a dime. The representatives fought to talk over each other as they touted the extraordinary benefits of this fine piece of equipment. The technician spun and whirled, moved forward and back and the Grillo, cute as it was, looked better suited for a Shriners parade than mowing an olive grove. I translated over the engine noise but all Roger wanted to do was hop on and try it himself. The technician took this quite seriously while I teetered between excruciating boredom and stifled laughter. Fabio issued instructions as though Roger were caring for his first born. You'd think he was getting ready to drive a specimen roadster on the open highway instead of a damn lawnmower in our backyard.

Roger nodded throughout the briefing until Fabio finally relinquished the controls. He kept a watchful eye while the two reps pummeled me with more details and features and benefits. The technician stood nearby, admiring Roger's motoring skills. After several runs, Roger turned off the engine, shaking his head. I explained that the Grillo was too loud, too big, too inefficient and too expensive. The reps tried to account for all the deficiencies while Fabio was visibly offended. He recovered his prize, taking it back to the delivery vehicle, while I was left to acknowledge the sales pitches. I stood firm and the Grillo left.

Days turned to weeks as we cast about for the perfect solution. Sleepless nights continued. Instead of turning to Romeo, we went to Bavicchi, the source of the Gator and riding mower and investigated various options. While not perfect, we eventually settled on a wider, 54-inch mower deck for the 355D riding mower. Changing mowers allowed the grass to be cut like grass and we were well on our way to achieving Roger's goal of a golf course fairway between the olives. The wider mower reduced mowing time. Instead of five passes for each five-meter row, the field could be clipped in four, achieving an impressive twenty percent savings.

The public is a fickle mistress and we were through with Monica. Antonio eventually found a buyer who took the Lamborghini and all her attachments. Roger didn't miss her too much except for the bragging rights. Even that pride was shelved in the interest of mown grass. The John Deere does the job, and future harvests will be made easier with grass in place. With that problem solved, I excused myself from daily mowing discussions to concentrate on really important matters like driving my air-conditioned car. The true and just order of life had been restored.

The World of Medicine

During our joined at the hip days, I occasionally thought about medical emergencies. I worried about how I would manage to drive us to Silvestrini hospital in Perugia or Augusto's hospital in Umbertide in the event Roger couldn't get behind the wheel. I envisioned gears grinding and the car stalling while I rolled backwards into impatient drivers. I could see Roger offering not so gentle encouragement and instruction to add to the certain confusion.

One morning Roger stormed into the house, calling my name followed by, "Nothing to worry about dear but you better grab some rags and a few band-aids." That's enough to get a heart racing. Armed with wire cutters and heavy duty leather gloves, Roger had been removing a rusty fence studded with barbed wire. The fence snapped back slashing his cheek and deeply slicing his nose. Blood trailed as I grabbed sterile cotton, hydrogen peroxide and bandages. He fought me the way a child does when attempting to wipe a runny nose. I suggested we have the wounds looked at and consider a tetanus shot. I was summarily rebuffed. Barely giving me enough time to slap on a band-aid, he spun from my reach to finish the task.

I shared the story with Mamma Ruta who recommended a tetanus shot. I told my morning walkers about the incident and Liana recommended a tetanus shot. Augusto came to collect the old fencing to use in his chicken coop and he recommended a tetanus shot. We were approaching unanimity here but Roger remained truculent. In a clever ploy designed to persuade Roger, Augusto asked when I was last inoculated against tetanus. Since it had been over ten years, he said I was in need of the same. Misery loves company.

On a day convenient for Augusto, we went to the *pronto soccorso,* emergency room, of his hospital in Umbertide, thirteen miles to our north. Much of the hospital was under construction for a modernizing face lift. The emergency room area was dark and noisy and arriving there was not easy; signage was minimal and dated. An attendant dressed in neon orange pants and jacket called us behind closed doors into a dimly lit examining room. Augusto and several technicians met us and one explained that we would each receive a series of three injections over several months' time. One technician readied a syringe, another completed an inoculation card and still another soaked a cotton ball in alcohol. Roger volunteered that I go first. I rolled up my sleeve and sitting on a gurney with a spotlight glaring on my arm, I received my shot. Delaying his injection for as long as he could, Roger eventually hopped on the gurney. As we redressed with sweaters and jackets, we thanked them for the efficient and professional medical care and were told to return in one month with our inoculation cards.

Our second and final visits went much the same. There was a slight hiccup on the second visit when the syringe-toting technician tried to get me to drop my pants for a shot in the rear. I refused but he insisted. Amusement playing on their faces, Roger and the others watched to see who would win this skirmish. I rolled up my sleeve and propped my arm on my hip explaining that the last shot had been in my arm. The tech didn't approve, saying it would be more effective the other way. He relented and everyone went back to their business once it was clear there would be no show.

Our next medical event came in the form of dentistry. I consulted with my orthodontist friend Liana about teeth cleaning. The *studio,* office, was tucked into an apartment building on a quiet side street. An intercom system permits access to the building as someone in the office releases a lock and the door remains open for a few seconds while we fumble to enter. We climbed the two flights of stairs in relative darkness; the lack of light still unsettling despite understanding the conservational motivations.

We entered the office to find a reception desk and small waiting room. No one is seated behind the desk – just a phone and appointment book. The waiting room is cramped. People already seated greet us with *Buongiorno* and shift to make room. The chairs are tiny; music plays and well-worn magazines are scattered across a glass coffee table. Roger chooses to stand and we both stare wide-eyed at some antique dental equipment occupying precious space. The cracked leather chair, chipped porcelain basin, worn rubber belts and foot-powered drill are intended to be decorative but we find it disconcerting, worrying about the modernity of technology we're about to encounter.

We don't know the protocol. We hear the sound of drills and muted voices from three exam rooms. Do we knock? Are we supposed to sign in? We had appointments but were all these people in front of us? Should we be completing paperwork? Roger wanted immediate answers but I was in favor of waiting until some medical type appeared. Every once in a while, an exam door opened and a technician escorted a patient to the desk, consulted the appointment book and provided a reminder card for a follow-up visit. Roger's sharp elbow urging me to trip the technician was ignored. She eventually caught my eye, quickly muttered, *"A presto"*, soon, before disappearing. Occasionally, a loud buzzer squawked and another hurried technician would bolt from an exam room to depress a button, giving the next victim access. The latest patient would greet everyone and new shifting would occur.

Just as Roger was about to walk out, demonstrating his well-known lack of *pazienza,* we were shown into an exam room. Language would dictate that we remain together. The technicians barely gave our offered dental records and X-rays a cursory glance, preferring their own exams and radiography.

I went first as seems to be the pattern in these medical matters. Much to Roger's dismay, I'm a poster child for perfect dental hygiene. The cleaning was unremarkable, the hygienist professional. The equipment was sleek and modern, nothing like the relic in the waiting room. As she worked, I glanced at the walls finding an eclectic mix of artwork that could only be found in an Italian dental office. There was a smattering of religious iconography oddly juxtaposed with several reclining female nudes. A wood crucifix adorned with a small olive branch hung above the door. The branch was dry but its leaves remained intact. I knew the branch had been placed there following Palm Sunday. Olive branches replaced palm fronds. All homes and businesses from Gina's dry cleaning shop to the police station to even this dentist's office displayed the olive branch. No separation of church and state here.

After the cleaning, dentist Giampaolo appeared for a standard exam. What was not standard was the certain knowledge that both dentist and hygienist were smokers; the tell-tale odor of smoke was an odd contrast to their daily labors.

It was now Roger's turn. A deep resentment of my dental health is rooted (pun intended) in his unfortunate oral condition. His discomfort in this setting was exacerbated by several factors. First, I was translating. Second, the reclining chair was too short so his head had no proper support while his feet uncomfortably dangled off the end. Last, they discovered that one of his implants was on the verge of failure. Giampaolo explained the problem so I could explain it to Roger. Each explanation meant probing the sensitive area, inflicting pain on a sore mouth and equally sore psyche. Not understanding the explanation first hand left him out of the loop and placed me squarely in his gun sight.

Giampaolo recommended a deep cleaning using a laser; a procedure that would have to be repeated every three weeks for several months. He hoped that laser cleaning would save the implant or at least delay its failure. Roger wanted to think about this but they were ready to begin. The dentist and hygienist donned protective goggles and eventually managed to strap a pair on Roger who was squirming uncomfortably. There weren't any goggles for me so I was told to face the wall. I was worried for both of us but Giampaolo and his assistant moved confidently forward and the whole thing seemed over before it started, at least from my wall staring, nude admiring perspective. Roger grumbled mightily but the laser process is working; his implant remains intact. We tried to pay but were rebuffed; payment could be discussed at some later date.

Even though the next medical event, a mammogram was mine alone, Roger accompanied me to the doctor's office. The *studio* was on the outskirts of Perugia, in an unfamiliar area of town. I foolishly scheduled my appointment for late afternoon which meant it would be dark. We got lost despite the verbal directions I had so painstakingly copied when making the appointment. The parking lot was full as the first floor of the building was a grocery store. Well versed in parking lot strategies, we maneuvered into a creative spot of our own. We announced ourselves via the intercom system and the door lock released. Dark stairwells were followed by dark hallways leading to the crowded waiting room.

As we entered, all eyes looked our way and we received a communal *Buonasera*. We responded in kind and most eyes turned back to magazines or newspapers but some lingered on Roger. On this mild winter day, he wore only a cotton shirt while everyone else remained bundled in the calendar mandating garb of sweaters, jackets and even a fur. Protocol stymied us again until a receptionist appeared to take my records. She returned shortly, handing me a post-it with a handwritten number. I stared at the post-it while noticing others in the room holding their own post-its. Obviously I would be called when my number was called but that was the problem. I couldn't read my number. Italian handwritten numbers are their own language which I had yet to master. The number one has a long tail in front, fours look like the letter **U**, fives could pass for an **S**. I watched carefully as the receptionist handed out the next number and craned my neck to read her post-it and in that way ciphered mine.

Once called, I trailed a technician into a room where I was asked to disrobe from the waist up. I sat on the edge of the exam table reading my book, holding a cloth in front of my chest, uncomfortably waiting. I mentally rehearsed words that would be useful in this setting. A knock on the door immediately preceded the entry of the doctor. He introduced himself, shaking my hand, unfazed by my partial nudity. The doctor was pleasant and upbeat and made small talk while I feigned a nonchalance I no more felt than if I had been sitting naked in church. As he chatted, he picked up a large camera and asked me to remove the cloth and raise my arms. This was too much. My puritanical sensibilities had collided directly with Mediterranean openness. "Look, I've come here for a mammogram and you're taking pictures?"

He explained that Italy has a completely different approach to breast exams than the States. I guess so. The camera recorded heat images. These baseline photos would be used for comparisons over time and they are just one of the tools used to study breast health. Cameras weren't the only difference. Routine screening included palpation and ultrasound along with the standard mammogram. The exam isn't over until it's determined that readable images are obtained. Any suspicious areas are re-imaged and all results are immediately read by the physician. There are no tension-filled days of uncertainty waiting for radiology to process results.

Now fully dressed, I was escorted to the doctor's office where he explained that everything was normal. He spoke rapidly as he created a folder with all the new images, results and hasty scribbles and handed the chart to me. I was to return in six months with my chart for a follow-up ultrasound exam, part of the standard process and included in today's price. Here I paid because I opted to go to a private *studio*. Considering all that had been done, the cost was reasonable. As we left his office, Roger appeared and introductions were made, handshakes exchanged. The last thing the doctor did was pat me on the shoulder, kiss me on both cheeks and wish me *Buon Natale*.

Another Winter

*I*t's true I wouldn't see the doctor before Christmas but we still had other landmark events to deal with before that holiday. First, there was olive harvest. Friends Linda and Mike came from the States to help but instead were rewarded with simply a vacation, something she desperately needed after bravely finishing her last round of radiation for breast cancer on their travel day.

The Easter freeze that blasted the flower buds last spring did as predicted and decimated the olive crop. We weren't alone with disappointing results. Mick, Roger and I finished our harvest in three hours. The weather was gloomy; a constant, bone-chilling drizzle. Olives shouldn't be picked wet or left in that condition but we planned to press immediately. Finding an open mill was a challenge. The *frantoio* we went to last year was closed; there wasn't enough business to justify opening. Eventually we found one in Piccione.

The contrast to our first year's bounty was striking. Last year we harvested four hundred kilos of olives from seventy-seven trees while this year we harvested sixty-eight kilos from six hundred seventy-seven trees. We asked for a separate press to have our own oil rather than combining it with someone else's. For a fee, the mill owners are willing to do this when the weight is close to the minimum required. Any other year he would have laughed but business was slow and he agreed. A small but mighty harvest delivered intensely flavorful oil that was worth the additional fee.

Though Linda and Mike missed the harvesting experience they reaped the rewards in the form of *bruschetta.* Nothing tastes better than freshly pressed oil heavily bathing crunchy toasted bread rubbed with fresh garlic and sprinkled with salt. As Mike was fond of saying, "This could only happen in 'Roger's World'."

Our next major event was Thanksgiving. The revolving door on our house was well greased; as Mike and Linda exited, Clayton and Shandi entered. They brought imports like canned pumpkin and offered assistance for hosting a traditional Thanksgiving dinner for twenty. We dined in the *salone rustiche* using a combination of tables and watched contentedly as Italians, Americans, Dutch and Canadians heartily embraced the spirit and the food of what we now called *Ringraziamento.*

We ate turkey, dressing, gravy, ham, mashed potatoes, vegetable side dishes, cranberry sauce, pumpkin pie. Only sweet potatoes were missing despite our searching. METRO claimed to have them but we met the produce man and explained that the *patata americana* he showed us was not a sweet potato despite the similar shape. I returned to *Gio* in the dreaded *centro* of Perugia as they insisted that they too had these American potatoes. Alas, they did not. I have no idea what root vegetable had been christened an American potato. I even tried cooking one but it was starchy, pale in color, bland and far removed from the natural sweetness associated with sweet potatoes. I think we'll just import our own next year.

Late fall is the season when *cappelletti* takes center stage. Last year I was occupied when Giuliana, Mary and others made the pasta but this year

I participated. The actual filling and shaping is the last step in a lengthy, time and labor consuming process that begins with butchering chickens. I appeared for the pasta portion, skipping the slaughter. Days in advance, Giuliana cooks the chicken with pork, beef and sausage, grinds it and binds the meats with eggs, cheese and seasonings for the filling. On *cappelletti* day, she leads the volunteer female workforce in a ritual that's existed for centuries.

When I arrive in Giuliana's pantry, work is in progress. Giuliana, Mary and five other women are operating as efficiently as a pit crew. Everyone at the large table has her own task with Giuliana directing their efforts. Earlier in the day, she made the pasta dough and let it rest. She now fed it through an electronic pasta maker attached to the edge of the table with a vise. The machine was a time saver normally eschewed by Giuliana in favor of a rolling pin. Using it almost nullifies the phrase, *fatto a mano* or made by hand. Today's large volume of pasta made the cheater a necessity if we had any hope of finishing before midnight.

Giuliana produced progressively thinner and thinner sheets of pasta; the goal was to see through each sheet. Another woman sliced the sheets into long strips. Each long strip was then cut into small squares about twice the size of a postage stamp. Another placed meat in the center of each square. The amount of filling was small, varying from the size of a pea to the size of a blueberry. The rest of the crew worked with the meat dabbed squares. Each square was folded into a triangle and two ends of the triangle are twisted back and pressed together forming the now recognizable little hat. The women continually shift positions around the table because the one slicing the pasta is in constant search of vacant table space on which to place new strips and squares. As little hats are formed, they are placed on plates, cutting boards, platters and any other large flat surface. Periodically, Renato appeared to move the pasta to other areas of the pantry to dry. Dialect-laden chatter filled the room without slowing the pace.

Breaking into this finely functioning operation was like breaking into a double-Dutch jump rope contest. I watched intently, studying the rapidly moving fingers expertly dabbing meat and folding squares into triangles and hats. The women made room for me and interrupted the flow to demonstrate proper folding. All eyes were on me as I grabbed my first meat dab and pasta square. The dab fell out of my hand, missing the square, landing on the table. They pretended not to notice. I inhaled and started again, all concentration. A ball bearing of meat on the center of the square, fold into a triangle, twist back the ends, start again. I made one, then two, then three. For my three, the others had made dozens and the women were ready to shift while I was still stuck on hat number four. I tried harder - meat, square, triangle, twist and again, meat, square, triangle, twist.

Daylight was long gone when we finished four hours and thousands of *cappelletti* later. By that time I had become proficient and could hold my own even listening in on the gossip that helped pass the time. Mary asked me to translate but the dialect was difficult. Occasionally I caught phrases. Each woman spoke about her mother's way of preparing *cappelletti.* Some add egg, others don't, some add prosciutto, some were aghast at the thought; some twisted the triangle ends back over their little finger to form a small opening, others tightly press the ends together to ensure there's not the slightest opening. The women talked about the proper number of *cappelletti* to be placed in each serving with broth. One said ten hats were sufficient and that raised a ruckus. Someone asked her if she intended to force her guests to go fishing for hats. Another said at least fifteen while Giuliana was in the twenty-range and a strong supporter of second servings.

The chatter confirmed we live in a very small town. All is known and subject to discussion. There was talk about the choice of attire worn in church. There was favorable reference to Roger greeting one woman's grandchild on the way home from school. I can just imagine what slipped through the dialect-ridden cracks.

We helped Giuliana clean the pantry. Dozens of plastic bags of *cappelletti* were sealed and frozen. I was exhausted more from concentration than physical labor. I couldn't wait to savor the little hats knowing that I had played a small role in their creation. I wondered whether mine would look like all the rest floating in the clear *brodo* or if they would stand out as being too large or misshapen.

Parties

These were party filled days. Valentina's parents, Clara and Raniero treated us to *pappardelle con sugo di cinghiale*, broad egg noodles with wild boar sauce. Clara, a self-taught cook who conducts many of our cooking classes, insisted on providing us with the hearty meal when Clayton and Shandi arrived. Raniero, the retired quality control director for Perugina chocolates, hunts wild boar, a destructive animal that is over-populated in the Italian countryside in much the same way deer are in parts of the

U.S. Hunting the dangerous tusked animal is Raniero's passion and not something done individually. Teams of hunters and their dogs gather during the winter months and the spoils are divided. Typically, the meat is braised, lending itself to long, slow cooking. It's fall-off-the-bone tender, not gamey and full of bold flavors from the wine and tomatoes used in the cooking process.

Knowing Valentina means that we've come to know the entire family. In addition to her warm and welcoming parents, we've met her brother Michele, his wife and their daughter. They all live together, help each other and support each other. As a former bookkeeper, Clara takes care of Valentina's accounting matters and looks after granddaughters Marta and newborn Chiara. She often cooks for the whole family. When he's not hunting, Raniero helps Valentina by assembling ceramic drawer pulls and bottle stoppers. Valentina's husband, Andrea, spends his off hours from his full-time automotive body repair job packaging Valentina's goods for overseas shipment. Michele helps Valentina with English as he studied in the U.K. and is quite proficient. This is family in the best sense of the word.

Such is the environment in which Mary, Don, Roger and I are invited to a dinner party to celebrate Chiara's baptism. The event rivaled a wedding reception with hundreds of guests and over twenty items in a buffet. We were the only Americans and were treated as honored guests. Roger was convinced that all family members had been briefed with orders to never leave us unattended. Graciously, we were handed off from Andrea to Clara to Michele and so on despite the many others requiring attention. It was a raucous, festive, high-spirited evening. Young children raced around the room; boys chased girls, girls chased boys, giggles and laughter bounced off the walls while the star of this event slept in serene beauty. It was close to midnight when the cake was cut and chocolate bonbons and baba au rhum were served. Sated and tired, we were among the first to leave and still the children played.

Our next big party was bittersweet; a farewell cocktail party for Mary and Don whose long-term Italian stay had come to an end. Their presence next door had become a fixture we wanted to be permanent. They had eased our way into Italy and we would soon be left without their company and assistance. Things would be different.

The concept of a cocktail party was difficult to convey. Thirty guests were invited for six-thirty, a time completely out of kilter with the strict Mediterranean dining schedule. I tried to explain that guests should arrive hungry and wives would be saved a night in the kitchen. There would be lots of heavy hors d'oeuvres and *prosecco.*

Mary looked beautiful as the star of her own party. It was an emotional night for both her and Don. The women had bought Mary a gift, photos were taken and Mary asked me to convey thanks and appreciation to everyone for having provided them with the experience of a lifetime. Despite unfamiliarity with cocktail parties, the Italians managed quite well. Buckets of *prosecco,* platters of meats, cheeses, dips, spreads, finger sandwiches and sweets disappeared in a flash.

Picture perfect winter days capped this holiday season. Crisp north winds brought fluttery horizontally flying snow. Fires burned in the *soggiorno* and *salone rustiche,* a Christmas tree from Antonio decorated with our manic flashing lights occupied a prominent position, *pungitopo* adorned various niches in the house. This was Currier and Ives, Umbrian style.

Caroline hosted Christmas dinner. Italian and American traditions co-mingled to provide a feast. Hundreds of our painstakingly hand-made little hats disappeared as everyone sought seconds. None, not even mine, were singled out as different.

After the lengthy meal, we remained at the table which became the gaming board for *Mercante in Fiera.* Each player took on his standard role; Renato as barker/banker, Augusto conniving and taunting, Ciccio studying all the players in search of a future partner for some serious card playing. Roger was central to the mix having made money off side bets and bluffing. It was lively, entertaining, comfortable.

New Year's Eve was celebrated closer to home this year. Ciccio and Gale hosted a dinner party that featured Calabrian specialties including fish and peppery spices; a striking departure from Umbrian cuisine. At midnight, we stood on their balcony, wrapped in coats, scarves and gloves and greeted the New Year with *prosecco* and spectacular fireworks from the surrounding towns.

And so it was, in this charming, bucolic and tranquil setting that we stepped into yet another year at *Le Vigne.*

Compiti

*B*ucolic and tranquil lasted all of one day. Crystal clear, blue sky mornings gave way to Euro weather; rains, dense fog, thunder and lightning. As long as it wasn't pouring daily walks continued. We covered our heads as the sodden condensation threatened to soak our hair more than a downpour. Heavy frost toppled budding wheat shoots. "Red sky at morning" carries the same negative connotation in Italy as elsewhere and while the aura of pink cotton candy fog surrounding hilltop churches looked frothy and confectionary, it was a certain harbinger of foul weather and the need to take warning.

In the midst of such gloom Roger left for the States. In Roger's World he can't leave the room without dictating a to-do list so imagine the list that covered an overseas stay. Roger drove to Fiumicino, while I jotted down the last minute additions to the already extensive list of projects that were to be completed prior to his return. The morning traffic was hellish, especially around the ring road that's been under construction since the days of Caesar. It felt strange getting into the driver's seat at the airport. We hadn't been apart for more than a few hours in over a year. Back in our career days, there was constant separation; days on end when we weren't even on the same continent let alone in the same state. Times had changed.

Leaving Fiumicino, I managed well through the narrow, roller coaster ring road and now approached the toll booth of the *Autostrada*, the easier part of the drive with its wide, multiple lanes and Autogrill stops. Something was wrong. The ticket lane I selected ceased dispensing tickets. I was sandwiched into a line-up with four cars in front and two behind. No attendant came to our rescue. We all needed to back out and select another lane. Communicating this concept from one vehicle to the next was cartoonish. There were gestures and grinding gears and the always helpful horn blowing. I proudly managed the reversal without hitting my car or anyone else's.

Two other note-worthy events happened on the drive home. First, I listened to the radio. Clayton dreaded being in the car with us because it was far too silent. Roger and I liked the quiet and often found the radio distracting when driving conditions were unfamiliar. Fiddling with the controls, bouncing from station to station must have been an indication of greater comfort. I learned that deejays are the same the world over. They offer a lot of blather and silliness in clipped slang requiring a fair amount of insider knowledge to comprehend. Today I understood the DJ's lame joke: What's the definition of a psychologist? He's the one looking at everyone else when a beautiful woman walks into the room.

My next big discovery took place at the Autogrill. Instead of ordering a decaf cap in my standard caffeine avoidance maneuver, I plunged and ordered a hot chocolate. I don't even like chocolate but during the winter I saw people ordering hot chocolates and they looked good. Good doesn't begin to describe it. The *barista* steamed milk and added cocoa to a cup that's larger than an *espresso* cup but smaller than a mug. It's served with a spoon which I tried to decline since I had no need for sugar. Turns out I needed it to eat, not drink this rich, molten ganache.

By the time I returned home, the phone was ringing. Giuliana wanted to check in; she was worried about me. She couldn't believe I would stay in this big house alone. She certainly wouldn't if Renato weren't around. She'd call her son or an aunt or someone to keep her and Yoshi company. She begged me to stay with her and while it was kind to be so worried over, I declined. I was to call her if I needed anything or changed my mind.

Walking with the girls the next morning, I encountered the same attitude. When Liana and Giovanna found out I had driven home from the airport alone and that Roger was out of the country, they were aghast. "Did you sleep, were you scared, what did you do for dinner, when is he coming back, you must stay with us, what are you going to do while he's gone?"

I answered all the questions which caused more tsking and tutting but when I responded to the final question describing Roger's list, they stopped in their tracks. Giuliana all but screamed, "He left you *compiti*?" They were astounded that I had homework. Every morning I bravely delivered a progress report. Giuliana thought I shouldn't do it; even Renato told me to say *basta.*

One evening while I watched a movie, Giuliana called. She'd heard an alarm and wanted to make sure it wasn't coming from our house. I assured her all was well but she didn't seem to believe me. Perhaps she had seen too many movies where the heroine responded to this question with a gun to her head.

Later Caroline called as Giuliana had told her about Roger's trip and my homework. We laughed off the concerns and talked about the excessive fear these Italian women have at the thought of being home alone. Augusto still spent nights on call at the hospital so she was used to it. Then again, she's American and has a different perspective even though she's lived in Italy all her adult life. Here, I had my own personal neighborhood watch program.

When I wasn't answering such phone calls or plowing through my *compiti,* I ran errands. On the way to the hardware store I stopped by the Faffa bakery for a *panino.* Antonella and Luigi invited me to join their family for lunch the following day. Word was out that Roger was gone and they too were worried. I could think of nothing better than eating a home-cooked meal with such kind people. I gladly accepted and offered to bring something. Luigi laughed. What are you going to bring a baker? Dessert? Bread? No, we need nothing.

Luigi's great-grandfather founded the bakery in 1851. His is one of only two authorized, certified wood-fired baking ovens in Umbria. It is with no small amount of pride that Luigi escorted Roger, me and our guests upon occasion through the inner workings of the bakery. It's a fascinating tour that comes alive in front of the oldest oven, the one with the large cast iron door made in Milan.

Here Luigi explains that his father operated the bakery at the time of the German occupation during World War II. The Germans were in retreat; an expulsion that took several years. The town of Ponte Valleceppi was small but strategic due to the bridge and its position on the Tiber River. Everyone was hungry. Soldiers' ribs protruded, people were reduced to eating cats; these were ugly days. The Germans immediately commandeered the bakery and a German captain oversaw the baking of bread.

The captain made it his business to be present when the loaves of bread were shoveled into the oven and when they came out. Everyday the count was precisely eighty loaves. Luigi's father was permitted to stand with the captain and the two young soldiers assigned the task of baking the bread. The captain recorded the daily count, writing on the wall to the right of the cast iron door, using a piece of charcoal. He would then leave to conduct other business, returning once the bread was baked to check the count. The number coming out had to square with the number that went in.

One day, one of the hungry young soldiers managed to slip in an extra loaf unbeknownst to the captain. Without breaking their rhythm, both soldiers continued to shovel in the remaining loaves. The captain grabbed a piece of charcoal and recorded the final count; eighty loaves had gone into the six hundred degree Fahrenheit oven. For some reason, the captain didn't leave the bakery that day. Luigi's father and the two soldiers exchanged knowing looks. Their lives were in danger. The captain would order their deaths if the bread count totaled eighty-one.

It was time to remove the bread from the oven. Each soldier alternated with his paddle, sliding the long loaves into wicker baskets. The count reached fifty, sixty, seventy. Luigi's father and the soldiers were panicky, sweat beading on their brows. Someone had to do something otherwise they would all be executed. Luigi's father distracted the captain by pointing out something else in the bakery. In the split second attention was diverted, one of the soldiers removed a loaf, shoving it inside his shirt beneath his apron. The captain regained his focus and continued the count. Eighty loaves appeared in the baskets. The numbers matched. The count was square.

The captain left and the soldier collapsed. Luigi's grandmother was called as the others tore open the man's shirt removing the hot loaf and a layer of skin. He suffered silently knowing that to cry out would bring attention and danger to him and the others. The grandmother treated the soldier with herbs and poultices. To notify a doctor or seek pharmaceuticals would have been suicide.

To hear Luigi tell this story is riveting. He explains matter of factly that while these Germans were not friends, one couldn't help but be connected with people in such circumstances. Eventually, the Germans moved on and Luigi's grandmother wondered whatever happened to the soldier she nursed back to health who called her *Nonna,* Grandma. Such was war. They never learned his fate.

Antonella suggested I meet her at the bakery so that she and I could drive the few short blocks to the house together. She gathered pastries, bread, several *antipasti,* closed and locked the sliding metal window grates and we left. Their home was warm and welcoming. We ate in the kitchen where the table had already been set and a fire built by oldest daughter Valentina.

Luigi sat at the head of the table and told me that family meals are important; a necessary time to learn things, discuss current events, family history, culture. Today, it is I who learn a great deal taking part in the comfortable discussion that covers a wide range of topics. This is an industrious, hard-working, respectful family; it is an honor and a pleasure to be in their company.

Valentina is studying fine arts at the University, majoring in *moderno.* Only in Italy can Renaissance be considered *moderno.* Younger daughter Elisa is studying economics and won't join us for lunch because she's taking an exam. School can take precedence over the family lunch. Valentina has a trained voice and has performed many times at the Basilica in Assisi. She inherited this talent from her father and has a gentle beauty, kind eyes and ready laugh similar to her mother's.

Luigi is usually at the bakery by four in the morning though other bakers arrive earlier. Antonella arrives between six-thirty and seven at which time the bakery is already packed with customers grabbing a quick breakfast *panino* before school or work. Three women work the chaotic counter. No one loses patience, everyone works quickly, efficiently and seemingly contentedly.

Our talk of current events centers on Parmalat and the scandal involving the company, the town and now all of Italy. They find it an embarrassment. They ask if I've ever been to Denver. Years ago, three women from Denver came to Luigi's bakery and spent a week learning how to bake bread and other Umbrian specialties. They returned to Denver, opened their own bakery and sell what they learned to make. Each year they send Luigi Christmas greetings. I ask who will run the family business in the future. Luigi and Antonella are hopeful one of the daughters and a future husband will remain involved.

Antonella has worked all morning yet we sit down to *antipasto, primo, secondo, contorno* and *dolce*. We have water, white wine made by Luigi, red wine that I brought and Vin Santo made by a friend. Lunch begins with finger sandwiches, some with thin slices of *salami*, others with tuna and artichoke and a small bowl of olives. The *primo* is *cappelletti alla Norcina*; the famous little hats served with a cream sauce and crumbled sausage. Next we enjoyed beef, thinly sliced with a nap of gravy and a side of steamed chicory seasoned with olive oil and onion. Dessert was a smattering of pastries from the shop; cream-filled shells, mini Napoleons and *strufoli*, a *carnevale* specialty that looked like an over-inflated doughnut with honey on top. Other than the *antipasti* and the dessert, this is a standard daily lunch.

Valentina clears the table and I'm practically body-slammed into my seat when I try to help. She stokes the fire before leaving to study. Luigi excuses himself, ready for his afternoon *pisolino*, nap, before returning to the bakery late in the afternoon.

I'm sure Antonella is tired but she wants to chat. I insist on grabbing a dish towel and we both companionably dry and put away the few remaining glasses. We talk about food and cooking and I ask if she'll share recipes. We sit at the cleared table and she writes the pasta and beef recipes, reviewing every line to make sure I understand. Finally, we walk downstairs to my car and after several sets of double cheek kisses and many thanks on my part, she guides me out of the tiny parking space to return home. Roger will be jealous that he missed the food, the company, the experience.

Flying free and therefore stand-by is a great perk that's also a juggling act requiring enormous flexibility. If the Atlanta-Rome flight is full, Roger could quickly switch to the Atlanta-Milan flight. From Milan, he can take a commuter to the Perugia airport. If the Atlanta flights aren't available, he could travel through New York or maybe Cincinnati. Whatever he decides, he has to notify me so I can leave *Le Vigne* in sufficient time to meet him early the next morning. Early evening flight departures and a six-hour time difference mean that I should be prepared for a phone call after midnight so I know what to do the next morning, which in this case is due to happen any minute.

For Roger's return, the stand-by gods smiled on us and he was scheduled to arrive in Fiumicino on time. He even enjoyed the benefit of what we called 'a big seat,' having secured a roomier business class seat on the overnight flight. This was a good thing. Roger in coach is not a pretty sight. I, too, was fortunate. Fortified with hot chocolate, the early morning drive to the airport went well. Perhaps it was the caffeine jolt but I held my assertive ground on the ring road, maintaining good time despite the mess.

Rather than parking, our plan called for me to circle until Roger called my cell at which time I'd know he'd be ready for pick up. His call came and he had made it through passport control. All he needed to do was collect his bags. Traveling to the States meant carry-on luggage but on his return he was loaded with purchases that didn't fit in a single carry-on. He'd call again once he had the bags.

I continued to circle, pausing illegally until the police neared when I would pull away and circle again. Roger finally called. Bad news. The baggage handlers had called a *sciopero* or strike. Their timing was designed to cause as much inconvenience and confusion as possible and they were successful. This was the prime time for international arrivals so thousands stood in baggage claim. It was now time to park.

I sat in the arrival area reading while waiting for news. Roger stood on the other side of the wall as there is no seating in baggage claim. *Che casino.* People were angry, confused, tired and frustrated. Announcements were few. It made no sense for us to leave. A return trip to Fiumicino was not a simple thing. The airline had no obligation to deliver our bags. We had no choice but to wait. Eventually airline ticket agents and supervisors unloaded baggage - four hours after landing.

Strikes are a way of life in Italy as they are in many other European countries. They're not particularly effective but definitely maddening and annoying, causing much intended disruption. Teachers strike, bus drivers strike, pharmacists strike, even doctors strike. They see it as their right to object to reduction in labor forces or demand pay increases or shorter hours. Alitalia was in dire financial freefall, seeking government assistance and yet various employee groups continued to strike. The company could no longer make any concessions; nothing was left to give.

Some strikes are announced well in advance. Others happened like this one, without warning. Strikes often occur on a Friday, conveniently delivering a three-day break to the downtrodden striker. Once, bus drivers went on strike on the first day of school forcing the cancellation of classes. Even in these circumstances public sympathies often lie with the strikers.

So it was one tired boy who eventually appeared outside of baggage claim. His eyes began to close as I recounted my adventures while he was away. I reviewed the status of my *compiti* and he dozed contentedly knowing the many tasks were complete. I spared him the knowledge that my friends had encouraged me to perform my own *sciopero*. That evening I rewarded the weary traveler with the comfort food from Antonella, here to provide you solace as well.

Rosbif (Serves 4)

2 lb. rump roast, tied
1 carrot, diced
1 rib celery, diced
1 onion, chopped
1 large clove garlic, minced
2 T. butter
2 T. olive oil
½ c. white wine
½ c. water or broth
1 small branch rosemary
S & P, flour for meat

Salt, pepper and lightly flour the meat. Melt butter and olive oil in heavy sauce pan and sear meat on all sides. Add vegetables, rosemary and wine and reduce heat. Let meat cook slowly, partially covered for about one to one and a half hours. Attend the meat frequently to baste and turn, adding more liquid as needed. Let meat rest before slicing. Can crush vegetables or strain and serve liquid over meat.

Penne alla Norcina (Serves 4)

Penne pasta
3 pork sausage links, skin removed and crumbled
½ c. heavy cream
Pinch hot pepper flakes
Parmigiano

While pasta is boiling in salted water, sauté sausage in fry pan. Add cream and pepper flakes and stir all together. Drain cooked pasta, reserving some liquid. Add pasta to sausage/cream mixture and blend thoroughly adding pasta liquid if needed. Add *parmigiano* and serve.

Vacation

Despite Roger's insistence last year that he'll never again return to the *questura,* the man had to eat his words as our *permessi* were due to expire. Once again, Antonio tried to save us from much of the hassle. He arrived at the *questura* early one morning and obtained a number. We raced into Perugia to meet him and he delivered the disturbing news. Procedures had changed. The rule of the day was one ticket number per person. Last year, one number worked for both of us. Today we spent the morning processing the paperwork for Roger.

We returned the following Monday at six. About thirty others were already in front of us. Roger and I took turns sitting on a little garden bench we brought for the two hour wait. As the clock approached eight, the line morphed into a blob and the blob moved as one toward the gate. I linked my arm through Roger's, appreciating his height. The shoving was rough and the meaning of the angry words clear despite the jumble of languages. At a minute after eight, we were given number ninety-eight. The cut-off is one hundred. Those outside the gate were left to fight another day.

Once again, this task was behind us. Our new *permessi* would be ready in sixty days and in the meantime we had temporary papers. It was time to focus on vacation. I can hear our friends now. "Vacation? What do you mean you're going on vacation? Your whole life's a vacation. You live in Italy, for crying out loud." Undeterred, we were going on vacation.

Mick had stayed at *Le Vigne* for brief periods during our absence but this stay would be longer. Now, the construction was complete and there was more house with greater responsibilities. Mick would continue to come to *Le Vigne* daily to work but we needed someone to stay full time. Ideally, we needed Italian speakers who had the flexibility to leave their own lives in limbo and step into ours. We wanted a mature couple who would take care of our home just as well if not better than their own. We needed people who were trustworthy, detail-minded, neat, orderly, responsible, handy and capable of exercising good judgment. What we really needed was to have our heads examined.

Where in the world would we find such people? We checked with friends here and in the States and endured the laughter that followed our request. Once the snorting subsided and our casual leads evaporated, we did what all sensible people do; we surfed the net and uncovered websites dedicated to house sitting.

Talk about the ultimate blind date. It's one thing to go out to dinner with a stranger, say goodnight and then return to the safety of home. It's quite another when that stranger never says goodnight and instead returns to the safety of the room next door. House-sitting websites posted thousands of profiles and we spent hours wading through hilarious, ridiculous, serious and at times heartbreaking resumes. Some were easy to reject: "I'm twenty-three, love yoga and eagerly anticipate all the free time I'll have to get in touch with my inner puppy. BTW, I love puppies and will take care of your pets as though they were people." Or, "Holistic health is my hobby and I'm anxious to explore the surrounding fields for herbs and natural remedies that will keep my soul at peace as I increase my appreciation for meditative states." Or, "I'm a fledgling screen writer and my wife is an actress and we are fond of home film-making and we've always wanted Italy as a backdrop to our artistic films." As Jay Leno said to Hugh Grant, "What were you thinking?"

I don't know what we were thinking but we were running out of time. Finally, we came across a promising lead. Karen and Wilfredo, originally from Argentina and now of New York were Italian speakers and readily available. We were lucky. They exceeded our wildest dreams, expertly took care of everything in our absence and best of all, became friends.

School Daze

We returned to Italy mid-March expecting better weather but winter refused to yield. Last summer was uncharacteristically hot and dry. So far this year was unusually wet. Well into April the rains continued. Our neighbors trotted out rhyming proverbs that covered every meteorological eventuality. *Marzo pazzerello.* Crazy March. *Se il Subasio ha il cappello, guarda il sole e prendi l'ombrello.* If Mount Subasio is wearing a hat, look at the sun but grab an umbrella. *I quattro aprilanti, quaranta giorni duranti.* If it rains on the fourth of April, expect forty more days of rain. An Italian Groundhog Day. Man, did it pour.

All our wonderful outdoor projects had to be delayed. Morning walks were postponed, olive pruning was postponed three times, field preparation and seeding were postponed, wall building was postponed, new masonry projects were postponed, vegetable and flower planting were postponed. Roger's *pazienza* was postponed.

Since walking was restricted, we joined Liana and Massimo twice a week for private exercise classes taught by Giorgio, a cute, young personal trainer from Bulgaria. We already knew Giorgio's sister, an equally cute aesthetician who comes to *Le Vigne* on demand to provide massages to our guests. We alternated class locations - one week at *Le Vigne* and the next week at Liana's. Each early morning session included strength training, cardio and stretching. In Italian, the words "personal trainer" are quite unique but I'll attempt a phonetic translation; "pair-so-knell tray-ner." That's in line with baby sitter which is just that or cream cheese which is known as Philadelphia or beep, as in recorded phone messages that say *lasciate un messaggio dopo il beep.*

I don't know how I convinced Roger to attend class. He took to them about as well as a cat to a bath. He was our class clown, inventing ways to shorten the session and reduce his participation. He was every "pair-so-knell tray-ner's" nightmare. After the first fifteen minutes, he claimed to have had enough; he'd pick this up again next year. When sunshine returns these classes will be history.

Roger and a classroom are antithetical. During his flying career, attending recurrent training or school on a new piece of equipment was faced with gritted teeth and inventive procrastination. It's no surprise then that last year's birthday gift of five private Italian lessons was received as though I provided a coupon for a free colonoscopy. I made the prospect enticing. Francesca, our television technician's girlfriend, was the instructor. She's a package one of our guests referred to as Barbarella; long blonde hair, short tight skirts, knee-high boots. Conversational classes would be conducted at *Le Vigne.* There would be little focus on verbs. Francesca and Roger were free to roam the property pointing at tractors and fruit trees, mind-numbing lawn mowers, saws and tools and any other nouns that intrigued him.

Poor Barbarella. She was no match for Roger who predictably drove the train or flew the plane or exercised any other metaphor to say he took charge. Thirty minutes into a ninety minute session, Roger would offer her a beer and he'd grab a gin and proudly point to the *ghiaccio*, ice, in his glass. He'd try to impress her with this word, one he's known for years. Despite his intransigence he was learning. He was ordering his own meals at Trilogy, chatting with owner Mara, even helping the guests with the menu. His comprehension was high and many times I could forego translations and simply ask, "Did you get that?"

Roger still avoided the phone but I've taught him repetitive patterns that make conversations easy to predict. Here's a typical phone call to our driver friend Roberto who handles our guests' transportation needs. Every call is answered with *pronto* which means ready but is the equivalent of hello. Next, I'll say, *"Ciao Roberto,"* and because Roberto has yet to recognize my voice, he'll say in the most haughty and indignant tone, *"Chi è,"* "Who is this?" *"Roberto, sono Joan,"* and he'll drop the haughty and veritably ooze his greeting, *"Ooooooo, Jo-wan, ciao, come stai?"* Then we'll amiably chat about our health and the weather and once we've covered the niceties, I move on to business. I start by saying, *"Ascolta,"* which means listen. I know Roberto has been doing just that but it's the trigger word indicating the true purpose of the call is about to be revealed. Roberto will say, *"Dimi tutto,"* "Tell me everything." I'll ask if he can come see us to discuss transportation logistics and he'll say, *"Ascolta, faciamo così,"* "Listen, let's do it like this." And we'll agree on a convenient date and time. That settled, I'll say *"Grazie, ciao,"* and he'll say, *"Niente, a dopo, salutami Roger, ciao,"* "It's nothing, see you later, say hi to Roger, bye." We do not hang up at this point. We must remain on the line, each saying *ciao* another four, five or six times. Just to be sure I've delivered the proper *ciao* quota, I keep saying it even after I've hung up.

The April rains concerned us. More than the cabin fever and inconvenience they imposed, we were approaching the May deadline for olive pruning. The task can begin as early as January but Roger wanted to participate in this horticultural event. Historically, Enzo pruned but we made special arrangements this year.

Totò, a friend of Caroline and Augusto's, is a professor at an agricultural trade school. He offered to bring a technical expert and his class of twenty students to prune our plants. It would take two days and we were to provide grilled sausages for lunch. We ordered rolls and cookies from Faffa and bought sausages from METRO. Three dates were scheduled and three dates were cancelled due to rain. Food orders were placed, then postponed.

Finally, a date was chosen and the class arrived. Totò and the expert were proficient and knowledgeable while the students were neophytes but so were we. The grill was started and the pruning began in earnest. Roger and I stood next to the expert. A handful of our youngest olives were pruned when the rain started. We had to stop. It was just a drizzle, but the rain exposed the freshly pruned branches to disease.

No one's hunger abated even though the work had stopped. Under cover of umbrella, we grilled sausages and tried to cover the rolls and cookies to prevent them from becoming sodden. We found protection under the extending branches of the old oak in the *piazza,* struggling to keep the active teens confined to a dry zone so as not to trample freshly planted sod near the grill. Since today was a wash, Totò suggested returning the following Friday.

The good news is that Friday's weather was perfect. The bad news is that the weather was perfect. Perfect weather meant projects. As if we didn't have enough going on with feeding the class and pruning the olives and expecting our first guests of the season that evening and the power company shutting off the electricity all morning, Roger had arranged for our three masons to appear at seven to begin construction on an outdoor *cantina* or cellar area.

Things were under control. We opted for *panini* rather than rolls and sausages so as not to have to fool with the grill. The sandwiches and standard order of cookies would be delivered by Faffa that morning. Pre-arrival shopping for the guests was done; the apartment was clean, ready and stocked with fresh flowers. Preparation of their arrival dinner was in the works.

Using hand gestures and sketches, Roger explained his construction plans to the masons who clamored for materials and supplies. The famous micro-manager couldn't leave so I was sent to the hardware store. While loading the car, I receive a panic call from Roger – the students have arrived with their own bread, sausages and demijohn of homemade wine. I'm to call Faffa and cancel the order. I call Antonella and explain the problem but it's too late; the sandwiches have been made and the delivery truck is on the way. Instead, she tells me how to freeze the sandwiches, assuring me they'll still be tasty and we won't need to prepare lunch for weeks.

When I return, the budding agronomists are in full swing. Most should consider a transfer to culinary school. Their attentions were focused on building a blazing fire, grilling the sausages, smoking cigarettes, tossing water bottles, using their cell phones and most importantly, guzzling the wine. Totò, strict disciplinarian that he is, seemed to find it charming and didn't mind being ignored when he asked the *ragazzi,* kids, to calm down.

The few serious students, the expert, Roger and I worked our way through the olives. The expert complimented us on the new grove. It won't be long before these young olives will develop into beautiful mature trees producing more olives and thus oil every year. He moved quickly from tree to tree, instantly analyzing its orientation, almost intuitively knowing the branches to remove. We were attentive as he generously shared his knowledge. I translated for Roger who eventually began to prune under the tutelage of the *maestro*. Olives do best with a southern exposure, they should be open in the center like a *cesta* or basket in order to receive as much sun and air circulation as possible. This year's olives grow off of last year's growth. The best advice came in the saying, "Make me poor and I'll make you rich." The more severe the pruning, the more flowers and therefore olives will result.

Roger asked the expert to look at our fruit trees, hedges, magnolias and other vegetation. It didn't take much prodding. The expert was full of advice, instructing Roger on maintenance, fertilization and irrigation while trimming and snipping. The students boarded the bus at two, anxious to leave but the *maestro* preferred to linger with his pruning soul mate. Finally it was time to leave. We thanked Totò, waved goodbye to the *ragazzi* and gave special thanks to our technical advisor.

With the pruning of the olives and the arrival of our first guests, vacation was officially behind us. Our availability calendar was filling steadily and our marketing successfully differentiated us from other vacation rentals. We'd had positive word-of-mouth but continued to track all leads.

An Atlanta travel agent who conducts Italian tours was intrigued with our property. She wanted to see *Le Vigne* herself before referring clients. We suggested she make *Le Vigne* an afternoon stop on her tour, perhaps between Assisi and Perugia and she embraced the idea. The itinerary to her clients read, "Enjoy lunch at a country villa and meet the couple who are living the dream." In a single phrase, we had gone from an afternoon stop to hosting a lunch for a busload of thirty tourists.

A flurry of activity ensued. We planned to keep things simple: informal outdoor lunch on the terrace overlooking Perugia, plastic plates, cups and cutlery, paper napkins, wine and water, tea sandwiches from Faffa, the ever popular rolls and grilled sausages, cookies and pastries.

Roger decided the *piazza* needed to be pressure-cleaned before the lunch. He turned into a prune; pressure-cleaning barefoot and in the rain. Enzo told him he'd be sick in the morning. I fretted about where thirty people would sit if we had to pull this party indoors and where to put sixty muddy shoes while guests roamed the house.

Anticipating good weather, we suggested the group arrive at noon so guests could look at the house and stroll the grounds before lunch. The weather held. This made things easier when the travel agent called at nine thirty to say they had already finished touring Assisi. Could we move lunch up a bit and meet the bus to lead them to *Le Vigne* as the driver didn't understand the directions we provided? Jeans still wet from pressure-cleaning, Roger left for Assisi while I organized the platters of food and Mick built a fire to begin grilling.

All was in order for the arrival and the thirty guests had a fine time. Some were a little more inquisitive than others. Closet doors and dresser drawers received unoffered inspection. We ate outdoors in the splendid sunshine; guests took pictures of themselves, the property and of us. They asked to hear our story; we explained *come mai* but in English.

The agent and her guests enjoyed their stop. As Roger and I waved, the bus pulled away while cameras continued to click. The bus rounded the corner and we scurried back to the *piazza* to clean up. In less than three hours a full house of guests were due. We reviewed the checklist: pre-arrival shopping, fresh flowers, chilled *prosecco,* chocolate candies, table set, finish the arrival dinner.

If only the busload could see us now. It took a whole lot of behind the scenes action to prop up the storied couple "living the dream." Bring it on. We were ready. Season two had begun.

The Great Outdoors

Piano, piano, the rains diminished and sunny days prevailed. Indoor exercise gave way to outdoor walks. Sometimes guests would join my walking group. A camera was always advised as views of monte Subasio, Perugia, the church in Colombella, the fields and rolling hills were picturesque and begged to be captured. *Pioppo* or poplar blossoms filled the sky with the warm-weather version of snowflakes. Fuzzy white petals carpeted the gravel roads and blanketed the streams like foaming bubbles at bath time.

A four-legged friend insisted on joining our group. The white lab we've named Pippo waits for us to round the corner. Hopping and frolicking, he then stretches, making that yawning sound that is close to human. The menagerie grows as Liana brings Flo, her Cavalier King Spaniel. Pippo barks at other dogs but if one returns the greeting he cowers behind the petite Flo.

A curious side-note regarding dogs. Most dog names are not Italian. I've met a Molly, Ronnie, Sofie, Charlie, Friskie, Genny, Igor, Toby, Bessie, Rocky, Lucky, Lola and Didi. I'm told these names were chosen because they're short and easy to remember. I hope that's the case. It's a better reason than thinking it's some sort of commentary about dogs and people, especially people with English names.

Winged friends announce their presence after the long winter. We found robins' nests tucked into the ivy and *merli,* blackbirds kicking up the dirt around the *piazza.* Our favorite bird is the *l'upupa,* named for the mournful repetitive chant that it makes. The sound is so unchanging and rhythmically spaced we thought it was a distant alarm clock that hadn't been turned off. The bird looks as odd as it sounds. It's brown with a white tail and has white wing tips interspersed with black horizontal stripes. It has a dark tuft of hair that looks gelled into place and a long pointed beak. It flies low and feeds on worms outside our kitchen window. It's a protected species according to our hunter masons who respect the wildlife and share reference books that classify the bird, its habits and surroundings.

We simply could not get enough outdoor time. While I walked in the morning, Roger rose progressively earlier to greet the sun. He's up with the *merli,* watering plants, deadheading geraniums, building walls and sorting rocks, all the while drinking double shots of *espresso.* Rural Umbria is very *tranquillo,* peaceful, calm, tranquil. But the sunrise sounds of nature are anything but peaceful. The birds are hungry and noisy – chickens, ducks, roosters, peacocks, geese, turkeys; all squawking. If they're awake, we should be too.

Roger envisioned more and more garden space. Areas left untended now became manicured, floral, weedless, pristine. The daffodils, tulips and iris of spring gave way to wisteria, cherries and jasmine. Roses were abundant, fragrant and varied. We planted. We planted like crazy. Hundreds of geraniums filled flowerbeds, window boxes and dozens of terra cotta pots. We drained Marina of petunias, impatiens, hydrangeas, daisies, vinca, verbena and marigolds. The ivy we planted in the *blochetti* walls had begun to take hold and cascade. The lavender was spectacular. The view around the tennis court was purple, the scent unmistakable and the air throbbed with the humming of bees. Herb pots near the kitchen are groaning with chives, oregano, parsley, thyme, basil and sage.

The olive grove is mowed to perfection. The sporadic volunteer poppy or sunflower growing next to an olive survives. The fields we leased to Grasselli were planted and harvested; the transition from green to gold to stubble happening all too quickly.

Flowers aren't the only plantings. We fought the snails and birds to successfully grow lettuces, radishes, zucchini, tomatoes, cucumber, eggplant, onions, potatoes, artichokes and Swiss chard. We overdid it on the zucchini. One variety is round and particularly prolific. We harvest daily and I've introduced zucchini bread into the Italian diet for our neighbors and included it in our guest welcome package to spread the wealth. I make zucchini casseroles, hot and cold soups, fritters, fried and stuffed flowers and salads. We eat it raw, steamed, sautéed. I comb cookbooks and the internet for new recipes and share bags full with Mick. I can't give it to anyone else; neighbors have their own surfeit.

One block wall, ten feet high and thirty feet long, is known as the strawberry wall. Over one hundred berry plants flourish, kissed by the sun. Our young guests run to the wall every morning to pick fresh berries for breakfast. Sometimes I gather enough to make *gelato* that's rich, creamy, divine.

Sun-ripened peaches and apricots lend themselves to *gelato* as well. Daily, Roger brings the fruit to the house in oversize pails. We eat them while they're still warm, juices dripping from hands and chins. When I'm not making *gelato*, I peel the fruit, add a little sugar and freeze small portions to enjoy during the winter months. We make sure the guests are well-stocked with this bounty but more remains. I ask Giuliana what to do with all this fruit. Martha Stewart without a rap sheet tells me to put up marmalade. It's easy, she says. All summer long, she'll put up marmalade, tomatoes, beans and more. She forgets I'm a city girl from Miami. I've never put up in my life. Where I come from we put up with, not put up.

We've enlisted Antonio to help us with corn. Corn, in Italy, is primarily a feed crop, a sacrilege according to Roger. Corn requires more garden space than we've created so Antonio's planted it in his garden based on Roger's drawings and instructions. The first harvest was small but going from plot to pot in eight minutes was a treat. A grind of salt and pepper and a slathering of butter on a half dozen ears brought back memories of summer cookouts. Antonio crinkled his nose at the pepper but liked everything else about it. Corn remains a work in progress.

Projects

Antonio continues to be our property angel. He smoothly transitioned from the various inside renovations to outside projects. He's become more comfortable in our presence. Occasionally, he'll drop the "*Lei*" formal address with me but it stands with Roger. He'll accept Roger's offer of a glass of wine following an afternoon's work. He'll even linger to chat about plants, vegetables and walls. He and Roger have settled into their own form of communication. They manage; Antonio's incredibly patient with Roger's Italian and understands more English than he admits.

Every once in a while a female guest nonchalantly asks about the attractive, well-dressed man who's working at *Le Vigne*. Even Roger's immediate response would be Antonio. Our *capo* is not a dandy and certainly not fussy but he's the only person I know who can change the oil in the Gator, replace a pump in a muddy two hundred foot well, dig lines of irrigation and reappear at the end of the day as impeccably groomed as when he started. There are no stains on his silk-blend shirt, no grime covering the Italian shoes. His shirt collar remains insouciantly but unaffectedly upturned. I'm convinced he is completely unaware of his capacity to appear as though he's walked off a magazine cover.

When Roger or I toil outdoors, it's obvious where we've been and what we've done. My forehead will be dirt streaked from pushing the hair out of my eyes, Roger's shirt will be salt stained from sweat. Dust and grime plume around us like Charles Schulz's Pigpen. We are as far removed from impeccably groomed as two people can be. Guests love the contrast.

We on the other hand love him. Antonio can accomplish just about anything and if he can't or chooses not to, he knows who can. Whoever he contacts to do the job is as reliable as he is. He's masterful in plumbing, heating, air, electricity, iron working, fencing, irrigation, masonry, carpentry and the ins and outs of the bureaucratic system. He's diligent, smart, honest, resourceful, unflappable and the ultimate answer to any difficult problem. He's our *capo* and a well-dressed one at that. We are lucky to be able to call him friend.

Antonio worked side-by-side with Roger and the masons all summer long. The outdoor *cantina* is finished and the bump that juts from the side of the house appears as though it's been there for hundreds of years. No longer am I the only one to access this hole in the wall. Roger can stand tall, not hit his head and comfortably roam around this new storage area with built-in shelves and benches. The next project was a circular brick and stone flowerbed to cover an old cistern. Then came the great wall of Umbria.

Roger's original idea was to create a small brick and stone retaining wall from the end of the *piazza* toward the back entrance of the property. He visualized hundreds of geraniums interrupted by *ortensia,* hydrangea, and the occasional lilac, forsythia and quince. As with many of Roger's ideas, this one grew in scope. Feature creep took over and irrigation was installed and the wall grew taller and longer. Roger lovingly micro-managed the selection and placement of every brick and stone. He had the masons use special bricks as decorative features. One stamped "Perugia" was prominently placed at eye level. Another, forever holding the paw print of a cat, occupied the prime spot on a step. Under his guidance, the masons created a face with eyes made from Leonardo da Vinci Euro coins and an upturned mouth made from the curve of a roof tile. The sixty meter long effort is now known as the face wall.

Within striking distance of the face wall is the back entrance of *Le Vigne*. The ugly white metal bar with a combination lock is gone. In its place is an attractive wood and iron gate that used to be the principal entry gate to *Le Vigne*. The masons built stone and brick columns and Antonio, electrician Giuliano and gate expert Federico installed the tracks and tubing to operate the gate electrically.

Roger and Antonio renamed the masons *bambini*. They cried every day for more supplies. We don't have enough sand, cement, bricks, or stones. We need rebar for foundations and wood for forms and nails for the wood. If we have to clean the bricks and stones ourselves that steals time from the actual masonry work. I became quite adept at heaving twenty-five kilogram bags of cement into the trunk of the car. Every morning Roger scrubbed bricks so an afternoon supply would be available. We set up shelving using saw horses and ladders and displayed the cleaned stones and bricks as though they were jewels in a Tiffany window. The masons called it self service and consumed everything in sight.

They were spoiled and didn't care for it if Roger pursued some other activity like mowing. I became their favorite runner, well known at the local building supply stores. They would send me for a few tubes of GG113 or some other esoteric item beyond my understanding in English let alone

Italian. Invariably, the GG113 would come in a variety of colors and I'd have to consult a mason for clarification. Meanwhile the shop owner would ask after Roger and send greetings.

I tolerated the hardware store and building supply store but had to be bribed to go to the Commie Mill. The family operating the Mill seems to have involved themselves in this cooperative more as hobby than business. The father is usually seated at the door in a lawn chair. He asks after Roger. When I say he's building walls or planting flowers or mowing the olive grove, Dad shakes his head saying, "Roger works too hard." There are rarely more than one or two customers and when the number exceeds three it gets confusing. The sister is well meaning but must defer to her brother about everything and he can't be interrupted if he's dealing with a customer. Even though the brother is the go-to guy what we want is rarely in inventory. He's always calling another Commie Mill for instructions to operate some tool I've been sent to purchase or the price of this must-have item. While he's on hold, he too asks after Roger, delivering the same works-too-hard head shake. I thank them and the very last thing I hear on the way out the door is "Say hello to Roger."

We have an insatiable appetite for brick so we're constantly searching. Luciano, Antonio and the masons are well trained spies, quickly reporting any brick sightings to Roger. One morning the masons pulled up to the gate driving a truck borrowed from Carlo, a mutual friend. The bed was loaded with bricks recovered from a distant construction site. We all pitched in to unload the trove.

Ever the joker, Roger had me tell the masons that we had just received a call asking if we had seen Carlo's truck in the area. Smiles disappeared, eyes widened, both men gulped. No, that can't be true. Really? Roger said yes, really. It was painful to watch and I couldn't keep up the ruse. I finally said he was kidding. "Roger, don't do that to us." Enzo thrust his hands in front of him, imitating shackled wrists and said, "I thought I would only see the sun again through little squares."

There were so many masonry projects on Roger's to-do list that our masons should have moved in. We installed a brick walkway leading to the bocce court. According to Enzo, it had the shape of a *prosciutto.* There was constant chatter when the masons were present and we had wide ranging discussions covering any number of topics.

Politics surfaced because the country was in the midst of election campaigning. Voters are made aware of the candidates and their positions through a variety of means. The most pervasive dissemination of information takes place in the form of posters that are publicly displayed on specially erected sign boards. In Italy, campaigning is limited to six weeks before the election. Wouldn't that be a great concept to export?

Every town is filled with hundreds of posters. Photos of the candidates, campaign slogans, hammers and sickles beg for attention in a crowded field. There are communists, socialists, rightists, leftists, greens, gays, laborists, moderates, democrats and unionists; over fifty parties seeking the popular vote. The posters peel and crack over time and become marred by graffiti. They're an unsightly mess but a highly effective way to get the message to the voting public.

Once we received a direct mail piece called *La Nuda Verità,* the naked truth, published by the "radical" party. Five naked men and one naked woman claimed that if elected they would "expose" the dirty deeds of past officials and clean up future politics.

Italian politics is best taken with a heavy dose of humor. Witness one of the most popular television shows called *Striscia la Notizia,* loosely meaning Exposing the News. It's a serious program that uncovers graft, corruption and other sordid political dealings. To lighten the load of such weighty matters, two gorgeous, scantily-clad girls assist the host in his important journalistic duties. In the States they'd be called bimbos; here the phrase is *tutte gambe, niente testa,* all legs, no head.

By the time the masons collected their tools, finished with self service and returned the borrowed cement mixer they had accomplished an impressive number of tasks using an equally impressive number of building materials. Luciano had made dozens of trips bringing sand and gravel. Piles of stone from previous renovation work and field collecting had vanished. Mountains of antique brick and almost two hundred bags of cement were required. I knew those bags well. The results were rewarding; from the face wall, to flowerbeds to bocce paths to gate columns, our masons did it right.

No New Projects

After all this activity, Roger declared a moratorium on new projects. I wasn't fooled. He'd send Antonio off on some mission like acquiring and planting thirty Leyland cypress along the lane behind the house and then tell me that the tree planting is not a new project but an offshoot of an ongoing one. He had Antonio replace some old fencing and install new around the entire property. It would keep the hunters and their dogs out in the fall and bring our stand of six majestic Mediterranean umbrella pines in. All this was described as merely a continuation of fencing projects started in his pre-tetanus shot days.

Roger continues to angle for his own *pollaio,* chicken coop. So far, I've been able to stave off this animal husbandry project. Most neighbors have a coop and I've urged him to consider these as his own. Roger spent many an afternoon talking to Augusto about his chickens; how they're cared for, what they eat, the level of egg production. Finally Augusto invited him to see the coop and its inhabitants. All Roger divulged upon returning was that I had to see this for myself.

Italians are quite talented at letting nothing go to waste. When it comes to constructing chicken coops even junk pile rejects are put to good use. Materials having no value under normal circumstances achieve vaunted status when their destination becomes a coop. Stalls defy engineering standards through ingenious application of a scrap of metal, rubber tubing, old fencing, bedsprings, plastic jugs, telephone cords, coat hangers, motorcycle parts, road signs, bath tubs, kitchen utensils, broken bowls. All of this is molded, tied, converted, adapted, reshaped or folded to create the most amazing animal living quarters. No wonder Augusto was so disappointed when he couldn't scavenge through our household shit on day one.

Caroline wants to publish a coffee table book featuring the Italian *pollaio.* Augusto's coop could be the cover story. There used to be a magazine for kids called *Highlights*, maybe it still exists. It was in every doctor's waiting room and always included the same game: try to locate specific objects hidden in the design of the bigger picture. For example, find the porcelain teapot in the school playground. Augusto's *pollaio* is just like this game. If you look long and hard enough, you'll find the porcelain teapot and the school playground.

Roger is fascinated. His grandfather invented the battery brooder which standardized, sanitized and revolutionized egg-laying. In fact, the company slogan was "She will lay the Arndt way." I am not making this up. Augusto's *pollaio* was so far removed from standardized that poor Grandad would roll over at the sight of these anarchist hens. But they were happy and Augusto was happy. And then there are the eggs. The eggs have the most amazing orange yolks imaginable and actually taste like eggs. As ridiculous as that sounds, Roger no longer eats eggs on return visits to the States. He says they have no flavor.

Chicken coops are labor intensive. Before we begin walking at seven every morning, Giuliana has already collected her orange-yolked eggs. She leaves the not insignificant task of feeding to Renato. She's not shirking responsibility; she has her own list of chores. Before *pranzo* each day she's got fresh pasta made along with a breakfast pastry for the next morning. Her house is decorated to the hilt by season. Christmas calls for trees and *presepe* and ornaments and pine wreaths and *pungitopo.* Easter calls for its own tree, perhaps a large quince branch that's forced to bloom indoors. The tree is decorated with hundreds of eggs that she has intricately hand-painted. Naturally, the intact egg shells come from her chickens and geese. Fall is all pumpkins and oddly shaped squash and summer is sunflowers and fresh herbs. If she's not making pizzas in her own wood-fired oven then she's creating tiered cakes for a friend's wedding reception or attending cooking classes in Assisi or designing dramatic flower arrangements after gathering greenery, twigs, abandoned bird nests and pine cones. If all else is done, she's putting up.

There are times Giuliana conducts cooking classes for our guests. I translate while she hand-cuts the *tagliatelle* she's rolled to see-through transparency with her mother's rolling pin. She then describes her hand-painted frescoes tastefully decorating several walls. She's sewn the curtains in the room we're in and lovingly displays a plush soft dish towel made with cloth that she and her mother wove years ago. All this takes place as she whips up a duck pâté; the duck being her own of course, herb-encrusted pork roast, roasted rosemary potatoes, sautéed spring vegetables, garden salad and *tiramisu* for fifteen people in less that two hours.

Giuliana rivals Roger in terms of energy level and would gladly purchase an old ruin if Renato gave her half a chance. Each time she decides on a new renovation project, Renato shoulders the responsibility that lasts for months. First there was the renovation of old animal stalls, then there was the new kitchen in the main house and now there's talk of adding an infinity pool.

Roger gets all twitchy himself at the thought of a ruin. How this would not be considered a new project requires imaginative and manipulative reasoning skills that only he can muster. It just so happened that talk of a ruin came our way. Anacleto, Antonio's oldest brother, stopped by *Le Vigne* recently to chat. He arrived on his little Vespa and introduced himself. We offered a coffee and walked around the property. Much had changed in the thirty years since he worked here planting oleander and hedges that had tripled in size. He complimented us on the olive grove, gardens, walls and pathways. It was clear Anacleto had a purpose to his visit but decorum called for us to speak of other things before getting down to business.

We talked about his family and his mother who is ninety, widowed, nearly blind and the mother of seven, grandmother of seven. She has good days and bad but is surrounded by loved ones. We spoke of the weather; last year's heat, this winter's rains. We talked about his name. He is the only Anacleto we've ever met. Finally he broached the subject.

These days, Anacleto helps maintain the gardens of a nearby home owned by three sisters. The sisters want to sell the house. He went to great pains to explain that he had no financial interest in the sale; he was simply bringing two parties together. Would we like to see the property?

The no-new-project rule was conveniently sidelined. Roger managed to communicate his interest without translation assistance. The three of us joined other brother Enzo on the short drive to *I Tigli,* The Lime Trees. The massive villa dating from 1359 was not quite a ruin but sorely needed attention. We soon lost track of rooms and structures. We're sure of this: many outbuildings, five kitchens, eleven bedrooms, eleven bathrooms, a small church, a carriage house and dilapidated greenhouses. There was an above-ground pool and a circular fishpond in the central driveway lined by the lime trees for which the property is named. Substantial oaks, certain to be centuries old, were so large that three of us holding hands could not encircle a trunk.

We had lived in Italy long enough to know that discussions regarding price should be approached in zigzag fashion. Roger knows no other way than straight ahead. Not surprisingly, no one had an answer but Anacleto promised to call us as soon as he knew. Roger can renovate anything and there was enough potential here to get his creative juices flowing. He finds it hard to resist the allure, the thrill, the challenge, the planning, the list-making that accompanies such a project.

Weeks later, Anacleto returned. He stood with us as we watered the bocce court in anticipation of guests playing that evening. We performed our ritual dance; we offered a coffee and discussed the weather before he felt the moment was right to divulge the price. He cleared his throat and reported the figure in *lire.* We made the conversion and it was staggering. The amount in *lire* was downright silly. I don't think I've ever seen so many zeroes, nine to be exact. The sisters wanted four billion *lire* or two million Euro or two point four million dollars.

For Roger, the allure of *I Tigli* was in the chase and once the numbers were reported we could easily decline. I was proud of myself for letting events unravel without stepping on the brakes. Now I could once again sleep without worrying about how we could possibly host, entertain, garden, clean, conduct change-overs, maintain the pool, tennis and bocce court, prepare arrival dinners, translate cooking classes, mow, do pre-arrival shopping, conduct tours, work with and for the masons and take on yet another property to renovate.

Recently, Roger's mother asked me where we like to sit and read and relax. Having been here she could readily visualize our home and wanted a mental image of us on the terrace or in the *soggiorno* or *salone rustiche*. I opened my mouth to answer and nothing came out. We never stand still.

So, in the end, even Roger wasn't terribly disappointed about *I Tigli*. He still had enough projects at *Le Vigne*, be they new or ongoing, to stimulate his active mind. Anacleto put on his white helmet and zipped away, seemingly unperturbed at not having made a sale. The four billion *lire* house was a good story but it quickly faded as we moved forward into deep summer and adventures with our guests.

Guests

*I*t is with the utmost gratitude and sense of good fortune that I report that *Le Vigne* is thriving as a self-catering vacation rental. Our early fears about locating customers, finding our niche and differentiating our product were overcome. We built it, they came. This is not intended as boastful and it was nowhere near as simple as that sentence makes it seem. We worked hard and our success has been greater than we could have imagined.

Thanks to word of mouth and creative marketing techniques we've hosted hundreds of guests, some more than once. Several have been European but most are from the States. We are booked well in advance and often find ourselves in the enviable position of declining reservations or suggesting alternative dates due to an almost full calendar.

In no small measure, success can be attributed to our participation in charitable auctions. Here's how it works. A week's stay at *Le Vigne* is featured at a fund-raising auction. We establish a minimum bid at a price lower than our standard rates but sufficient to cover expenses. Normally, *Le Vigne* is the biggest ticket item in the auction, raising the most funds and more than one week is auctioned. It's a win for all. The bidders win a fabulous week in Italy, the charity wins by receiving all monies over the minimum bid and we win by receiving exposure to our target market. After investing in travel ads and linking with websites and offering commissions to travel agents all of which resulted in *poco niente*, auctions have become our sole form of advertising.

We've supported cancer research, a symphony orchestra, scholarship foundations, private schools, hospitals, Operation Smile, YMCA, Alzheimer research, organizations supporting mentally challenged young adults and at-risk teenagers. In the process, we have met amazing people with wide-ranging talents, interests and careers. *Le Vigne* has given us entrée to people and places we never would have known otherwise. Deep and abiding friendships have been the bonus result.

Participating in these auctions is the reason most of our guests are from the States. A map of the country would show heavy representation from Georgia, Pennsylvania, Florida, California and Mississippi. The links between these States and others would look like Delta's route map. American guests tend to appreciate the hands-on approach that has become our trademark, a distinguishing feature of the type of hospitality we provide. A vacation at *Le Vigne* can be a turn-key, no stress event where all needs are catered to from airport arrival to departure. Knowledge of the Italian language and familiarity with restaurants, guides, drivers, points of interest, artisans, vineyards, specialty shops, *sagre*, chefs and wine bars give us an insider's edge. Our guests reap the benefits.

Our trademark is a double-edged sword. It is a huge customer draw but one that ties us closely to our guests. Our friends in the same business are surprised by our level of involvement. Their approach is to take the money, hand over the key and make sure the guests are out the following week in sufficient time to change sheets and hand over the key again. That's certainly one approach. Sometimes the ties that bind are comfortable, pleasant, relaxed. It's as though we've known these guests for years and we could continue to be in each other's company easily. Other ties are not so pleasant; one week can seem an eternity.

It takes all kinds and if we had any doubts regarding this banality we shouldn't be in the hospitality industry. Innkeepers, concierge and bed & breakfast owners should form a union whose code would be to protect identities, habits and idiosyncrasies of guests. Behavior would call for us to be discreet, not betray surprise at any bizarre action, to patiently explain the same thing from day to day, week in, week out without conveying boredom, annoyance or condescension. Once a year, union members could meet to vent, compare notes in secrecy and then return to three hundred sixty-four days of confidentiality and discretion.

We belong to no such union. We are not duty-bound to any blood oaths. I'm here to dish a little dirt, to bring you alongside and marvel at some of the outrageous things people do. While it's not all like that, every now and then we must take a few seconds, collect our thoughts and restrain all urges to immediately evict. A friend once insightfully asked, "To what extent is it fun and to what extent is it work?" The simple answer is that it becomes work when guests behave badly.

Most have been utterly charming. Once on Italian terrain, they meld into our world. They make an effort to try new foods, learn a few Italian phrases, celebrate, not condemn, the differences between cultures. They are respectful and inquisitive.

There are those who deliver gifts upon arrival, buy generous and lovely presents during their stay or treat us to lunch or dinner. An artist gave us a framed painting of *Le Vigne* based on photos from our website. Thoughtful guests have written in advance offering to bring supplies we're unable to get here. Many more deliver important intangible gifts in the form of humor, companionship and intelligent conversation.

Ours is a home environment not a hotel. There are those who considerately treat their stay as if they are occupying the guest bedroom down the hall rather than renting some stranger's villa. They eagerly want to demonstrate their appreciation to their hosts, perhaps making their beds every morning or cleaning the kitchen every day. They feel at home, pitching in to help weed the garden or deadhead flowers. Despite our objections, they insist on stripping beds on departure day and remaking them in advance of arriving guests. This is above and beyond.

My favorite guest stories involve children as they have an interesting take on life at *Le Vigne*. Our friends Miriam and Brad have twin boys and the family visited when the twins were eleven. This was the boys' first overseas trip. They began in England before traveling to Italy. It was an exciting adventure that included dining at the Tower of London, visiting Westminster Abbey and Big Ben, touring Rome's Forum and Coliseum. Back home, the boys were asked by a friend what it was like "over there in Italy." "Well," Ryan began, "first, they drink blood orange juice." Reed continued, "and their kitchens have no toe space," the presence of which he demonstrated by kicking his foot under his own kitchen counter. In unison, they agreed that the most fun they had was learning to drive our Gator and sliding down the muddy hill the masons created while constructing the face wall. Miriam loved it - she and Brad had exposed the boys to the majesty of London and the wonders of ancient Rome yet the twins' lasting impressions are blood orange juice, kitchen toe space and playing in the mud.

Providing new experiences to children whose lives are overly scheduled and consumed by Game Boys, televisions and computers has been rewarding. How many children had their first driving experience in the Gator under Roger's watchful eye? How many children, young at heart like Mamma Ruta and Roger's mother delighted at the blast of air through their hair while Roger drove them through the olive grove at top speed? How many children helped me make *gelato* using freshly picked strawberries, peaches or apricots? How many were compelled to divulge the addition of chopped Perugina chocolate bars as the "secret" ingredient in our ice cream concoction? How many asked for more zucchini bread or helped me in its preparation? How many stood on chairs to reach the counter and make lemonade from our own baseball-size, sugary sweet lemons?

How many read books in the hammock or helped mow the grass or worked side-by-side with Roger building block walls? How many carried buckets to the apricot and fig trees; eating with one hand, picking with the other? How many made special drawings for our bulletin board, learned how to swim or twirl pasta or ordered their own *pizza margherita*? How many joined a pick-up soccer game at a *sagra* without knowing a word of Italian or climbed into bed at night trying to bring the six-foot long dolphin float with them? How many painted ceramic plates or cups with Valentina; the artistry, patience and affection serving as common language? How many told their parents they wanted to forever be known as Roger? How many, on departure day, threw their arms around my neck, nuzzling in to ask when they could return? However many it was, it was nowhere near enough. To witness the purity of joy and discovery in such simple things is gratifying. Even more rewarding, parents tell us it's the best vacation they ever had as a family.

Less rewarding are the experiences with children who lack any discipline in their lives at home - the three angels who pulled all the geraniums out of the flower beds, the boys who denied walking into our living space to take a basketball from a corner of the room, those who left tennis balls and rackets strewn on the court when play ended. Fortunately, there aren't many of the super-spoiled.

Strangely, guests want to compete for the pejorative award. "Are we the worst guests you ever had?" "Are we the most demanding, are we the highest maintenance?" As in *King Lear,* the King's declaration of being mad made him sane. He was only truly mad when he said he wasn't. In similar fashion, the worst guests are those who never think to ask the question; the ones who bring their alcoholic brawling to new heights while on vacation, those whose screaming tantrums and foul-mouthed tirades accompanied by shattered bottles and slamming doors make Martha and George in *Who's Afraid of Virginia Woolf?* look like June and Ward Cleaver.

Aside from the outright lunatics, the next most difficult guest type is the intolerant. A pleasant traveling experience calls for an open mind, flexibility and adaptability. The intolerant morosely wants to know why dinner is so late, why the shops are always closed, why restaurants don't have American food, why he has to use Euro instead of dollars and best of all, why these people don't speak English. Some guests are just quirky. We've had a lot of women bring clothes they have no intention of keeping. Vacation is a time to jettison. We learned about this habit only after trying to track down half a dozen to return their belongings. Sometimes our possessions grow legs. Odd things disappear, like a bread basket, kitchen utensils, books, a corkscrew. Perhaps they're inadvertently thrown away.

Some guests are wasteful but oblivious to the waste. Guests turn on an air conditioner, open the windows and doors and then leave for the day. Instead of making use of the glorious summer sun for drying, guests wash clothes at night and run the dryer all night long. They'll grocery shop as though they're here for months, overload the fridge and then abandon large quantities of untouched food. Not to be too much of an environmental zealot, their carbon footprint is anything but dainty.

Some events are comical. On arrival we make it clear that our *orto* is readily available for guest use. Late one afternoon, a guest collected tomatoes, eggplant and herbs. Roger was watering nearby and asked what he planned to prepare. A special pasta sauce was on the menu. He cheerfully waved several branches of greenery in Roger's direction, saying, "And this bunch of fresh basil is going to be the perfect finishing touch." Exercising a rare display of simultaneous facial and verbal restraint, Roger directed him to the pot of basil on the patio. Instead of basil, our guest had procured a bountiful harvest of green pepper tops.

One of our rare European guests was a family from Scandinavia. They arrived in early March when the weather is typically cold and capricious. They knew the pool wasn't heated but they wanted to be sure it would be available for use. We thought it odd but decided their polar blood was stout enough to handle the low temperatures.

The week before the family's arrival, Roger's mother Nancy was scheduled for a knee replacement. Roger flew to Pittsburgh to be with her and help Dana. Reviewing the two-page, single-spaced list of *compiti* he left behind, I couldn't help wondering whether Nancy and Roger conspired to select this precise week for delivery of her new knee. The list was a monster, loaded with deceptively simple-sounding little gems like "clean the pool" and "finish your book."

Last fall, the masons removed the cracked tile that formed the entire pool coping. They replaced the tile with travertine that is not only beautiful but impervious to the freeze damage that caused the original tile breakage. The pool remained uncovered all winter. Without pumps, filters or chlorine to keep it clean and sparkling, it was a stagnant, murky lagoon.

Antonio opened the drain late one afternoon. Early the next morning a portion of the olive grove was flooded and the pool was empty except for the foot-thick layer of leaves, muck and algae-green ooze coating the bottom. Mission Impossible called for us to remove the muck, scrub the pool, repair a broken pump, refill the pool, adjust the chemicals and have it pristine in time for our guests' arrival. Four of us donned knee-high rubber boots and elbow-length rubber gloves. We began at the shallow end, making dozens of trips to remove bucket-loads of compost-worthy gunk. By the time we arrived at the deep end, the nine-foot trips up and down the ladder became vertigo-inducing.

Once the leaves were removed, we used brushes and an interesting mix of acids and other chemical compounds to scrub every inch of the pool interior. If the EPA had seen this exercise we would have been issued hazmat suits. Storm clouds threatened but eventually the sky cleared to brilliant sunshine. The reflection on the pool lining was blinding. We were quite a sight in sunglasses, boots and gloves. We worked through the afternoon while Antonio repaired the pump. At eight that evening, he finished tacking down loose areas of the liner with silicone and began filling the pool. All was right with the world by the time Roger returned and the guests arrived.

Predictably, nary a Scandinavian toe entered the pool. The family could not get warm enough. The wood stove burned constantly. Radiators glowed orange and the auxiliary room heating units were set on high heat, max fan.

Often we accompany our guests to restaurants and it can be completely enjoyable or thoroughly disagreeable. Picky eaters, parents or children, are difficult. The demand for me to translate ten pages of a menu and ultimately find nothing appealing is irritating.

That said, I can't tell you how many four-hour wine tastings, lazy afternoon lunches and long nights under the stars we've spent with our guests.

It's perpetually enjoyable to uncork a fine *Sagrantino*, the signature wine of Umbria. It's a pleasure to reveal Corys' sublime *tagliatelle con asparagi e fragole,* homemade pasta with asparagus and strawberries, or L'Osteria del Bosco's *dolce della Mamma,* Luigi's mother's dark chocolate dessert or *risotto con melone* from Lo Spedalicchio. This restaurant has been renamed "Oh, my spleen is leaking so," by our friend Karen who visited to celebrate her fiftieth birthday. That's as close as she could get to pronouncing the tongue-twister and it's a pretty fair approximation. From fine dining experiences such as these to *porchetta* at the local market, guests indulge in gastronomic pleasures because we're able to lead them there.

Vicariously participating in our guests' discoveries has been touching as they search for family roots and histories. To celebrate their fortieth wedding anniversary, Anita and Charlie brought their children and grandchildren to the land of their ancestors. We easily accommodate seven people, nine if we use our personal guest bedroom, ten if we put a sofa bed into service. This crowd totaled fifteen; seven under the age of twelve. Bodies were everywhere. Parents slept with children three or four to a bed. Extra mattresses covered limited floor space. There was constant motion. A non-stop hum permeated *Le Vigne*. Anita called them the cicadas; her term, not mine.

One day we joined the family on a drive to Montefollonico to visit Andrea, Anita's cousin, his wife and their three boys. Montefollonico is the small historic Tuscan town where Anita's father was born. For Anita it was an emotional experience – entering the church where her father was baptized, recognizing the door of his childhood home from photographs she had seen over the years. With Andrea's help she chatted with a few of the older residents who had known her father. Now her grandchildren were running up and down the same cobbled streets with their distant cousins. They had found a common language simply by being children playing on a hot summer day.

We gathered for *pranzo* at a local restaurant. Twenty relatives arranged themselves on the outdoor steps and Roger and I took photo after photo with at least six cameras. Inside, a long table was set. Cousin Andrea had arranged the menu, taking the painful ordering process out of the equation.

Strange things happen in large family gatherings. The toddler who normally refuses to eat tomato sauce is covered with tell-tale red stains on her cheeks, in her hair, on her tee-shirt. At the far end of the table a language mix-up between *basta* and *pasta* resulted in unordered platters of *pasta* being served. No worries. The additional food vanished.

Parents and grandparents were proud and it was moving to watch Anita and Charlie surrounded by family. Three generations united in the land of the father, grandfather, great grandfather or uncle made for a satisfying day filled with accomplishment and continuity. The continuity extends to us. We now have a connection to Montefollonico. Andrea, visits us every fall when Charlie comes to help with our olive harvest. He dines with us and gets caught up on family stories. Memories were made that summer's day and they have become part of our mutual family lore.

Jaye and Bill spent a few days with us recently. One overcast Sunday morning they traveled to Le Marche, the region to the east of Umbria, in search of her grandmother's roots. Armed only with her grandmother's name and the name of the small village where she was born, they launched on the two hour drive east. Castelvecchio is just like many other small towns in Italy. The center consists of one main *piazza* and a single narrow road leads into and out of town. Two or three-story brick and stone buildings line the road and block the sunlight to the few shops below. The church is always at the physical and spiritual center.

They arrived in Castelvecchio just as church services were ending. As in a fairy tale, the sun broke through the clouds as they stood on the church steps. Blindly, they chose someone to speak to using a combination of gestures, family names, English, a little Italian. That person led them to someone else with the same surname as Jaye's grandmother. The second stranger was not related but invited them to her home where they were asked to join that family for lunch. Their host made phone calls to try and locate someone who was indeed family. She succeeded and directed Jaye to that home.

As Jaye entered this distant relative's house, she noticed a photo on the wall. It was grainy, black and white and filled with people dressed formally for a wedding. Jaye recognized it immediately. She has the same picture in her home. In the line-up of squinting faces was Jaye's grandmother. So many years later, so many miles apart yet the day's events aligned perfectly to connect family members previously unconnected. Promises to write and keep in touch and share photos and family stories were somehow communicated in a jumble of languages and hugs. Jaye's emotional high was infectious and her family story became ours to tell.

Guests like to shop and ceramics and artwork rank high on the purchase list. When we travel to the States, we see these items proudly displayed as memories of special vacations. We find Umbria and *Le Vigne* transplanted into everyday American life whether it's seeing a beautiful framed photograph of our home on display or bottles of *Le Vigne* olive oil in kitchens. Valentina's plates or spoon rests or clocks or platters splash *Ricco Deruta,* Deruta's famous flowery design or Perugia's *Grifo,* griffin logo across American homes.

Oil paintings and water color scenes of cypress trees and poppy-filled hillsides are difficult for guests to resist. In Cortona, art purchases are made from Marco and sister Paola, owners of *Galleria d'Arte Nocchia.* Their exquisite taste is evident in the selection of art, frames and the restoration of the gallery itself, featuring an Etruscan well and the ancient remains of the town's communal oven. The gallery ships worldwide and there's great satisfaction in our being able to connect the trans-Atlantic dots from ceramics to oil to art.

In the end, the significant question remains, is it work or is it fun? On balance it's more fun. We've helped create indelible memories for guests and ourselves. When asked what they remember most their answers vary. Some say it's touring the historic cities of Perugia, Gubbio, Assisi, Spoleto or Orvieto with Marco Bellanca. There's no doubt he's the best guide in Umbria – knowledgeable, dramatic, impassioned and able to entertain a six-year-old or a sixty-year-old equally. The wine enthusiasts might say it's time spent at Marco Molesini's *enoteca,* wine shop, in Cortona's *Piazza della Repubblica,* where the owner conveys his expertise regarding Tuscan wines in superb English. Others indulge their senses in Umbrian vintages featured in Spello where Drinking Wine proprietor Maurizio hosts wine tasting luncheons in his charming *enoteca.*

Morning walks through the Umbrian hills, a fifty-fifth birthday extravaganza complete with food, music, dancing and fireworks, a previously unknown talent for *bocce,* an ability to drink red wine without suffering a headache due to the absence of sulfites in these limited, boutique-production wines, dancing and lip-synching the soundtrack of *Chicago,* rolling pasta or gnocchi by hand, sleeping with the windows wide open on a cool summer night, guests trying to "Italianize" their names, the common request that we adopt them; all this and more tip the scale to the side of fun.

And for those we'd like to evict? Eventually we're able to do even that. For in the end they are guests and their stay is finite and with a little *pazienza,* sometimes a lot, they're gone. The fun ones, new friends and memories, can't be far behind.

Mek Mek

I have stories to share about Mick. Since he started working at *Le Vigne* two weeks after we moved here we've all grown into this property and each other together. From the very start Mick's been unfailingly polite and respectful. I'm always Ma'am, Roger is always Sir. There's not a job that he hasn't readily agreed to undertake and we've had our share of disagreeable ones.

Mick is reticent and shy in our presence. I'm sure he's not this timid among his peers. We're used to his quiet nature but it drove Mike batty when he and Linda visited for the puny harvest. Mike made it his personal quest to elicit streaming commentary from Mick. His quest failed. The result was streaming commentary from Mike.

Over time Mick has relaxed to reveal a sly wit. The verbosity is relative. When Mike visits he continues to find the quiet oppressive but since we're in Mick's company daily we know the difference. I wouldn't call him a chatterbox but there's more to the day's conversation than "Good morning, Ma'am, good morning, Sir."

Mick left the Philippines in search of work. "There are no jobs in my country, Sir." The sentence explains the sizeable Filipino population in Perugia. Leaving the Philippines meant leaving a young daughter. From his *Le Vigne* earnings, Mick sent money by way of the child's mother. For a while he talked about getting married to the mother but that talk ceased. Time and distance proved too much for the relationship. The mother became involved with someone else and it broke Mick's heart, mostly at being further removed from the little girl. The baby's picture is with him always. She's precious – smiling, bright eyes, full head of dark hair, very fancy dress.

The little girl's smile is Mick's. When he grins, those bright whites can be seen from across the *piazza*. Roger teases him unmercifully just to get to see that smile. "What gang are you in Mick? That tattoo on your wrist must stand for some super secret underworld oath. Better get rid of that earring, Mick. No earrings allowed in Roger's World. Mick, why did you say all those mean things about Mrs. Arndt?" As he denies all, backpedaling while removing the earring, he resorts to his favorite habit. He grabs the neck of his shirt, pulls it in front of his mouth and tilts his head downwards to cover a giggle. Arriving at this point wasn't easy; sort of like pulling some of those pearly whites.

Mick's been with us through every step of renovating, planting, building, cleaning and re-cleaning *Le Vigne*. He's learned how the grounds should look, how the apartment should be arranged, how clothes need to be ironed, how the olive grove should be mowed, how the compost should be tossed from the kitchen daily. He removed tons of rubble, dug the holes for many of the six hundred olive trees, weeded around those trees, watered thousands of plants, contributed his share of sweat into building the block walls that are almost a quarter mile long, often worked six-day weeks, shoveled buckets of sand, compost, dirt and stones for every project and did it all with that wonderful, beautiful, face-breaking smile. His attitude is worth gold. His sense of pride and accomplishment is evident.

When guests arrive, he greets them and carries their luggage to the apartment. We introduce him but often guests erroneously assume he's Italian and doesn't speak English. We set the record straight but perhaps they're too jet-lagged to focus because days later someone will say, "Wow, his English is really good." One guest thought him to be Japanese, another Mexican. Roger took to calling him Mickey-san or Pedro and Mick would alternately bow or say, *"Sí, Señor."* Always with that smile.

In his earliest days with us, I prepared Mick's lunch. I tried to determine his food preferences but since these were the early days it was impossible to elicit a response. After six weeks he started bringing his own lunch. I didn't know whether to be offended or relieved so I was neither. Lunchtime is his time and he's found private spots on the property to hide, eat lunch and text message. Sometimes the spots aren't so private – catnapping in a hammock when the guests are off the property or snoozing in the Trooper when it's chilly.

Roger and I are cell phone challenged but like all young people, Mick is technology savvy. He's our go-to guy for DVDs, TVs, speaker systems, decoders, phones and other apparati that youth are pre-programmed to comprehend. We share our DVD library and he provides one word reviews. His tastes tend toward action and adventure; *Kill Bill, Saw, Con Air.* I don't really worry about *Tea with Mussolini* disappearing for days on end.

Roger insisted Mick watch *The Great Escape* but Mick always found another movie he'd rather borrow. Reluctantly he told Roger that it was "too old school." Roger was crushed. After a series of rainy winter days when no outdoor work was possible and all indoor work was done, Roger called for movie time. They watched *The Great Escape* together, installment-style. Mick had no choice. His verdict? "I was wrong Sir, it was really good."

Roger's been a father figure to Mick. He taught him to use all kinds of equipment from mowers to blowers, how to build a fire and clean the fireplace, how to control a burn pile. Mick learned to drive the Gator thanks to Roger. There were some hairy moments around the *piazza* in the beginning. I thought Roger would be flung from the passenger seat from speed, erratic braking and centrifugal force. Now Mick owns that machine. There have been life lessons as well dealing with money management or the dangers of cigarette smoking. He no longer smokes. Mick admires Roger and has taken to calling him Boss. He's fiercely protective of the Boss, a trait that particularly pleases me.

Mick is a huge basketball fan and plays in the Filipino league in Perugia. Who knew there was such a thing? Mick and Carlo are on the same team and Cesar is a player/coach. Basketball season afforded us greater conversational opportunities. Every Monday morning started with a recap of the previous day's game. His team won often, Mick was frequently high scorer and at the end of one season, he had won the league MVP as a point guard. After sheer erosional effort on our part, Mick invited us to a few games.

One hot Sunday afternoon, we arrived with an outdoor game in progress. We were impressed at the hundreds of Filipinos of all ages in attendance. It was a lively setting and a true community - small children ran around the courts, others dribbled their own basketballs emulating the older players, relatives and friends cheered, foes jeered, gorgeous young girls dressed for attention flirted and giggled.

We were immediately noticed as we took our seats along the sidelines. Several clues gave us away. We're not Filipino and Roger is a foot taller than anyone else. At courtside, an announcer with a microphone is reporting play-by-play and color commentary, assisted by a scorekeeper. The announcer is speaking in a non-stop fluid blend of Tagalog, English and Italian. Smiling, he looks our way and we return the greeting.

We're trying to get our bearings, determine the score, see if Mick is playing when the announcer, in "Heeeeere's Johnny" style says, "And now, ladies and gentlemen, introducing the employer of Mick from the United States, Mr. Roger aaaaaand...," he's looking at me and obviously struggling for a title when he settles on, "aaaaand Mom!" All eyes turn to us, everyone applauds and the announcer turns back to the game.

Mick's jersey says Mek^2 and he's number eleven. Mick's grandfather used to call him Mek Mek, hence the square. Sometimes the announcer calls Mick number twenty-two, doubling (not squaring) his number. The announcer loves the microphone, "...and heeeeeere's Mek Mek, short but terrible," or "He scores!" or rarely, "He shoots and it's...ohhhhh, no good."

Our presence that day was probably a little distracting. Our team lost and Mick wasn't on top of his game. After the final buzzer, Mick brought his mother, Carlo and Cesar over and introduced us. He then returned with drinks and two small aluminum containers. The trays were filled with Filipino food, a blend of mussels, octopus, vegetables and noodles. "Here, Ma'am, Boss, these are on me for coming to watch me, well...suck today" – a virtual discourse from our normally taciturn employee.

The following Sunday promised a major competition. A huge rivalry existed between Mick's team and the team from Rome. The bad guys had a history of playing dirty. We arrived during the first period and received friendly greetings from a few recognizable faces. Once again the announcer acknowledged us; we had become Mr. Roger and Mom. Concession stands flanked the court and Roger asked for a beer. The vendor refused to take Roger's money, "Compliments of the Filipino community, Sir."

From the start, the game seemed off kilter. There was no strong sense of rhythm; neither side could gain traction. Mistakes were being made by both teams. One of our players scored for Rome. A series of fouls on both sides disrupted momentum. Our opponents were keying on Carlo when something happened. There was a skirmish at the far end of the court and Mick and Carlo were at the center; fists flying, whistles screeching, a jumble of arms and legs flailing. Spectators erupted from their seats and rushed the court. Coaches, refs and parents tried to separate entangled bodies. Mick's mother, all five feet of her, levitated from the sidelines and launched into the fray. The scorekeeper called time and the announcer resorted to fast-paced Tagalog. The Thrilla wasn't in Manila, it was here in Perugia.

Edgily separated for the moment, the teams stood in two tight circles surrounded by dozens of advisors. Everyone was talking and gesturing, angry faces were flushed, sweat dripped off players, refs and fans. The announcer turned, focused on us and with a slight shrug said, "Sometimes these things can happen, even in the NBA." The confusion and tension continued for close to fifteen minutes. Finally, Carlo stormed off the court followed by Mick who was followed by Cesar. Play resumed.

We still had no idea what actually happened when Carlo approached us and said "Sorry for the inconvenience." Mick did the same and so did their feisty mother. Would someone please fill us in? Mick explained that an opponent attacked Carlo and he had to defend his brother. Mick's team was penalized and the team leaders decided to throw Carlo out of this game and the next. Everyone found the penalty unfair and too harsh so Mick and Cesar quit in protest.

It seemed a shame but during our Monday morning recap Mick took it in stride. The season was almost at its end and Mick had other things on his mind. He had met a girl living in Milan and the absence of Sunday games would give him time to visit. They would meet in Florence, a mid-point for both. Good for him, he's young and needed some fun. There was always next year for basketball. We were happy to see a new twinkle in his eye and an even broader smile.

A little P.S.: A twinkle in the eye is all well and good as long as the eye doesn't lose focus. One Monday morning Mick called me while I was walking to say he wouldn't be coming to work that day because he was "experiencing bird flu-like symptoms." Between raspy coughs, I tried to find out more but the connection was as weak as his voice and then both were gone.

When I returned home, I told the Boss who promptly called Mick, informing him he'd been watching too much TV. Mick giggled, blowing his cover. "Having a nice time in Florence, Mick?" Hacking cough followed, stifling another giggle. "I'd suggest you appear at *Le Vigne* as soon as physically possible or you'll be experiencing more than bird flu." In nothing short of a miracle, Mick showed up by noon in remarkably good health.

Here was just another life lesson for Mek Mek - not a good idea to trifle with the Boss.

The Mediterranean Pines

There's a process in Italy known as *denuncia*. It is an official complaint. Italians are *denuncia* crazy. Everyone and anyone can be denounced; likewise everyone and anyone can do the denouncing.

The white road leading to our house, the one that appeared on our must-have criteria list has lost its charm over time. The choking dust during the summer and mud during the winter are annoying inconveniences. The real problem is a particularly hazardous area that is deeply rutted and pot-holed. The road is private property and each neighbor should contribute to its maintenance. A five-year struggle over road upkeep that began long before our arrival has resulted in no action other than continued deterioration, especially in the hazardous zone. We've replaced many tires and readjusted headlights dozens of times. We're told we can denounce the neighbors living nearest the bad zone to seek restitution. These are our friends. Can't we come to agreement to jointly repair the road? Endless meetings take place, the same ground is covered and nothing changes. Threats to denounce are rife. It's a true *casino.*

Such is the backdrop to one busy Saturday in late August. It is change-over day – one group of guests leaves and the next arrives. The outgoing guests had been here for two weeks. Both washing machines were slowly churning. Two loads of bed and bath linens had already been pegged. The warm sun and strong breeze made quick work of drying. Mick and I split the ironing of sheets; a task normally reserved for Gina. But this was *ferragosto* and our reliable, professional launderer was on holiday along with most everyone else in Italy. Saint Gina is appreciated all season long; we missed her greatly during vacation.

Every Saturday is a race against the clock. All hands were at work. Even visiting Mamma Ruta pitched in to set the table as the rest of us divided the labor that included stocking the apartment with basic necessities and fresh flowers, vacuuming, dusting, mopping, scrubbing bathrooms, checking light bulbs, emptying the fridge, making beds. Incoming guests were expecting an arrival dinner so dinner preparations were underway. Countless trips were made to get rid of trash or remove cleaning supplies or bring in dry towels. We criss-crossed each other up and down, down and up.

Not surprisingly, Roger created a Prussian-style spreadsheet to catalogue all the basics for stocking the apartment. Lacking the pith helmet and the stick but not the swagger, the Boss swoops in for the final survey: seven boxes of Kleenex, check; twelve rolls of toilet paper, check; two rolls of paper towels, four moisturizing lotions, eight soaps, kitchen soap, laundry detergent, ice in the freezer, *pecorino* cheese on the counter, *salami*, bread, fresh fruit, milk, *prosecco,* juice, Perugina chocolates...check, check, check, check, check.

In the thick of all this activity, I hear the front gate bell. Racing around the apartment, I lean out the green bedroom window but can't determine who's at the gate. By the time I pick up the intercom phone the driver is back in the car so I simply press the button that automatically opens the gate. I have just given access to a police car and two policemen.

Roger likes to say that I'm a wreck in the face of authority. In my defense, I found it a little unnerving to be approached by two policemen in a language that is not my native tongue. I scamper down the steps while Roger casually comes from behind. The policemen greet us, show us identification and ask to speak with the owners. All right, I admit it. I was a wreck in the face of authority. Nervously, I respond that we're the owners and ask what's going on.

The police are holding official paperwork which they allow us to read. I try to absorb the legalese but I'm obviously taking too long. One of the policemen simply says it's a *denuncia*. Oh. My. God. We've been denounced. My mind is racing. I have no idea why we're being denounced but I'm certain we'll be deported. Absurdly, I wonder who's going to prepare the arrival dinner and feed the guests.

In excessively flowery language, the formal complaint claims we've installed illegal fencing along the drive leading to *Le Vigne*. Even more egregious than the fencing transgression is the fact that we enclosed six majestic centuries-old Mediterranean umbrella pines. The *denuncia* claims we had no right to do so, calling the fencing offensive and an eyesore that can no longer be tolerated.

We are stunned, shocked. We feel betrayed and can't believe someone's taken this action against us. We've been denounced and demand to know who in the world has filed such a complaint. Is it a neighbor, a friend, a stranger? Could it be someone I pass every morning on my walk? Worse yet, could it be one of my walking companions? Obviously it's someone in our very midst, someone who sees the work being done here, someone geographically close taking notice of goings-on at *Le Vigne*. Who could it be?

We steel ourselves for the news and ask the policemen. Shock becomes indignation in a flash. The policemen hem and haw and can't quite bring themselves to answer, instead pushing the paperwork back our way, pointing to the signature area. The document is signed, *Cittadini rispettosi delle regole,* respectful citizens of the law. That's all it says. There are no names, no surnames written in capital letters followed by first names in lower-case; no scribbled illegible signatures. In other words, the *denuncia* is anonymous. These are our brave, heroic, valiant and respectful citizens who have stood up to right the wrongs perpetrated against an appreciative, law abiding public.

We are hurt, surprised, taken back. My tremble in the face of authority has given way to a sputtering series of questions...how can they do this, what are you going to do, who cares what these people think, why can't we just throw this away? Meanwhile Roger looks like one of those cartoon characters; faces that transform into steam whistles, vapor blasting from both ears.

Our anonymous respectful citizens are wrong. The fencing is on our property. It replaced older fencing that was also on our property. Most importantly, the well-loved, dramatic and impressive centurion pines are unequivocally on our property. Beyond that, what business is it of anyone's what we do with our land? Moreover, why do the police have to waste their time responding to an anonymous complaint? Since it is in fact anonymous, to whom exactly are they going to respond?

The policemen shuffle their feet and hang their heads. They sheepishly acknowledge, "Yes, *Signori*, we know they are cowards, but we have to make an official response to the proper authorities." We walk into the cool office as they ask for and we produce documentation, drawings and plats that clearly indicate the fencing and trees are on our property. They study, discuss, point fingers and then ask for copies of all this paperwork which we gladly provide. We willingly share the name and number of Francesco, our *geometra* so everything can be verified with him.

After readily providing so much documentation, we're surprised when the policemen won't allow us to make a copy of the complaint. Is this not public knowledge? Yes. Is this *denuncia* not specifically directed against us? Yes. Why can't we have a copy? This fact cannot be explained to anyone's satisfaction. Roger is particularly miffed and no amount of questioning on his part or translating on mine changes their stance. I do manage to obtain the name and phone number of one of the policemen and jot down some of the language from their paperwork. Before leaving, they promise to follow-up with our *geometra* and then wish us *buona giornata*.

Mick and Mamma Ruta show their faces from behind corners where they've been lurking, mildly concerned about their own deportations. Roger explains while I reluctantly call Antonio who's at the beach with the family. Roger wants him to know about the *denuncia*. Unflappable and never a wreck in the face of authority, our *capo* is gracious and polite. Besides, he is the authority. There is no hint of irritation at interrupting his vacation nor the slightest concern about my story. I remain frazzled. "Can you believe these anonymous citizens," I demand, followed by all my other rhetorical questions. He allows me to vent and once I've worn myself out, says "Well, that's the way things can be done here. *Pazienza.*"

Antonio will call Francesco and fill him in on the situation. "Truth be told," he says, "while you're clearly within your rights to install the fencing and enclose the pines, we probably should have Francesco create all the proper drawings and requests for conducting this work."

"Requests?" I screech. "But the work's already been completed."

"That's OK," he tells me. "It can all be done retroactively. Now, let's talk about more important things. Are you coming to visit us at the beach while we're on holiday?"

Leave it to Antonio to place things in perspective. We finish the apartment cleaning, finalize dinner preparations and begin to think about a drive to the coast. We'll show Mamma Ruta the Adriatic, have a nice seafood lunch and visit Antonio and his family in a relaxed setting far removed from busybodies.

It's hard to dismiss the image of these people. How did this come about? Did they meet late at night, in some cramped smelly pig stall, a lantern swinging from the rafters, casting faint light over their conspiratorial heads? Each one in turn goading the other, their spirits emboldened by swilling homemade wine. Once they decide to denounce us anonymously, their moral rectitude grows and they've worked themselves into a fevered pitch of civil disobedience. They are resolved, they are united. They will denounce!

One night, I dreamt that we won the fencing battle but lost the war. Francesco filed all the proper paperwork and everything was in good order. But someone had defaced the fence. Spray-painted in neon orange were the heartbreaking words, "American Go Home." I awake drenched in sweat and decide I really have to let this thought go. It's time to learn some lessons from Antonio; time to shelve this little worry bead. Accept it; that's the way things can be done here. It was only a dream, nothing's been spray-painted, no one's overtly behaving differently. The stoic Mediterranean pines remain as silent observers inside the fence. Neither they nor we are ever likely to learn who our respectful citizens are despite being in our very midst.

Puglia

*I*t's ironic that our guests often see more of Italy than we do. Hosting responsibilities leave us little free time so a recent last-minute cancellation gave us a chance to enjoy a brief sojourn to the south.

We've had a long-standing invitation from Caroline and Augusto to visit them in Puglia, the spur of the Italian boot. In addition to their home around the corner from us and an apartment in Venice, our neighbors own a small home in Mattinata overlooking the ocean. We finally accepted.

Puglia is very different from Umbria – it's desert-like, mountainous, craggy, barren. There's an almost Grecian aspect to the look of these

Southern coastal towns: the preponderance of whitewashed houses with blue accents, the blinding sunlight striking the sea, the weathered older women dressed in black. Not only is the topography different, so is house construction. While Umbria is filled with renovated *casa coloniche* such as ours, Puglia lays claim to the renovated *pagliaio* or straw barn. They are distinctive, small, low ceilinged, white, domed structures. Once a *pagliaio* or two could be picked up for a song but Puglia has been discovered and the prices are soaring toward Tuscan levels.

Puglia has olive trees but the philosophy regarding pruning, growth and harvesting is entirely different. The trees are left to grow tall with no effort to open the center to create the basket. Since it's difficult to reach the upper limbs, harvesting isn't done by hand. Nets are placed under the trees and the olives are allowed to ripen and fall. Once the tree has dropped its fruit, the nets are collected and the olives are taken to the mill to be processed. Truthfully, the oil is not as good as that in Umbria because pressing ripe olives translates to a higher percentage of water than oil. There's a reduction in flavor; it's milder, more insipid, but the quantity is considerably greater. Quantity matters. Italy can't produce enough olive oil for its own consumption so the country imports oil from Spain and Greece. Thus, Italy is able to export its best olive oil. Haven't we become the experts?

Augusto and Caroline's Puglia home is a *pagliaio.* It is small but comfortable even in the heat of late summer. The thick walls and dome cool the interior. Roger's head is in constant danger due to the squat ceilings; even I'm at risk in the bathroom. Removing headers in this house would mean changing the roof line of the *pagliaio.* Fortunately, we're not in the market.

Augusto is from Puglia and many of his relatives still live in the area. On the first evening we join his brothers, a sister, spouses, nieces, nephews, boyfriends and girlfriends at dinner in the *centro.* There's a relaxed camaraderie among family members reflected in the non-stop conversation. The talk is part Italian, part dialect, part shorthand. Settings like these make me question my ability to understand any Italian. I mention it to Caroline who claims it's difficult even for her after all these years.

Augusto has selected the restaurant, his favorite. The owner is a childhood friend who's easing out of the business, allowing a son to manage things. The transition gives the owner the luxury of greeting the familiar patrons, chatting over coffee, offering complimentary appetizers and *prosecco.* He can relax while the son does the heavy lifting.

We sit outside after a complicated shifting of tables from the narrow sidewalk to the equally narrow street. A constant stream of motorcycles and cars adds to the hustle and bustle of waiters and patrons and pedestrians. Occasionally a driver tucks in his side mirror so as not to make contact with diners. Sometimes it takes a combination of tucked mirrors and scooted chairs. The setting is action-packed but delightful. People are friendly, it's warm, the night is clear, the stars are shining and the food is plentiful and tasty. The seafood menu offers a refreshing change from our Umbrian diet.

The next morning we walk into town to Augusto's favorite *pasticceria* for coffee and a *cornetto,* a horn-shaped, cream-filled pastry. The bar owner, the waitress, the *barista,* are all glad to see Augusto back in Mattinata. Again we sit outdoors, chatting amiably. Augusto reads the local paper, sharing current events with Roger. Caroline and I watch passersby and discuss the day's plans.

For lunch, we wander from shop to shop and buy cheeses, tomatoes, olives, *salami* and bread. We return to the *pagliaio* and sit on the tree-shaded patio facing the glistening sea. A herd of scrappy goats provides entertainment. Methodically, they work on clearing a nearby hillside, the bells on their necks ringing as they skitter in one direction or another.

Roger and I are very relaxed and our friends make it easy to be in their company. We move at a leisurely pace, having no agenda, no tight schedule. We drive to nearby towns to visit the outdoor markets. We sample *Puglia bomba*, a fiery tomato and pepper-based sauce bottled in unmarked jars. Small quantities of the sauce are added to pastas, soups, toasted breads. Small is key. This bomb will peel paint.

A plucky young girl sells us the *bomba* and suggests other necessities: strands of dried peppers, massive jars of pickled vegetables, specialty liqueurs. She's very persuasive and we buy more than we need. Augusto engages her in a discussion about education. This is late summer and she's not focused on school. He encourages her to study hard when classes resume. She agrees but street learning holds greater appeal.

Augusto is not the mean, old dumpster guy we first met. He's caring and gentle and very soft spoken. He's attentive to our every medical matter from tetanus shots to head colds. Caroline can be flapped but Augusto is unflappable. He calls her *Cicchi,* an endearment that has no literal meaning but conveys affection. He's not a curmudgeon but a pussycat. He dislikes the concept when I out him, preferring to foster the gruff exterior.

One afternoon we meet Simonetta and Guido, owners of a *pagliaio* just a few doors down from our hosts. Simonetta is in her sixties and her husband in his seventies. Age hasn't deterred them from undertaking two ambitious renovation and building projects. The more massive of the two is a place in the mountains, in a spot so remote that supplies and equipment are transported to the site by helicopter.

The other is land close to the sea that's been in Simonetta's family for years. She remembers time she spent there in her youth. They invited us to see this property. We began the journey late in the afternoon so that we could see a beautiful sunset and still return to our vehicles before dark. We drove partially up a mountainside and pulled off the road to leave the cars; we would walk the rest of the way.

It was here I realized I'd made a tactical error in shoe selection. While I wasn't sporting some spiky, pointy-toed Italian sandal, I was wearing flip-flops. I would have been better served by steel-toed hiking boots or thigh-high Wellies. Plus, I was carrying a purse. A bit of a girly-girl in a hiking environment.

There was no turning back now. We followed our hosts along a steep narrow path that falls away sharply to the sea far below. Simonetta and Guido spent every day in April clearing the path and now found it completely covered again with grasses and brambles and wild *rucola,* rocket. We sampled the *rucola* while we walked. It is my favorite green and it tastes so much better than the rocket in the States. It's stronger and more pungent but not bitter. This wild version is even better; there's a slight sweetness to it. We crushed the rocket as we walked and it reminds us of other fresh herbal scents – just mown thyme or mint. Augusto, a farmer at heart, told us he's tried many times to transplant this wild version from Puglia to Umbria with no success. Thanks to the ease of traveling, I conclude there's nothing wrong with nature restricting a delicacy to its indigenous setting.

We walked about half a mile before coming into a clearing and a patch of level land. I'm relieved to walk away from the steep drop. Here we found a small three-room hut made of stone. Inside there was a rusted American jerry can, a remnant from World War II. Simonetta told the story of her grandmother, a strong and practical woman who raised her children and grandchildren alone. Her husband had taken off for America. Twenty years later he returned to Puglia but there was little talk of what he'd done in all that time. Perhaps he had been jailed or taken on a new wife or had children. All that time in America meant he knew how to speak English which came in handy, allowing him to help the U.S. soldiers in the area who were forcing the Germans north. Simonetta's grandmother also helped the Americans by taking in laundry in exchange for food.

This is hearty stock. It must partly explain how Simonetta and her husband have the desire, will, determination and drive to convert this small pile of stones into something habitable. Even Roger is astounded at the force required to complete this task. If this is the easier of the two renovations, we have a hard time envisioning the helicopter project. All this and at their ages. *Complimenti.*

From this high vantage point the ocean views are dramatic. Simonetta reminisced about her childhood when she would stand on the cliff and watch schools of dolphin frolic past. She remembers distinctly hearing snippets of conversations from fishing boats far out at sea. This has always been a quiet, peaceful spot and remains so today.

The setting sun brought a slight chill. We'd lingered and the long walk back to the cars would be in the dark. Roger wondered why we couldn't climb straight up the hill to the paved road rather than returning along the narrow path in the dark. Discussion ensued about the merits of each choice but eventually the Italians decided on the path. Roger preferred his idea and wanted to try the new route. Clad in inappropriate flip-flops, I had a decision to make. Resolved, I slung my purse across my shoulder and blindly followed my hero.

Behind the hut is a steep incline covered in dense brush. There's no semblance of a path and the grass is waist-high. Roger leads the way, finding stones on which to stand. I follow, stepping over or under barbed wire, grasping tufts of grass to pull myself forward. He offers encouragement and a strong arm upon occasion. I don't look back, fearful of tumbling hundreds of feet into the sea. I think about Roger's survival school training while remaining light on my feet. If I dwell on this whole concept I get a little dizzy at the thought of the height, the terrain, the remote locale. My mantra is there are no snakes, there are no snakes, there are no snakes.

It's very quiet and I wonder if we're going in the right direction. It's cooler and darker now, the barbed wire more difficult to see. Off in the distance we hear a car change gears making its way up the mountain. Finally, we reach the top of the hill but instead of finding guard rails and road beyond, looming before us is a concrete embankment twice Roger's height. We walk parallel to the embankment to a point where it eventually begins to descend. Roger thinks he can scramble to the top. I'm reluctant to let him go but he promises not to leave me behind.

I continue along at the bottom of the embankment with Roger walking five feet above me. The wall is smooth and there's no place to gain purchase and pull myself up. The height of the embankment doesn't change. From his perspective, Roger sees that it will soon start to rise once again and this position is my best chance at arriving roadside. At his urging, I lift my arms above my head, he grabs hold and begins to pull me up. Like a rag doll with feet dangling, I'm plucked from the grasses above the embankment and railing and deposited gently on the roadside.

We're reunited and euphoric. We're celebrating with high-fives, hooting, hugs and pats on the back. Giddily we walk back to our car, surprised to see that we're the first to arrive. We sit on a ledge, munching wild *rucola,* listening to the waves. My heart is no longer racing, my legs have stopped shaking. Soon we hear our friends' voices. We thank them for revealing this spot, wish them great success and return to Mattinata.

That night I slept well, grateful to have survived the Outward Bound experience intact. More than anything else, I'm relieved to know that renovation via helicopter holds zero appeal to either one of us.

Calabrone

Saturday changeover days remained hectic but this past Saturday rivaled our infamous Saturday with the police. The usual cleaning, mopping, laundry, dusting and arrival dinner preparation was underway. Mick scurried up and down the stairs, Roger cross-checked the spreadsheet, I set the table and Antonio was in the garden working on irrigation problems.

Roger decided today would be a good day to light a fire in the *soggiorno* to get the dampness out of the air. The neatly stacked kindling caught easily and the small flame grew steadily stronger. He asked me to open the kitchen door because the flue didn't seem to be drawing properly. We had done this all last winter so I didn't find it an unusual request. Leaving the door open for a minute or so was normally enough to get the smoke rising up the flue instead of backing up into the room.

Today was different. Our little trick wasn't working and smoke curled around the mantle to the ceiling. I opened all the other doors but the problem seemed to be more than just a bad draw. Roger can't understand the blockage. As he nears the fireplace he hears sizzling and notices a few insects circling the hearth. I turn to open more doors when Roger lets loose with an impressive string of epithets. When I look inside, he's waving his arms, flapping a rag, swinging, running and ducking around the *soggiorno*. I can't wait to find out what's provoked this fancy footwork.

The instigators are the dreaded *calabrone,* hornets. The word is not to be confused with *Calabrese,* the people from Calabria, the toe of the Italian boot. Although Antonio, who by now has swooped in to help with his own share of rag flapping, says there can be very little difference between the two. The hornets must have spent the entire summer building a hive in the chimney. They were not the least bit appreciative of the sudden warmth and smoke. I now know what "mad as a hornet" means.

Between swats, Antonio tells us the hornets can be quite dangerous. The sting from just one has the toxic equivalence of a bite from a venomous snake. Hundreds are swarming and the smoke is thick and acrid. Fearing anaphylactic shock, I ducked out of the room to watch the action from a distance. Roger accuses me of exaggerated hyperbole (there's a perfect example right there) but I must say these hornets are huge; about the size of a hummingbird. From the outside, I could see swarms dive-bombing the chimney and flying in and out all the open doors.

Mick joined the fun, appearing with an aerosol can of wasp spray. He wisely handed it to Antonio who periodically shot a stream into the fireplace producing a remarkable pyrotechnics display. I'm convinced the chimney is going to explode and release a hail storm of bricks and stone. The hive isn't budging, the hornets continue to swarm and the smoke is now billowing.

Antonio tells us there's an environmental agency that will make house calls to take care of problems just like this. We urge him to make the call. A recording suggests we call again on Monday. The hornets have little regard for this being Saturday. A second can of spray has done nothing to diminish the threat but it's done a fine job of inciting the flames. As a last resort, Antonio calls the Perugia fire department.

In no time a truck and five firemen arrive. They calmly survey the situation and the Captain issues orders. They bring in ladders and two of the firemen remove their standard uniforms and don puffy suits. They look like astronauts or beekeepers. The other firemen assist them by latching the suits and helmets and loading tank sprayers onto their backs. Meanwhile, the Captain is left with the all important job of readying a technologically advanced weapon – he ties a rope around a brick. The moon suit guys climb the ladders and approach the chimney humming with hornets. They spray clouds of poison from their tanks but the hornets continue to circle. This lasts ten minutes with an occasional squadron of *calabrone* breaking through but eventually they succumb; the spray is too much.

One moon suit descends, grabs the high-tech weapon and re-ascends. The brick is thrown into the chimney and raised and lowered and raised and lowered like a pile driver until the hive is finally destroyed. Inside the house, great gray sheets of papier mache-like hive fall into the flames. A few fierce hornets manage to survive but the threat has passed. The pile-driver brick is removed and the firemen have saved the day.

The firemen remove their suits and chat amiably as they stow their equipment. We offer them coffee or water, wine or beer but they decline. Their radio crackles with calls. The Captain wants to know our story, asking "*Come mai?*" When he learns we're American he slaps Roger on the back, asking whether the insects were *Calabrone Americani.* "No," Roger replied, *"Calabrone Francesi,"* much to the delight of the firemen. We thank them profusely, shaking hands, appreciating their nonchalant professionalism in the face of our minor crisis. The Captain's well-attuned ear picks out their call letters from the indistinguishable radio monotone and they're off. The truck has barely left the drive before Roger and Antonio have devised a mesh chimney covering to preclude future infestations.

The Empire

Even a normal Saturday is not dull. Along with everything else, Saturday is market day in Ponte Valleceppi. We often make an early morning run to buy produce and *porchetta* for our guests and flowers and planting vegetables from a vendor named Marco who works the market circuit with his mother and father.

Marco's a scruffy character, covered in tattoos, dreadlocks and a rough beard. Instead of finding him at his stall, he's usually next to the *porchetta* wagon drinking an early morning *vino.* He smiles seeing Roger, revealing gaps where teeth once were, and relinquishes his shady spot until later asking what we need to buy that day. His product is good and so are his prices. He's knowledgeable and he's been to *Le Vigne* so he knows what's required to fill the garden and vegetable beds, pots and block walls. Roger demands a *sconto* but after all the purchasing we've done, it now happens automatically. Maybe it's too much *vino* but he often calls Roger, George. Roger doesn't think it has anything to do with the juice; it's simply the jumble of similar letters that causes the confusion and it happens often, even with people he's known for years. Roger's corrected him so many times that Marco finally wrote Roger's name inside his cash drawer, a well-worn wooden cigar box, to help jog his memory.

Our *giardino* and *orto* continue to grow. The fall *orto* contains fennel, onions, lettuces, and garlic. The fall *giardino* has been converted from impatiens and geraniums to pansies and cyclamen with tulip, iris and daffodil bulbs interspersed for the spring. The flowerbed next to the pool requires thirty-six pansies, cyclamen or geraniums depending on the season and the enclosed cistern calls for seventy. There are flower pots around the pool, some on the terraces, pots on the stairs leading to the apartment, hanging baskets, window boxes, flower beds at the back of the house, pots near the barbeque and all along the *piazza*. There are dozens of roses, azaleas, hydrangeas and rhododendrons. There are the herb pots and the massive plantings of ivy, lavender and rosemary for the block walls.

We fold down the seats in the station wagon to make room for the flower trays. I get in the passenger seat and Roger hands me the fruit and *porchetta* and a rhodie or azalea or orchid. It doesn't end there; everything must be planted in amended and tilled soil. Then the plants must be watered and nurtured and weeds pulled and spent blooms dead-headed.

This is a labor intensive property so you can understand my incredulity when Roger told me he thought *Le Vigne* was low maintenance. What planet are you on? For a while, the planet was Roger's World but of late, Roger's taken to calling these sixteen acres his empire. He even held a self coronation and declared himself Emperor. There's probably some psychobabble name for his megalomaniacal condition but we're all humoring him. Frankly, the guests love it.

Roger and I work side-by-side on our low maintenance empire and still we're unable to accomplish all that needs to be done. We originally hired Mick to clean this six bedroom, four bathroom, two kitchen, four story house but the Emperor has exercised his right of imminent domain, usurping most of Mick's time for outdoor activities. Urgent pleas on the part of the Empress (What else would I be called?) for a few minutes of Mick's time for indoor cleaning are resented and go largely unheeded. It took a lot of scepter banging on my part to make it clear I meant business.

Emma

We agreed to find some part-time help and knew right where to turn. In our never-ending search for bricks we had spotted a pile next to a house near the main road. Emma refused us the bricks but offered her cleaning services should we ever need help with "that big house you live in up there."

So Emma joined the empire to clean two mornings a week. She was not genteel or refined but she was hard working. She wasn't afraid of getting her hands dirty or ringing a chicken's neck. We still didn't have chickens but she did and she'd report all the tasks she'd accomplished before arriving at our house and that frequently included a neck ringing or two.

Emma spoke non-stop in a dialect that was heavily laced with profanity. I was the only one who came close to understanding her. Roger had no clue what Emma said and Mick avoided her. Clayton and Mamma Ruta were downright terrified of Emma. Mom hid in her room while Mick and Roger hid in the gardens. Clayton hadn't yet learned to duck the dervish; he wanted to know why Emma kept talking when he couldn't respond.

At the end of her first day Emma tracked Roger down and approached him with outstretched arms to give him a big hug and kisses on both cheeks. She was wearing one of those sleeveless wrap-around house dresses and had worked up quite a sweat. He scrunched his eyes closed to receive his medicine while I smirked in the background. Watching her leave, he begged me, "Please tell me that won't happen every time she comes."

One day we took our guests to Cortona. As we left the *piazza,* Roger gave Mick last minute instructions that included a few tasks for Emma. Mick cringed but was polite, "Sir, you're not going to leave me alone here with that woman, are you?"

Emma had an answer for everything. Roger would point out cobwebs and she'd act like the *calabrone.* Her defenses would rise and she'd rant about how spiders just grow in this environment and even if you clean them, they grow right back and what makes you think she didn't try to clean them, she knows how to keep a clean house. We'd ask her to clean the windows and she'd stand barefoot on chairs to reach the upper panes. Roger bought her a step ladder but she refused to use it. If the weatherman even mentioned the word rain, she'd dismiss the window washing task; *non vale la pena,* it's not worth it.

Emma was divorced or separated, it was never clear which. She told me she had to look out for herself, she couldn't trust anyone, especially some man who might up and leave. She was always in search of work, rubbing sticks together to try and start things. She did not approve of my side-by-side working arrangement with Roger. Building walls, moving block, hefting crates of bottles should be left to someone else. I should sit back as the lady of the house and have Roger hire others to do the work.

Eventually, Emma's need for full-time, regular employment led her to find another job. She pursued that on her own and it was important to her that we understood her reasons for leaving. We certainly did and it was probably just as well. Translating between Roger and Emma was a test of wills that Roger would eventually win simply because he's the Emperor. She made for good stories but the clash was too great to remain workable for long.

Daniela

All of which leads us to Daniela. If ever there were such a thing as human sunshine it would burst forth in this sprite of a woman. Daniela is married to Alfio, our carpenter, and they have a ten-year-old, Lorenzo. She has become as indispensable in our lives as Mick. There is no one on the planet or in the empire who has a more positive outlook on life than Daniela. She is unbridled joy, all smiles and giggles. Daniela's a talker too but as far removed from Emma's stevedore mouth as the Madonna. She's a diamond in the rough, Eliza Doolittle come to life.

She knows no English. In the beginning, I translated everything but now she and Roger have their own language. She speaks of herself in the third person, like Jimmy, that basketball playing character on *Seinfeld.* "What do you want Daniela to do? Should Daniela water the plants this morning? Daniela will bring some fresh eggs tomorrow. Daniela will show you how she makes artichokes. Do you want Daniela to work on Saturday?"

She's diligent, trustworthy, strong, hardworking, prompt and willing to undertake any task. She sings and whistles and finishes her work quickly, looking for the next assignment. The Emperor has claimed her for his crew and she too builds walls, gardens, makes dirt and waters plants when she's finished indoors. She's trim and fit but could eat all day long. No fruit tree is safe in her presence. She tries to sneak an apple or fig but Roger always catches her. She claims he's like *prezzemolo,* parsley; he turns up everywhere. Our chocolate candy bowl is plundered daily. She is an unabashed flirt, purposely and boldly leaving the *cioccolatini* wrappers on Roger's desk so he'll know she was the thief.

Anytime we leave *Le Vigne* for more than a day, she asks for a postcard from our destination. She's not alone in that regard; half of Colombella is plastered with our postcards. From the *pasta fresca* store to Faffa's bakery to the post office, the town displays our cards from as far afield as Florida, California, Texas, Casablanca, St. John and Jackson. I must say, finding postcards in Jackson, Mississippi, is no easy feat. Not only are they difficult to find they're less than attractive. Yet here they are, half a world away in tiny downtown Colombella.

Infuriatingly, recipients thank Roger for sending the postcards when his participation might have been limited to the burdensome task of stamp procurement. He's not the one writing cheery greetings in Italian or addressing twenty cards from every U.S. stop, but he gladly accepts the kudos, chuckling while I fume. *Mamma mia!*

When we travel for extended periods I'm absolutely petrified that Daniela will have found permanent employment in our absence. We want only the best for her but make her swear that she won't leave us the way we've left her. She insists she'll always be here. In my heart of hearts I believe her. I think she enjoys us and *Le Vigne* as much as we do her.

Following one of our long winter trips, we found a lovely pink azalea on the doorstep. Mick told us it was from Daniela. Attached to the plant was a card from the entire family. Daniela's words are simple, heartfelt and the essence of all that is Daniela:

Ben Tornati. Il mondo è grande ma la casa è ancora piu grande. Welcome home. The world is big, but home is even bigger.

Olives, again

Life in Italy is measured by harvests and we've just completed our third. This year's was different and more the way I imagine a harvest should be. Our crop was so bountiful that we needed more hands than those we could tap locally. We turned to the States and invited friends with whom we have a very long, loving and laugh-filled history. The team is now known as the International Harvesters and they claim the harvest as their own, refusing to relinquish their spots even to paying clientele. While there may be some rotation among players, positions are grandfathered.

Linda and Mike returned and actually got to harvest olives. She remains healthy and tells us that the prospect of the harvest gets her through the year. Mike is impressed with how much Mick has opened up but he's still too quiet. Daniela is overwhelmed by Mike's running commentaries regardless of topic. In her third person way she says Daniela works but Mike is all blah, blah, blah.

Carol and Mike arrived again. Carol likes the delayed morning start of the harvest. It gives her enough time to drink lots of strong coffee, do her hair and makeup and put on rhinestone-encrusted jeans and gloves before she has to pick olive one. As she likes to say, quoting Dolly Parton, "It takes a lot of money to look this cheap." Her Mike is a rock. He's as dry as they come and the perfect foil to other Mike's outsized shenanigans.

Dianne and Pat are fine pickers. She's a tom-boy who loves to sing and dance, surprising all of us with a mildly risqué show after a hard day's work. Pat's a retired pilot who's even drier than Mike. The Pat, Mike and Mike trio is capable of heaping an inordinate amount of grief on the Emperor's head. Dianne's no slouch in this regard either.

Charlie, a frequent guest, owns the best Italian market in Atlanta. As a result of his contacts, the *Le Vigne* olive harvest made it into print in a gourmet magazine feature article that is linked on our website. While Charlie harvested, Anita stayed in Atlanta to make sure the market ran smoothly in Charlie's absence.

Don is Roger's best friend and knows the Emperor inside and out. He has been by Roger's side through every cockamamie idea Roger ever had. He gripes and grunts and groans but wouldn't miss this or any other project the Vark decided to pursue.

Lisa and Albert travel to *Le Vigne* from the postcard-challenged city of Jackson. Lisa is a petite, charming, elegant Southern belle who can get just as down and dirty as the rest of us. Albert is my Coca-Cola colleague from years back who initially intimidated the entire team. A late night, a lot of wine and a bucket load of unmerciful prodding led by Linda's Mike changed all of that. Mike's verdict: "Albert's really loosened up." Albert is our documentarian and has photographed and edited a spectacular showcase DVD of the harvest and our season's high jinks.

Several others floated in and out of the mix. Melody, a slightly homesick American student doing her semester abroad in Florence, spends many weekends with us. She is Raymond and Eydie's niece. Raymond, Roger and Don were in pilot training together and sadly Raymond is gone. Any family of theirs is ours as well. Mary and Don have returned from the States for six weeks of vacationing and they'll lend an olive harvesting hand when not touring. Cameron and her boyfriend joined the harvest and she says she can check this off her list. Cameron was not nearly as enamored with harvesting as the rest of us and in an effort to evenly distribute family labor wants to make sure Clayton gets a harvest under his belt. Mick, Daniela and I round out the team.

Weeks before the harvesters arrive I bake dozens of apple or *cachi* muffins and loaves of zucchini bread. I stock the freezer with gallons of hearty soups and chili. I plan our menus in advance, choosing comfort foods and meals that can be prepared quickly; roast chickens, baked pastas, vegetable casseroles, grilled sausages, pork tenderloins. There's always a night or two at Trilogy and *porchetta* for lunch on market days.

Under normal circumstances, most of the harvesters are beer drinkers. In Italy however it's all *vino.* We discovered Goretti *cantina* on the outskirts of Perugia and purchase their *vino sfuso*, bulk wine. It has become our house wine, the one we use for arrival night dinners and cooking classes. Many vineyards sell bulk wine but Goretti is the only one to have cleverly transformed the way the wine is dispensed. Think of a gas station with four gleaming red and chrome pumps, each with LED displays showing cost per liter. Here is fuel of a different sort. Instead of *benzina,* gas, or *gasolio,* diesel, there's a white, two reds and a rosé. Five liter bottles are filled using shiny hoses with trigger nozzles. Three such bottles are crimp capped, put into a handy crate and loaded into the car. The pump prints a receipt summarizing the purchase and the wine is paid for at the cashier. There's even a frequent drinker card and the wine prizes beat the hell out of any Sidis' delicious point rewards.

I thought having thirty liters of wine on hand would be enough for the International Harvesters. I was wrong. We made more trips to Goretti during the harvest and as much as everyone liked the wine, I think they wanted to return just to say "fill 'er up."

Picking olives doesn't require a steep learning curve. Roger made sure new harvesters were familiar with a few pointers before he considered them qualified:

1. Using both hands, run fingers down an olive-filled branch, pulling the fruit, letting the olives fall onto the tarp below.
2. Pick all olives regardless of color – green, red, brown, black. Strive to pick just the olives, avoid stems and leaves.
3. Watch foot placement. Once the olives begin to gather on the tarp, shifting positions must be done carefully so as not to crush any fruit.
4. Watch out for the olive leaves. The points of the leaves are very sharp and can cause serious eye injury.
5. Don't be like Eve and allow an Adam to tempt you with eating an olive directly from the tree. Olives are extremely bitter. You'll never forget the awful taste nor forgive the one who lured you into sampling the fruit.

This is a highly competitive group of friends. For the older trees heavily-laden with fruit, two teams are formed. It's best to work side-by-side to better goad and trash-talk the other team. As the tarp is placed around each new tree, the team approaches to work in a pattern that has its own natural rhythm. Think of a May pole dance with the tree as the pole and each person evenly placed around the tree with the branches serving as the ribbons attached to the center. Taller team members reach high, shorter ones low or at eye level, each stretching without foot movement. The olives plop onto the tarp, sometimes bouncing off a head or slipping into a pocket to be discovered later.

Like locusts, a team can strip a large full tree in thirty minutes. Once a tree is done all branches are surveyed for blind spots and hidden fruit. Mick or Daniela scamper into the center to release hidden or unreachable olives. Despite all the many eyes, inevitably a few remain. As Enzo taught us; they're for the birds.

The dance steps are more delicate now as each person tiptoes away from the tarp. The edges of the tarp are gathered taking care not to lose any olives, a *cassetta* is dragged closer, a corner of the tarp placed in the crate and all the collected olives are rolled into the crate. The team moves to the next May pole to begin the dance again.

Despite the competition, the work is communal and satisfying. The weather is appropriately seasonal, chilly and windy. As the sun grows stronger and we work harder, layers are peeled and tossed on the ground, in the Gator or along block walls.

Shortly before one, a few of us leave to prepare *pranzo.* I heat the soup while someone gathers mugs, spoons and napkins. Cheeses, cold cuts, grain bread, olives and the all important *vino rosso* round out the rest of the meal. At the stroke of one, I ring the cast iron bell, a gift from Pittsburgh friends, and the harvesters quickly appear. A mountain of muddy footwear is left in a jumble at the door while sock-clad feet pad around the sun-filled *soggiorno* to grab a steaming mug of soup and some wine.

It's a fast but filling lunch. The dishwasher is quickly loaded, the food put away and we're back at it for several more hours until the chill and dampness return. The previously jettisoned sweaters, jackets, hats and vests are suddenly in demand. All are gathered now as we fold tarps and place them in a dry spot for the evening.

The day's work hasn't ended, we've simply moved on to the next stage. Mamma Ruta has got to be happy she was here for harvest one not harvest three. Roger insisted we clean the olives, removing all stems and leaves that inadvertently were collected in the tarps. We set up shop in the *salone rustiche* aided by wine, music and a roaring fire. Once again we split into teams and the lies and stories flow. When an olive hits the ground instead of the inside of a crate, team members maturely cry, "Olive down, olive down." Careful scurrying in pursuit of the runaway fruit follows; no one wants to crush an olive that's made it this far.

Shoulders aching, hands and fingernails stained from sorting, wine continuing to flow, the day's harvest eventually becomes pristine. Roger collects the heavy crates, nesting them one atop the other. Moisture is the olives' enemy so we direct large fans at the crates. As the indoor work ends, we break from the group one by one to enjoy a hot shower before dinner. The combination of fresh air, physical labor, camaraderie, wine and good food guarantee a sound night's sleep.

After several such days, we finished the harvest and were ready to press. The mill in Bosco where we pressed the first year had no openings but I secured an appointment at the mill in Piccione, last year's mill. We loaded the vehicles with crates and caravanned to the mill. I thought Roger would cry when he walked inside.

In the short span of one year a startling transformation had taken place and we had witnessed the evolution. Italy's inclusion in the European Union called for many changes not the least of which was compliance with certain production and hygiene standards for olive oil production. During the preceding summer, mills invested hundreds of thousands of Euro in new equipment to meet the standards. Cold press was gone. Gone were the hemp mats and hydraulic presses. Most granite grinding wheels were gone although the mill in Bosco still retained this charming relic. The mill in Piccione was filled with banks of shiny stainless steel equipment that magically took the olives, bathed them, crushed them and spun them in large centrifuges to eventually become emerald green oil.

The process that once took six hours was now reduced to two. We watched as workers dumped the crates into the chute and olives shimmied away to become oil. There was a fair amount of pointing from the locals with regard to our fastidious nature. Once again our higher yield (the weight ratio of olives to oil) justified the extra time and effort. The results for year three are: twenty-one *cassette*, 1,065 pounds of olives, eighty-five liters of oil.

One of the many appealing things about growing olives is the instant gratification it provides – harvest, process, and immediately savor the tasty oil. This is in direct contrast to harvesting wine grapes which is a messy, smelly, bee-infested, dirty, stain-inducing process without instant gratification and no guarantees.

Unlike most wines, olive oil doesn't improve with age. It has a maximum shelf life of eighteen months so it's best enjoyed young and peppery and biting. We consume all of our oil within a year of harvest. Olive oil will degrade near heat or in sunlight so avoid the temptation to keep it next to the cooktop or oven or on a windowsill.

While the new mills have lost their Old World charm on the technical side, the fireplaces for toasting *bruschetta* and grilling sausages along with the cups for drinking someone's homemade vintage remain. Much to the dismay of another patron, we burned the bread but drenching it with newly spun liquid gold more than made up for any charred edges. We toasted ourselves for having completed a successful harvest, loaded the empty crates and full stainless steel tanks into the car and returned home.

Once home we make our own *bruschetta*:

Toast slices of Italian bread in the oven or fireplace.
Pierce toasted bread slices with the tines of a fork.
Lightly rub each slice with a freshly cut red garlic clove.
Grind coarse salt over each slice.
Generously pour freshly pressed oil on top.
Be prepared with a napkin to catch oil as it drizzles down the chin.

The grind of salt is important. It adds flavor to Umbrian bread historically made without salt. Throughout the centuries, emperors, the Papacy and other leaders levied taxes on this valuable commodity. Wars were fought over salt. The people rebelled against the taxes and sought ways to reduce their dependence. While salt was necessary for preserving meats, independent and frugal Umbrians decided it was unnecessary in making their daily bread.

Unsalted bread grows stale and hardens quickly but the resourceful peasant wives would not let it go to waste. Place a slice of hard, day-old bread in the bottom of a bowl, pour a hearty bean and leftover vegetable soup on top, drizzle olive oil to finish and the meal is complete. This is the famous soup known as *ribollita* or reboiled. During the summer months, the stale bread would be torn into small pieces, tossed with tomatoes, onions, cucumbers and olive oil to create *panzanella*.

This style of cooking is known as *cucina povera*. Literally meaning poor kitchen, it is central Italy's answer to soul food or down-home cooking. It is peasant cooking, simple fare making use of basic ingredients: flour, water and perhaps an egg to make pasta, seasonal garden vegetables, on rare occasions a chicken, on religious holidays, a lamb. Meals had to be prepared quickly as all hands were required to work the land. While the need for farmhands has diminished, *cucina povera* remains as does unsalted bread.

Bruschetta has been imported to the States, in most cases with admirable results. However restaurant owners and servers should be taken to task for the incorrect pronunciation they've imposed on the American public. They insist on turning the *ch* into a *sh* sound as in *shoe.* Proper pronunciation is *brew-sket-a*, with the accent on the second syllable and a hard *k* sound not a *sh* sound. Here's a simple trick; every *ch* in Italian is pronounced as a hard *k* – always, no exceptions. Everyone seems to be able to say *chianti* correctly. I've never heard anyone say *she-on-tee*, not even Hannibal Lecter.

We're often asked if our oil is first press and extra virgin. All table oil is created from the first press. A second press takes place with the remaining pulp. The small amount of oil released isn't food grade. Instead, it's used for soaps, lotions and creams. Oil is considered extra virgin if it contains less than one percent acid and virgin if the acid content is between one and three percent. Anything greater than three percent is used for packing fish. All of the olive oil produced in the Silver Coast is considered extra virgin.

As we prepare slice after slice of *bruschetta* surrounded by our friends, I can't help but reflect on our first harvest. We've just passed the three-year mark of our life in Italy and the progress the mills have made in olive pressing technology serves as a parallel to our progress. It's hard to believe we've been here long enough to be nostalgic for the old ways. Looking back we were so ignorant. Our famous "absence of intellect" was profound and manifested itself in everything we saw or did or wanted to do. It took time but we learned, slowly, sometimes painfully. Now our visitors reap the benefits of our hard-earned knowledge the easy way. We filter the stems and leaves and deliver a pure, concentrated slice of Italian life.

Antonella visited the other day, collecting our pruned rosemary for use in the bakery. She admired our many gardens and stone walls and the hundreds of olive trees that have grown visibly. She placed her hand on my shoulder, saying, "*Avete seminato bene qui in Italia.*" The phrase conveyed her approval - you have been planted well, you are rooted in Italy. Indeed.

Ringraziamento

It's Thanksgiving morning and the turkey is in the oven. That's a simple enough statement that belies the effort required to get it there. Several weeks ago, I ordered a nine kilogram turkey (about twenty pounds) from the local butcher in Colombella. I specified *"Un tacchino completamente pulito,"* a completely clean bird. There was no need to have the head or feet.

Late last night, Don and Roger picked up the bird and it was a good thing two of them went on this errand. The butcher apologized but the smallest turkey was fourteen kilograms or thirty pounds. It looked prehistoric with brontosaurus-size drumsticks and gargantuan breasts. The butcher had dutifully followed instructions about the head and feet. It never occurred to me to specify sans feathers.

Shandi had been my constant kitchen companion all week. There was not a single task she shirked. A fork didn't hit the sink before she had it washed, dried and ready for an encore. It's amazing how many onions are needed for this meal. Shandi cut and cried over every one. She patiently sautéed pound after pound of sausage for dressing. She grated large blocks of cheddar, her knuckles narrowly escaping the shredding.

It wasn't as though the turkey was covered in fluffy feathers but enough pin feathers remained to be unappetizing – they had to go. I wouldn't have blamed Shandi if she suddenly developed a rare avian allergy but she stayed and we attacked the job purposefully. Neither of us had any experience with feather plucking. We tried pulling the tenacious remains with our fingers but gave that up after a few painful minutes. We decided tweezers would work much better so we grabbed our makeup bags. Conscious of sanitation and hygiene we made a big display of sterilizing our instruments and approached the onerous task with renewed intent. Note to file regarding next year's turkey: no head, no feet, no feathers.

Now that the turkey was clean I worried about it fitting in the oven. First I had to get it inside the Reynolds oven bag imported from Atlanta. After some clever rack juggling and a little heavy lifting, the bird squeezed into the bag and the bag squeezed into the oven. Clayton will enjoy watching Renato carve this year's bird. He calls the restaurant owner a piranha for his skill and speed at stripping the carcass.

We are honored that Renato chooses today as the only day of the year to close Corys. His wife Laura and his eighty-eight year old mother, lovingly known as the *Generale,* join him as do his employees. Giuseppe is the maitre d' and Renato's much needed right hand man. A Lebanese Christian, Giuseppe fled his country due to religious persecution. He planned to be a pharmacist but that career was shelved; now he's a sommelier and restaurateur whose English is an added benefit to Renato.

Eva is Giuseppe's Albanian wife who's taken over many of the cooking responsibilities from Laura. It took years but Eva finally managed to bring her two young children, Leda and Denis to Italy. The immigration process was difficult but ultimately successful thanks to Renato's repeated appearances at the *questura.* The children arrived at the end of the school year. They are brave and they are sponges; already making friends and speaking Italian.

Renato and Laura now have children in their lives. Leda and Denis call the General *Nonna* and Renato and Laura are *zio e zia.* They are guileless, loving, respectful, kind children who are appreciative of their new lives and adoring of their adoptive aunt and uncle. Laura picks the children up from school and Renato helps them with their homework. The children do not go to sleep without calling their aunt and uncle to say good night. At the restaurant, they help set tables, display baskets of freshly collected *funghi,* greet us and our guests with open loving arms and the increasing list of English words they've learned.

These will not be our only Italian guests. Our neighbors will arrive along with Giancarla, the owner of Lo Spedalicchio. Augusto and his daughter Francesca will come without Caroline, who's in New Jersey. Antonio and his family and Enzo and his wife are included. Rossana and Roy whom we recently met at a wine-tasting dinner in Perugia will join us; she's from Milan, he's from Minnesota. Thanksgiving at *Le Vigne* is an international affair. Our Irish friends, Abigail and Ralph are invited and so are our Dutch friends, Wendy and Frits. Melody is already here and Mary and Don have returned from their Italian travels to lend a hand with preparations. Sadly, Lisa and Albert left yesterday because of her mother's sudden and grave illness.

Twenty-eight guests are expected today. Clayton and Roger have filled the *salone rustiche* with five festively set tables and chairs. The cyclamen centerpieces are destined to be planted later but now add their brightness to the room that shimmers with silver and crystal. The scene is warm and comfortable with a fire already burning. An American flag is on display and California wines will be decanted early. Clayton's custom designed place cards featuring our olive grove will guide guests to their seats.

The smells of Thanksgiving have been wafting through the house all week: crumbled sage for the dressing, cinnamon and pumpkin spices for pies and sweet potatoes, cranberry and oranges for tart, fresh relish, onions and celery sautéing. These are the aromas that broadcast this holiday in no uncertain terms. I rely on the International Harvesters for imports to ensure the menu remains traditional. The ever elusive sweet potatoes, cranberries, rutabagas, turnips, pecans, cheddar cheese, pumpkin pie filling, graham cracker crumbs and even plastic oven bags fill our friends' suitcases on the trip eastbound. Once emptied, there's now room for Italian purchases to travel westbound. While only one oven bag is needed for the turkey, the extras are distributed to Renato, Giancarla and Giuliana who have become converts to this roasting method, a process unfamiliar to Italians.

We'll begin our feast with appetizers in the *soggiorno*: *prosecco,* crab dip, olives, *pecorino* and the spicy roasted pecans known as Winkler's Nuts. For dinner we'll have turkey, ham, gravy made by Mamma Ruth and Dianne, dressing, cranberry relish, fresh bread, mashed potatoes and rutabaga, sweet potatoes, squash casserole, even cheese grits. Abigail and Ralph are bringing fresh bread and his mother's classic turnip casserole. For dessert there's an apple and cranberry crisp, Cinzia's *biscotti della nonna*, Abigail's carrot cake, Don Winkler's pumpkin pie, Rossana's Mont Blanc, a desert that looks like the snow-covered mountain for which it's named and Giuliana's *panna cotta* and *tiramisu*. There will be more food than we can possibly eat. Every year I plan to cut back and every year I fail. Thanksgiving is a dinner that takes the longest to prepare and the least amount of time to eat.

Our international mix of guests has adopted this holiday as their own. They no longer struggle over the concept and instead accept and expect it as part of the late fall lead-in to Christmas and Epiphany. It is the bounty, the warmth, the celebration of togetherness, the now traditional foods that combine to make this an anticipated holiday for all of our guests regardless of nationality.

In these moments before guests arrive and the house is filled with laughter and a multitude of languages, before Denis and Leda charmingly offer to take guests' coats and scarves, before the *prosecco* is poured and the turkey is carved as though vacuumed and toasts are made and the buffet line begins, I'm able to reflect on how grateful we are for the bounty we have received – food, family, friends and a world that allows us to cross cultures and share traditions that would otherwise remain isolated. We bring Thanksgiving to Italy and Italy has given us so very much in return.

Christmas is only a month away and we'll return to the States during the winter. We'll visit and travel and re-charge our batteries before hosting again next spring. Even now, two-thirds of the calendar is full. This means we've achieved our goals, we've been successful, our capital P projects have been completed. There's been so much progress, so much change.

Change came over us slowly. Our eyes see the world differently. I can't pinpoint the day this happened. We ceased being the recently arrived tourists. We became residents and our daily lives have become the norm. We've progressed, learned the ways of this land, lost our innocence and much of our ignorance. A trip to the grocery store is a utilitarian event, not an adventure of discovery and wonder. We are road-savvy so a drive to the industrial zone of Perugia is no longer terrifying or fraught with accusatory exchanges about missed turns and poor directions. Monica Bellucci is a sweet memory. We've sold our miniature though mighty expensive mulcher. We learned it's easier to burn the pruned olive branches than laboriously feed them into the little machine. We find little odd about only now signing documents requesting permission to install fencing and enclose the Mediterranean pines. It seems routine that the work was completed ages ago, the paperwork a mere formality.

While life in Italy is now our norm, in no way has it become wallpaper. We understand how blessed we are to occupy sixteen heavenly acres with every view being postcard perfect. The steepled images of Perugia, seen from our bedroom window morning and night, remain striking. The seasonal changes revealed during my daily walks remain life-affirming. The sunsets over Perugia in winter and the northern hills in summer are majestic. I open my eyes and my heart daily to this beauty; none of it taken for granted.

There was a time when both feet remained firmly on American soil and we peeked at life in Italy. Then there came a day when we straddled the ocean. After a while, both feet landed in Italy and the peek was back at America and the footprints we left behind. When we travel to the States we often feel like tourists. Some things are familiar but there are differences. When did washers and dryers double in size and start talking to each other? When did children begin to seemingly levitate through grocery aisles, shoes equipped with blinking wheels gliding them to their destination? When did 866 become a toll-free prefix? When did television programming change to cruel judging of singing and dancing competitions and reality shows? From Costco to WalMart, how did everything become supersized? And why?

Antonella sees we are rooted but, as comfortable as our feet are in Italy,

I notice Roger's feet are restless. With the big projects behind us and the to-do list shrinking, the challenges diminish. It is ironic that his comfort level is in direct proportion to his challenge level. He needs the challenges to survive. He is Edison's quintessential dissatisfied man.

The dissatisfaction translates to a need for another project. That something has yet to be defined. For the first time in his life Roger must factor age into his equations and this doesn't please him. Whatever is next must strike the right balance between desire and physical ability. It is a difficult reality to accept.

Not far from Perugia is the small hilltop town of Solomeo. An enterprising visionary, Brunello Cucinelli, perfectly restored this castle-village jewel and chose the site as headquarters for his world renowned cashmere manufacturing operations. He devoted years to the effort and it's hard to imagine him not being forever connected to the town. Yet he says, "I am the steward of the place, not the owner. Should we leave, Solomeo will go on."

And so too, *Le Vigne*. If Roger is restless, then so must I be. It won't happen tomorrow. This future project remains very tentative, a kernel of a thought, a premonition that forecasts a possibility that change may be in the winds. It is a sobering thought nonetheless. How will we ever leave *Le Vigne*? I suppose in the same way Cucinelli will leave Solomeo. We are merely stewards here and others will follow.

Some day but not today. Today the oven timer is buzzing and it's time for big bird to rest before Renato carves. I hear the front gate; the guests are arriving. The time for reflection is behind me. As Roger so romantically and poignantly put it seconds after we pronounced our wedding vows, "Let's eat."

So it's time for both feet to be planted firmly in the moment and focus on this grand day. Whatever the future holds is so vague as to not even coalesce into a place or a plan. In the meantime, what is very clear is the over-arching lesson of our life in Italy...*pazienza.*

Epilogue – Fall 2008

It's hard to believe we're about to begin our seventh year in Italy where we remain firmly and happily ensconced. There have been enough projects for Roger to be stimulated and content in his role as a dissatisfied man. Marketing *Le Vigne* as a vacation rental continues to be a major focus and to date we've hosted over five hundred guests. We've been successful, taking bookings two years in advance.

Since Thanksgiving 2004, Delta Air Lines has entered and exited bankruptcy, flaying the retired pilots' pensions in the process. Retirement has a whole different cast to it these days; more along the lines of the hoofers in *A Chorus Line;* "I really need this job." We've turned *Le Vigne* into a little marketing machine selling mugs, note cards and aprons featuring our logo or images of the property.

Our biggest export and greatest source of pride is our olive oil. We've been blessed with increased annual abundance as the trees mature. Last year's yield was more than the total of the previous five years; 3,256 pounds of olives and almost 300 liters of oil. Stateside, *Le Vigne* oil can be sampled at Charlie Augello's E. 48th Street Market in Dunwoody, Georgia. This year's harvest is anticipated to be the best yet; International Harvesters are already confirmed. The olive grove and our centuries old Mediterranean pines are the key distinguishing landmarks denoting our property from a distance.

Roger continues to design and build both block and masonry walls and steps. Gardens grow and vegetable plots flourish. Dahlias are planted in the Clayton garden, named for the son who is an expert in growing these tubers. Asters thrive in the Cameron garden; the seed packets were her gift so she gets the credit. Roger's mother Nancy and traveling companion friend Claire contributed the specimen olive that commands center stage on the fruit tree level overlooking the large grove. We've introduced okra and kohlrabi to Italy and reduced our zucchini crop to a manageable three a day. We continue to harvest great Jersey tomatoes grown from imported seeds and add vegetables such as green beans, peas, potatoes, Brussels sprouts and cauliflower the size of basketballs. Corn remains an annual adventure.

We've requested the "permissions" to demolish the dilapidated green metal sheds and build an equipment storage building. Forever pushing the envelope, Roger plans to sneak a few extras into this building that will cover two levels and include a *limonaia.* We'll soon be "making the works" again and crews of masons, electricians, plumbers, carpenters and deliverymen led by Antonio will ensure rampant activity for months.

The "technical building" with our pool equipment is targeted for renovation, elevating valves and pumps, sealing leaks and adding solar panels to heat the water for the temperate shoulder months. We've converted the pool from chlorine to salt water thus eliminating harsh and costly chemicals and stinging, blood-shot eyes.

Modern technology has slowly crept into our lives. Our vehicles are now graced with GPS navigational devices. Had these existed sooner, much of our driving torment would have been eliminated. Even more remarkable, ADSL broadband and wireless routers have made their way to Colombella Alta. We can now join the rest of the world and watch a two minute YouTube clip without painful protracted buffering.

The six-year odyssey to graduate from dial-up was a wild ride with upbeat salesmen promising coverage while dejected technicians informed us otherwise. Back and forth we went. Once I talked to a customer service agent named Mauro and on a whim asked if he spoke English. "Yes," he replied. I began my tale of woe and he occasionally interjected a 'yes.' After a few inappropriately placed affirmatives, my euphoria abated. "Mauro, do you really understand English?" "Yes," he replied, "I love you." Charming Mauro admitted those were the only words he knew in English.

On a blisteringly hot August day, our *strada bianca* was finally paved. We joined Renato on one side and Federico on the other to continue an uninterrupted ribbon of black asphalt. It is smooth and dust-free; a true pleasure.

Mick and his girlfriend from Milan are now living in Perugia. They have a son, Kyle Andrei. Roger lobbied hard for him to be named Roger. He's known as Andrei but the name Kyle came from a former guest; a precious six year old who adored me while his sisters adored Roger. We attended Andrei's baptism along with hundreds of others including (I kid you not) eighteen godmothers and godfathers. At the reception, Mick made sure we were first in the buffet line while we made sure we were first to leave. Mick needed to enjoy himself without the Boss and Mom nearby.

Last summer was marked by weddings and receptions. Italian weddings are everything they're cracked up to be; extravaganzas with gorgeous brides, handsome grooms and casts of thousands. A morning wedding was followed by a five hour, seated and served lunch. I lost track of the number of courses after the tenth. In the evening, a buffet dinner was served with all new guests. Music, cake, *prosecco,* dancing and bawdy pranks continued into the wee hours, long after we were gone.

While weddings and babies promise new beginnings, the circle of life must have its endings. Roger's fathers Bill Arndt and Dana Criswell passed away after living long, full lives. Neither one ever saw *Le Vigne*. On this side of the Atlantic, our local priest Don Gilberto died. His successor, Don Franco has already come a callin' to perform the annual Easter house blessing. It's amusing to watch Roger explain our good-for-a-lifetime version.

I still walk every morning alone or with guests or with Giuliana, Liana and Giovanna. Twice a week the girls work out with everyone's favorite "pair-so-knell tray-ner"; a luxury I have no time for. The boisterous Pippo, once a fixture on morning rounds, is conspicuously absent of late. Word is he's been denounced or rather his owner was. Occasionally he's spotted but always leashed, head bowed, *moscio, moscio,* disheartened and dejected. Whatever he did must've been bad. The gossip has yet to work its way up the hill to reveal the transgression.

Speaking of denounce, we got in on the act ourselves. Under cover of darkness, thieves removed seven hundred feet of our fencing and stole or broke seventy fence posts. The fencing bordered our woods and was in place for less than a day. No one saw or heard anything and the *denuncia* with the *Carabinieri* is merely an exercise; we hold no illusions about apprehending the culprits. The prime suspects are hunters seeking unfettered access to the woods. We'll rebuild, this time claiming protection of the land as a floral or fauna preserve. The Emperor has spoken.

The Euro just celebrated its sixth anniversary and continues to pummel the dollar. In June 2002, when we made the initial deal to buy *Le Vigne,* the Euro was $.88. By the time we completed the *atto* in October it had gained an additional ten cents and by the end of the year stood at $1.02. While it will forever be a moving target, today it's a hammer at $1.56. Despite its sixth year in existence, the Euro remains a novelty and Italians continue to speak in *vecchie lire.*

Shutter management has been further refined. We've learned how to keep the interior cooler during the hot summer months. At five or six in the morning we open all doors, screens and windows to allow the cool air to enter. When the first ray of sunlight strikes the building, we close the shutters *and* windows. We used to think it was an advantage leaving the windows open but the hot air entered and cool air vanished. Closing the windows works.

On the calendar flipside, we've reduced our heating fuel costs thanks to Alfio's new custom-made windows and doors; thirty-nine of them. The double-pane glass and perfect seal keep warm air inside and rain outside. Roger designed them without mullions allowing more light and splendid views to flood the interior.

Roger had another fine meal eating his words. We suffered through the *permesso* renewal again. We're told that the next time we can apply for a *carta di soggiorno,* valid for ten years. The process is certain to change.

Unchanged is the comforting constancy of Antonio's presence in our lives. Steadfast and unwavering, Valentina and her family provide the same. Corys has changed owners yet still delivers an exceptional dining experience thanks to Giuseppe and Eva. Renato and Laura remain our dear friends. Change happens. In Atlanta, Michael Tuohy recently sold Wood Fire Grill to return to the West Coast and open another restaurant. Abigail and Ralph have sold their property and left Italy. Wendy and Frits happily remain, having bought, renovated and sold three magnificent properties since we first met.

Amidst the change, there are certain constants. Roger still wants his own chicken coop and I continue to divert his attention. His latest live animal project is one he and Giuliana conspire about incessantly; they want to raise a few sheep. Renato and I pretend not to listen which forces them both to talk about buying and renovating some neighboring ruins. We ignore those schemes too.

Plants and flowers are purchased in ever-increasing quantities and we rely on Marina for geraniums, impatiens, petunias, begonias, violas and cyclamen depending on the season. She's warmed over the years, particularly after discovering she and Roger celebrate the same birthday. Roger brought a bottle of *prosecco* to the greenhouse on a hot August day, sharing a gift that delivered more surprised pleasure than bubbles. When Roger appeared as promised the following year, she grinned broadly and exclaimed, "You said you'd do it and you did it!" The unmistakable wrapping and ribbons of a pastry tray gave away her anticipation of the event and on a table swept clear of potting soil and seed packets we poured *prosecco,* ate *biscotti* and toasted future communal birthdays.

Pazienza is still the national catchphrase and Roger is still the number one recipient of this admonition. His Italian continues to improve; *lui* orders his own pizzas from Dani at Trilogy but he tends to rely on his *stampella,* crutch, aka, me, because it's easier.

New flavors and culinary delights have come our way. *"Ogni morte di papa,"* (literally every death of a pope but the equivalent of once in a blue moon), our mechanic Paolo calls us to race to the bottom of the hill. The cheese lady is making her rounds in Colombella selling artisan aged *pecorino* from the back of her Fiat Panda. She plunges her cheese iron, a special T-shaped tool, into a wheel, turns it and extracts a core sample. We taste the salty morsel as she replaces the end of the plug to keep the wheel airtight. She weighs the wheel using a hand-held scale; the kind always depicted with the Libra astrological sign, wraps the cheese in paper and scribbles the price on top using a stubby pencil. Blue moons don't come often enough. As an aside, a pope has died since our arrival and Italy won the World Cup provoking a rare display of national rather than provincial pride.

Every Easter promises delivery of *Torta di Pasqua,* the traditional cheese bread made only in Umbria. The egg bread loaded with chunks of *parmigiano* is the size of a hat box and we're always blessed with three. Mason Sergio's wife Carla provides one that's delivered still warm. Our driver Roberto and his wife Katiuscia deliver her version, her *nonna's* recipe, decorated with an olive leaf in the center. Not least is my indefatigable and multi-talented neighbor Giuliana who manages to bake her *torte* in between hand-painting goose eggs and creating a *lasagna* lighter and more delicate than a crepe. Remember, in Italy it often comes down to food.

. . .*Le Vigne* thrives and so do we. Active, engaged and dissatisfied in all the right ways, we remain enchanted with this country and our Emperor is ready to seize yet another day. Our Italian lessons continue but the bottom line is clear; we are still living the dream.